DATE DUE

HIGHSMITH 45-220

UNITED STATES RELATIONS WITH RUSSIA AND THE SOVIET UNION

A Historical Dictionary

David Shavit

Greenwood Press
Westport, Connecticut • London

Library of Congress Cataloging-in-Publication Data

Shavit, David.
    United States relations with Russia and the Soviet Union : a
historical dictionary / David Shavit.
      p.   cm.
    Includes bibliographical references.
    ISBN 0–313–28469–5 (alk. paper)
      1. United States—Relations—Russia—Dictionaries. 2. Russia—
Relations—United States—Dictionaries. 3. United States—
Relations—Soviet Union—Dictionaries. 4. Soviet Union—Relations—
United States—Dictionaries. I. Title.
E183.8.R9S487   1993
303.48'273047—dc20   93–9313

British Library Cataloguing in Publication Data is available.

Library of Congress Catalog Card Number: 93–9313
ISBN: 0–313–28469–5

First published in 1993

Greenwood Press, 88 Post Road West, Westport, CT 06881
An imprint of Greenwood Publishing Group, Inc.

Printed in the United States of America

∞™

The paper used in this book complies with the
Permanent Paper Standard issued by the National
Information Standards Organization (Z39.48–1984).

10 9 8 7 6 5 4 3 2 1

For Ronnie Wesley Knepper
and Eli Robin Reshef

Contents

Abbreviations   ix

Place Names   xi

Chronology   xiii

Introduction   xvii

The Dictionary   1

United States Chiefs of Diplomatic Missions in Russia and the Soviet Union   207

List of Individuals by Profession and Occupation   209

Bibliographical Essay   217

Index   225

Abbreviations

ACAB	*Appleton's Cyclopaedia of American Biography* (New York, 1888–1901)
ACDA	*Arms Control and Disarmament Agreements: Texts and Histories of Negotiations* (Washington, D.C., 1990)
BDAC	*Biographical Directory of the American Congress, 1774–1971* (Washington, D.C., 1971)
BRDS	*Biographical Register of the Department of State*
CA	*Contemporary Authors* (Detroit, 1962–)
CB	*Current Biography*
DAB	*Dictionary of American Biography* (New York, 1928–)
DADH	*Dictionary of American Diplomatic History,* John E. Findling. Rev. ed. (Westport, Conn., 1989)
DAMIB	*Dictionary of American Military Biography,* ed. Roger J. Spiller (Westport, Conn., 1984)
DANB	*Dictionary of American Negro Biography,* ed. Rayford W. Logan and Michael R. Winston (New York, 1982)
DH	*Diplomatic History*
DINRT	*Dictionary of International Relations Terms* (Washington, D.C., 1987)
DSB	*Dictionary of Scientific Biography* (New York, 1970–1976)
EAFP	*Encyclopedia of American Foreign Policy: Studies of the Principal Movements,* ed. Alexander DeConde (New York, 1978)

EAIE	*Encyclopedia of American Intelligence and Espionage: From the Revolutionary War to the Present,* G.J.A. O'Toole (New York, 1988)
McDonald	*U.S.-Soviet Summitry: Roosevelt through Carter,* John W. McDonald, Jr. (Washington, D.C., 1987)
MERSH	*Modern Encyclopedia of Russian and Soviet History,* ed. Joseph L. Wieczynski (Gulf Breeze, Fla., 1976–)
NAW	*Notable American Women* (Cambridge, Mass., 1971–1980)
NCAB	*National Cyclopaedia of American Biography* (New York, 1898–).
NYT	*New York Times*
PolProf	*Political Profiles,* ed. Nelson Lichtenstein (New York, 1976–1978)
RR	*Russian Review*
S	*Supplement*
SR	*Slavic Review*
USNIP	*United States Naval Institute Proceedings*
Weihmiller	*U.S.-Soviet Summits: An Account of East-West Diplomacy at the Top, 1955–1985,* Gordon R. Weihmiller (Lanham, Md., 1986)
WWA	*Who's Who in America*
WWIN	*Who's Who in Engineering*
WWWA	*Who Was Who in America*

Place Names

Current Name	Former Name
Dnepropetrovsk	Ekaterinoslav
Kuibyshev	Samara
Nizhni Novgorod	Gorki, 1932–1991
Russia, 1991–	Russia, –1917
	Soviet Russia, 1917–1924
	Soviet Union, 1924–1991
St. Petersburg, 1991–	St. Petersburg, –1917
	Petrograd, 1917–1924
	Leningrad, 1924–1991
Sverdlovsk	Ekaterinburg

Chronology

1762–1796	Tsarina Catherine II (the Great)
1783	First Russian colony founded in Alaska
1799	Russian-American Company received its charter
1801–1825	Tsar Alexander I
1812	Ross Colony founded north of San Francisco
1824	Russian-American Convention signed
1825	Decembrist uprising
1825–1855	Tsar Nicholas I
1830–1831	Polish revolution
1832	Russo-American Treaty of Commerce and Navigation signed
1838	First Russian railroad built
1853–1856	Crimean War
1855–1881	Tsar Alexander II
1861	Emancipation of the serfs
1863	Russian fleets in New York and San Francisco
1863–1864	Second Polish Revolution
1865–1876	Russian advance in Central Asia; conquest of the khanates of Kokand, Bokhara, and Khiva
1867	Russia sold Alaska to the United States
1875–1878	Russian-Turkish War
1881	Transcaspian region annexed
1881–1894	Tsar Alexander III
1891	Trans-Siberian Railway begun

1891–1892	Great famine
1894–1917	Tsar Nicholas II
1903	Kishinev pogrom
1904–1905	Russo-Japanese War
1905	Treaty of Portsmouth
1905–1906	Revolution in Russia
1917	Nicholas II abdicated; provisional government; Bolshevik Revolution; Root Mission to Russia
1917–1920	Russian Railway Service Corps in Siberia
1917–1924	V. I. Lenin, Premier of Soviet Russia
1918	Treaty of Brest-Litovsk
1918–1919	Allied intervention in North Russia
1918–1920	Civil War
1918–1920	Allied intervention in Siberia
1920	War with Poland
1921–1922	Great famine
1921–1923	American Relief Administration (ARA) in Soviet Russia
1921–1929	New Economic Policy (NEP)
1922	Treaty of Rapallo between Soviet Russia and Germany; formation of the Union of Soviet Socialist Republics
1922–1953	Joseph Stalin, General Secretary of the Communist Party
1924	Death of Lenin
1928–1932	First Five-Year Plan
1929	Leon Trotsky exiled from the Soviet Union;
1933	Roosevelt-Litvinov Agreements signed; United States recognized the Soviet Union
1933–1938	Second Five-Year Plan
1937–1938	Purges; show trials
1939–1940	Russo-Finnish war
1941	Germany invaded the Soviet Union
1943	Teheran conference
1945	Yalta conference; Potsdam conference
1946	Azerbaijan crisis

1948–1949	Berlin blockade crisis
1951	First Soviet atomic bomb exploded
1953	"Doctors' Plot"; death of Stalin; uprising in East Germany
1953–1964	Nikita S. Khrushchev, General Secretary of the Communist Party
1955	Warsaw Pact formed; Geneva summit
1956	Hungarian revolt; Soviet intervention in Hungary
1957	Sputnik I, Soviet earth satellite, fired into orbit
1958–1959	Berlin crisis
1958–1964	Nikita S. Khrushchev, Premier of the Soviet Union
1959	Khrushchev visited the United States; Washington summit
1960	RB–47 incident; U–2 incident; Paris summit
1961	First manned Soviet space flight; Berlin Wall constructed; Vienna summit
1962	Cuban missile crisis
1963	Limited Test Ban Treaty (LTBT) signed; "Hot Line" Agreement signed
1964–1977	Leonid I. Brezhnev, General Secretary of the Communist Party
1967	Glassboro summit
1968	Soviet intervention in Czechoslovakia
1971	Accident Measures Agreement signed
1972	Moscow summit; SALT I treaty signed; Anti-Ballistic Missile (ABM) Treaty signed; Incidents at Sea Agreement signed; Basic Principles Agreement (BPA) signed; U.S.–Soviet Commercial Agreements signed
1973	Washington summit
1974	Moscow summit; Vladivostok summit; Threshold Test Ban Treaty (TTBT) signed
1975	Apollo-Soyuz Test project
1976	Peaceful Nuclear Explosions (PNE) Treaty signed
1977–1982	Leonid I. Brezhnev, President of the Soviet Union
1979	Vienna summit; Soviet invasion of Afghanistan
1980	Olympic games in Moscow boycotted

1980–1988	Afghanistan crisis
1982–1984	Yuri Andropov, General Secretary of the Communist Party
1983	KAL 007 incident
1984–1985	Konstantin Chernenko, General Secretary of the Communist Party
1985–1991	Mikhail Gorbachev, General Secretary of the Communist Party; Gorbachev launched *Glasnot* and *Perestroika*
1985	Geneva summit
1986	Reykjavik summit
1987	Washington summit; Intermediate-Range Nuclear Forces (INF) Treaty signed
1988	Moscow summit; Ballistic Missile Launch Notification Agreement signed
1989	Malta summit; Soviets withdrew from Afghanistan
1989–1991	Mikhail S. Gorbachev, President of the Soviet Union
1990	Washington summit
1991	Moscow summit; dissolution of the Soviet Union; START I Treaty signed
1993	Moscow summit; START II treaty signed

Introduction

The U.S. economy of the eighteenth century depended on Russia for certain products, including hemp, flax, iron, candles, and animal fats. Although Russia was England's ally during the Revolutionary War, it did not send troops to North America to aid England, but it also refused to recognize the United States and to receive the first U.S. diplomatic mission. Independence enabled Americans to trade directly with Russia. The first two ships flying the U.S. flag arrived in St. Petersburg in 1783, and by 1797 one hundred American vessels visited Russia. In 1803, Levett Harris became the first U.S. consul in St. Petersburg, and in 1809 John Quincy Adams became the first U.S. minister to Russia to present his credentials to the Russian tsar. Only in 1832 was Russia willing to sign a commercial treaty with the United States, but U.S. trade with Russia remained of little significance for a long time.

Friendly relations between the United States and Russia continued into the period of the Civil War and culminated in Russia's sale of Alaska. Russian excesses in its Siberian exile system and its treatment of its Jewish population, as well as conflict over East Asia, ended a century of friendship and led to the abrogation of the commercial treaty in 1913.

The Bolshevik victory in Russia in 1917 made the rivalry between the United States and Soviet Russia also an ideological one. The United States, together with its Allies, intervened in the Russian Civil War. When the Bolsheviks won, the United States refused to recognize the Soviet Union and continued with its policy of nonrecognition until 1933. The United States, however, was willing to provide aid to Soviet Russia during the famine of 1921–1923, and business relations between the two countries continued even during the period of nonrecognition.

The German invasion of the Soviet Union in 1941 brought an alliance and cooperation between the United States and the Soviet Union. Lend-Lease was one of the major components of this cooperation, and U.S. and Soviet leaders met several times to coordinate their actions and to reach agreements about the future. The end of World War II resulted in increased tensions between the

Soviet Union and the United States—the two superpowers of the postwar period. Confrontation between the two powers rose and ebbed over the next forty years.

The Cold War was conducted through means short of direct military conflict. It was a long period of competition and confrontation with brief periods of cooperation and conciliation. At times tensions relaxed—when policies of peaceful coexistence and détente were adopted. At other times, tensions increased. When the Soviet Union tried to increase its influence beyond Eastern Europe, the United States took various measures to counteract and contain such influence and aggression. The two superpowers formed rival military alliances, conducted propaganda wars, intervened in weaker states, and carried on a dangerous and expansive arms race. Successive summit meetings and negotiations led to various agreements and treaties to limit and reduce the arms race and improve the relations between the two countries.

This dictionary covers all U.S. relations with Russia and the Soviet Union up to the present day. It includes entries on the events, policies, summit meetings, treaties, individuals, institutions, organizations, and business firms involved in the whole gamut of these relations. Presidents, secretaries of state, diplomats, arms control and disarmament negotiators, and others who played significant roles in the political and economic relations between the two countries have been included in the dictionary, as well as individuals who played a role in the industrial, commercial, scientific, social, and cultural relations between the two countries, such as military and naval officers, public and government officials, merchants and businessmen, engineers, journalists, and travelers.

Books that provide additional information about the relations between the United States and Russia and the Soviet Union are listed in the Bibliographical Essay. Cross-references are indicated by an asterisk appearing before a name or topic for which there is a separate entry.

Several librarians and archivists, as well as family members of some of the individuals discussed in the dictionary, provided assistance in compiling this work. Without their help, it would have been far less complete. Special thanks are due to the staff of the Interlibrary Loan Office of Northern Illinois University, DeKalb, Illinois.

UNITED STATES RELATIONS WITH RUSSIA AND THE SOVIET UNION

A

ABBE, CLEVELAND (1838–1916). Meteorologist, born December 3, 1838, in New York City. Abbe graduated from the City College of New York and studied at the University of Michigan. He served with the U.S. Coast Survey in Cambridge, Massachusetts, from 1860 to 1864. He worked at Pulkovo Observatory in Pulkovo, Russia, from 1864 to 1866. His Russian stay and his personal connections with Russian scientists provided a point of contact between the American and Russian scientific communities. He served as director of the Cincinnati Observatory from 1868 to 1870, joined the Weather Service of the U.S. Signal Corps in 1871, and was the first regular official weather forecaster of the U.S. government. Died October 28, 1916, in Washington, D.C. *References*: Cleveland Abbe Papers, Manuscript Division, Library of Congress; Truman Abbe, *Professor Abbe and the Isobars: The Story of Cleveland Abbe, America's First Weatherman* (New York, 1955); *DAB*; *DSB*; *NCAB* 8:264; Nathan Reingold, "Cleveland Abbe at Pulkovo: Theory and Practice in the Nineteenth Century Physical Sciences," *Science American Style* (New Brunswick, N.J., 1991), pp. 96–109; and Nathan Reingold, "A Good Place to Study Astronomy," *Library of Congress Quarterly Journal of Current Acquisition* 20 (1963): 211–17.

ABBE, JAMES EDWARD (1883–1973). Photographer, born July 17, 1883, in Alfred, Maine, and grew up in Newport News, Virginia. A self-taught photographer, he was a free-lance photographer in Virginia from 1913 to 1917 and then a reporter for the *Washington Post*. He established a studio in New York City in 1917, went to Europe in 1924, and established a studio in Paris. He went to Russia in 1932, becoming the first Western photographer for whom Joseph Stalin willingly posed. He wrote *I Photograph Russia* (New York, 1934). He was later a free-lance photojournalist in Colorado and in Spain during the Spanish Civil War. He was coauthor of *Around the World in Eleven Years* (New York, 1936). He was a rancher in Colorado and Wyoming from 1937 to 1945, a reporter on KLX Radio in San Francisco from 1945 to 1950, and a television critic for the *Oakland Tribune* from 1951 until his retirement in 1961. Died November 11, 1973, in San Francisco. *References*: Turner Browne and Elaine Partnow, *Macmillan Biographical Encyclopedia of Photographic Artists and Innovators* (New York, 1983); Colin Naylor, ed., *Contemporary Photographers* (Chicago, 1988); and *NYT*, November 13, 1973.

ABM TREATY (1972). Treaty between the United States of America and the Union of Soviet Socialist Republics on the limitation of anti-ballistic missile systems, signed in Moscow on May 26, 1972. The treaty limited each country to only two anti-ballistic missile (ABM) deployment sites, so restricted and so located that they could not provide a nationwide ABM defense or become the basis for developing one. Each country thus left unchallenged the penetration capability of the other's retaliatory missile forces. Both countries also agreed to limit qualitative improvement of their ABM technology. The treaty also provided for a U.S.-Soviet Standing Consultative Commission. The **PROTOCOL TO THE TREATY**, signed in Moscow on July 3, 1974, further limited each country to only one ABM deployment site. *References*: ACDA; Mathew Bunn, *Foundation for the Future: The ABM Treaty and National Security* (Washington, D.C., 1990); Mark T. Clark, "The ABM Treaty Interpretation Dispute: Partial Analyses and the Forgotten Context," *Global Affairs* 2 (Summer 1987): 58–79; Regina Cowen, Bhupendra Jasani, and Walter Stutzle, eds., *The ABM Treaty: To Defend or Not to Defend?* (Oxford, 1987); William J. Durch, *The ABM Treaty and Western Security* (Cambridge, Mass., 1988); Raymond L. Garthoff, *Policy versus the Law: The Reinterpretation of the ABM Treaty* (Washington, D.C., 1987); and Alan Platt, "The Anti-Ballistic Missile Treaty," in Michael Krepn and Dan Caldwell, eds., *The Politics of Arms Control Treaty Ratification* (New York, 1991), pp. 229–77.

ACCIDENTS MEASURES AGREEMENT (1971). Agreement on measures to reduce the risk of outbreak of nuclear war between the United States and the Union of Soviet Socialist Republics, signed in Washington on September 30, 1971. The two countries pledged to take measures to maintain and improve their organizational and technical safeguards against accidental or unauthorized use of nuclear weapons, to immediately notify the other country should a risk of nuclear war arise in cases of accidental, unauthorized, or unexplained incidents, and to give advance notification of any planned missile launches outside the territory of the launching party. Hot line was to be used in situations requiring prompt clarification. *References*: ACDA; and Barry M. Blichman, "Efforts to Reduce the Risk of Accidental or Inadvertent War," in Alexander L. George, Philip J. Farley, and Alexander Dallin, eds., *U.S.-Soviet Security Cooperation: Achievements, Failures, Lessons* (New York, 1988), pp. 466–81.

ACHESON, DEAN GOODERHAM (1893–1971). Secretary of state, born April 11, 1893, in Middletown, Connecticut. Acheson graduated from Yale University and Harvard Law School. He served in the U.S. Navy during World War I. He practiced law in Washington, D.C., until 1941. He was undersecretary of the treasury in 1933, assistant secretary of state from 1941 to 1945, and undersecretary of state from 1945 to 1947. He resumed law practice from 1947 to 1949. He was secretary of state from 1949 to 1953. He rejected the possibility of negotiation with the Soviet Union, believing that the USSR was not ready to bargain, and accepting the inevitability of a bipolar world. His major goals were to contain Communist expansion and to develop a strong military presence so that the United States could force the Soviet Union to negotiate on its own terms. He resumed law practice in 1953. He wrote *Morning and Noon* (Boston, 1965), *Sketches from the Life of Men I Have Known* (New York, 1959), and *Present at the Creation: My Years in the State Department* (New York, 1969). Died December 12, 1971, in Randy Spring, Maryland. *References*: Dean G. Acheson Papers, Harry S. Truman Library, Independence, Mo.; Dean G. Acheson Papers, Yale University Library; Douglas G. Brinkley, *Dean Acheson: The Cold War Years, 1953–1971* (New Haven, Conn., 1992); *CB* 1949; *DADH*; Norman Graebner, "Dean G. Acheson," in Norman Graebner, ed., *An Uncertain Tradition: American Secretaries of State in the Twentieth Century* (New York, 1961), pp. 267–88; Walter Isaacson and Evan Thomas, *The Wise Men: Six Friends and the World They Made* (New York, 1986); David S. McLellan, *Dean Acheson: The State Department Years* (New York, 1976); David S. McLellan and David Acheson, eds., *Among Friends: Personal Letters of Dean Acheson* (New York, 1980); *NYT,* October 13, 1971; *PolProf: Truman*; and Gaddis Smith, *Dean Acheson* (New York, 1972).

ACKERMAN, CARL WILLIAM (1890–1970). Journalist, born January 16, 1890, in Richmond, Indiana. Ackerman graduated from Earlham College and Columbia University. He was a reporter for United Press International in 1915, special writer for the *New York Tribune* in 1915–1916, and correspondent in Mexico, Spain, France, and Switzerland for the *Saturday Evening Post* in 1917–1918. He was a correspondent in Siberia for the *New York Times* in 1918–1919 and wrote *Trailing the Bolsheviki: Twelve Thousand Miles with the Allies in Siberia* (New York, 1919). He was director of foreign news service for the *Philadelphia Ledger* from 1919 to 1921, president and head of public relations of Carl W. Ackerman, Incorporated, from 1921 to 1930, and dean of the Graduate School of Journalism of Columbia University from 1931 to 1970. Died October 9, 1970, in New York City. *References*: Carl William Ackerman Papers, Manuscript Division, Library of Congress; *CA*; and *NYT,* October 10, 1970.

ADAMS, JOHN QUINCY (1767–1848). Diplomat, secretary of state, and president of the United States, born July 11, 1767, in Braintree (later Quincy), Massachusetts. Adams graduated from Harvard College and was admitted to the bar in 1790. He served as secretary to his father, John Adams, U.S. minister to France, and then to Francis Dana in St. Petersburg from 1781 to 1783. He was U.S. minister to the Netherlands from 1794 to 1797 and minister to Prussia from 1797 to 1801. He served in the U.S. Senate from 1803 to 1808. He was U.S. minister to Russia from 1809 to 1814. He became friendly with the tsar, participated in the social life of St. Petersburg, and was successful in furthering the interests of the United States. He chaired the commission that negotiated the Treaty of Ghent, which ended the War of 1812. He was secretary of state from 1817 to 1825 and president of the United States from 1825 to 1829. He served in the U.S. House of Representatives from 1831 until his death. Died February 23, 1848, in Washington, D.C. *References*: John Quincy Adams Papers, Massachusetts Historical Society, Boston; Charles Francis Adams, *Memoirs of John Quincy Adams Comprising Portions of His Diary from 1795 to 1848* (Philadelphia, 1874); Samuel F. Bemis, "John Quincy Adams and Russia," *Virginia Quarterly Review* 21 (1945): 553–68; Samuel F. Bemis, *John Quincy Adams and the Foundation of American Foreign Policy* (New York, 1949); *DAB*; *DADH*; Marion Mainwaring, *John Quincy Adams and Russia: A Sketch of Early Russian-American Relations as Recorded in the Papers of the Adams Family and Some of Their Contemporaries* (Quincy, Mass., 1965); and *NCAB* 5:73.

AFGHANISTAN CRISIS (1980–1988). Following a coup by left-wing opposition groups, and in order to keep control of the Afghani government by the Soviet Union, Soviet armed forces entered Afghanistan in December 1979. It was the first occasion since 1946 of Soviet ground troops being used in any number outside the Communist bloc and the first time the Soviet Union had involved a Third World and nonaligned country. The United States was alarmed at the possibility that an outside power would attempt to gain control of the Persian Gulf region, but it did little except boycott the 1980 Olympic games in Moscow, build up its military forces in the Persian Gulf, and provide funds and some arms to the insurgents in Afghanistan, U.S.-Soviet relations deteriorated to their lowest level since the *Cuban Missile Crisis. The Soviet army was unable to achieve a victory and withdrew from Afghanistan in 1988. *References*: Milan Hauner and Robert L. Canfield, eds., *Afghanistan and the Soviet Union: Collision and Transformation* (Boulder, Colo., 1989); Amin Saikal and William Maley, *Regime Change in Afghanistan: Foreign Intervention and the Politics of Legitimacy* (Boulder, Colo., 1991); and Amin Saikal and William Maley, eds., *The Soviet Withdrawal from Afghanistan* (Cambridge, Eng., 1989).

AGRO-JOINT. See AMERICAN JEWISH JOINT AGRICULTURAL CORPORATION

ALASKA PURCHASE (1867). In 1866, the Russian government offered to sell Russian America to the United States. It was a financial liability to the Russian government, but Tsar Alexander II and his advisers also thought that the sale would cement Russo-American ties and lead to a formal military alliance against Great Britain. Negotiations were conducted by Edouard de Stoeckl, the Russian minister to the United States, and Secretary of State *William H. Seward. A treaty was signed on March 30, 1867, under which the United States purchased Alaska for $7.2 million in gold. The U.S. Senate ratified the treaty on April 9,

1867, and the U.S. House of Representatives appropriated the necessary funds in July 1868. *References*: *DADH*; Victor John Farrar, *The Annexation of Russian America to the United States* (New York, 1937); James R. Gibson, "The Sale of Russian America to the United States," in S. Frederick Starr, ed., *Russia's American Colony* (Durham, N.C., 1987), pp. 271–94; Ronald J. Jensen, *The Alaska Purchase and Russian-American Relations* (Seattle, Wash., 1975); David Hunter Miller, *The Alaska Treaty* (Vestal, N.Y., 1981); Richard Emerson Neunherz, "The Purchase of Russian America: Reasons and Reactions" (Ph.D. diss., University of Washington, 1975); and Archie W. Shiels, *The Purchase of Alaska* (Fairbanks, Alaska, 1967).

ALBERT KAHN COMPANY. Industrial architects, formed in 1902 by Albert Kahn (1869–1942), with his brothers Julius and Moritz. At the request of the Soviet government in 1928, it participated in the industrialization program of the first Five-Year Plan, involved in building 521 factories in twenty-five cities at a cost of two billion dollars. The majority were designed in Moscow, where the Kahn staff, under the charge of Moritz Kahn, trained thousands of Soviet engineers in American industrial architecture. The Moscow office was dissolved in 1932. *References*: Detroit Institute of Arts, *The Legacy of Albert Kahn*, with an essay by W. Hawkins Ferry (Detroit, 1970); Grant Hildebrand, *Designing for Industry: The Architecture of Albert Kahn* (Cambridge, Mass., 1974); and George Nelson, *The Industrial Architecture of Albert Kahn, Inc.* (New York, 1939).

ALDRIDGE, IRA FREDERICK (1807–1867). Actor, born probably July 24, 1807, in New York City. Aldridge began his acting career at the African Theater in New York City and made his debut in England in 1824, remaining there until 1852 and becoming one of the leading tragedians of his time. In 1852, he went on his first continental tour. He went to Russia in 1858, performed in St. Petersburg, Moscow, and the provinces, and made several tours through much of European Russia. He directly influenced the art of a number of Russian actors. He became a citizen of Great Britain in 1863. Died August 7, 1867, in Lodz, while on a tour of Poland. *References*: *DAB*; *DANB*; Herbert Marshall and Mildred Stock, *Ira Aldridge, the Negro Tragedian* (Carbondale, Ill., 1958).

AMERICAN COMMITTEE ON EAST-WEST ACCORD. A nonprofit citizens' group interested in all aspects of the Soviet-American relationship. Founded in 1974 as an informal group, the American Committee on U.S.-Soviet Relations, it was formally chartered in 1977. The committee was established to strengthen public understanding of initiatives to control and reduce nuclear arms and to encourage mutually beneficial programs in science, culture, and nonmilitary trade. *Reference*: *DINRT*.

AMERICAN EXPEDITIONARY FORCES IN NORTH RUSSIA. Because of pressure from the other Allies, U.S. forces, numbering approximately five thousand, intervened in North Russia in August 1918. The purpose of the intervention was to protect military supplies in Murmansk and Archangel, to guard the Murmansk-Petrograd Railroad, and to aid the counterrevolutionaries. U.S. forces left North Russia in June 1919. *References*: Richard M. Doolen, *Michigan's Polar Bears: The American Expedition to North Russia, 1918–1919* (Ann Arbor, Mich., 1965); Richard Goldhurst, *The Midnight War: The American Intervention in Russia, 1918–1920* (New York, 1978); Dennis Gordon, ed., *Quartered in Hell: The Story of the American North Russian Expeditionary Force, 1918–1919* (Missoula, Mont., 1982); E. M. Holliday, *The Ignorant Armies: The Anglo-American Archangel Expedition, 1918–1919* (London, 1958); Chester V. Jackson, "Mission to Murmansk," *USNIP* 95 (February 1969): 82–89; John W. Long, "American Intervention in Russia: The North Russian Expedition, 1918–1919," *DH* 6 (1982): 45–67; Benjamin D. Rhodes, *The Anglo-American Winter War with Russia, 1918–1919: A Diplomatic and Military Tragicomedy* (Westport, Conn., 1988); and Leonid I. Strakhovsky, *Intervention at Archangel: The Story of Allied Intervention and Russian Counter-Revolution in North Russia, 1918–1920* (Princeton, N.J., 1944).

AMERICAN EXPEDITIONARY FORCES IN SIBERIA. U.S. forces intervened in Siberia in August 1918, with some seven thousand troops. The stated purpose of the intervention was to guard military stores and to assist in the evacuation of the Czech troops who were withdrawing to the East. In reality, they were sent to Siberia to serve as a deterrent to Japanese ambitions there and to preserve the territorial integrity of Russia. The troops assumed responsibility for the Trans-Siberian Railroad east of Lake Baikal. They left Siberia in April 1920. *References*: Richard Goldhurst, *The Midnight War: The American Intervention in Russia, 1918–1920* (New York, 1978); George F. Kennan, *Soviet-American Relations, 1917–1920, Vol. 2: The Decision to Intervene* (Princeton, N.J., 1958); Sylvian G. Kindall, *American Soldiers in Siberia* (New York, 1945); Judith A. Luckett, "The Siberian Intervention: Military Support of Foreign Policy," *Military Review* 44 (April 1984): 54–63; Robert James Maddox, *The Unknown War with Russia: Wilson's Siberian Intervention* (San Rafael, Calif., 1977); Betty Miller Unterberger, *America's Siberia Expedition, 1918–1920: A Study of National Policy* (Durham, N.C., 1956); and John Albert White, *The Siberian Intervention* (Princeton, N.J., 1950).

AMERICAN FRIENDS SERVICE COMMITTEE (AFSC). Established in 1917 by the American Society of Friends to put into practice traditional Quaker concern with relief. The first party of the AFSC went to Russia in 1917 and worked in Samara. The office was closed in 1918. The *AFSC* returned in 1920 as part of the *American Relief Administration (ARA) but continued to work after the ARA withdrew. The AFSC withdrew from the Soviet Union in 1927.

References: American Friends Service Committee Archives, Haverford College; John Forbes, *American Friends and Russian Relief, 1917–1927* (Philadelphia, 1952); Mary Hoxie Jones, *Swords into Ploughshares: An Account of the American Friends Service Committee, 1917–1937* (New York, 1937); and Richenda C. Scott, *Quakers in Russia* (London, 1964).

AMERICAN INTERVENTION IN RUSSIA. See AMERICAN EXPEDITIONARY FORCES IN NORTH RUSSIA and AMERICAN EXPEDITIONARY FORCES IN SIBERIA

AMERICAN JEWISH JOINT AGRICULTURAL CORPORATION (AGRO-JOINT). Founded in 1924 by the *American Jewish Joint Distribution Committee (JDC) to promote the agricultural settlement of Jews in the Soviet Union. It developed a project of three million acres of land in the Ukraine and the Crimea, populated by a quarter-million Jews, and trained petty traders and unskilled workers as farmers and artisans. It ended its activities in the Soviet Union in 1938, and the corporation was dissolved in 1952. *References*: Agro-Joint Archives, American Jewish Joint Distribution Committee Office, New York City; *MERSH*; Evelyn Morrisey, *Jewish Workers and Farmers in the Crimea and Ukraine* (New York, 1937); Allan L. Sagedan, "American Jews and the Soviet Experiment: The Agro-Joint Project, 1924–1937," *Jewish Social Studies* 43 (Spring 1981): 153–64; and *The Universal Jewish Encyclopedia* (New York, 1936), 1:253–56.

AMERICAN JEWISH JOINT DISTRIBUTION COMMITTEE, INC. (JDC). Founded in 1914 by several Jewish relief committees to coordinate relief efforts for Jews in Palestine and Eastern Europe and help displaced persons and other civilians suffering from the conflict. Russia and the Soviet Union were a limited focus of its attention, but it continued to operate in the Soviet Union until about 1938. *References*: American Jewish Joint Distribution Committee Archives, New York City; Herbert Agar, *The Saving Remnant: An Account of Jewish Survival* (New York, 1960); Oscar Handlin, *The Continuing Task: The American Jewish Joint Distribution Committee, 1914–1964* (New York, 1964); Moses A. Leavitt, *The JDC Story: Highlights of JDC Activities, 1914–1952* (New York, 1953); Michael Miller, "The Ukraine Commission of the Joint Distribution Committee, 1920, with Insight from the Judge Harry Fisher Files," *Jewish Social Studies* 49 (1987): 53–60; and Jerome C. Rosenthal, "Dealing with the Devil: Louis Marshall and the Partnership between the Joint Distribution Committee and Soviet Russia," *American Jewish Archives* 39 (April 1987): 1–22.

AMERICAN NATIONAL RED CROSS. Founded in 1881 and chartered by an act of Congress in 1905 to carry a system of national and international relief. An extensive Red Cross mission accompanied the *Root Mission to Russia in 1917, carried an extensive mission in Petrograd, and left in 1918. Another mission was dispatched to Archangel in 1918, and a third mission worked in Siberia from 1918 to 1920, with headquarters in Vladivostok. *References*: American National Red Cross Records, National Archives, Washington, D.C.; Foster Rhea Dulles, *The American Red Cross: A History* (New York, 1950); and Claude E. Fike, "The Influence of the Creel Committee and the American Red Cross on Russian-American Relations, 1917–1919," *Journal of Modern History* 31 (1959): 93–109.

AMERICAN RELIEF ADMINISTRATION (ARA). Chartered by the U.S. Congress on February 25, 1919, to provide famine relief to Europe. *Herbert Hoover served as head of the agency. *Walter Lyman Brown, head of ARA in Europe, negotiated in August 1921 an agreement with Soviet Russia. It was the first full-scale involvement of Americans with the Soviet government. The first contingent of the Russian unit arrived in Moscow in August 1921 to begin operations in Soviet Russia. *William N. Haskell served as director of the Russian unit. By August 1922, over ten million people were fed daily. As conditions in Soviet Russia began to improve, the Soviet government tried to obtain greater control of the relief operations, and ARA operations were terminated on July 10, 1923. *References*: American Relief Administration Archives, Hoover Institution Archives, Stanford, Calif.; Harold H. Fisher, *The Famine in Soviet Russia, 1919–1923: The Operations of the American Relief Administration* (New York, 1927); Frank A. Golder and Lincoln Hutchinson, *On the Trail of the Russian Famine* (Stanford, Calif., 1927); Robert W. McElroy, *Morality and American Foreign Policy: The Role of Ethics in International Affairs* (Princeton, N.J., 1992), ch. 3; Benjamin M. Weissman, "The After-Effects of the American Relief Mission to Soviet Russia," *RR* 29 (1970): 411–21; and Benjamin M. Weissman, *Herbert Hoover and Famine Relief to Soviet Russia, 1921–1923* (Stanford, Calif., 1974).

AMERICAN-RUSSIAN CHAMBER OF COMMERCE. A Russian-American Chamber of Commerce was established in 1914 by a group of Moscow entrepreneurs, and a U.S. section, the American-Russian Chamber of Commerce was incorporated in New York in 1916. It had virtually ceased operation by the end of 1920. It was reestablished in New York City in 1926, to foster trade and promote the economic, commercial, and industrial relations between the Soviet Union and the United States. The Moscow office, reopened in 1927, maintained contact with various economic and political departments of the Soviet government. The chamber prepared regular newsletters on Soviet exports, finances, production, railway operations, and lists of sailing between the countries and issued special reports on Soviet economic life, including *Economic Handbook* *of the Soviet Union* (New York, 1931) and *Handbook of the Soviet Union* (New York, 1936). The chamber closed its offices in 1940. *References*: James K. Libbey, "The American-Russian Chamber of Commerce," *DH* 9 (1985): 233–48; and *MERSH*.

AMERICAN SOCIETY FOR CULTURAL RELATIONS WITH RUSSIA. Established in 1926 to bring together those who were interested in Russian life and culture, to promote cultural intercourse between the two countries and especially the interchange of students, doctors, scholars, artists, scientists, and teachers, and to collect and diffuse information in both countries on developments in science, education, philosophy, art, literature, and social and economic life. It took a lead in promoting cultural intercourse during the late 1920s. By 1930, it was referring to itself as the American-Russian Institute, though it did not incorporate under that name until 1936. *Reference*: American Society for Cultural Relations with Russia Records, Files of the Library for Intercultural Studies, New York University Library, New York City.

AMERICAN SPECIAL MISSION TO RUSSIA. See ROOT MISSION TO RUSSIA

AMERICAN TRACTOR BRIGADE. Originally named Friends of Soviet Russia Agricultural Relief Unit, organized in the early 1920s by *Harold Ware. The brigade of tractors, accompanied by ten Americans, mostly farmers, arrived at the Toikino state farm in Sarapulskii County, Perm Province, in the Ural Mountains, in 1922. They seeded Toikino's land in rye and wheat and trained Russians to operate and maintain the tractors and the other equipment. They left the tractors as a gift when they returned to the United States later that year. *Reference*: *MERSH*.

ANDERSON, PAUL B. (1894–1985). Association official, born December 27, 1894, in Madrid, Iowa. Anderson graduated from the University of Iowa and studied at Oxford University. He served with the *Young Men's Christian Association (YMCA) in Shanghai, China, from 1913 to 1917. He was director of war prisoners' aid in Russia and Siberia in 1917–1918 and was private secretary to *John R. Mott on the *Root Mission to Russia in 1917. Charged with spying by the Russian authorities, he was forced to leave Russia in 1918. He was senior secretary of the European section of the North American YMCA and director and editor of the Russian YMCA Press, first in Berlin and then in Paris. He set up a large YMCA service to Russian émigrés. He was a consultant to the National Council of Churches, initiating and leading numerous high-level church delegates to Moscow. He wrote *Russia's Religious Future* (London, 1935) and *People, Church, and State in Modern Russia* (New York, 1944). Died June 26, 1985, in Black Mountain, North Carolina. *References*: *Christian Century* 102 (August

14–21, 1985): 730; Richard H. Marshall, ed., *Aspects of Religion in the Soviet Union, 1917–1967* (Chicago, 1971); *SR* 45 (1986): 188–89; and *WWWA*.

ANTI-BALLISTIC MISSILE TREATY. See ABM TREATY

APOLLO-SOYUZ TEST PROJECT (ASTP). A joint mission of American and Soviet space teams, Apollo and Soyuz, which met in orbit on July 17, 1975, to test an international docking system and joint flight procedures. *References*: Edward Ezell and Linda Ezell, *The Partnership: A History of the Apollo-Soyuz Test Project* (Washington, D.C., 1978); and David D. Finley, "The United States and the Soviet Union in Space," in Nish Jamgotch, Jr., ed., *U.S.-Soviet Cooperation: A New Future* (New York, 1989), pp. 111–31.

ARLE-TILZ, CORETTI (c. 1870–after 1943). Singer, born Coretta Alfred, c. 1870, in New York City. Alfred sang in the choir of a Baptist church in Harlem, New York. In 1901, she joined the "Louisiana Amazon Guards," a vaudeville troupe of black women, which toured Europe until 1904. The troupe arrived in Moscow in 1904, performed in theaters in St. Petersburg and Moscow for a year, and disbanded in 1905 because of revolutionary activities in Russia. She remained in Russia, attending the St. Petersburg Conservatory and later the Moscow Conservatory. After 1920, she sang professionally as Coretti Arle-Tilz. She toured extensively for more then two decades, particularly in the Scandinavian countries and Eastern Europe. She attracted wide attention in the 1920s with her debut in the title role of Verdi's *Aïda* in Kharkov and again during World War II when she toured Russian army camps singing concerts of spirituals for Russian troops. Died after 1943 in Moscow. *Reference*: Eileen Southern, *Biographical Dictionary of Afro-American and African Musicians* (Westport, Conn., 1982).

ARTHUR G. MCKEE AND COMPANY. Consulting engineers and contractors, of Cleveland, organized in 1915 by Arthur Glenn McKee (1871–1956). From 1931 to 1933, the firm assisted in designing and building the huge steel works at Magnitogorsk, the largest single undertaking in the Soviet Union's First Five-Year Plan.

AUSTIN COMPANY. A building and general contracting business, incorporated in 1904 in Cleveland under the name of Samuel Austin and Son Company. The name was changed to the Austin Company in 1916. Involved in the engineering and building of industrial buildings, the company initiated the development of basic types of industrial structures and designed and erected numerous industrial plants of all types. In 1929 it obtained a contract to design and supervise the construction of an automobile factory and workers' city for sixty thousand inhabitants in Nizhni Novgorod; it constructed the buildings from 1930 to 1932. *References*: The Austin Company Archives, Cleveland, Ohio; and Martin Greif,

The New Industrial Landscape: The Story of the Austin Company (Clinton, N.J., 1978).

AUTONOMOUS INDUSTRIAL COLONY "KUZBAS." See KUZBAS COLONY

AZERBAIJAN CRISIS (1946). The first major post–World War II crisis between the United States and the Soviet Union. In 1945 the USSR established the Autonomous Republic of Azerbaijan in North Iran. Pressure from the United States and Great Britain forced the Soviet Union to withdraw its forces in 1946. *References*: Louise L'Estrange Fawcett, *Iran and the Cold War: The Azerbaijan Crisis of 1946* (Cambridge, Eng., 1992); Gary R. Hess, "The Iranian Crisis of 1945–46 and the Cold War," *Political Science Quarterly* 89 (1974): 117–46; Richard Pfau, "Containment in Iran, 1946: The Shift to Active Policy," *DH* 1 (1977): 359–72; J. Philip Rosenberg, "The Cheshire Ultimatum: Truman's Message to Stalin in the 1946 Azerbaijan Crisis," *Journal of Politics* 41 (1979): 933–40; Robert Rossow, Jr., "The Battle for Azerbaijan, 1946," *Middle East Journal* 10 (1956): 17–32; and James A. Thorpe, "Truman's Ultimatum to Stalin on the 1946 Azerbaijan Crisis: The Making of a Myth," *Journal of Politics* 40 (1978): 188–95.

B

BAGBY, ARTHUR PENDLETON (1794–1858). Public official and diplomat, born in 1794 in Louisa County, Virginia. Bagby settled in Claiborne, Monroe County, Alabama, in 1818. He studied law and was admitted to the bar in 1819. He practiced law, served in the state house of representatives in 1821, 1822, 1824, and from 1834 to 1836, served in the state senate in 1825, was governor of Alabama from 1837 to 1841, and served in the U.S. Senate from 1841 to 1848. He was U.S. minister to Russia in 1849. His arrival in St. Petersburg was preceded by a large shipment of alcohol. Arriving drunk, he remained so for much of his stay. Died September 21, 1858, in Mobile, Alabama. *References*: Arthur Pendleton Bagby Papers, Alabama Department of Archives and History, Montgomery; *BDAC*; *DAB*; *DADH*; and *NCAB* 10:428.

BAKER, HENRY DUNSTER (1873–1939). Consul and editor, born February 26, 1873, in Attleboro, Massachusetts. Baker graduated from Yale University. He was a member of the editorial departments of the *Chicago Tribune,* the *New York Evening Post,* and the *Commercial West* (Minneapolis) until 1904. He served as consul in Hobart, Nassau, and Bombay from 1907 to 1914. He traveled through Siberia in 1909. He was commercial attaché at the embassy in St. Petersburg from 1914 to 1916. He was consul in Trinidad from 1916 to 1927, when he resigned, and was publisher and editor of the *Commercial West* until 1935. Died September 13, 1939, in Durham, North Carolina. *References*: Henry Dunster Baker Papers, Duke University Library, Durham, N.C.; and *WWWA*.

BAKER, JAMES ADDISON, III (1930–). Secretary of state, born April 28, 1930, in Houston, Texas. Baker graduated from Princeton University and University of Texas at Austin Law School and served in the U.S. Marine Corps. He practiced law in Houston. He managed *George Bush's campaign for the U.S. Senate in 1970, was undersecretary of commerce in 1975–1976, and directed Gerald Ford's presidential campaign in 1976 and George Bush's presidential campaigns in 1980 and 1988. He served as chief of staff to President

*Ronald Reagan from 1981 to 1985 and was secretary of the treasury from 1985 to 1988. He was secretary of state from 1989 until 1992. His interaction with leaders of the Soviet Union took U.S.-Soviet relations to a new stage of intimacy and cooperation. He encouraged a careful and prudent American response to the collapse of Soviet rule in Eastern Europe and to economic and political reforms in the Soviet Union. He backed President Bush's impulse to continue supporting Mikhail S. Gorbachev even when the Soviet leader's weaknesses were becoming clear, but he underestimated the power of nationalism in the Soviet Union. He resigned in August 1992, to become White House chief of staff and oversaw Bush's presidential reelection campaign. *References*: *CB* 1982; and *WWA*.

BALLISTIC MISSILE LAUNCH NOTIFICATION AGREEMENT (1988). Agreement between the United States of America and the Union of Soviet Socialist Republics on notification of launches of intercontinental ballistic missiles and submarine-launched ballistic missiles, signed in Moscow on May 31, 1988. Expanding on the agreements between the two countries under the *Accident Measures Agreement and the *Nuclear Risk Reduction Centers Agreement, each country would notify the other, no less than twenty-four hours in advance, through the Nuclear Risk Reduction Centers, of the planned date, launch area, and area of impact of any launch of an Intercontinental Ballistic Missile (ICBM) and Submarine-Launched Ballistic Missile (SLBM). *Reference*: ACDA.

BARGAINING CHIP. A phrase used since 1968 and defined as any military force, weapons system, or other resource, present or projected, that a country expresses a willingness to downgrade or discard in return for a concession by a particular rival. Since the Nixon administration believed that the Soviet Union signed *SALT I only because the United States had approved the development of the ABM, the Poseidon submarine, and the Minuteman III missile systems, it asked Congress to approve, as a bargaining chip for SALT II, the development of the Trident submarine, the B–1 bomber, and the Cruise missile. The bargaining chip strategy has been attacked because it is too expensive to develop weapons just to trade them away at the negotiating table and because it is inflammatory to the arms race to develop weapons systems just as a hedge in case negotiations should fail. *References*: Robert J. Bresler and Robert C. Gray, ''The Bargaining Chip and SALT,'' *Political Science Quarterly* 92 (1977): 65–88; and *DINRT*.

BARGHOORN, FREDERICK CHARLES (1911–1991). Political scientist, born July 4, 1911, in Queens Village, New York, and grew up in Dayton, Ohio. Barghoorn graduated from Amherst College and Harvard University. He worked for the State Department during the 1930s and was press attaché at the U.S. embassy in Moscow from 1943 to 1947. From 1949 to 1951, he headed a federal project interviewing Soviet defectors in analyze Soviet government and society. He was a member of the department of political science at Yale University after 1947 and professor of political science after 1956. He wrote *The Soviet Image* *of the United States: A Study in Distortion* (New York, 1950), *Soviet Russian Nationalism* (New York, 1956), *The Soviet Cultural Offensive: The Role of Cultural Diplomacy in Soviet Foreign Policy* (Princeton, N.J., 1960), *Soviet Foreign Propaganda* (Princeton, N.J., 1964), *Politics in the USSR* (Boston, 1966), and *Détente and the Democratic Movement in the USSR* (New York, 1976). He became the center of an international incident in 1963 when Soviet officials jailed him in Moscow on espionage charges and released him only under pressure from President John F. Kennedy. Died November 21, 1991, in Woodbridge, Connecticut. *References: NYT,* November 26, 1991; *PolProf: Kennedy*; and Thomas F. Remington, ed., *Politics and the Soviet System: Essays in Honour of Frederick C. Barghoorn* (Basingstoke, Eng., 1989).

BARKER, WHARTON (1846–1921). Banker, born May 1, 1846, in Philadelphia. Barker graduated from the University of Pennsylvania. He served in the Union army during the Civil War. In 1866, he began work with the banking firm of Barker Brothers and Company, becoming a member of the company in 1868. In 1878, the Russian government appointed him its special financial agent in the United States and entrusted him with the building of four cruisers in American shipyards. He went to Russia in 1879 to advise the country on the development of the coal and iron mines north of the Sea of Azof; for his services he was knighted by Tsar Alexander II. He returned to Russia in 1880 and again in 1892, attempting to gain concession to construct the middle sections of the Trans-Siberian Railroad. He compiled *Reports and Correspondence, Relating to Projected Coal and Iron Industries in Southern Russia* (N.p., 1881). He retained his interest in the family banking firm but also organized the Investment Company and the Finance Company of Philadelphia. Died April 8, 1921, in Philadelphia. *References*: Wharton Barker Papers, Manuscript Division, Library of Congress; *DAB*; *NCAB* 1:368; *NYT,* April 9, 1921; and George Queen, "Wharton Barker and Concessions in Imperial Russia, 1878–1892," *Journal of Modern History* 17 (1945): 202–14.

BARNES, RALPH W. (1899–1940). Journalist, born June 14, 1899, in Salem, Oregon. Barnes graduated from Willamette and Harvard universities. He was a reporter for the *Brooklyn Daily Eagle* from 1924 to 1926 and for the *New York Herald Tribune* in 1926 and was a member of the editorial staff of the *New York Herald* in Paris from 1926 to 1929. He was a foreign correspondent for the *New York Herald Tribune* after 1930, serving in Moscow from 1931 to 1935. Killed November 18, 1940, in an airplane crash near Danilovgrad, Yugoslavia. *References: NYT,* November 20, 1940; and *WWWA*.

BASIC PRINCIPLES AGREEMENT (BPA) (1972). Agreement on basic principles of mutual relations between the United States and the Union of Soviet Socialist Republics, signed by President *Richard M. Nixon and General Secretary Leonid I. Brezhnev on May 29, 1972, in Moscow. It was a sort of charter defining the basis for the further development of détente. The two sides agreed to hold periodic high-level meetings, to continue efforts to limit armaments, and to develop economic, scientific, and cultural ties between the two countries on a long-term basis in order to strengthen their relationship. *Reference*: Alexander L. George, "The Basic Principles Agreement of 1972: Origins and Expectations," in Alexander L. George, ed., *Managing U.S.-Soviet Rivalry: Problems of Crisis Prevention* (Boulder, Colo., 1983), pp. 107–17.

BATES, LINDON WALLACE (1858–1924). Civil engineer, born November 19, 1858, in Marshfield, Vermont. Bates attended Yale University. He was assistant engineer for North Pacific and Oregon Pacific railways and was the contractor engineer or manager on railway, dock, and terminal contracts in Oregon, Washington, Montana, Kansas, Illinois, Louisiana, and California for transcontinental railways or their subsidiary companies and on the Chicago Drainage Canal. He was retained from 1896 to 1902 by the Belgian government to prepare reports and projects for the improvement of the port of Antwerp, and he worked on the enlargement of the Suez Canal. He was consulted by the Russian government on deepening the mouth of the Volga River and on improving the harbors of the Black Sea ports. He was later involved in projects in the Danube River; Queensland, Australia; Shanghai; Galveston, Texas; the Panama Canal; Korea; Trinidad; and Peru. Died April 22, 1924, in Paris, France. His son, **LINDON WALLACE BATES, JR**. (1883–1915), a civil engineer, traveled in Russia in 1896, made a midwinter sled journey in Siberia and Mongolia in 1908, and wrote *The Russian Road to China* (Boston, 1910). *References*: *NCAB* 11:81; *NYT,* June 9, 1915; NYT, April 23, 1924; and *WWWA*.

BEAL, FRED ERWIN (1896–1954). Worker, born in Lawrence, Massachusetts. Beal went to work in a textile mill at age fourteen and was active in the textile strikes of 1912 and 1922. He joined the Communist party in 1922. With six other strike leaders, he was convicted of conspiracy after the killing of the police chief in Gastonia, North Carolina, in a skirmish at union headquarters in 1929. He fled to the Soviet Union in 1929, saying afterward that he was ordered by the Communist party to jump bail and flee there. He headed the political instruction apparatus for foreign employees at the Kharkov Tractor Factory and wrote *Foreign Workers in a Soviet Tractor Plant: A Pictorial Survey of the Life of Foreign Workers and Specialists during the Period of Socialist Construction, 1931–1932* (Moscow, 1933). Disillusioned, he returned to the United States in 1931 and became an avowed anti-Communist. He served four years of a seventeen-year prison sentence. He wrote *Proletarian Journey: New England, Gastonia, Moscow* (New York, 1937), in which he gave a detailed account of his life at the Kharkov factory. He later lectured and wrote *The Red Fraud, an Exposé of Stalinism* (New York, 1949). Died November 14, 1954, in Lawrence, Massachusetts. *Reference*: *NYT*, November 16, 1954.

BEAM, JACOB DYNELEY (1908–). Diplomat, born March 24, 1908, in Princeton, New Jersey. Beam graduated from Princeton University and studied at Cambridge University. He joined the foreign service in 1931 and served in the U.S. consulate in Geneva in 1933–1934 and in the embassy in Berlin from 1934 to 1940. He was a member of the political advisory staff of the Supreme Headquarters of the Allied Expeditionary Force (SHAEF) from 1944 to 1946 and was chief of the Central European Division of the State Department in 1948–1949. He served in the embassy in Jakarta, Indonesia, from 1949 to 1951 and was minister-counselor at the embassy in Moscow in 1952–1953, deputy director of the Policy Planning Staff of the State Department from 1953 to 1956, U.S. ambassador to Poland from 1957 to 1961, assistant director of the International Relations Bureau of the Arms Control and Disarmament Agency from 1962 to 1966, and ambassador to Czechoslovakia from 1966 to 1969. He was U.S. ambassador to the Soviet Union from 1969 to 1973 but played a minor role in policy-making and negotiations between the United States and the Soviet Union, and his influence was peripheral. He retired in 1973 and wrote *Multiple Exposure: An American Ambassador's Unique Perspective on East-West Issues* (New York, 1978). *References*: *CB* 1959; *DADH*: *PolProf: Eisenhower*; and *Polprof: Nixon/ Ford*.

BEATTY, BESSIE (1886–1947). Journalist, born January 27, 1886, in Los Angeles. Beatty attended Occidental College. She began as a reporter for the *Los Angeles Herald* in 1904 and served on the editorial staff of the *San Francisco Bulletin* from 1908 until 1917. She was special correspondent for *Good Housekeeping* and *Hearst's International* magazine in Russia in 1917 and got an exclusive interview with V. I. Lenin. She wrote *The Red Heart of Russia* (New York, 1918). She was editor of *McCall's Magazine* from 1918 to 1921. She went to Soviet Russia again in 1921, as special correspondent for *Hearst's Magazine* and *Good Housekeeping*. She was later director of the National Label Council, engaged in publicity work for welfare and cultural groups, and was a commentator on radio station WOR in New York City from 1940 until her death. Died April 6, 1947, in Nyack, New York. *References*: Bessie Beatty Papers, New York Public Library; *CB* 1944; *NYT*, April 7, 1947; and Ishbell Ross, *Ladies of the Press* (New York, 1936), pp. 580–83.

BEEUWKES, HENRY (1881–1956). Physician, born August 29, 1881, in Jamesburg, New Jersey. Beeuwkes graduated from Johns Hopkins University School of Medicine. He entered the U.S. Army in 1909 and served in the Army Medical Corps. He served during World War I. He was medical director of the *American Relief Administration in Soviet Russia from 1921 to 1923, where he helped to rehabilitate many hospitals and dispensaries. He resigned from the army in 1924 and was director of the West African Yellow Fever Commission organized by the Rockefeller Foundation from 1924 to 1934. He organized and commanded Valley Forge General Hospital in Phoenixville, Pennsylvania, during

World War II. Died January 31, 1956, in Bay Pines, Florida. *References*: *Journal of the American Medical Association* 161 (May 5, 1956): 85; and *NYT*, February 2, 1956.

BERDAN, HIRAM (1823–1893). Inventor, born in 1823 in Plymouth, Michigan, and grew up near Rochester, New York. Berdan attended Hobart College and was then apprenticed to a machine shop in Rochester. He served in the Union army during the Civil War, commanding a regiment of sharpshooters, which he organized and which was armed with a repeating rifle that he had invented. He went to Russia in 1865 and spent several years superintending the manufacture of his rifle there for the Russian government. The standard rifle introduced into the Imperial Russian Army in 1868 was named the "Berdanka." In 1888, he returned to the United States and sued the United States for infringing his patents in the Springfield rifle, for which the court of claims awarded him a hundred thousand dollars in 1892. Besides his rifle, he had several other inventions. Died March 31, 1893, in Washington, D.C. *References*: *ACAB*; *The Biographical Dictionary of America* (Boston, 1906); *NYT*, April 1, 1893; and Alexander Tarsaidze, "Berdanka," *RR* 9 (1950): 30–36.

BERKMAN, ALEXANDER (1870–1936). Anarchist and author, born November 21, 1870, in Vilna, Russia, and grew up in St. Petersburg and Kovno, Russian Lithuania. He came to the United States in 1887 and became deeply involved in the activities of radical Jewish labor groups in New York City. In 1892, he attempted to assassinate Henry C. Frick, general manager of the Carnegie Steel Company, during the Homestead steel strike. He was convicted and sentenced to twenty-two years in jail, served fourteen years, and was released in 1906. He returned to the anarchist movement, opposed U.S. entry into World War I, was arrested and found guilty of conspiracy to obstruct the operation of the selective service law, was sentenced to two years in jail, and was deported (with *Emma Goldman) to Soviet Russia in 1919. Although he sympathized with the Russian Revolution in its early stages, once he was in Soviet Russia, his enthusiasm cooled, especially after the suppression of the Kronstadt sailors' demonstration in 1921, and he finally left Soviet Russia in 1922. He wrote *The Kronstadt Rebellion* (Berlin, 1922), *The Russian Revolution and the Communist Party* (Berlin, 1922), *The Russian Tragedy* (Berlin, 1922), *Anti-Climax: The Concluding Chapter of My Russian Diary* (Berlin, 1925), and *The Bolshevik Myth, Diary 1920–22* (London, 1925). The last work was one of the first radical criticisms of the Soviet experiment. He lived in Germany until 1930 and later in France. Committed suicide June 28, 1936, in Nice, France. *References DAB S2*; Richard Drinnon and Anna Maira Drinnon, eds., *Nowhere at Home: Letters from Exile of Emma Goldman and Alexander Berkman* (New York, 1975); William Nowlin, "The Political Thought of Alexander Berkman" (Ph.D. diss., Tufts University, 1980); and *NYT*, July 2, 1936.

BERLIN BLOCKADE CRISIS (1948–1949). On June 24, 1948, the Soviet Union stopped all land travel to the western sector of Berlin in response to the Allied decision to begin forming a German government in the western zones of Berlin to ensure West Germany's economic and political alignment with the West. Although military challenge was considered by the United States, it was rejected in favor of an airlift to supply Berlin. On May 12, 1949, the Soviet Union concluded that the blockade had failed and lifted it. *References*: Richard Collier, *Bridge across the Sky: The Berlin Blockade and Airlift, 1948–1949* (New York, 1978); Walter Philipps Davison, *The Berlin Blockade: A Study in Cold War Politics* (Princeton, N.J., 1958); M. Steven Fish, "The Berlin Blockade of 1948–1949," in Alexander L. George, ed., *Avoiding War: Problems of Crisis Management* (Boulder, Colo., 1991), pp. 195–221; Daniel F. Harrington, "The Berlin Blockade Revisited," *International History Review* 6 (1984): 88–112; Eric Morris, *Blockade: Berlin and the Cold War* (London, 1973); Avi Shlaim, *The United States and the Berlin Blockade, 1948–1949: A Study in Crisis Decision-Making* (Berkeley, Calif., 1983); and Ann Tusa and John Tusa, *The Berlin Airlift* (New York, 1988).

BERLIN CRISIS (1958–1959). Premier Nikita Khrushchev demanded, in November 1958, discussions on European security, a nuclear-free Germany, and the end of the four-power occupation status for Berlin. He threatened that the Soviet Union would agree to a separate peace treaty with East Germany, but the West refused to give in. The Berlin problem was on the agendas for the *Washington Summit of 1959, *Paris Summit of 1960, which collapsed, and the *Vienna Summit of 1961, which failed to resolve the problem. The erection of the Berlin Wall in August 1961 ended the crisis. *References*: *DADH*; and Jack M. Schick, *The Berlin Crisis, 1958–1962* (Philadelphia, 1971).

BERLIN WALL CRISIS (1961). In August 1961, the Soviet and the East Germany authorities erected a wall between East and West Berlin to prevent East Germans from escaping to the West. The United States did not actively respond to the building of the wall. The Berlin Wall came down in 1990. *References*: Curtis Cate, *The Ides of August: The Berlin Wall Crisis, 1961* (New York, 1978); Honore M. Catudal, *Kennedy and the Berlin Wall Crisis: A Case Study in U.S. Decision Making* (Berlin, 1980); *DADH*; Norman Gleb, *The Berlin Wall: Kennedy, Khrushchev, and the Showdown in the Heart of Europe* (New York, 1986); Jack M. Schick, *The Berlin Crisis, 1958–1962* (Philadelphia, 1971); and Robert M. Slusser, *The Berlin Crisis of 1961: Soviet-American Relations and the Struggle for Power in the Kremlin, June-November 1961* (Baltimore, 1973).

BESS, DEMAREE CAUGHEY (1893–1962). Journalist and editor, born July 28, 1893, in Kansas City, Missouri. Bess attended Occidental College (Los Angeles) and graduated from the University of Iowa. He was instructor of English at Assiut College (Egypt), joined the British forces in Palestine during World War I, and later served with the American Red Cross in Palestine and Syria.

He returned to the United States in 1919, worked for the *Minneapolis Tribune* and then for the *Los Angeles Times,* was news editor of the *Japan Advertiser* in Tokyo in 1927–1928, traveled throughout China from 1928 to 1931, and was manager of the North China bureau of the United Press, based in Peking. He was Far Eastern chief and correspondent for the *Christian Science Monitor* in the Soviet Union and Europe from 1931 to 1938. His years in the Soviet Union were spent traveling throughout the country, from the Arctic Circle to the Black Sea. He wrote (with John D. Littlepage) *In Search of Soviet Gold* (New York, 1938). He was foreign correspondent for the *Saturday Evening Post* in 1938, stationed in Europe, and was later its associate editor until his death. Died June 2, 1962, in New York City. *References: CB* 1943; and *NYT,* June 3, 1962.

BEVERIDGE, ALBERT JEREMIAH (1862–1927). Public official and author, born October 6, 1862, in Highland County, Ohio. Beveridge graduated from Asbury College (now DePauw University) and was admitted to the bar in 1887. He practiced law in Indianapolis after 1887 and became involved in Indiana Republican politics. He served in the U.S. Senate from 1899 until 1911. He went to Russia in 1901 and wrote *The Russian Advance* (New York, 1903), which sold twenty thousand copies within six weeks. He later had a career as a historian. Died April 27, 1927, in Indianapolis. *References: BDAC;* Claude G. Bowers, *Beveridge and the Progressive Era* (Boston, 1932); John Braeman, *Albert J. Beveridge: American Nationalist* (Chicago, 1971); *DAB; DADH;* and *NYT,* April 28, 1927.

BILLINGS, FRANK (1854–1932). Physician, born April 2, 1854, in Highland, Iowa County, Wisconsin. Billings attended the state normal school in Platteville, Wisconsin, and graduated from the Chicago Medical College. He practiced medicine in Chicago after 1881. He was assistant demonstrator in Chicago Medical College (later Northwestern University Medical School), professor of physical diagnosis from 1887 to 1892, professor of medicine from 1892 to 1898, and professor of medicine at Rush Medical College from 1898 to 1924. He was also professor of medicine at the University of Chicago from 1905 to 1924. He went to Russia in 1917 as chairman of the American Red Cross commission to that country. He was medical adviser to the provost marshal-general and later chief of the Division of Reconstruction in the Surgeon-General's Office during World War I. Died September 20, 1932, in Chicago. *References: Chicago Tribune,* September 21, 1932; *DAB S1;* Edwin Frederick Hirsch, *Frank Billings: The Architect of Medical Education, an Apostle of Excellence in Clinical Practice, a Leader in Chicago Medicine* (Chicago, 1966); and *NCAB* 223:345.

BOGEN, BORIS DAVID (1869–1929). Social worker, born in Moscow and came to the United States in the early 1890s. Bogen graduated from New York University. He taught at the Hebrew Technical School of the Educational Alliance from 1896 to 1900, was principal of the Baron de Hirsch Agricultural School in Woodbine, New Jersey, from 1900 to 1904, was superintendent of the United

Jewish Charities in Cincinnati from 1904 to 1913, and was field secretary of the Conference of Jewish Charities after 1913. After the outbreak of World War I, he was involved in relief activities in Poland and Russia for the *American Jewish Joint Distribution Committee from 1917 to 1924. Died June 30, 1929. His autobiography, *Born a Jew* (New York, 1930), was published posthumously. *References*: Boris D. Bogen Papers, American Jewish Archives, Hebrew Union College, Cincinnati; *Encyclopaedia Judaica* (Jerusalem, 1971), 4:1169–70; *Jewish Social Service Quarterly* 6 (1929): 39–40; and Zosa Szajowski, *The Mirage of American Jewish Aid in Soviet Russia, 1917–1939* (New York, 1977), ch. 9.

BOHLEN, CHARLES EUSTIS ("CHIP") (1904–1974). Diplomat, born August 30, 1904, in Clayton, New York. Bohlen graduated from Harvard University. He joined the foreign service in 1928. He served in the U.S. embassy in Moscow in 1934–1935 and from 1938 to 1941. He was White House liaison officer of the State Department and also State Department counselor. He was U.S. ambassador to the Soviet Union from 1953 to 1957. His appointment stirred controversy because of the opposition of Senator Joseph McCarthy. In Moscow, he served mainly as reporter on internal changes in Russia after the death of Joseph Stalin, advising Secretary of State *John Foster Dulles that neither one-man rule nor extensive political purges were going to return. He was U.S. ambassador to the Philippines from 1957 to 1959, ambassador to France from 1962 to 1968, and deputy undersecretary of state for political affairs in 1968–1969. He wrote *The Transformation of American Foreign Policy* (New York, 1969), and *Witness to History, 1929–1969* (New York, 1973). Died January 1, 1974, in Washington, D.C. *References*: Charles Eustis Bohlen Papers, Manuscript Division, Library of Congress; Thomas G. Corti and T. Michael Ruddy, "The Bohlen-Thayer Dilemma: A Case Study in the Eisenhower Administration's Response to McCarthyism," *Mid-America* 72 (1990): 119–33; *DADH*; Daniel F. Harrington, "Kennan, Bohlen, and the Riga Axioms," *DH* 2 (1978): 423–37; Walter Isaacson and Evan Thomas, *The Wise Men: Six Friends and the World They Made* (New York, 1986); Eduard M. Mark, "Charles E. Bohlen and the Acceptable Limits of Soviet Hegemony in Eastern Europe: A Memorandum of 18 October 1945," *DH* 3 (1979): 201–13; *NYT*, January 2, 1974; and T. Michael Ruddy, *The Cautious Diplomat: Charles E. Bohlen and the Soviet Union, 1929–1969* (Kent, Ohio, 1986).

BOKER, GEORGE HENRY (1823–1890). Author and diplomat, born October 6, 1823, in Philadelphia. Boker graduated from Princeton University, studied law, but was never admitted to the bar. He embarked on a literary career, writing plays and poetry. He was U.S. minister to Turkey from 1872 to 1875 and minister to Russia from 1875 to 1878. He developed a personal friendship with the tsar and persuaded the Russian government to participate in the Centennial Exposition. Later he helped establish the Union League of Philadelphia and served as its president and was president of the Fairmount Commission. Died January

2, 1890, in Philadelphia. *References*: Edward Sculley Bradley, *George Henry Boker, Poet and Patriot* (Philadelphia, 1927); *DAB*; *DADH*; and *NYT*, January 3, 1890.

BOVT, VIOLETTE (1927–   ). Dancer, born May 1927, in Los Angeles. Bovt grew up in Moscow and attended the Bolshoi school there after 1935. She performed with the Stanislavsky and Nemirovich-Danchenko Theatre in the 1950s and 1960s. *Reference*: Barbara Naomi Cohen-Stratyner, *Biographical Dictionary of Dance* (London, 1982).

BRECKINRIDGE, CLIFTON RODES (1846–1932). Public official and diplomat, born November 22, 1846, near Lexington, Kentucky. Breckinridge attended Washington College (Lexington, Va.) and served in the Confederate army and Confederate navy during the Civil War. He was a cotton planter in Arkansas from 1870 to 1883. He served in the U.S. House of Representatives from 1883 to 1894. He was U.S. minister to Russia from 1894 to 1897. He was mostly concerned with the treatment of Jews by the Russian government and spent much effort on behalf of Jews, but with little success. Died December 3, 1932, in Wendover, Leslie County, Kentucky. *References*: *BDAC*; Dorsey D. Jones, "Breckinridge: An Arkansas at the Court of the Tsar," *Arkansas Historical Quarterly* 1 (1942): 193–205; *NCAB* 8:191; and James F. Willis. "An Arkansan in St. Petersburg: Clifton Rodes Breckinridge, Minister to Russia, 1894–1897," *Arkansas Historical Quarterly* 38 (1979): 3–31.

BROOKS, ERASTUS (1815–1886). Journalist, born January 31, 1815, in Portland, Maine. Brooks was apprenticed to a compositor and then attended Brown University. He was a reporter for the *Haverhill* (Mass.) *Gazette,* correspondent in Washington for a group of papers from 1835 to 1840, and editor of *Haverhill Advertiser*. In 1843 he visited Russia, the first American journalist to cover the country. He wrote vivid articles, which were widely appreciated. He later joined in the management of the *New York Express* and then assumed complete control of the newspaper from 1852 until his death. Died November 25, 1886, in Staten Island, New York. *References*: *DAB*; *NCAB* 6:47; and *WWWA*.

BROWN, NEILL SMITH (1810–1886). Public official and diplomat, born April 18, 1810, in Giles County, Tennessee. Brown studied at the Maury County Manual Labor Academy, then studied law, and was admitted to the bar in 1834. He practiced law in Pulaski, Tennessee. He participated in the Seminole War in Florida in 1836, served in the Tennessee House of Representatives from 1838 to 1844, and was governor of Tennessee from 1848 to 1850. He was U.S. minister to Russia from 1850 to 1853. His critical assessment of Russia in his reports was fresh and direct. He served again in the state house of representatives from 1856 to 1870 and then practiced law in Nashville until his retirement in 1872. Died January 30, 1886, in Nashville. *References*: Neill Smith Brown

Papers, Tennessee State Library and Archives, Nashville; Joseph O. Baylen, "A Tennessee Politician in Imperial Russia, 1850–1853," *Tennessee Historical Quarterly* 14 (1955): 227–52; *BDG*; and *NCAB* 7:209.

BROWN, WALTER LYMAN (? –1951). Mining engineer. Brown graduated from the University of California. He started his mining career in San Francisco in 1903 and worked in Mexico, California, Idaho, and Alaska. He then worked at the New Modderfrontein and Crown mines in South Africa and was assistant manager (and later manager) of a mine in the Gold Coast. In 1916, he joined the Commission for Relief in Belgium and conducted many delicate negotiations in The Hague during World War I. After the war, he continued the work of relief in Central Europe and supervised it from headquarters in London until 1923. In 1920, he negotiated with Maxim Litvinov of the Soviet Russian government for relief of the famine in Soviet Russia. At the request of *Herbert Hoover, he went to Riga to meet the Bolshevik representatives and reached an agreement detailing the future operations of the relief operations in Soviet Russia. He later conducted additional negotiations in Soviet Russia. He also concluded negotiations for Lena Goldfields Company and the Aluminum Company of America. After 1934, he was president of Carson Hill Gold Mining Corporation in California and later developed and operated Know Hill Mines in Washington. Died September 5, 1951, in Carmel, California. *Reference*: *Engineering and Mining Journal* 152 (December 1951): 117–18.

BROWN, WILLIAM ADAMS, JR. (1894–1957). Economist, born November 14, 1894, in New York City. Brown graduated from Yale and Columbia universities. He was a member of the *Committee on Public Information in Russia from 1917 to 1919 and wrote *The Groping Giant: Revolutionary Russia as Seen by an American Democrat* (New Haven, Conn., 1920). He worked in the family banking firm of Brown Brothers and Company in New York City from 1919 to 1926 and was assistant professor of economics at Brown University from 1928 to 1936, associate professor from 1936 to 1941, and professor from 1941 to 1946. He went to the Soviet Union in 1930 to study Soviet economic experiments in the industrial and agricultural fields. He served in the Economics Studies Division of the State Department from 1943 to 1946 and was a member of the senior staff of Brookings Institution after 1946. Died April 19, 1957, in Washington, D.C. *References*: *NCAB* 43:137; and *NYT*, April 20, 1957.

BROWNE, LOUIS EDGAR (1891–1951). Journalist, born October 20, 1891, in Lynn, Massachusetts. Browne attended the U.S. Naval Academy but left in 1912 to become a journalist. He was Washington correspondent for the *New York Herald* in 1913 and war correspondent for the *Chicago Daily News, New York Globe,* and Philadelphia Bulletin during World War I. He was in Soviet Russia in 1917–1918 and was later the representative of the *Chicago Daily News* in the Middle East. He was executive secretary of the *American-Russian Chamber of Commerce from 1929 until 1940. He compiled *Economic Handbook of the Soviet Union* (New York, 1931) and *Handbook of the Soviet Union* (New York, 1935). He was in charge of the Russian section of the Military Intelligence in the War Department in Washington during World War II. Died February 10, 1951, in Gainesville, Florida. *References*: *NYT,* February 11, 1951; and *WWWA.*

BRYANT, LOUISE (1885–1936). Journalist, born December 5, 1885, in San Francisco. Bryant attended the universities of Nevada and Oregon. She married *John Reed in 1917. She was in Soviet Russia in 1917–1918, in the early days of the Russian Revolution, and wrote many articles about it for the Hearst newspapers. In Moscow and Petrograd, she met and interviewed every Soviet official of importance. She wrote *Six Months in Russia: An Observer's Account of Russia before and during the Proletarian Dictatorship* (New York, 1918) and *Mirrors of Moscow* (New York, 1923). She married *William C. Bullitt in 1923, but they were divorced in 1930. Died January 6, 1936, in Paris, France. *References*: Virginia Gardner, *"Friend and Lover": The Life of Louise Bryant* (New York, 1982); Barbara Gelb, *So Short a Time: A Biography of John Reed and Louise Bryant* (New York, 1973); and *NYT,* January 10, 1936.

BRZEZINSKI, ZBIGNIEW KAZIMIERZ (1928–   ). Educator and government official, born March 28, 1928, in Warsaw, Poland, and emigrated to Canada in 1938. Brzezinski came to the United States in 1953 and was naturalized in 1958. He graduated from McGill and Harvard universities. He was assistant professor of government and research associate at the Russian Research Center of Harvard University from 1956 to 1960, associate professor at Columbia University from 1960 to 1962, and professor of public law and government and director of the Research Institute on International Change at Columbia University from 1962 to 1977 and again after 1981. He wrote *The Permanent Purge: Politics in Soviet Totalitarianism* (Cambridge, Mass., 1956) and *Ideology and Power in Soviet Politics* (New York, 1962), was coauthor of *Political Power: USA/USSR* (New York, 1964), and edited *Dilemmas of Change in Soviet Politics* (New York, 1969). He was special assistant for national security affairs to President Jimmy Carter from 1977 to 1981. Suspicious of Soviet intention, he insisted that the Soviets were pursuing détente to create favorable conditions to acquire power in Third World countries, and he held them responsible for all such crises. He wrote *Power and Principle: Memoirs of the National Security Adviser, 1977–1981* (New York, 1983). *References*: *CA*; *DADH*; and *WWA.*

BUCHANAN, JAMES (1791–1868). Diplomat, secretary of state, and president of the United States, born April 23, 1791, near Mercersburg, Pennsylvania. Buchanan graduated from Dickinson College, studied law, and was admitted to the bar in 1812. He practiced law, served in the Pennsylvania legislature from 1814 to 1816 and in the U.S. House of Representatives from 1821 to 1831. He was U.S. minister to Russia in 1832–1833. He negotiated the Russian-American

Commercial Treaty of 1832. He served in the U.S. Senate from 1834 to 1845 and was secretary of state from 1845 to 1849, U.S. minister to Great Britain from 1853 to 1856, and president of the United States from 1857 to 1861. Died June 1, 1868, near Lancaster, Pennsylvania. *References*: James Buchanan Papers, Historical Society of Pennsylvania, Philadelphia; *DAB*; *DADH*; *James Buchanan's Mission to Moscow, 1831–1833: His Speeches, State Papers, and Private Correspondence* (New York, 1970); Philip D. Klein, *President James Buchanan* (University Park, Pa., 1962); and *NCAB* 5:1.

BUEL, JAMES WILLIAM (1849–1920). Author and journalist, born October 22, 1849, in Golconda, Pope County, Illinois. Buel began working in his father's tannery at the age of eight and was later clerk in his father's shoe and leather store. He attended the University of Illinois and studied law. He went West in 1870, started a small weekly newspaper in Spring Hill, Kansas, and was reporter and editorial writer on various Kansas City and St. Louis papers. He wrote his first book in 1878 and later wrote some twenty historical works. He traveled in Russia and Siberia in 1882 and visited the most important mines of Siberia. His book *Russian Nihilism and Exile Life in Siberia: A Graphic and Chronological History of Russia's Bloody Nemesis, and a Description of Exile Life in All Its True but Horrifying Phases, Being the Results of a Tour through Russia and Siberia Made by the Author* (San Francisco, 1883) was officially forbidden by the Russian government because of its revelations of convict life. Died November 16, 1920, in San Diego, California. *References*: *NCAB* 7:75; and *WWWA*.

BULLARD, ARTHUR (1879–1929). Journalist and author, born December 8, 1879, in St. Joseph, Missouri. Bullard attended Hamilton College. He was probation officer for the New York Prison Association in New York City from 1903 to 1906. In 1904 he went abroad, spent some time in Switzerland with Russians, learning Russian, and then went to Russia to write, for American magazines, of the revolutionary forces stirring among the Slavs. He spent time in Moscow and St. Petersburg. He served as press representative of the Friends of Russian Freedom in America from 1905 to 1907 and was war correspondent for *Outlook* during the Balkans War in 1912–1913 and of *Outlook, Century,* and the *Atlantic* during World War I. In 1917 he became a member of the *Committee on Public Information and was sent to Russia to organize its activities there. He remained for nearly two years, suffering to severe illness as a result of hardships encountered in Siberia. He was chief of the Russian division in the State Department from 1919 until 1921. He wrote *The Russian Pendulum: Autocracy, Democracy, Bolshivism* (New York, 1919). He was editor of *Our World* in 1923–1924 and representative of the League of Nations Non-Partisan Association in Geneva, Switzerland, after 1925. Died September 10, 1929, in Geneva, Switzerland. *References*: Arthur Bullard Papers, Princeton University Library, Princeton, N.J.; *NCAB* 21:392; Stephen Vaughn, ''Arthur Bullard and the Creation of the Committee on Public Information," *New Jersey History* 97 (1979): 45–53; and *WWWA*.

BULLITT, WILLIAM CHRISTIAN (1891–1967). Diplomat, born January 25, 1891, in Philadelphia. Bullitt graduated from Yale University and attended Harvard Law School. He joined the State Department in 1917 as chief of the Bureau of Central European Information, where he supplied data on the Russian Revolution for President *Woodrow Wilson. He was a member of the U.S. delegation to the Paris Peace Conference and was sent by President Wilson on a secret mission to Moscow to confer with Soviet leaders on peace-related issues, but his proposals were ignored by Wilson. He wrote *The Bullitt Mission to Russia* (New York, 1919). He was in private business from 1919 to 1933. A long-standing advocate of Soviet recognition, he was U.S. ambassador to the Soviet Union from 1933 to 1936, the first ambassador after the establishment of diplomatic relations. He soon became disillusioned and embittered over the behavior of the Soviet government and became an advocate of a hard line toward the Soviet Union. He was U.S. ambassador to France from 1936 to 1940 and was special representative of the president in North Africa and the Middle East during World War II. Died February 15, 1967, in Neuilly, France. *References*: Will Brownell and Richard N. Billings, *So Close to Greatness: A Biography of William C. Bullitt* (New York, 1987); Orville H. Bullitt, ed., *For the President, Personal and Secret: Correspondence between Franklin D. Roosevelt and William C. Bullitt* (Boston, 1972); *DAB S8*; *DADH*; Beatrice Farnsworth, *William C. Bullitt and the Soviet Union* (Bloomington, Ind., 1967); *NCAB* D:35; and *NYT*, February 16, 1967.

BURRELL, GEORGE ARTHUR (1882–1957). Chemical engineer, born January 23, 1882, in Cleveland, Ohio. Burrell graduated from Ohio State University. He was a chemist with the U.S. Geological Survey from 1904 to 1908, in charge of mine gas, natural gas, and petroleum investigation for the U.S. Bureau of Mines in Pittsburgh from 1908 to 1916 and consulting engineer in 1916–1917. He directed the chemical research division of the Chemical Warfare Service of the U.S. Army during World War I. He was an engineering consultant to the chemical, natural gas, and petroleum industries from 1919 to 1943. He founded the Burrell Technical Supply Company in Pittsburgh in 1923, serving as president until 1952 and as its chairman of the board until his death. He was retained by the Soviet government in 1930–1931 to modernize the Soviet natural gas industry and worked in the oil town of Grozny in the Caucasus. He wrote *An American Engineer Looks at Russia* (Boston, 1932). He was president of the Atlantic States Gas Company from 1936 to 1954 and vice-president of the Commonwealth Gas Corporation from 1942 to 1954. Died August 16, 1957, in New York City. *References*: *NCAB* 46:228; and *NYT*, August 18, 1957.

BUSH, GEORGE HERBERT WALKER (1924–   ). Public official and president of the United States, born June 12, 1924, in Milton Massachusetts. Bush served in the U.S. Naval reserves during World War II and graduated from Yale University. He moved to Texas, entered the oil industry, and founded the Zapata Petroleum Corporation and later the Zapata Offshore Company. He served in the U.S. House of Representatives from 1967 to 1971 and was U.S. ambassador to the United Nations from 1971 to 1973, chief of the U.S. liaison office in the People's Republic of China in 1974–1975, and director of the Central Intelligence Agency in 1976. He was vice-president of the United States from 1981 to 1989 and president from 1989 to 1993. He encouraged the improvement of relations with the Soviet Union and met President Mikhail S. Gorbachev in Malta in 1989, in Washington in 1990, and in Moscow in 1991, signing several agreements, including a trade agreement and an agreement to destroy 80 percent of chemical weapons stocks. He also met with Boris Yeltsin, president of Russia, in 1991, 1992 and 1993. He signed the *START I treaty in 1991 and the START II treaty in 1993. His interaction with Soviet leaders took U.S.-Soviet relations to a new stage of intimacy and cooperation. He supported the revolution of 1989 in Eastern Europe, and the republics emerging from the collapse of the Soviet Union, and he continued to support Gorbachev even when the Soviet leader's weaknesses were becoming clear. *References*: Joseph G. Whelan, *Soviet Diplomacy and Negotiating Behavior, 1988–90: Gorbachev-Reagan-Bush Meetings at the Summit* (Washington, D.C., 1991), pp. 149–211.

BUSH, RICHARD JAMES (fl. 1865–1899). Surveyor, born in Massachusetts. Bush served in the Civil War. He was a surveyor for the *Russian-American Telegraph Expedition in Siberia from 1865 to 1867. He wrote *Reindeer, Dogs, and Snow-Shoes: A Journal of Siberian Travel and Explorations Made in the Years 1865, 1866, and 1867* (New York, 1871).

BYRNES, JAMES FRANCIS (1879–1972). Public official and secretary of state, born May 2, 1879, in Charleston, South Carolina. Byrnes studied law and was admitted to the bar in 1903. He edited the *Aiken* (S.C.) *Journal and Review* from 1903 to 1907, practiced law, and became involved in politics. He was prosecutor for the Second Circuit of South Carolina from 1908 to 1910, served in the U.S. House of Representatives from 1911 to 1925, practiced law from 1925 to 1930, and served in the U.S. Senate from 1931 to 1941. He was justice of the U.S. Supreme Court in 1941–1942, head of the Office of Economic Stabilization in 1942–1943, and director of the Office of War Mobilization from 1943 to 1945. In 1945, he attended the *Yalta Conference as a personal adviser to President *Franklin D. Roosevelt. He was secretary of state from 1945 to 1947. He accompanied President *Harry S. Truman to the *Potsdam Conference. Initially, his policy was based on compromise and openness in order to maintain the wartime alliance, but the principle of compromise soon floundered in the growing hostility between the United States and the Soviet Union after the end of the war. His firmness with the Soviets was evident in the *Azerbaijan Crisis, and he became an important architect of the hardened attitude toward the Soviet Union. He wrote a memoir, *Speaking Frankly* (New York, 1947), and an autobiography, *All in One Lifetime* (New York, 1958). He was governor of South Carolina from 1951 to 1955. Died April 9, 1972, in Columbia, South Carolina. *References*: James Francis Byrnes Papers, Clemson University Library, Clemson, S.C.; Richard D. Burns, "James F. Byrnes," in Norman A. Graebner, ed., *An Uncertain Tradition: American Secretaries of State in the Twentieth Century* (New York,1961), pp. 223–44; Kendrick A. Clements, ed., *James F. Byrnes and the Origins of the Cold War* (Durham, N.C., 1983); George Curry, *James F. Byrnes* (New York, 1965); *DADH*; J. F. Karl, "Compromise or Confrontation: James F. Byrnes and United States Policy towards the Soviet Union, 1945–1946" (Ph.D. diss., University of Toronto, 1976); Robert L. Messer, *The End of an Alliance: James F. Byrnes, Roosevelt, Truman, and the Origins of the Cold War* (Chapel Hill, N.C., 1982); *NYT*, April 10, 1972; and Patricia Dawson Ward, *The Threat of Peace: James F. Byrnes and the Council of Foreign Ministers, 1945–1946* (Kent, Ohio, 1979).

C

CALDER, JOHN KNIGHT (1882–1946). Industrial engineer, born October 8, 1882, in Ingersoll, Ontario, Canada. Calder was employed by various construction companies in Pittsburgh, Chicago, and Toronto from 1902 to 1918 and was partner in an automobile sales agency in Ingersoll, Ontario, from 1918 to 1924. He was job superintendent with Bryant and Detweiler Company of Detroit after 1924, supervising the construction of many buildings of the River Rouge plant of the Ford Motor Company. Engaged by the Soviet government in 1929, he went to the Soviet Union as a consulting engineer. He supervised the construction of tractor plants in Stalingrad and Cheliabinsk, a blast furnace in Magnitogorsk, the Salta bridge plant, and the beginning of a large copper smelting plant at Lake Balkhash. Around each of these plants, he helped build a complete modern city. He was then appointed adviser to the central Soviet agency handling all new construction and was later supervisor of the Soviet Steel Building Trust. The hero of the play *Tempo* by Nikolai Pogodin was modeled after him. He returned to the United States in 1935 and resumed his association with Bryant and Detweiler as general superintendent until his death. Died November 16, 1946, in Detroit, Michigan. *References*: Maurice Hindus, ''Pinch Hitter for the Soviets,'' *American Magazine* 113 (April 1932): 31–33, 134–36; *NCAB* 35:40; and *NYT*, November 17, 1946.

CALDWELL, JOHN KENNETH (1881–1982). Diplomat, born October 16, 1881, in Piketon, Ohio. Caldwell graduated from Berea College. He was appointed student interpreter in Japan in 1906, was vice- and deputy consul general and interpreter in Yokohama, and was assistant Japanese secretary in the embassy in Japan from 1909 to 1914. He was consul in Vladivostok from 1914 to 1920. He was consul in Kobe, Japan, in 1920–1921, and was Japanese secretary at the embassy in Tokyo in 1921. He served on special duty in Chita, Siberia, in 1921. He was assistant chief of the Division of Far Eastern Affairs in the State Department in 1925–1926, representative of the secretary of state on the Federal Narcotics Control Board from 1925 to 1930, and chairman of the U.S. delegation to the Conference on Limitation of Manufacture of Narcotics Drugs in Geneva in 1931. He was U.S. consul general at Sydney and at Tientsin, China, from 1932 to 1942 and U.S. minister to Ethiopia from 1943 until his retirement in 1945. Died June 27, 1982, in Carmel, California. *References*: John Kenneth Caldwell "Memoirs," Hoover Institution Archives, Stanford, Calif.; and *WWWA*.

CAMERON, SIMON (1799–1889). Public official and diplomat, born March 9, 1799, in Lancaster County, Pennsylvania. He was an apprentice printer, became editor of the *Bucks County Messenger* in 1821, worked in a Washington printing house from 1822 to 1824, and bought the *Harrisburg Republican* in 1824. He became involved in state and national politics and served in the U.S. Senate from 1845 to 1849 and again from 1857 to 1861. He was secretary of war in 1861–1862. He was named U.S. minister to Russia and was virtually exiled to St. Petersburg because of complaints about his mishandling of the War Department and his advocacy of policies contrary to those of President *Abraham Lincoln. He was in Russia only three months (June-September 1862), although he did not formally resign until 1863. While in St. Petersburg, he maintained tsarist support of the Union. He served again in the U.S. Senate from 1867 to 1877. Died June 26, 1889, in Dinegal Springs, near Harrisburg, Pennsylvania. *References*: Simon Cameron Papers, Manuscript Division, Library of Congress; Simon Cameron Papers, Historical Society of Dauphin County, Harrisburg, Pa.; Erwin S. Bradley, *Simon Cameron: Lincoln's Secretary of War* (Philadelphia, 1966); *DAB*; *DADH*; Lemar L. Libhart, "Simon Cameron's Political Exile as United States Minister to Russia," *Journal of the Lancaster County Historical Society* 72 (1968): 189–228; and *NCAB* 3:437.

CAMPBELL, GEORGE WASHINGTON (1769–1848). Public Official and diplomat, born February 9, 1769, in Tongue, Sutherlandshire, Scotland, and brought to Mecklenburg County, North Carolina, in 1772. Campbell graduated from Princeton College, studied law, and was admitted to the bar. He practiced law in Knoxville, Tennessee. He served in the U.S. House of Representatives from 1803 to 1809, was a judge of the state supreme court of errors and appeals from 1809 to 1811, served in the U.S. Senate from 1811 to 1814, and was secretary of the treasury from 1814 to 1818. He was U.S. minister to Russia from 1818 to 1820, the first of several purely political appointments to the Russian post, appointments of men who had no diplomatic experience. Three of his children died of typhus in St. Petersburg within one week, and he became depressed and performed little diplomatic business of note. Died February 17, 1848, in Nashville, Tennessee. *References*: George Washington Campbell Papers, Manuscript Division, Library of Congress; *DAB*; and Weymouth Tyree Jordan, *George Washington Campbell of Tennessee, Western Statesman* (Tallahassee, Fla., 1955).

CAMPBELL, THOMAS DONALD (1881–1966). Agriculturist, born February 19, 1881, in Grand Forks, North Dakota. Campbell graduated from the University of South Dakota and studied at Cornell University. He was general manager of the Grand Forks Street Car Company from 1906 to 1910. He joined the Torrance-Marshall Company in 1910, which was engaged in farming and the development of large land tracts, and then headed a subsidiary company that managed the firm's ranching properties. After 1917, he was involved in a program to convert idle Indian lands in the West into wheat farms. He organized Campbell Farming Corporation in 1923, with headquarters in Hardin, Montana, and served as its president until his death. Recognized as an authority on mechanized farming, he was invited by the Soviet government in 1929 to advise on the development of an agricultural program in its First Five-Year Plan. During his stay in the Soviet Union, more than seventy-five hundred acres of farming land were put under cultivation according to his plans. He returned to the Soviet Union in 1931, and Russian agricultural delegations frequently visited his Montana farm. He wrote *Russia: Market or Menace?* (New York, 1932). Died March 18, 1966, in Pasadena, California. *References*: H. Drache, "Flower in the Plains," *Agricultural History* 51 (1977): 78–91; J. K. Howard, "Tom Campbell: Farmer of Two Continents," *Harper* 198 (March 1949): 55–63; *NCAB* 54:86; and *NYT*, March 19, 1966.

CANTACUZENE, JULIA DENT GRANT (1876–1975). Socialite, born June 7, 1876, in the White House, granddaughter of President Ulysses S. Grant. She met Prince Michael Cantacuzene, a lieutenant in the Russian guards cavalry, in Cannes, France. They were married in 1899, and she became Princess Cantacuzene and Countess Speransky. She lived in the Cantacuzene estates in central Ukraine. The prince became a major general during World War I. The couple was forced to flee Russia in 1917 and came to the United States. They went back in Russia briefly, when General Cantacuzene joined the staff of the White Russian Admiral Aleksander Kolchak. She wrote *Revolutionary Days: Recollections of Romanoffs and Bolsheviki, 1914–1917* (Boston, 1919), *Russian People: Revolutionary Recollections* (New York, 1923) and *My Life Here and There* (New York, 1921). In 1934, she obtained a divorce. She became a leader in Washington society and frequently held court at her home for Washington's large White Russian colony. Died October 5, 1975, in Washington, D.C. *Reference*: NYT, October 7, 1975.

CARTER, JAMES (JIMMY) EARL, JR. (1924–   ). Public official and president of the United States, born October 1, 1924, in Plains, Georgia, and grew up in Archery, Georgia. Carter attended Georgia Southwestern College and graduated from the U.S. Naval Academy in 1946. He served in the U.S. Navy from 1947 until 1953, when he resigned to run his family farm in Plains. He served in the Georgia state senate from 1963 to 1966 and was governor of Georgia from 1970 to 1975. He was president of the United States from 1977 to 1981. Determined to end the Cold War, he pressed the Soviet Union on human rights and moved to evolve the arms-control limitation talks into reduction talks. He signed SALT II in 1979 but withdrew the treaty in 1980, following the Soviet intervention in Afghanistan. He retaliated against the Soviet Union with a grain embargo and an Olympic boycott. He returned to the assertive themes of the early Cold War, and U.S. relations with the Soviet Union deteriorated. He wrote *Keeping Faith: Memoirs of a President* (New York, 1982). *References*: Coral Bell, *President Carter and Foreign Policy: The Costs of Virtue* (Canberra, 1982); Alexander Moens, *Foreign Policy under Carter: Testing Multiple Advocacy Decision Making* (Boulder, Colo., 1990); Gaddis Smith, *Morality, Reason, and Power: American Diplomacy in the Carter Years* (New York, 1986); and Richard C. Thornton, *The Carter Years: Toward a New Global Order* (New York, 1991).

CHAMBERLIN, WILLIAM HENRY (1897–1969). Journalist, born February 17, 1897, in Brooklyn, New York. Chamberlin graduated from Haverford College. He was reporter for the *Philadelphia Public Ledger* in 1917–1918, assistant magazine editor of the *Philadelphia Press* in 1918, and assistant to the book editor of the *New York Tribune* from 1919 to 1921. He was the Moscow correspondent of the *Christian Science Monitor* from 1922 to 1934 and also correspondent of the *Manchester Guardian*. Initially a sympathizer with the Soviet regime, he turned into one of its bitterest enemies during the years he spent in the Soviet Union, and he assailed the Soviet system and communism in many books. He wrote *Soviet Russia: A Living Record and a History* (Boston, 1930), *The Soviet Planned Economic Order* (Boston, 1931), *Russia's Iron Age* (Boston, 1934), *The Russian Revolution, 1917–1921* (New York, 1935), and *Collectivism: A False Utopia* (New York, 1937). He was foreign correspondent of the *Christian Science Monitor* in Japan from 1935 to 1939 and France in 1939–1940. After 1940, he was a free-lance lecturer and writer, contributing editor of the *New Leader*, and editorial contributor to the *Wall Street Journal*. He wrote *The Confessions of an Individualist* (New York, 1940), *The Ukraine: A Submerged Nation* (New York, 1944), *The Russian Enigma: An Interpretation* (New York, 1943), *Beyond Containment* (Chicago, 1953), and *The Evolution of a Conservative* (Chicago, 1959). Died September 12, 1969, in Samaden, near St. Moritz, Switzerland. *References*: William Henry Chamberlin Papers, Providence College Library, Providence, R.I.; *CA*; Robert Hobbs Mayers, "William Henry Chamberlin: His Views on the Soviet Union" (Ph.D. diss., Indiana University, 1973); *NYT*, September 15, 1969; and *RR* 29 (1970): 1–5.

CHASE NATIONAL BANK. Founded in New York City in 1877. During the 1920s and 1930s, there was a close connection between the Chase National Bank and the Soviet government. The bank was a leader in the Soviet credit business, advancing the Soviet Union thirty million dollars of revolving credit in 1926. It also acted as agent for the Soviets during the 1930s and was later Moscow Narodny's correspondent in New York. Chase merged with Equitable Trust in 1930 and with the Bank of Manhattan in 1955 to form the Chase Manhattan

Bank. It opened an office in Moscow in May 1973, the first American bank to do so. *Reference*: John Donald Wilson, *The Chase: The Chase Manhattan Bank, N.A., 1945–1985* (Boston, 1986).

CHURCHMAN, JOHN (1753–1805). Scientist, born May 29, 1753, in East Nottingham, Chester County, Pennsylvania. Churchman was self-taught. He worked as a surveyor and conceived a design for improving magnetic observations. He was in England from 1792 until 1796. He was elected to the Russian Imperial Academy of Sciences in 1795. In 1804, he visited St. Petersburg, where he was well received by the authorities, and he spent the winter there. He was again in England from 1803 to 1805. Died July 17, 1805, at sea, during a voyage from England to the United States. *Reference*: NCAB 9:287.

CLAY, CASSIUS MARCELLUS (1810–1903). Public official and diplomat, born October 19, 1810, in Madison County, Kentucky. Clay attended Transylvania University and graduated from Yale University. He studied law but never practiced. He served in the Kentucky state legislature in 1835, 1837, and 1840 and was governor of Kentucky from 1849 to 1853. He was U.S. minister to Russia in 1861–1862 and again from 1863 to 1869. Despite his eccentric, jealous behavior and numerous social gaffes, he was successful in maintaining the pro-Union attitude of the Russian government. During the Polish insurrection, he communicated U.S. support of Russian actions and sent information back to Washington about the resources of Alaska, thus aiding the purchase of that territory. He retired in 1869 and wrote an autobiography, *The Life of Cassius Marcellus Clay: Memoirs, Writings, and Speeches* (Cincinnati, 1886). Died July 22, 1903, in Madison County, Kentucky. *References*: Cassius Marcellus Clay Papers, Filson Club Library, Louisville, KY.; *DAB*; *DADH*; *NCAB* 2:311; H. Edward Richardson, *Cassius Marcellus Clay: Firebrand of Freedom* (Lexington, Ky., 1976); James R. Robertson, *A Kentuckian at the Court of the Tsars: The Ministry of Cassius Clay to Russia, 1861–62 and 1863–69* (Berea, Ky., 1935); and David L. Smiley, *Lion of Whitehall: The Life of Cassius M. Clay* (Madison, Wis., 1962).

CLAY, JOHN RANDOLPH (1808–1885). Diplomat, born September 29, 1808, in Philadelphia and grew up in Roanoke, Virginia. Clay studied law and was admitted to the bar in 1829. He was secretary of legation in St. Petersburg from 1830 to 1837 and again from 1845 to 1847. He was secretary of legation in Vienna from 1838 to 1845. He was chargé d'affaires in Peru from 1847 to 1853 and minister to Peru from 1853 to 1860. Died August 15, 1885, in Philadelphia. *References*: NCAB 12:80; and George Irvin Oeste, *John Randolph Clay: America's First Career Diplomat* (Philadelphia, 1966).

COLD WAR. The term describing the state of relations between the United States and the Soviet Union in the period following the end of World War II until the end of the 1980s. The Cold War was conducted through various means, including diplomatic maneuvers, political pressure, propaganda, and threat of force, but short of direct military force, and led to tension and hostility between the two superpowers, struggling for world supremacy. The threat of massive nuclear retaliation and the nuclear holocaust that would follow deterred the two countries from recourse to "hot war." *References*: J. L. Black, *Origins, Evolution, and Nature of the Cold War: An Annotated Bibliographic Guide* (Santa Barbara, Calif., 1986); Lynn Etheridge Davis, *The Cold War Begins: Soviet-American Conflicts over Eastern Europe* (Princeton, N.J., 1974); *EAFP*; John Lewis Gaddis, *The United States and the Origins of the Cold War, 1941–1947* (New York, 1972); Patrick Glynn, *Closing Pandora's Box: Arms Races, Arms Control, and the History of the Cold War* (New York, 1992); Michael J. Hogan, ed., *The End of the Cold War: Its Meaning and Implications* (Cambridge, 1992); William G. Hyland, *The Cold War: Fifty Years of Conflict* (New York, 1992); Walter LaFeber, *America, Russia, and the Cold War, 1945–1990* (New York, 1991); Thomas G. Patterson, *Meeting the Communist Threat: America's Cold War History* (New York, 1988); Thomas G. Patterson, *On Every Front: The Making of the Cold War* (New York, 1979); Hugh Thomas, *Armed Truce: The Beginnings of the Cold War, 1945–46* (New York, 1987); Kenneth W. Thompson, *Interpreters and Critics of the Cold War* (Washington, D.C., 1978); and Daniel Yergin, *Shattered Peace: The Origins of the Cold War and the National Security State* (Boston, 1977).

COLE, FELIX (1887–1969). Diplomat, born October 12, 1887, in St. Louis, Missouri. Cole Attended the University of Wisconsin, graduated from Harvard and George Washington universities, and was admitted to the bar. He was a reporter and editorial writer for the *Boston Herald* from 1911 to 1913. He was with an automobile business in St. Petersburg in 1913–1914 and with a publisher there in 1914–1915. He became clerk in the U.S. consulate in Petrograd in 1915, was vice-consul in Petrograd from 1915 to 1917, and was consul in Archangel from 1917 to 1919. He was acting chief of the Russian Division in the State Department in 1920. He was later consul in Bucharest and Sydney, consul general in Warsaw and Frankfort-on-the-Main, counselor of legation in Riga, Kovno, and Tallinn, consul general in Riga, Algiers, Rabat, and Monrovia, minister to Ethiopia from 1945 to 1947, and the first U.S. ambassador to Ceylon in 1948–1949. He retired in 1950. Died July 23, 1969, in Montclair, New Jersey. *References*: *BRDS*; *NYT*, July 25, 1969; Benjamin D. Rhodes, "A Prophet in the Russian Wilderness: The Mission of Consul Felix Cole at Archangel, 1917–1919," *Review of Politics* 46 (1984): 388–409; and *WWWA*.

COLEMAN, FREDERICK WILLIAM BACKUS (1874–1947). Diplomat, born May 17, 1874, in Detroit. Coleman graduated from the University of Michigan. He practiced law in Detroit from 1899 until 1906 and was counsel and representative of a French manufacturing company in London, England, from 1906 to 1910. He was vice-president of the Minneapolis City Fuel Company from 1915 to 1921. In 1914–1915, he was in Norway, Sweden, and Russia as attorney for American coal interests at Spitsbergen. He served in the U.S. Army during World War I. He was the first U.S. minister to Estonia, Latvia, and Lithuania from 1922 to 1931, living in Riga, Latvia. He negotiated and signed treaties of extradition, friendship, commerce, consular regulations, arbitration, and conciliation with the three republics. At Riga, he served as the main American "listening post" to the Soviet Union at that time. His dispatches to Washington provide detailed and accurate reports of events in the Soviet Union and suggest a deep understanding of events there. He was U.S. minister to Copenhagen from 1931 to 1933, when he resigned. Died April 2, 1947, in Bronxville, New York. *References*: *NCAB* 33:518; *NYT,* April 3, 1947; and *WWWA.*

COLLINS, PERRY MCDONOUGH (1815–1900). Explorer, born in Hyde Park, Dutchess County, New York. Collins studied law in New York City. He practiced law in New York City and then worked for a steamship company in New Orleans from 1846 to 1849. He went to California in 1849, practiced law in Sonora, Tuolumne County, and was involved in real estate and other commercial ventures. In 1853, he became associated with the American-Russian Commercial Company. He was the U.S. commercial agent to the Amur River in Siberia, explored the area between St. Petersburg and Irkutsk in 1856–1857, and wrote an account of his journey, *A Voyage down the Amoor: With a Land Journey through Siberia, and Incidental Notices of Manchuria, Kamschatka, and Japan* (New York, 1860). He returned to Moscow in 1858–1859. He was involved in the *Russian-American Telegraph Expedition of Western Union Telegraph Company from New York through Siberia to Europe, popularly known as the Collins Overland Line, in 1866–1867, when the project was canceled following the laying of the Atlantic cable. He later settled in New York City. Died January 18, 1900, in New York City. *References*: *NYT,* January 20, 1900; Charles Vevier, "The Collins Overland Line," *PHR* 28 (1959): 237–53; and Charles Vevier, "Introduction," in Charles Vevier, ed., *Siberian Journey: Down the Amur to the Pacific, 1856–1857* (Madison, Wis., 1962).

COLTON, ETHAN THEODORE (1872–1970). Association official, born November 22, 1872, in Palmyra, Jefferson County, Wisconsin. Colton graduated from Dakota Wesleyan University and studied at the University of Chicago and Columbia University. He was traveling secretary in the student department of the International *Young Men's Christian Association (YMCA) from 1900 to 1904, secretary of the foreign department from 1904 to 1915, associate general secretary from 1915 to 1924, and executive secretary from 1926 to 1932. He organized the YMCA service in Russia and Siberia in 1917 and directed relief for the Russian intelligentsia, a project centered in Paris, from 1922 to 1925. In 1925–26, he was administrative secretary of the combined work of the American and Canadian YMCAs in the Russia-Baltic areas. He retired in 1932 but was an executive for YMCA War Prisoners' Aid in camps in the United States during World War II. He was coauthor of *The Russia We Face Now* (Washington, D.C., 1953) and wrote *Forty Years with Russians* (New York, 1940) and *Memoirs of Ethan T. Colton, Sr., 1872–1952* (n.p., 1952). Died May 21, 1970, in Montclair, New Jersey. *References*: Ethan Theodore Colton Papers, Hoover Institution Archives, Stanford, Calif.; Ethan Theodore Colton, "With the Y.M.C.A. in Revolutionary Russia," *RR* 14 (1955): 128–39; and *WWWA*.

COMMITTEE ON PUBLIC INFORMATION ("CREEL COMMITTEE"). Set by executive order of President *Woodrow Wilson in 1917, with George Creel as chairman, and responsible for uniting American support behind World War I effort. In the autumn of 1917, it established a war cable service to Petrograd, a motion picture service, a lecture bureau, and a pamphlet program for Russia. Although primarily set up as an agency for wartime propaganda and censorship, it got involved in military and political intelligence. The committee's personnel in Russia tried successfully to influence U.S. policy toward Russia. *References*: Claude E. Fike, "The Influence of the Creel Committee and the American Red Cross on Russian-American Relations, 1917–1919," *Journal of Modern History* 31 (1959): 93–109; and James R. Mock and Cedric Larson, *Words That Won the War: The Story of the Committee on Public Information, 1917–1919* (Princeton, N.J., 1939).

COMMITTEE ON THE PRESENT DANGER. A nonprofit citizens' group, founded in 1976, that viewed the principal threat to U.S. security to be the Soviet drive for dominance based on an unparalleled military buildup. The committee argued for a stronger U.S. military position and more defense spending to counter the Soviet buildup. A number of the committee's members were prominent in the administration of President *Ronald Reagan. It published *Alerting America: The Papers of the Committee on the Present Danger*, ed. Charles Tyroler II (Washington, D.C., 1984). *References*: *DINRT*; Beth Ann Ingold, "The Committee on the Present Danger: A Study of Elite and Public Influences, 1976–1980" (Ph.D. diss., University of Pittsburgh, 1989); and Jerry Wayne Sanders, *Peddlers of Crisis: The Committee on the Present Danger and the Politics of Containment* (Boston, 1983).

CONTAINMENT. U.S. strategy after World War II was to prevent the territorial expansion by the Soviet Union while avoiding a major war, and containment was the central element of this strategy. The term was devised by *George Frost Kennan in his article in the July 1947 issue of *Foreign Affairs*. Characterizing the Soviet Union as an expansionist society, the article stated that the United

States had to "contain" the Soviet Union in the areas of Eastern Europe already under its control and frustrate its expansionism, a policy that would lead to the collapse of the communist regime in the Soviet Union. Containment involved establishing military alliances with Western Europe and Japan and deploying U.S. armed forces in Europe and East Asia. *References*: Terry L. Deibel and John Lewis Gaddis, eds., *Containing the Soviet Union: A Critique of U.S. Policy* (Washington, D.C., 1987); *EAFP*; Thomas H. Etzold and John Lewis Gaddis, eds., *Containment: Documents on American Policy and Strategy, 1945–1950* (New York, 1978); John L. Gaddis, "Containment: A Reassessment," *Foreign Affairs* 55 (1977): 874–87; John L. Gaddis, *Strategies of Containment: A Critical Appraisal of Postwar American National Security Policy* (New York, 1982); Deborah Welch Larson, *Origins of Containment: A Psychological Explanation* (Princeton, N.J., 1985); and David S. McLellan, "Who Fathered Containment?" *International Studies Quarterly* 17 (1973): 205–26.

CONVENTIONAL ARMS TRANSFER TALKS (CAT). See U.S.-SOVIET CONVENTIONAL ARMS TRANSFER TALKS

COOLIDGE, ARCHIBALD CARY (1866–1928). Historian, born March 6, 1866, in Boston, Coolidge graduated from Harvard College and the University of Freiburg (Germany). Coolidge was acting secretary of legation in St. Petersburg in 1890–1891, private secretary to the U.S. minister to France in 1892, and secretary of legation in Vienna in 1893. He was an instructor in history at Harvard University from 1893 to 1899, assistant professor from 1899 to 1908, and professor after 1908. He introduced the first course in Russian history at Harvard University in 1894, which is considered the beginning of formal history of Russian studies in the United States. In 1895, he presented the first paper on Russia given at an annual meeting of the American Historical Association. He was director of the university library from 1911 until his death. He was editor-in-chief of *Foreign Affairs* from 1922 to 1927. In 1918, he served as special agent of the United States in Sweden and northern Russia. In 1921, he served as negotiator for the American Red Cross with the Soviet government, arranging for the distribution of supplies to the famine-stricken Soviet people. Died January 14, 1928, in Boston. *References*: Robert Francis Byrnes, *Awakening American Education to the World: The Role of Archibald Cary Coolidge, 1866–1928* (Notre Dame, 1982); Harold Coolidge and Robert Lord, *Archibald Cary Coolidge: Life and Letters* (Boston, 1932); *DAB*; *DADH*; and *NCAB* 12:58.

COOPER, HUGH LINCOLN (1865–1937). Hydrological engineer, born April 28, 1865, in Seldon, Minnesota. Cooper was apprenticed to an engineer in 1882. He was first involved in bridge design, but in the mid–1890s his interests turned to hydroelectric engineering. From 1896 to 1904, he designed and supervised the construction of hydroelectric plants in Brazil, Mexico, and Canada. He was a consultant in New York City after 1905, designing major hydroelectric plants in North and South America, and was a consultant on the Aswan Dam in Egypt in 1914 and 1928. He served in the U.S. Corps of Engineers during World War I. After the war, he directed the construction of Wilson Dam in Muscle Shoals, Alabama. In 1926, he was employed by the Soviet government to study the project at Dnieprostroi, which he designed in 1927. Until 1932 his company supplied advice and direction on building the power station, and he served as chief consulting engineer of the Dnieprostroi Dam construction project, one of the largest single enterprises built during the first Soviet Five-Year Plan and the biggest dam in the world at the time. It became the most successful undertaking of the First Five-Year Plan. He was the first foreigner to receive the Order of the Red Army, the highest honor bestowed by the Soviet government. Died June 24, 1937, in Stamford Connecticut. *References*: *DAB S2*; Harold Dorn, "Hugh Lincoln Cooper and the First Détente," *Technology and Culture* 20 (1979): 322–47; and *NCAB* 33:174.

COULTER, HERBERT MCKAY (1877–1939). Physician, born November 22, 1877, in Huntington, near Montreal, Quebec, Canada. Coulter attended Cheffey College (Ontario) and graduated from the University of Minnesota School of Medicine. He practiced medicine in Azusa, California, from 1904 to 1911, and in South Pasadena, California, after 1911. He was also medical director of the Boys' and Girls' Aid Society, a private charity orphanage, after 1911, was medical director of all public schools in South Pasadena from 1916 until his resignation shortly before his death, and was director of nutrition for the Los Angeles Hospital from 1922 to 1926. He served on the medical staff of the Good Samaritan Hospital in Los Angeles. He went to Siberia in 1919, with the Siberian Commission of the American Red Cross, and served as resident superintendent of the Petrograd Refugee Children's Colony on Russian Island near Vladivostok. When the colony was evacuated to Finland in 1920, he accompanied it. Died June 16, 1939, in South Pasadena, California. *Reference*: *NCAB* 44:151.

COUNCIL OF FOREIGN RELATIONS. A private foreign policy research organization, created in 1921. By World War II, a close relationship with the State Department had developed. After the war, the council helped define the U.S. policy of containment of the Soviet Union. Suspicious of Soviet intentions, and concerned that the Soviet Union threatened U.S. interests, the council called for a tough assertion of U.S. military and economic power toward the Soviet Union. "The Sources of Soviet Conduct," written by "X" (*George Frost Kennan) and published in its journal, *Foreign Affairs,* in 1947, was called one of the most influential magazine articles ever published. *References*: Council on Foreign Relations Archives, New York City; Robert D. Schulzinger, *The Wise Men of Foreign Affairs: The History of the Council on Foreign Relations* (New York, 1984); and Larry Shoup and William Minter, *Imperial Brain Trust: The Council on Foreign Relations and the United States Foreign Policy* (New York, 1977).

COUNTS, GEORGE SYLVESTER (1889–1974). Educator, born December 9, 1889, near Baldwin City, Kansas. Counts graduated from Baker University (Kan.) and the University of Chicago. He was head of the Department of Education at Delaware College (Newark), professor of secondary education at the University of Washington until 1920, associate professor of secondary education at Yale University from 1920 to 1924 and professor from 1924 to 1926, associate director of the International Institute from 1927 to 1932, and professor of education at Teachers College of Columbia University from 1927 to 1956. The foremost systematic student of Soviet education, he made trips to the Soviet Union in 1927, 1929, and 1936, observing schools, collecting source materials, and interviewing leading educators. He wrote *A Ford Crosses Soviet Russia* (Boston, 1930), *The Soviet Challenge to America* (New York, 1931), and *Challenge of Soviet Education* (New York, 1957) and was coauthor of *Country of the Blind: The Soviet System of Mind Control* (Boston, 1949). Died November 10, 1974, in Belleville, Illinois. *References*: George Sylvester Counts Papers, Southern Illinois University Library, Carbondale; *CA*; *CB* 1941; Lawrence J. Dennis and William E. Eaton, eds., *George S. Counts: Educator of a New Age* (Carbondale, Ill., 1980); Gerald L. Gutek, *George S. Counts and American Civilization: The Educator as Social Theorist* (Macon, Ga., 1984); *NCAB* F:190; *NYT*, November 11, 1974; and *SR* 34 (1975): 218–19.

CRANE, CHARLES RICHARD (1858–1939). Businessman and philanthropist, born August 7, 1858, in Chicago. Crane served the Crane Company in Chicago in various capacities until 1894, was vice-president from 1894 to 1912, and was president from 1912 until 1914, when he sold his interests to his brother. In 1898, he assisted in organizing the Westinghouse Air Brake Company in Russia. He made twenty-five trips to and through Russia between 1890 and 1937 and was mostly intrigued by Russian cultural life. He was in Russia during the revolution of 1905, and again in 1917, and was a member of the *Root Mission to Russia. He was a member of the King-Crane Commission to the Middle East in 1919 and was U.S. minister to China in 1920–1921. Died February 15, 1939, in Palm Springs, California. *References*: *DADH*; *NCAB* 30:211; *NYT*, February 16, 1939; and Albert Parry, "Charles R. Crane: Friend of Russia," *RR* 6 (Spring 1947): 20–36.

CRAWFORD, JOHN MARTIN (1845–1916). Physician and translator, born October 18, 1845, in Herrick, Pennsylvania. Crawford graduated from Lafayette College. He taught Latin and mathematics in Cincinnati, Ohio, from 1871 to 1879, studied at three medical schools in Cincinnati, and served as registrar of the Pulte Medical College from 1881 to 1889. He translated the Finnish Epic *Kalevala* and later the Estonian epic *Kalevipoeq* into English. He was U.S. consul general in Russia from 1889 to 1894. He was involved in the negotiations between the Russian government and the administration of the World's Fair in Chicago, and in this connection he translated into English and edited *The In-*

dustries of Russia (St. Petersburg, 1893), prepared by the Russian government for the Columbian Exposition. He was engaged in merchandising, manufacturing, and banking in Cincinnati. Died August 11, 1916, in Cincinnati. *References*: *DAB*; and *NCAB* 23:338.

CUBAN MISSILE CRISIS (1962). To increase its offensive capability against the United States, and to obtain concessions, the Soviet Union installed medium-range ballistic missiles in Cuba in 1962. U.S. aerial reconnaisance planes confirmed the existance of the missiles in October 1962. President *John F. Kennedy placed a quarantine on Cuba, to prevent further delivery of Soviet missiles to Cuba, and presented an ultimatum to the Soviet Union to dismantle and remove the missiles already in Cuba. The Soviets agreed to the demands on October 28, 1962, and in return, the United States pledged not to invade Cuba. *References*: Elie Abel, *The Missile Crisis* (New York, 1968); James G. Blight, *The Shattered Crystal Ball: Fear and Learning in the Cuban Missile Crisis* (Savage, Md., 1990); James G. Blight and David A. Welch, *On the Brink: Americans and Soviets Reexamine the Cuban Missile Crisis* (New York, 1989); Dino A. Brugioni, *Eyeball to Eyeball: The Inside Story of the Cuban Missile Crisis*, ed. Robert F. McCort (New York, 1991); Lester H. Brune, *The Missile Crisis of October 1962: A Review of Issues and References* (Claremont, Calif., 1985); Herbert S. Dinerstein, *The Making of a Missile Crisis: October, 1962* (Baltimore, 1976); Robert Divine, ed., *The Cuban Missile Crisis* (New York, 1988); *EAIE*; Raymond L. Garthoff, *Reflections on the Cuban Missile Crisis* (Washington, D.C., 1989); Alexander L. George, ''The Cuban Missile Crisis,'' in Alexander L. George, ed., *Avoiding War: Problems of Crisis Management* (Boulder, Colo., 1991), pp. 222–68; Richard M. Leighton, *The Cuban Missile Crisis of 1962: A Case Study in National Security Crisis Management* (Washington, D.C., 1978); and Robert Smith Thompson, *The Missiles of October: The Declassified Story of John F. Kennedy and the Cuban Missile Crisis* (New York, 1992).

CURTIN, JEREMIAH (1840–1906). Author and linguist, born September 6, 1838 or 1840, in Greenfield, near Milwaukee, Wisconsin. Curtin graduated from Harvard University. His acquaintance with some of the officers of the Russian fleet that came to the United States in 1864 led him to accept their invitation to go to Russia. He served as a translator in St. Petersburg and was later assistant secretary of the legation until 1870. He then traveled in Eastern Europe and Asia, apparently in the service of the Russian government. He conducted research for the Bureau of American Ethnology from 1883 to 1891, then traveled around the world, collecting myths of various peoples. He wrote *Myths and Folk-Tales of the Russians, Western Slavs, and Magyars* (Boston, 1890), *Fairy Tales of Eastern Europe* (New York, 1914), and *Wonder Tales from Russia* (Boston, 1921). Died December 14, 1906, in Burlington, Vermont. *References*: Jeremiah Curtin Papers, Milwaukee County Historical Society, Milwaukee, Wis.; *DAB*; *NYT*, December 15, 1906; Frederick I. Olson, ''The Story of Jeremiah Curtin,''

Historical Messenger of the Millwaukee County Historical Society 9 (March 1953): 3–7; Joseph Schafer, ed., *Memoirs of Jeremiah Curtin* (Madison, Wis., 1940); and H. B. Segel, "Sienkiewicz's First Translator, Jeremiah Curtin," *SR* 24 (1965): 189–214.

D

DALLAS, GEORGE MIFFLIN (1792–1864). Public official and diplomat, born July 10, 1792, in Philadelphia. Dallas graduated from Princeton University, studied law, and was admitted to the bar in 1813. He was clerk in the U.S. Treasury Department and practiced law in Philadelphia after 1816. He was deputy attorney general for the city and county of Philadelphia, was elected mayor, and then served as district attorney from 1829 to 1831. He served in the U.S. Senate from 1831 to 1833 and was attorney general of Pennsylvania from 1833 to 1835. He was U.S. minister to Russia from 1837 to 1839, where he focused his attention on trade in the Pacific. He resumed the practice of law, was vice-president of the United States from 1844 to 1848, and was U.S. minister to Great Britain from 1856 to 1861. Died December 31, 1864, in Philadelphia. *References*: *BDAC*; John M. Belohlavek, *George Mifflin Dallas: Jacksonian Politician* (University Park, Pa., 1977); *DAB*; Susan Dallas, ed., *Diary of George Mifflin Dallas, While United States Minister to Russia, 1837–1839, and to England, 1856 to 1861* (Philadelphia, 1892); and *NCAB* 6:268.

DANA, FRANCIS (1743–1811). Diplomat, born June 13, 1743, in Charlestown, Massachusetts. Dana graduated from Harvard, studied law, was admitted to the bar in 1767, and practiced law. He was a member of the Massachusetts Council from 1776 to 1780, a delegate to the Continental Congress from 1777 to 1779, and secretary of legation in France in 1780. He was appointed U.S. minister to Russia in 1780 and resided in St. Petersburg from 1781 to 1783. He did not present his credentials, never met Tsarina Catherine II, rarely met members of the Russian Foreign Ministry, and was ignored by the court. His mission was a failure, and he returned to the United States in 1783. He was chief justice of the supreme court of Massachusetts from 1791 to 1806. Died April 25, 1811, in Cambridge, Massachusetts. *References*: Francis Dana Papers, in Dana Family Papers, Massachusetts Historical Society, Boston; William Penn Cresson, *Francis Dana: A Puritan Diplomat at the Court of Catherine the Great* (New York, 1930); *DAB*; and *NCAB* 3:240.

DANENHOWER, JOHN WILSON (1849–1887). Naval officer and explorer, born September 30, 1849, in Chicago, Illinois. Danenhower graduated from the U.S. Naval Academy in 1870. He served in the European Squadron, with the USS *Portsmouth* surveying party in the North Pacific, and in the Naval Observatory until 1878. He joined the *Jeannette* Arctic expedition in 1878, acting as its executive officer. The trip to the Arctic began in 1879, but the ship was crushed in the ice in 1881, and the party, dragging its boats and provisions over the ice, moved toward the Siberian mainland. When open water was reached, the party set out for the Lena Delta in three boats. His boat, under the command of George W. Melville, reached the eastern Lena Delta and was rescued. He returned to the United States in 1882. He wrote *Lieutenant Danenhower's Narrative of the "Jeannette"* (Boston, 1882). He later acted as assistant commander of cadets at the U.S. Naval Academy. Committed suicide, April 20, 1887, in Annapolis. *References*: *DAB*; *NCAB* 3:284; and *NYT*, April 21, 1887.

DANILOFF, NICHOLAS (1934–   ). Journalist, born December 30, 1934, in Paris, France. Daniloff graduated from Harvard University and Magdalen College, Oxford. Reporting for United Press International, he was staff member in London in 1959 and bureau manager in Geneva, Switzerland, in 1960–1961. He was then *U.S. News and World Report* correspondent in Moscow. He was seized by KGB agents in Moscow in August 1986 on a trumped-up charge, in retaliation for the FBI's arrest of a Soviet spy in New York City, and was released after thirteen days in jail. He was later a congressional and diplomatic correspondent in Washington, D.C. He wrote *Kremlin and the Cosmos* (New York, 1972) and *Two Lives, One Russia* (Boston, 1988). *References*: *CA*; and William L. Chaze, "A Frame-up in Moscow," *U.S. News and World Report* 101 (September 15, 1986): 18–19.

DAVIES, JOSEPH EDWARD (1876–1958). Lawyer and diplomat, born November 29, 1876, in Watertown, Wisconsin. Davies graduated from the University of Wisconsin and was admitted to the Wisconsin bar in 1901. He practiced law in Watertown. He served as prosecuting attorney for Jefferson County, Wisconsin, from 1903 to 1907 and practiced law in Madison from 1907 to 1912. He was U.S. commissioner of corporations from 1913 to 1915, was chairman and then vice-chairman of the Federal Trade Commission from 1915 to 1918, served as economic adviser to President *Woodrow Wilson during the Paris Peace Conference, and then practiced law in Washington, D.C. He was U.S. ambassador to the Soviet Union from 1936 to 1938. He succeeded in negotiating a United States–Soviet trade agreement. His own impressions of Russia were positive. Assessing the Soviet Union's economic, political, and military capabilities, he concluded that the country was basically peace-loving. He believed that the United States and the Soviet Union could find a basis for joint action in pursuit of common interests. He wrote *Mission to Moscow* (New York, 1943), which became a best-seller and was made into a movie. He was U.S. ambassador to Belgium from 1938 to 1940. He resumed law practice in 1940 in Washington, D.C. During World War II, he spoke and wrote in an effort to dispel U.S. prejudice against the Soviet Union and its leaders and to convince Americans of the importance of the Russian front. In 1943, he acted as President *Franklin D. Roosevelt's special envoy, with the rank of ambassador, to confer with Joseph Stalin on preliminary arrangements for the *Teheran Conference. In 1945, he was a special envoy, with the rank of ambassador, of President *Harry S. Truman to confer with Prime Minister Winston Churchill regarding plans for the *Potsdam Conference, and he served as a member of the U.S. delegation to the conference. Died May 9, 1958, in Washington, D.C. *References*: Joseph E. Davies Papers, Manuscript Division, Library of Congress; Keith David Eagles, ''Ambassador Joseph E. Davies and American-Soviet Relations, 1937–1941'' (Ph.D. diss., University of Minnesota, 1966); Elizabeth Kimball MacLean, *Joseph E. Davies: Envoy to the Soviets* (New York, 1993); Elizabeth Kimball MacLean, ''Joseph E. Davies and Soviet-American Relations, 1941–1943,'' *DH* 4 (1980): 73–93; *NCAB* 61:215; *NYT*, May 10, 1958; Richard H. Ullman, ''The Davies Mission and United States–Soviet Relations, 1937–1941,'' *World Politics* 9 (1957): 220–39; and Robert C. Williams, *Russian Art and American Money, 1900–1940* (Cambridge, Mass., 1980), ch. 7.

DAVIS, ARTHUR POWELL (1861–1933). Hydraulic and irrigation engineer, born February 9, 1861, near Decatur, Illinois, and grew up near Junction City, Kansas. Davis graduated from the State Normal School (Emporia, Kan.) and the Corcoran Scientific School of Columbia College (later George Washington University). He was assistant topographer at the U.S. Geological Survey from 1882 to 1884 and topographer from 1884 to 1904, conducting surveys and explorations in Arizona, New Mexico, and California. He was hydrographer in charge of all stream measurements from 1895 to 1897, U.S. hydrographer for the Isthmian Canal Commission from 1898 to 1901, and later consulting engineer in the construction of the Panama Canal. He was chief engineer of the U.S. Reclamation Service from 1906 to 1914 and director from 1914 to 1923. In 1911, he was engaged by the Russian government to investigate the irrigation of the Kara Kum Desert, lying to the south and west of the Amu Darya River in Turkestan. In 1914, he made a survey and investigation of the Huai River Conservancy Project in China. He was chief engineer and general manager of the East Bay Municipal Utility District in Oakland, California, from 1923 to 1929. In 1930, he was engaged by the Soviet government as chief consulting engineer for irrigation in Turkestan and Transcaucasia. He described his observations in the January 1932 issue of *Civil Engineering*. Died August 7, 1933, in Oakland, California. *References*: *DAB S1*; *NCAB* 24:116; and *NYT*, August 8, 1933.

DAVIS, JEROME (1891–1979). Educator, born December 2, 1891, in Kyoto, Japan, to American missionary parents. Davis graduated from Oberlin College, Union Theological Seminary, and Columbia University. He was secretary to Wilfred Grenfell in Labrador in 1915. He carried out war work in Russia for the world's committee of the *Young Men's Christian Association (YMCA) from 1916 to 1918 and visited World War I prison camps in Russia in 1917 on a mission for the YMCA. He was in Russia during the Russian Revolution, became a friend of V. I. Lenin's, and was entertained at the Kremlin many times. He was associate professor of sociology at Dartmouth College from 1921 to 1924 and professor of practical philanthropy at the Yale Divinity School from 1924 to 1937, president of the American Federation of Teachers from 1936 to 1939, and director of prisoner of war camps in Canada for the world's committee of the Young Men's Christian Association from 1940 to 1943. He was a correspondent in Russia in 1943–1944. He founded Promoting Enduring Peace, Incorporated, in Woodmont, Connecticut, in 1952 and was an executive director until 1960. In June 1957, he led a group of Americans on a visit to the Soviet Union, where they were granted an interview with Nikita S. Khrushchev, and in 1970 he visited Premier Aleksei N. Kosygin with another group. He wrote *Behind Soviet Power* (New York, 1946) and *A Life Adventure for Peace: An Autobiography* (New York, 1967). Died October 19, 1979, in Olney, Maryland. *References*: Jerome Davis Papers, University of Oregon Library, Eugene; *CA*; and *NYT*, October 24, 1979.

DAVIS, MALCOLM WALTER (1889–1970). Journalist, born September 18, 1889, in Hartford, Connecticut. Davis graduated from Yale and Columbia universities. He was a journalist with the *Springfield* (Mass.) *Republican* from 1911 to 1913 and with the *New York Evening Post* from 1913 to 1916 and from 1920 to 1922, served in World War I in prisoner relief work in Scandinavia and Russia, and lived in Russia from 1916 to 1919. He was managing editor of *Our World Magazine* from 1922 to 1924, executive director of the Council on Foreign Relations from 1925 to 1927, editor of Yale University Press from 1927 to 1931, and executive of the Carnegie Endowment for International Peace from 1931 to 1951. Died November 14, 1970, in New York City. *References*: Malcolm Walter Davis Papers, Columbia University Library, New York City; Warren F. Kuehl, *Biographical Dictionary of Internationalists* (Westport, Conn., 1983); and *NYT*, November 15, 1970.

DEANE, JOHN RUSSELL (1896–1982). Army officer, born March 8, 1896, in San Francisco. Deane attended the University of California. He was commissioned second lieutenant in the infantry in 1917, served with the 14th Infantry in the United States and Panama from 1917 to 1923, and was instructor of military tactics at the Oakland School from 1923 to 1927 and at the infantry school of the 29th Infantry from 1927 to 1932. He was with the 15th Infantry in Tientsin, China, from 1932 to 1934, the 3rd Infantry in 1934–1935, and the

1st Brigade in New York City from 1936 to 1938. Deane was an instructor at the Command and General Staff College from 1938 to 1941 and served with the Office of Combined Chiefs of Staff in the War Department from 1941 to 1943. He was head of the U.S. military mission to Moscow from 1943 to 1945. He was responsible for the administration of *Lend-Lease assistance to the Soviet Union and for the coordination of U.S. land, sea, and air activities with those of the Soviet Union. He retired in 1946, with the rank of major general. He wrote *The Strange Alliance: The Story of Our Efforts at Wartime Cooperation with Russia* (New York, 1947). He was later president of the Italian Swiss Colony. Died July 14, 1982, in Charleston, South Carolina. *References*: Joseph G. Whelan, *Soviet Diplomacy and Negotiating Behavior: The Emerging New Context for U.S. Diplomacy* (Boulder, Colo., 1983), pp. 125–47; and *WWA*.

DELAFIELD, RICHARD (1798–1873). Military engineer, born September 1, 1798, in New York City. Delafield graduated from the U.S. Military Academy in 1818 and was commissioned second lieutenant. He was an engineer on the construction of fortifications and defenses at Hampton Roads, Virginia, from 1819 to 1824, at the Plaquemine Bend on the Mississippi River from 1824 to 1832, and on the Atlantic Coast defenses from 1845 to 1855. He was superintendent of the U.S. Military Academy from 1838 to 1845 and again from 1856 to 1861. In 1855, he was a member of the military commission to the Crimea and the theater of war there. He prepared *Report on the Art of War in Europe in 1854, 1855, and 1856* (Washington, D.C., 1860). He served during the Civil War and was in command of the Corps of Engineers and in charge of the Engineer Bureau in Washington from 1864 to 1866. He retired in 1866, with the rank of major general. Died November 5, 1873, in Washington, D.C. *References*: *DAB*; and *NCAB* 11:29.

DE LONG, GEORGE WASHINGTON (1844–1881). Naval officer and explorer, born August 22, 1844, in New York City. De Long graduated from the U.S. Naval Academy in 1865. He served on the USS *Canandaiqua* and on the USS *Junniata*. Enthusiastic for Arctic research, he interested James Gordon Bennett, and they fitted the steamer *Jeannette* for a voyage through the Bering Strait to the Arctic in 1879. The ship was caught in an ice pack about twenty-five miles east of Herald Island and drifted to the northwest for over twenty-one months. It was finally crushed by heavy ice floes and sank. De Long abandoned ship in an orderly fashion, salvaging most of the provisions and equipment, and began a retreat southward toward the Siberian coast. For over two months, he and his men fought their way over a frozen sea. When open water was reached, the party embarked in three boats for the Lena Delta. His boat reached the northern arm of the river and landed in uninhabited country, and the entire crew died from starvation and exposure toward the end of October 1881. His body was found the next spring by *George Wallace Melville and was brought to the United States. His journal was later edited by his widow, Emma De Long, as

The Voyage of the Jeannette: The Ship and Ice Journals of George W. De Long
(Boston, 1883). *References*: *DAB*; and *NCAB* 3:282.

DENNY, HAROLD NORMAN [HOBBS] (1889–1945). Journalist, born
March 11, 1889, in Des Moines, Iowa. Denny graduated from Drake University.
He was a reporter and editorial writer on the *Des Moines Register, St. Paul
Pioneer Press, Minneapolis Tribune, New York Tribune, Chicago Tribune* (Paris
edition), and other newspapers from 1913 to 1922. He served as an enlisted man
in the infantry in the U.S. Army during World War I and was wounded. He
was a reporter with the *New York Times* from 1922 until his death. He was its
Moscow correspondent from 1934 to 1939 and covered Moscow treason trials
and Soviet purges from 1936 to 1938. He was a war correspondent during World
War II. Died July 3, 1945, in Des Moines, Iowa. *References*: *NCAB* 34:300;
and *WWWA*.

DÉTENTE. A term describing U.S.-Soviet policy as it developed under President *Richard M. Nixon and *Henry Kissinger. The policy stressed direct
cooperative dealings in areas that were formerly competitive, but it avoided
ideological accommodation. Areas affected by détente included promoting arms
control—particularly by slowing down the nuclear arms race—easing Central
European tensions, avoiding direct military confrontation in areas such as the
Middle East, and fostering closer economic, social, and cultural ties. *References*:
Coral Bell, *The Diplomacy of Détente: The Kissinger Era* (New York, 1977);
Eleanor Lansing Dulles and Robert Dickson Crane, eds., *Détente: Cold War
Strategies in Transition* (New York, 1965); *EAFP*; Louisa Sue Hulett, *Decade
of Détente: Shifting Definitions and Denouement* (Washington, D.C., 1982);
Fred Warner Neal, ed., *Détente or Debacle: Common Sense in U.S.-Soviet
Relations* (New York, 1979); Richard Pipes, *U.S.-Soviet Relations in the Era
of Détente* (Boulder, Colo., 1981); and Albert L. Weeks, *The Troubled Détente*
(New York, 1976).

DEWEY, JOHN (1859–1952). Educator, born October 20, 1859, in Burlington,
Vermont. Dewey graduated from the University of Vermont and Johns Hopkins
University. He taught philosophy at the Universities of Minnesota and Michigan
and was head of the Department of Philosophy, Psychology, and Pedagogy at
the University of Chicago from 1894 to 1904. Establishing the Laboratory School
there in 1896, he was its director until 1904. He was professor of philosophy
at Columbia University from 1904 until his retirement in 1930. He visited the
Soviet Union in 1928 as a member of a private delegation studying Soviet
education, and his articles were republished as *Impressions of Soviet Russia and
the Revolutionary World: Mexico, China, Turkey* (New York, 1929). Died June
1, 1952, in New York City. *References*: John Dewey Papers, Southern Illinois
University Library, Carbondale; *DAB S5*; George Dykhuizen, *The Life and Mind
of John Dewey* (Carbondale, Ill., 1973); *NCAB* 40:1; and *NYT,* June 2, 1952.

DITSON, GEORGE LEIGHTON (1812–1895). Author, born August 5, 1812, in Westford, Massachusetts. Ditson studied medicine in Boston. When his health failed, he went on a sea voyage to Egypt and India. He was U.S. consul in Nuevitas, Cuba, in the 1840s and taught English in a college in Puerto Príncipe (Camagüey) in 1842–1843. He traveled in Russia in 1847–1848, claiming to be the first foreigner in Circassia after its penetration by Russia, and wrote *Circassia; or, A Tour to the Caucasus* (New York, 1850). He later studied medicine at the University of Vermont and became involved with the Theosophical Society. Died January 29, 1895, in Albany, New York. *References*: *DAB*; and *NCAB* 13:440.

DOBELL, PETER (?–1855). Merchant, born in Ireland. Dobell came with his family to the United States and attended the University of Pennsylvania. He went to Kamchatka with two merchant ships in 1812. He traveled from Kamchatka to St. Petersburg in 1813. He became a Russian citizen in 1818 and served as Russian consul in Manila in 1818 but was not accepted by the Spanish authorities. He went back to Kamchatka in 1821 but returned to St. Petersburg in 1828. He wrote *Travels in Kamchatka and Siberia, with a Narrative of Residence in China* (London, 1830) and *Russia as It Is, and Not as It Has Been Represented* (London, 1833). *References*: Nikolai N. Bolkhovitinov, "Vydvizhenia i proval proektov P. Dobela (1812–1821 gg.)" [The promotion and failure of Peter Dobell's schemes (1812–1821)], *Amerikanskii Ezhegodnik* 1976 (Moscow, 1976), pp. 264–81; Albert Parry, "First Americans in Siberia," *Travel* 87 (June 1946): 18–22; and *Russky Biografichesky Slovar'* (St. Petersburg, 1905), 6:468–69.

DODER, DUSKO (1937–   ). Journalist, born July 22, 1937, in Yugoslavia and emigrated to the United States. Doder graduated from Washington University (St. Louis) and Columbia University. He was a reporter for the Associated Press in New York City, in Concord, New Hampshire, and in Albany, New York, from 1965 to 1968, foreign correspondent in Moscow for United Press International from 1968 to 1970, assistant foreign editor of the *Washington Post* from 1970 to 1973, chief of the East European bureau from 1973 to 1976, assistant foreign editor from 1978 to 1981, and Moscow correspondent after 1981. He wrote *Shadows and Whispers: Power Politics inside the Kremlin from Brezhnev to Gorbachev* (New York, 1986). *References*: *CA*; and *WWA*.

DOLE, NATHAN HASKELL (1852–1935). Author, editor, and translator, born August 31, 1852, in Chelsea, Massachusetts, and grew up in Norridgewock, Maine. Dole graduated from Harvard University. He was preceptor of the Derby Academy (Hingham, Mass.) from 1876 to 1878, newspaper correspondent in New York City in 1880–1881, and art and music editor of the *Philadelphia Press* from 1881 to 1887. He was literary adviser to the publishing firm of Thomas Y. Crowell and Company in Boston from 1887 until 1901. He was among the earlier translators who introduced Russian literature to American readers. He edited and enlarged *A Popular History of Russia from the Earliest Times to 1880* (Boston, 1880–1882) and wrote *Young Folk's History of Russia* (Boston, 1881). He translated a number of Leo Tolstoy's novels and other Russian writings and wrote *The Life of Count Lyof N. Tolstoi* (New York, 1911). Died May 9, 1935, in Yonkers, New York. *References*: *DAB S1*; *NCAB* 13:554; and *NYT,* May 10, 1935.

DORR, RHETA LOUISE CHILDE (1866–1948). Author and journalist, born in Omaha, Nebraska. Dorr was editor of the woman's department of the *New York Evening Post* from 1902 to 1906 and the first editor of the *Suffragist,* organ of the Congressional Union (later the National Woman's Party). She went to Europe in 1906 on her first foreign assignment and visited Russia during the social and political unrest there. She served as war correspondent for the *New York Evening Mail* and for a syndicate of twenty-one newspapers during World War I and as a foreign correspondent with headquarters in Prague. She was again in Russia in 1917 and denounced bolshevism in *Inside the Russian Revolution* (New York, 1917). She wrote an autobiography, *A Woman of Fifty* (New York, 1924). Died August 8, 1948, in New Britain, Pennsylvania. *References*: John Jakes, *Great Woman Reporters* (New York, 1969), pp. 91–113; *NAW*; and *NYT,* August 9, 1948.

DOWNS, WILLIAM RANDALL, JR. (1914–1978). Journalist, born August 17, 1914, in Kansas City, Kansas. Downs graduated from the University of Kansas. He was a reporter for newspapers and the United Press in Kansas City, Kansas, from 1937 to 1939, foreign correspondent for the United Press in London from 1939 to 1942, and reporter for the Columbia Broadcasting System (CBS) from 1942 to 1962. He was stationed in Moscow from 1942 to 1944 and covered the battle of Stalingrad. He was diplomatic correspondent in Rome from 1956 to 1962. He was network correspondent for the American Broadcasting Corporation (ABC-TV) from 1964 until his death. Died May 4, 1978, in Bethesda, Maryland. *References*: William R. Downs Papers, Georgetown University Library, Washington, D.C.; *CA*; and *Washington Post,* May 4, 1978.

DREISER, THEODORE (1871–1945). Author, born August 27, 1871, in Terre Haute, Indiana. Dresier attended Indiana University and then became a newspaper reporter and free-lance writer. His first novel, *Sister Carrie,* appeared in 1900, and he finally achieved recognition and success with *An American Tragedy* in 1925. He toured Russia in 1927–1928 and wrote *Dreiser Looks at Russia* (New York, 1928). Died December 28, 1945, in Hollywood, California. *References*: Theodore Dreiser Papers, University of Pennsylvania Library, Philadelphia; *DAB*; Ruth Epperson Kennell, *Theodore Dreiser and the Soviet Union, 1927–1945: A First-Hand Chronicle* (New York, 1969); *NCAB* 34:58; and W. A. Swanberg, *Dreiser* (New York, 1965).

DROPSHOT PLAN. The U.S. plan for world war with the Soviet Union, prepared by a committee of the Joint Chiefs of Staff in 1949 with the authority and knowledge of President *Harry S. Truman. The main military planning production of the times, it was the outcome of the menacing events of the first years of the Cold War. *Reference*: Anthony Cave Brown, ed., *Dropshot: The United States Plan for War with the Soviet Union in 1957* (New York, 1978).

DUGGAN, STEPHEN PIERCE (1870–1950). Educator, born December 20, 1870, in New York City. Duggan graduated from City College of New York and Columbia University. He was professor of political science at City College from 1910 to 1928. He founded and organized the Institute of International Education in 1919 and was its director until his retirement in 1946. It specialized in the promotion of exchange scholarships between the United States and other nations. He went to Moscow in 1925, at the request of the Soviet government, to establish a program of student-professor exchanges. He wrote *A Professor at Large* (New York, 1943). Died August 13, 1950, in Stamford, Connecticut. *References*: Institute of International Education News Bulletin 26 (October 1950): 3–7; *NCAB* 38:308; and *NYT*, August 19, 1950.

DULLES, JOHN FOSTER (1888–1959). Secretary of state, born February 25, 1888, in Washington, D.C., and grew up in Watertown, New York. Dulles graduated from Princeton University, attended George Washington University Law School, studied at the Sorbonne (Paris), and was admitted to the bar in 1911. He practiced law in New York City after 1911, specializing in international law. He became a partner in 1918 and a senior partner in 1927. He served on the War Trade Board during World War I and was counsel to the reparations section of the American Commission to Negotiate Peace in 1919. He was special representative to negotiate the Japanese Peace Treaty in 1950–1951. He was secretary of state from 1953 until 1959. Opposing the *Containment policy, he called for massive retaliation against Communist aggression and for the liberation of East European countries from Soviet power by peaceful means. But the United States followed the principle of Containment and did not contest Soviet power and influence in Eastern Europe. Dulles also resisted negotiations with the Soviets. He resigned in 1959 because of ill health. Died May 24, 1959, in Washington, D.C. *References*: John Foster Dulles Papers, Princeton University Library, Princeton, N.J.; *DAB S6*; *DADH*; Louis L. Gerson, *John Foster Dulles* (New York, 1967); Michael A. Guhin, *John Foster Dulles: A Statesman and His Times* (New York, 1972); Ole R. Holsti, "Cognitive Dynamics of Image of the Enemy: Dulles and Russia," in David J. Finlay et al., eds., *Enemies in Politics* (Chicago, 1967), pp. 25–96; Townsend Hoopes, *The Devil and John Foster Dulles* (Boston, 1973); Richard H. Immerman, ed., *John Foster Dulles and the Diplomacy of the Cold War* (Princeton, N.J., 1990); Hans J. Morgenthau, "John Foster Dulles," in Norman A. Graebner, ed., *An Uncertain Tradition: American Secretaries of States in the Twentieth Century* (New York, 1961), pp. 289–308; *NYT,* May 25, 1959; Ronald W. Pruessen, *John Foster Dulles: The Road to Power* (New York, 1982); and Mark G. Toulouse, *The Transformation of John Foster Dulles* (Macon, Ga., 1986).

DUNCAN, ISADORA (1878–1927). Dancer, born May 27, 1878, in San Francisco. Duncan began dancing at an early age, first in San Francisco and later in Chicago and New York. She then went to London, Paris, and other parts of Europe, opening a dancing school for children in Berlin. In 1921, she was invited by the Soviet government to open the school in Moscow. She was given an empty palace, where she gathered forty pupils. In 1922, she married the poet Sergei Esenin, who later left her. She left Russia in 1924 and resided in France. She wrote an autobiography, *My Life* (London, 1927). Died September 14, 1927, in Nice, France. *References*: Frederika Blair, *Isadora: Portrait of the Artist as a Woman* (New York, 1986); *DAB*; Irma Duncan and Allan Ross MacDougall, *Isadora Duncan's Russian Days and Her Last Years in France* (New York, 1929); Lillian Loewenthal, *The Search for Isadora: Tracking the Legend and Legacy of Isadora Duncan* (Princeton, N.J., 1992); Gordon MacVay, *Isadora and Esenin* (London, 1980); *NCAB* 22:159; and Ilya Ilyitch Schneider, *Isadora Duncan: The Russian Years* (London, 1968).

DURANTY, WALTER (1884–1957). Journalist, born May 25, 1884, in Liverpool, England. Duranty graduated from Emmanuel College, Cambridge. In 1914, he became a reporter for the Paris bureau of the *New York Times*. He was a war correspondent during World War I, attached to the French army. In 1919–1920, he covered famine and political unrest in the Baltic states and gathered news about the Soviet Union. In 1920, he returned to the Paris bureau. He went to the Soviet Union in 1921 with the *American Relief Administration. He became Moscow correspondent of the *New York Times* in 1922 and remained in the Soviet Union until 1941. He was traveling correspondent between 1934 and 1941, returning to Russia for four to five months every year. He became well-known for personally influencing Soviet-American relations. He obtained two private interviews with Joseph Stalin in the early 1930s. He worked for U.S. recognition of the Soviet Union and defended the major Moscow purge trials of the 1930s but misreported this story. He failed as a political analyst, sympathizing with Stalin's acts. He wrote *Duranty Reports Russia,* edited by Gustavus Tuckerman, Jr. (New York, 1934), *I Write as I Please* (New York, 1935), *The Kremlin and the People* (New York, 1941), *U.S.S.R.: The Story of Soviet Russia* (Philadelphia, 1944), and *Stalin and Co.: The Politburo—the Men Who Run Russia* (New York, 1949) and was coauthor of *Red Economics* (Boston, 1932). He also wrote *Search for a Key* (New York, 1943), the autobiographical novel *One Life, One Kopeck: A Novel* (New York, 1937), and short stories in *The Curious Lottery and Other Tales of Russian Justice* (New York, 1929) and *The Gold Train and Other Stories* (London, 1938). Died October 3, 1957, in Orlando, Florida. *References*: James William Crowl, *Angels in Stalin's Paradise:*

Western Reporters in Soviet Russia, 1917 to 1937, a Case Study of Louis Fischer and Walter Duranty (Lanham, Md., 1982); *DAB S6*; *NYT*, October 4, 1957; and S. J. Taylor, *Stalin's Apologist: Walter Duranty: The New York Times's Man in Moscow* (New York, 1982).

DURBROW, ELBRIDGE (1903–   ). Diplomat, born September 21, 1903, in San Francisco. Durbrow graduated from Yale University and studied at Stanford, Dijon, and The Hague. He joined the foreign service in 1930 and served in the U.S. embassy in Warsaw in 1930, in Bucharest in 1932, and in Moscow from 1934 to 1937. He was consul in Naples in 1937–1938, served in the U.S. embassy in Rome in 1940 and in Lisbon in 1941, and was assistant chief of the Eastern European Division of the State Department from 1942 to 1944 and its chief from 1944 to 1946. He was counselor of embassy in Moscow from 1946 to 1948, member of the faculty of the National War College from 1948 to 1950, chief of the Division of Foreign Service Personnel from 1950 to 1952, minister counselor in Rome from 1952 to 1954, deputy chief of mission and consul general in Singapore from 1955 to 1957, U.S. ambassador to Vietnam from 1957 to 1961, alternate U.S. representative to the North Atlantic Council from 1961 to 1967, and adviser to the commander of the Air University at Maxwell Air Force Base in 1967–1968. He retired in 1968 and was director of Freedom Studies Center in Reston, Virginia, after 1971. *Reference: DADH*; and *WWA*.

DURLAND, KELLOGG (1881–1911). Social worker, born March 13, 1881, in New York City. Durland studied at Harvard University, the University of Edinburgh, and Ecole des Hautes Etudes Sociales (Paris). He worked as a coal miner in Scotland in 1901 to study mining conditions and made special investigations into child labor abuses in Pennsylvania coal mines in 1902. Disguised as an emigrant, he studied the immigration question in 1905. He traveled in Russia during the revolution of 1905 as a contributor to *Collier's, Harper's Weekly, Review of Reviews, Boston Transcript,* and *New York Evening Post.* He was arrested by the Russian authorities for associating with Russian revolutionaries and was imprisoned. He wrote *The Red Reign: The True Story of an Adventurous Year in Russia* (New York, 1907). He was later a writer and lecturer on events and conditions in Russia. Died November 18, 1911, in Boston. *References: NYT*, November 22, 1911, and *WWWA*.

E

EASTMAN, MAX FORRESTER (1883–1969). Author and editor, born January 4, 1883, in Canadaigua, New York. Eastman graduated from Williams College and attended Columbia University. In 1912, he was elected editor of the *Masses,* a socialist monthly, which he transformed into a lively left-wing periodical. Eastman opposed American entry into World War I and was a leader of the antiwar movement in 1917–1918. In 1917, the government put the *Masses* out of business by denying it second-class mailing privileges, and he was indicted for conspiring to obstruct military recruiting, but two juries in succession failed to agree on a verdict. He founded the *Liberator* in 1918. He went to the Soviet Union in 1922 to see the great ''experiment'' in action. There he learned Russian, met many leading Bolsheviks, and sided with Leon Trotsky in the struggle for power following V. I. Lenin's death. He left the Soviet Union in 1924, taking with him a copy of ''Lenin's Testament,'' in which Lenin warned against Joseph Stalin and named Trotsky as his heir. Eastman published parts of it in *Since Lenin Died* (New York, 1925), an attack on the new Soviet leadership, which he believed was betraying the revolution. He returned to the United States in 1927 and continued to serve as Trotsky's translator and literary agent. He supported himself by lecturing. In the 1930s, he was attacked by Stalin, who called him a ''gangster of the pen,'' the only American writer so named. He wrote *Stalin's Russia and the Crisis of Socialism* (New York, 1940). In the 1940s, he moved steadily to the Right. He joined *Reader's Digest* in 1941 as a roving editor and became a contributor to the *National Review*. He made translations from Russian, edited anthologies, and made a film documentary of the Russian Revolution. He wrote his memoirs, *Enjoyment of Living* (New York, 1948) and *Loves and Revolution: Journey through an Epoch* (New York, 1964). Died March 25, 1969, in Barbados. *References*: Max Eastman Papers, Lilly Library, Indiana University, Bloomington; *CA*; Milton Cantor, *Max Eastman* (New York, 1970); *CB* 1969; *DAB S8*; *NYT,* March 26, 1967; William L. O'Neill, *The Last Romantic* (New York, 1978); and *Polprof: Eisenhower.*

EATON, CYRUS STEPHEN (1883–1979). Businessman, born December 27, 1883, in Pugwash, Nova Scotia, Canada, and came to the United States in 1900. Eaton graduated from McMaster University (Toronto). In 1905, under the auspices of John D. Rockefeller, he started a long and successful business career. He settled in Cleveland and became a naturalized citizen in 1913. He was involved in steel, rubber, and paint concerns and in various other enterprises, was associated with the East Ohio Gas Company, and organized Canada Gas and Electric Corporation. In 1912, he began extensive activity in the American utility industry and formed the Continental Gas and Electric Company, which consolidated a number of electric and gas companies. He joined Otis and Company, an investment bank, in 1916. He reorganized Trumbull Steel Company in 1925, formed Cliffs Corporation in 1929, organized Republic Steel Corporation in 1930, led in the formation and reorganization of other midwestern companies, and was chairman of the board of the Chesapeake and Ohio Railroad. He established Pugwash conferences in 1954, which were held annually during the 1950s and 1960s for Soviet and U.S. scientists. He visited the Soviet Union many times, advocating stronger ties between the two countries, especially in the area of trade. Died May 9, 1979, near Cleveland, Ohio. *References*: Cyrus Eaton Papers, Western Reserve Historical Society, Cleveland; *CB* 1948; Joseph Finder, *Red Carpet* (New York, 1983); M. Allen Gibson, *Beautiful upon the Mountains: A Portrait of Cyrus Eaton* (Windsor, Nova Scotia, 1977); Marcus Gleisser, *The World of Cyrus Eaton* (New York, 1965); E. J. Kahn, Jr., "Communists' Capitalist," *New Yorker* 53 (October 10, 1977): 50–86, 53 (October 17, 1977): 54–87; *NCAB* C:88; *NYT*, May 11, 1979; and *PolProf: Kennedy*.

EDDY, HARRIET GERTRUDE (1876–1966). Librarian, born February 19, 1876, in Lexington, Michigan. Eddy graduated from Albion College and attended the University of Chicago. She was principal of a high school in Elk Grove, California, from 1906 to 1909. She served on the staff of the State Library of California from 1909 to 1918, organizing the county libraries in the state. She was state organizer and teacher in the Agricultural Extension Service of the University of California from 1918 until her retirement in 1941. She was invited to the Soviet Union in 1927 and again in 1931 as a consultant to the Ministry of Education, to analyze Soviet libraries and suggest solutions. She traveled throughout the Soviet Union, working out a program for unification of library services for the entire country. She wrote of her experiences in the January 15, 1932, issue of *Library Journal*. Died December 3, 1966, in Napa, California. *Reference*: *California Librarian* 28 (January 1967): 54–55.

EDGAR, WILLIAM CROWELL (1856–1932). Journalist and editor, born December 21, 1856, in LaCrosse, Wisconsin. Edgar was employed in a St. Louis business house from 1874 to 1882. He was manager of *Northwestern Miller* (Minneapolis) in 1882 and its editor from 1886 to 1924. He established the *Bellman* in 1906 and was its editor and manager until 1919, when it discontinued publication. He was president of Miller Publishing Company until his retirement in 1924. In 1891, he organized a private program of famine relief to Russia, in which American millers gave a shipload of flour for the relief of Russian peasants. He personally superintended its collection, shipment, and distribution. He wrote *The Russian Famine of 1891 and 1892* (Minneapolis, 1893). In 1914, he directed a relief movement in Belgium and served as a member of the Commission for Relief in Belgium during World War I. Died December 2, 1932, in Maxine-on-St. Crois, Minnesota. *References*: William Crowell Edgar Papers, Minnesota Historical Society, St. Paul; *NYT,* December 3, 1932; Harold F. Smith, "Bread for the Russians: William C. Edgar and the Relief Campaign of 1892," *Minnesota History* 42 (Summer 1970): 54–62; and *WWWA.*

EISENHOWER, DWIGHT DAVID (1890–1969). Army officer and president of the United States, born October 14, 1890, in Denison, Texas. Eisenhower graduated from the U.S. Military Academy in 1915. He served in the Office of the Chief of Staff in Washington, D.C., in the Philippines, and in the War Plans Division of the army's staff headquarters in Washington, D.C. He was commander of the U.S. forces in Europe in 1942–1943 and Allied commander-in-chief from 1943 to 1945. He was army chief of staff from 1945 to 1948. He retired in 1948, with the rank of general of the army, and was president of Columbia University until 1950, when he was recalled to active duty, and was commander of the forces of the North Atlantic Treaty Organization (NATO) until 1952. He was president of the United States from 1953 until 1961. As a counter to Soviet expansionist moves, he allowed Secretary of State *John Foster Dulles to construct a network of alliances to meet further Communist expansion with the threat of massive retaliation. He was willing to begin negotiations with the Soviet Union toward a mutual reduction of armament, but distrust on both sides was high, and there was little to negotiate. He met with Premier Niklai A. Bulganin in the summit conference in Geneva in 1955 and made his *"Open Skies" proposal, whereby the two countries would permit aerial surveillance of each other's territories and military activities. The proposal was rejected by the Soviets. The results of the 1959 meeting with Nikita S. Khrushchev in Washington were minimal. The planned summit conference in Paris in 1960 was canceled by Khrushchev after the *U–2 incident—the downing of a reconnaissance airplane in May 1960—and Eisenhower's attempt to dismiss the incident. He wrote *Mandate for Change, 1953–1956* (Garden City, N.Y., 1963) and *Waging Peace, 1956–1961* (Garden City, N.Y., 1965). Died March 28, 1969, in Washington, D.C. *References*: Stephen E. Ambrose, *Eisenhower, Vol. 2: President, 1952–1969* (New York, 1984); Michael R. Beschloss, *Mayday: Eisenhower, Khrushchev, and the U–2 Affair* (New York, 1986); Blanche Wiesen Cook, *The Declassified Eisenhower* (Garden City, N.Y., 1981); Robert A. Divine, *Eisenhower and the Cold War* (New York, 1981); Elmer Plischke, "Eisenhower's 'Correspondence Diplomacy' with the Kremlin: Case Study in Summit Diplomatics," *Journal of Politics* 30 (1968): 137–59; and Thomas F.

Soapes, "A Cold Warrior Seeks Peace: Eisenhower's Strategy for Nuclear Disarmament," *DH* 4 (1980): 57–72.

EMERSON, GEORGE H. (?–1950). Railway engineer. Emerson began as a water boy with Great Northern Railroad in 1880, was apprenticed at its St. Paul shops from 1882 to 1887, and was boilermaker from 1887 to 1890, fireman and engineer in the Dakota division from 1890 to 1895, locomotive foreman in Glasgow, Montana, from 1895 to 1897, general shop foreman and master mechanic of the Dakota and Northern divisions from 1897 to 1900, general master mechanic of the Western district from 1900 to 1903, superintendent of motive power from 1903 to 1910, assistant general manager from 1910 to 1912, and general manager after 1912. He was colonel in the U.S. Army, commanding officer of the *Russian Railway Service Corps, and chief inspector of the Inter-Allied Technical Board. He described his experiences in the June 24, 1920, issue of *Railway Age*. He joined the Baltimore and Ohio Railroad in 1920, and served as its chief of motive power and equipment for the Baltimore and Ohio Railroad, until his retirement in 1942. Died January 12, 1950, in Baltimore. *References*: George H. Emerson Papers, Hoover Institution Archives, Stanford, Calif.; *NYT,* January 14, 1950; and *WWWA*.

EQUITABLE LIFE ASSURANCE SOCIETY OF THE UNITED STATES. Established in 1859 and began to do business in Russia in 1890. The Soviet government terminated its activities in Soviet Russia in 1919. *References*: Archives, New York Life Insurance Company, New York City; William Alexander, *A Brief History of the Equitable Life Assurance Society of the United States: Seventy Years of Progress and Public Service, 1859–1929* (New York, 1929); and Roscoe Carlyle Buley, *The Equitable Life Assurance Society of the United States, 1859–1964* (New York, 1967).

F

FARNEY, GEORGE WIMBOR (1872–1941). Mining and metallurgical engineer, born March 21, 1872, in Rostov, Russia, and came to the United States in 1895. Farney graduated from the Michigan School of Mines. He was employed by the International Steam and Pump Company. He went to Russia in 1901 as consulting engineer and general manager for Russia of the Worthington Pump Company of London and held this position until 1917. He was also chief engineer of the E. Tillman and then the Paul Boeckel companies, from 1904 to 1912. He was in charge of the construction of many important public works and plants, including a large copper electrolytic plant in the Ural mountains, a bridge over the Don River, the first incinerator plant and an asbestos manufacturing works in St. Petersburg, waterworks for the city of Nikolayev, and oil refineries in Baku. He also acted as consulting engineer to mining companies in Russia and China. He served in the U.S. Army during World War I. He was president and treasurer of the Jireh Food Company, near Morris Plains, New Jersey, from 1919 until 1936. Died September 1, 1941, in Sea Cliff, Long Island, New York. *Reference*: *NCAB* 30:531.

FARSON, [JAMES SCOTT] NEGLEY (1890–1960). Journalist, born May 14, 1890, in Plainfield, New Jersey. Farson attended the University of Pennsylvania. He was a munitions salesman and adventurer, selling oil in New York, chains in Manchester, arms in Moscow, and trucks in Chicago from 1914 to 1917. He went to Russia to sell army and navy supplies to the tsarist government and was witness to the Russian Revolution. He served with the Royal Flying Corps in World War I, was wounded in a plane crash near Cairo in 1918, and spent two years recuperating in British Columbia. He served as foreign correspondent for the *Chicago Daily News* from 1924 to 1933 and was in the Soviet Union in 1928–1929. He wrote *Black Bread and Red Coffins* (New York, 1930), *Caucasian Journey* (London, 1951), and his memoirs, *The Way of a Transgressor* (New York, 1936) and *A Mirror for Narcissus* (New York, 1957). Died December 12, 1960, near Georgeham, North Devon, England. *References*: *DAB S6*; and *NYT*, December 14, 1960.

FAYMONVILLE, PHILIP RIES (1888–1962). Army officer, born April 30, 1888. Faymonville graduated from Stanford University and the U.S. Military Academy in 1912 and was commissioned second lieutenant in the Coast Artillery Corps. He served on the Mexican border and in the Philippines before World War I and in the Ordnance Corps during World War I. He was chief ordnance officer of the American Expeditionary Forces in Siberia in 1918–1919. He also served as judge advocate of the forces and was a member of the Inter-Allied War Materials Committee. He was in charge of prisoners of war repatriation in Germany in 1920 and was ordnance officer of the Ninth Corps in San Francisco. In 1922–1923, he was an American military observer in Chita, the capital of the short-lived Far Eastern Republic, an artificial buffer state that the Soviet government erected between itself and Japan. He was assistant military attaché in Tokyo in 1923–1924 and was attaché from 1924 to 1926. He was military attaché in Moscow from 1934 until 1939. He served on the technical staff of the chief of ordnance in Washington and then with the Fourth Army in San Francisco from 1939 until 1941. He returned to the Soviet Union in 1941 as chief of the U.S. Supply Mission to the Soviet Union and was then *Lend-Lease representative in Moscow, assuming responsibility for all problems related to military aid until 1943. He retired, with the rank of brigadier general, in 1948. Died March 29, 1962, in San Francisco. *References*: J. S. Hernson and J. O. Baylen, "Col. Philip R. Faymonville and the Red Army, 1914–1943," *SR* 34 (1975): 483–505; J. D. Langer, "The 'Red General': Philip R. Faymonville and the Soviet Union, 1917–1952," *Prologue* 8 (Winter 1976): 211–14; Anatole G. Mazour, "Philip R. Faymonville," *California Historical Society Quarterly* 42 (1963): 82–84; and *NYT*, March 31, 1962.

FELL, EDWARD NELSON (1857–1928). Mining engineer, born August 27, 1857, in Nelson, New Zealand. Fell graduated from the Royal School of Mines (London). He was manager of St. John del Rey Gold Mining Company in Brazil, of drainage and development enterprises in Florida, of Huntsville Manufacturing Company in Alabama, and of the Athabasca Gold Mines in British Columbia until 1902. He was manager of Spaasky Copper Mines in Siberia from 1902 to 1908 and director of a mining company near the Ishim River in Kazakhstan. He wrote *Russian and Nomad: Tales of the Kirghiz Steppes* (New York, 1916). He was later manager of Fellsmere Farms Company in Florida and of iron mines at Andrews, North Carolina. Died in Warrenton, Virginia. *References*: *NYT*, April 1, 1928; and *WWIN*.

FEW, SIMON (1810–1882). Steamboat captain, born October 18, 1810, in Chester, Pennsylvania. Few moved to St. Louis, Missouri, and was steamboat engineer on the Mississippi River until 1853 and steamboat captain on the Missouri River from 1853 to 1859. He prospected for gold in Colorado and New Mexico from 1859 to 1861, when he went back to steamboating. In 1875, he superintended the building of two boats in San Francisco and shipped them to the mouth of the Amur River, where he had them put together by convicts and took them twenty miles up the river. He was employed by a company of Russian merchants in Siberia until 1877. He later made several trips around the world and farmed in Kickapoo Township, Kansas. Died November 1, 1882, in Fort Leavenworth, Kansas. *References*: Simon Few Papers, Jackson County Historical Society, Independence, Mo.

FISCHER, LOUIS (1896–1970). Journalist and author, born February 29, 1896, in Philadelphia. Fischer graduated from the Philadelphia School of Pedagogy. He served in the British Army's Jewish Legion during World War I. He was a writer for the *New York Evening Post* in Moscow in 1922–1923 and foreign correspondent of the *Nation* in the Soviet Union from 1923 to 1935. He portrayed the changes brought by the revolution in the most favorable light and deliberately covered up the severity of Soviet social and economic conditions in certain cases. He wrote *Machines and Men in Russia* (New York, 1932), *Soviet Journey* (New York, 1935), and *Men and Politics: An Autobiography* (New York, 1941). He left the Soviet Union in 1936, served with the International Brigades in Spain, and then returned to the United States. He later became a free-lance writer and world traveler. He wrote *The Life and Death of Stalin* (New York, 1952), *Russia Revisited: A New Look at Russia and Her Satellites* (Garden City, N.Y., 1957), *The Life of Lenin* (New York, 1964), *Fifty Years of Soviet Communism* (New York, 1968), *Russia's Road from Peace to War: Soviet Foreign Relations, 1917– 1941* (New York, 1969), and *The Road to Yalta* (New York, 1972) and was coauthor of *The God That Failed* (New York, 1950). He was research associate and visiting lecturer at the Woodrow Wilson School of Public and International Affairs, Princeton University, after 1961. Died January 15, 1970, in Hackensack, New Jersey. His wife, **BERTHA MARKOOSHA FISCHER**, wrote *My Lives in Russia* (New York, 1944). *References*: Louis Fischer Papers, Princeton University Library, Princeton, N.J.; *CA*; James William Crowl, *Angels in Stalin's Paradise: Western Reporters in Soviet Russia, 1917 to 1937, a Case Study of Louis Fischer and Walter Duranty* (Lanham, Md., 1982); *DAB S8*; *NYT*, January 17, 1970; and A. Raucher, "Beyond the God That Failed: Louis Fischer, Liberal Internationalist," *Historian* 44 (1982): 174–89.

FISHER, HAROLD HENRY (1890–1975). Historian, born February 15, 1890, in Morristown, Vermont. Fisher graduated from the University of Vermont. He served in the U.S. Army during World War I. He served with the *American Relief Administration (ARA) in Soviet Russia in 1922 and was also chief of the history department of the ARA. He wrote *The Famine in Soviet Russia, 1919– 1923: The Operations of the American Relief Administration* (New York, 1927). He taught history of Stanford University from 1924 until his retirement in 1955. He wrote *America and Russia in the World Community* (Claremont, Calif., 1946) and *The Communist Revolution: An Outline of Strategy and Tactics* (Stanford,

Calif., 1955) and was coauthor of *Soviet Russia and the West, 1920–1927: A Document Survey* (Stanford, Calif., 1957). He was vice-chairman and then chairman of the Hoover Institution of War, Revolution, and Peace at Stanford University from 1924 until his retirement in 1955. He was professor of international relations at San Francisco State College from 1955 to 1960. Died November 15, 1975, in Palo Alto, California. *References*: *CA*; *NYT*, November 17, 1975; *RR* 35 (1976): 231–32; and *WWWA*.

FISHER, MIERS, JR. (1787–1813). Merchant, member of a Philadelphia Quaker family. Fisher was involved in the St. Petersburg commission business from 1809 to 1813, establishing Miers Fisher and Company, the first American merchant house in St. Petersburg, in 1811. *Reference*: Miers Fisher, Jr., Papers, American Philosophical Society Library, Philadelphia.

FORCED REPATRIATION. At the *Yalta Conference, the United States and Britain agreed to return to the Soviet Union over two million Soviet war refugees without reference to their individual wishes, primarily to ensure the Red Army's repatriation of nearly fifty thousand American and British servicemen liberated in Eastern Europe. *References*: Nicholas Bethell, *The Last Secret: The Delivery to Stalin of Over Two Million Russians by Britain and the United States* (New York, 1974); Mark Elliott, *Pawns of Yalta: Soviet Refugees and American's Role in Their Repatriation* (Urbana, Ill., 1982); Mark Elliott, "United States and Forced Repatriation of Soviet Citizens, 1944–47," *Political Science Quarterly* 88 (1973): 253–75; Julius Epstein, *Operation Keelhaul: The Story of Forced Repatriation from 1944 to the Present* (Old Greenwich, Conn., 1973); and Nikolai Tolstoy, *The Secret Betrayal* (New York, 1977).

FORD MOTOR COMPANY. Created in 1903 and began shipping tractors to the Soviet Union in 1920. It signed a contract with the Soviet government in 1929 to provide plans for the erection and equipment of a plant to produce cars and trucks as part of the Soviet Union's First Five-Year Plan. It gave the Soviet government the rights to make and use Ford Machinery and sent engineers and foremen to the Soviet Union. The contract was canceled in 1935. *References*: Ford Archives, Henry Ford Museum, Dearborn, Mich.; Floyd J. Fithian, "Soviet-American Economic Relations, 1918–1933: American Business in Russia during the Period of Nonrecognition" (Ph.D. diss., University of Nebraska, 1964); Allan Nevins and Frank Ernest Hill, *Ford: Expansion and Challenge, 1915–1933* (New York, 1956), appendix: "The Russian Adventures," pp. 673–83; and Mira Wilkins and Frank Ernest Hill, *American Business Abroad: Ford on Six Continents* (Detroit, Mich., 1964).

FOX, GUSTAVUS VASA (1821–1883). Public official, born June 13, 1821, in Saugus, Massachusetts. Fox graduated from the U.S. Naval Academy in 1841. He served in the U.S. Navy from 1841 to 1856. He resigned in 1856 and was an agent of the Bay State Mills in Lawrence, Massachusetts. He was chief clerk of the Navy Department in 1861 and assistant secretary of the navy from 1861 until 1866. In 1866, he was sent by President Andrew Johnson to Russia as bearer of a congratulatory resolution of the American people at the escape of Tsar Alexander II from the attack by an assassin. Fox was escorted to Russia by a fleet and received a hospitable and elaborate reception by the tsar. A narrative of the expedition, prepared by his secretary, J. F. Loubat, was published as *Narrative of the Mission to Russia, in 1866, of the Hon. Gustavus Vasa Fox, Assistant Secretary of the Navy* (New York, 1873). Fox was later agent of the Middlesex Company in Lowell, Massachusetts, and then joined the firm of Mudge, Sawyer, and Company in Boston. Died October 29, 1883, in New York City. *References*: Gustavus Vasa Fox Papers, New York Historical Society, New York City; Gustavus Vasa Fox Papers, Division of Political History, Smithsonian Institution, Washington, D.C.; Virginia Woodbury Fox, "Diary," 1866, in Levi and Charles Levi Woodbury Papers, Manuscript Division, Library of Congress; I. M. Casanowicz, "The Gustavus Vasa Fox Collection of Russian Souvenirs in the United States National Museum," *Proceedings of the United States National Museum*, vol. 38, no., 1725; *DAB*; and *NCAB* 8:355.

FRANCIS, DAVID ROWLAND (1850–1927). Public official and diplomat, born October 1, 1850, in Richmond, Kentucky. Francis graduated from Washington University (St. Louis). He became a commission and grain merchant in St. Louis in 1870 and then founded his own commission company. He served as mayor of St. Louis from 1885 to 1889, as governor of Missouri from 1889 to 1893, and as secretary of the interior in 1896–1897. He was U.S. ambassador to Russia from 1916 to 1918. After the Russian Revolution, he supported the provisional government but sent misleading reports on the strength of this government. Although ordered not to deal directly with the Bolshevik government, and given permission to return to the United States, he stayed on and moved the embassy from place to place. He left Russia in 1918, on a stretcher. He wrote *Russia from the American Embassy, April 1916–November 1918* (New York, 1921). Died January 15, 1927, in St. Louis. *References*: David Rowland Francis Papers, Missouri Historical Society, St. Louis; Jamie H. Cockfield, ed., *Dollars and Diplomacy: Ambassador David Rowland Francis and the Fall of Tsarism, 1916–1917* (Durham, N.C., 1981); *DAB*; *DADH*; Gilbert C. Kohlenberg, "David Rowland Francis: American Businessman in Russia," *Mid-America* 40 (1958): 195–217; *NCAB* 24:322; and *NYT*, January 16, 1927.

FRANCIS, JOSEPH (1801–1893). Inventor and businessman, born March 12, 1801, in Boston. Francis was engaged in developing unsinkable rowboats from 1816 to 1819 and later continued to experiment in the development and manufacture of lifeboats. He went abroad in 1855. For the Russian government, he constructed a fleet of light-draft corrugated iron steamers, which were transported unassembled over the Ural Mountains to the Aral Sea in Siberia. There they were assembled and successfully put into service. He later established a factory for corrugated iron steamers in Russia. He returned to the United States in 1863. Died May 10, 1893, in Cooperstown, New York. *References*: Joseph Francis

Papers, Division of Natural History, Smithsonian Institution, Washington, D.C.: *DAB*; *NCAB* 10:88; and *WWWA*.

FREYN ENGINEERING COMPANY. Industrial design company, established in Chicago in 1914 by Henry Joseph Freyn (1876–1956). The company was chiefly engaged in international consulting work. As a leading designer of steel mills in the late 1920s, it agreed to build eighteen new iron and steel mills and rebuild some forty outdated metallurgical plants in the Soviet Union. It also permitted Soviet engineers access to its archives and to its design technology. The agreement was called "the first milestone in the transfer of western metallurgical technology to the Soviet Union." The company began preparing the plans for the Kuznetsk steel mill for the Gipromez State Institute in 1927, and a group of its engineers resided in the Soviet Union from 1929 to 1933, when the contract was terminated.

FRIEDLANDER, ISRAEL (1876–1920). Communal leader, born September 6, 1876, in Kovel, Poland, and grew up in Warsaw. Friedlander attended the Hildesheimer Rabbinical Seminary (Berlin) and Berlin University and graduated from the University of Strasbourg. He came to the United States in 1904 and was professor of biblical literature and exegesis at the Jewish Theological Seminary (New York City). He was also chairman of New York City's Bureau of Jewish Education. In 1919, he undertook a mission, on behalf of the Joint Distribution Committee, to the war-ravaged Jewish communities of Eastern Europe. He visited Poland and then toured the Russian countryside, at the time immersed in Civil War. He was murdered, with Rabbi Bernard Cantor (1892–1920), on July 5, 1920, by bandits near Yarmolinez, in the Ukraine. *References*: Israel Friedlander Papers, Jewish Theologial Seminary of American Library, New York City; *American Jewish Year Book* 23 (1921–1922): 65–79; *Encyclopaedia Judaica* (Jerusalem, 1971); and Baila Round Shargel, *Practical Dreamer: Israel Friedlander and the Shaping of American Judaism* (New York, 1985).

FRIENDS OF SOVIET RUSSIA. Official name: The Society of Friends of Soviet Russia. Founded in 1921, working under the direction of the American Communist Party, it was a front organization that appealed to the American left, farmers, labor unions, and worker organizations of various political persuasions. Its political objectives were diplomatic recognition of the Soviet Union by the United States, establishment of trade relations between the two countries, and dissemination of literature to counter the negative information in the American press about the Soviet government and the Soviet Communist Party. It was also involved in collecting food, money, and clothing for Soviet citizens suffering during the famine of 1921–1922. It supported the activities of *Harold Ware. *Reference*: *MERSH*.

FROST, GEORGE ALBERT (1843–1907). Artist, born December 27, 1843, in Cambridge, Massachusetts. Frost studied at the Belgian Royal Academy. He traveled through Siberia in 1867 as a member of the *Russian-American Telegraph Expedition. He also accompanied *George Kennan on his investigatory trip through Siberian prisons in 1885. Died November 13, 1907, in Cambridge, Massachusetts. *Reference*: *NYT*, November 14, 1907.

G

GANTT, WILLIAM ANDREW HORSLEY (1893–1980). Psychologist, born October 18, 1893, in Wingina, Virginia. Gantt graduated from the Universities of North Carolina and Virginia and studied at University College (London). He was chief of medicine of the *American Relief Administration in Petrograd in 1922–1923. He was affiliated with the Research Institute of Experimental Medicine of the physiologist Ivan Petrovich Pavlov in Leningrad from 1924 to 1929 and was the last American to study under Pavlov. He was later the leading American authority on the Pavlovian principle of conditioned reflexes. He translated Pavlov's *Lectures on Conditioned Reflexes* (New York, 1928–1941). He was psychiatrist at the Johns Hopkins Hospital in Baltimore after 1930, director of the Pavlovian Laboratory at Johns Hopkins University from 1930 to 1964, and director of the Pavlovian laboratory at the Veterans Administration Hospital in Perry Point, Maryland, from 1950 to 1974. He wrote *Russian Medicine* (New York, 1937). Died February 26, 1980, in Baltimore, Maryland. *References*: *American Psychologist* 36 (1981): 417–19; *CA*; and *NYT*, February 28, 1980.

GARST, ROSWELL (1898–1977). Agriculturist, born June 17, 1898, in Coon Rapids, Iowa. Garst attended Iowa State and Northwestern universities and the University of Wisconsin. In 1917, he took over the management of his father's farm. He founded the Garst and Thomas Hybrid Corn Company of Coon Rapids, Iowa, in 1930 and developed it into one of the leading producers of hybrid corn seed. The first group of Russian farm experts visited his farm in 1955, and he visited the Soviet Union later that year. He gained national prominence in 1959 when Premier Nikita Khrushchev visited his farm during a tour of the United States. He traveled several more times to the Soviet Union; several Russian agricultural ministers visited his farm to study American farming techniques; and he sold the Russians both hybrid corn and grain sorghum seed. Died November 5, 1977, in Carroll, Iowa. *References*: *CB* 1964; Harold Lee, *Roswell Garst: A Biography* (Ames, Iowa, 1984); Richard Lowitt and Harold Lee, eds.,

Letters from an American Farmer: The Eastern European and Russian Correspondence of Roswell Garst (Dekalb, Ill., 1987); and *NYT,* November 7, 1977.

GAYLORD, FRANKLIN AUGUSTUS (1856–1943). Association official, born May 1, 1856, in Glenwood, near Yonkers, New York. Gaylord graduated from Yale University and Union Theological Seminary, studied at the College de France (Paris), and was ordained in 1881. He was general secretary of the *Young Men's Christian Association (YMCA) in Paris, France, from 1887 to 1893 and pastor of Trinity Congregational Church in New York City from 1895 to 1899. He went to Russia in 1899, was general secretary of the Russian YMCA in St. Petersburg from 1899 to 1911, and was director of the Russian Society for Moral and Physical Development of Young Men from 1911 to 1918. He was secretary of the American Hospital for wounded Russian soldiers in 1916, secretary of the International Committee of the YMCA in 1918–1919, and representative of the International Committee of the YMCA in Odessa in 1919–1920. Died August 14, 1943, in West Englewood, New Jersey. *References*: Franklin A. Gaylord, "Breaking into Russia," in Frank W. Ober, ed., *James Stokes: Pioneer of Young Men's Christian Association* (New York, 1921), pp. 107–22; *NYT,* August 15, 1943; and *WWWA.*

GENERAL ELECTRIC COMPANY. Established in 1892 as a result of a merger between the Thompson-Houston Company and the Edison General Electric Company. Its subsidiary, International General Electric (IGE) signed a contract in 1917 with a Russian company for technical assistance and entered the Russian electrical industry, establishing in Kharkov a factory that manufactured light bulbs. The factory was nationalized in 1918. General Electric continued contact with the Soviet market through its European affiliates. In 1928, IGE signed a contract with the Soviet Union to sell the Soviets electrical products providing lengthy credits. It supplied the generators installed in the power plants at the Dnieprostroi Dam. It also provided technical assistance to the Soviet electrical industry and was involved in developing production facilities for the manufacturing of electrical equipment. *Reference*: Floyd James Fithian, "Soviet-American Economic Relations, 1918–1933: American Business in Russia during the Period of Nonrecognition" (Ph.D. diss., University of Nebraska, 1964), ch. 8.

GENEVA SUMMIT (1955). Summit meeting between President *Dwight D. Eisenhower, Prime Minister Anthony Eden, Premier Edgar Faure, and Premier Nikolai A. Bulganin on July 18–23 in Geneva. The United States aimed to reduce Cold War tensions and to define crucial world problems, including German unification, European security, disarmament, and East-West contacts, which would then be delegated to foreign ministers for negotiation. Eisenhower presented his *"Open Skies" proposal which called for an exchange of military blueprints among nations and allowed aerial reconnaissance of military installations. The plan was rejected by General Secretary Nikita S. Khrushchev as an attempt to spy on the Soviet Union. A final communique directed the foreign ministers to pursue negotiations, but these talks eventually collapsed. The "Spirit of Geneva," a sense that it was possible for Cold War enemies to meet and discuss problems, lasted for some time. *References*: *DADH*; *McDonald*; and *Weihmiller*.

GENEVA SUMMIT (1985). Summit meeting between President *Ronald Reagan and General Secretary Mikhail S. Gorbachev on November 19–21, 1985, in Geneva. The two leaders signed an agreement that a nuclear war must not be fought and could not be won and that neither side would seek military superiority. It was decided that air service would be resumed between the two countries and that new consulates would be opened. But the chief result was the resumption of talks on arms control. *Reference*: Joseph G. Whelan, *Soviet Diplomacy and Negotiating Behavior, 1979–88: New Tests for U.S. Diplomacy* (Washington, D.C., 1988), pp. 237–336.

GILDER, WILLIAM HENRY (1838–1900). Journalist, born August 16, 1838, in Philadelphia. Gilder served in the Union army during the Civil War. He later became involved in journalism in Newark, New Jersey. In 1878–1879, as a correspondent of the *New York Herald,* and second in command, he accompanied Lieutenant Frederick Schwatka on an expedition to King-William Land to discover the bodies or the records of the Sir John Franklin expedition. In 1881, James Gordon Bennett organized an expedition to search for the *Jeannette,* and he accompanied the expedition of the *Rodgers* as correspondent for the *New York Herald.* After a long cruise in the Arctic Ocean and an exploration of the islands of Herald and Wrangel, the *Rodgers* was destroyed by fire at St. Lawrence Bay in Eastern Siberia. Gilder proceeded along the coast to Nizhni-Kolymsk and thence to Irkutsk to telegraph the news of the loss of the *Rodgers.* At Nizhni-Kolymsk he learned of the destruction of the *Jeannette* and met a courier carrying sealed reports of *George W. Melville, who had discovered the bodies of the expedition. He broke open the sealed reports and forwarded the news to the *New York Herald.* After a journey across Siberia to Nizhni-Novgorod, he returned to the United States. *Ice-pack and Tundra: An Account of the Search for the Jeannette and a Sledge Journey through Siberia* (New York, 1883) was a collection of his articles, illustrated by many of his own drawings. He later visited Borneo and Cochin China. He was editor of the *Newark Sunday Standard* and later the *Trenton Sunday Times* and then joined the staff of the *New York Journal.* Died February 5, 1900, in Morristown, New Jersey. *References*: *DAB*; *NCAB* 3:287; and *WWWA*.

GILMORE, LANIER KING ("EDDY") (1907–1967). Journalist, born May 28, 1907, in Selma, Alabama. Gilmore attended Washington and Lee University and Carnegie Institute of Technology. He was a reporter for the *Atlanta Journal* from 1928 to 1932 and the *Washington* (D.C.) *Daily News* from 1933 to 1936. He worked for the Associated Press after 1936, in its Washington Bureau from

1936 to 1940 and in the London Bureau in 1940–1941. He served in the Moscow Bureau from 1941 to 1953 and was chief of the Moscow Bureau from 1943 to 1954. He succeeded in obtaining an interview with Joseph Stalin in 1946. His wartime romance with Tamara Chernashova, a dancer with the Bolshoi Ballet, continued despite obstacles put between foreigners and Russian citizens. Chernashova was banished by the regime, but through the good offices of Wendel L. Wilkie, she was returned to Moscow, where the couple were married. Gilmore was able to leave the Soviet Union with his wife only after the death of Stalin. He worked in the London bureau after 1954. He wrote *Me and My Russian Wife* (Garden City, N.Y., 1954), *Troika* (London, 1961), and *After the Cossacs Burned down the Y* (New York, 1964). Died October 5, 1967, in East Grinstead, England. *References*: *CA*; *CB* 1947; *NYT*, October 7, 1967; and *WWWA*.

GINZBERG INCIDENT (1894–1896). John Ginzberg was a citizen of the United States and of Glasgow, Montana. Although he left Russia at age fourteen, he was arrested by the Russian authorities in 1894 when he returned for a visit. Accused of escaping military service, he was imprisoned in a Russian jail. His arrest and imprisonment became a subject of protracted negotiations between the U.S. Department of State and the Russian Foreign Office. He was finally released in 1896. *References*: William S. Wallace, "A Montanan in Russo-American Relations: The Case of John Ginzberg," *Pacific Northwest Quarterly* 40 (1949): 35–43; and William S. Wallace, "Notes and Documents: A Russian Incident, 1894–1897," *American Jewish Historical Quarterly* 39 (1949): 67–86.

GLASSBORO SUMMIT (1967). Summit meeting of President *Lyndon B. Johnson and Premier Aleksei N. Kosygin from June 23 to 25, 1967, in Glassboro, New Jersey. Johnson wanted to avoid the accelerated arms race that he believed would follow the refinement and deployment of Anti-Ballistic Missile (ABM) systems; to achieve agreement on arms shipments to the Middle East so as to avoid the U.S. sale of Phantom jets to Israel; and to explore whether or not serious peace negotiations with Hanoi were possible. Some headway was made on the nonproliferation treaty and on an ABM agreement, and two weeks after the summit the two sides accepted the first two articles of the nonproliferation agreement. *References*: Robert D. Bole, *Summit at Holly Bush* (Glassboro, N.J., 1969); *McDonald*; and *Weihmiller*.

GLENNON, JAMES HENRY (1857–1940). Naval officer, born February 11, 1857, in French Gulch, California. Glennon attended the University of California, graduated from the U.S. Naval Academy in 1878, and was commissioned ensign in 1882. He was assigned to USS *Ranger* and served as part of a force engaged in a North Pacific survey from 1881 to 1885. He served in the Spanish-American War and the Philippine-American War, was in charge of gun development in the Bureau of Ordnance of the U.S. Navy Department in Washington from 1904 to 1907, commanded the USS *Virginia* from 1910 to 1912, and commanded the Navy Yard and was superintendent of the Naval Gun Factory in Washington, D.C., from 1915 to 1917. In 1917, he was the Navy Department representative with the *Root Mission to Russia. He made a trip to Sebastopol to inspect the Russian Black Sea Naval Command and discovered that a mutiny had taken place on the battleships and that all officers were under arrest. He persuaded the mutineers to restore their officers. He was commandant of the 13th Naval District in Seattle, Washington, and of the 3rd Naval District in New York City until his retirement, with the rank of rear admiral, in 1921. Died May 29, 1940, in Washington, D.C. *References*: NCAB 42:650; and C. J. Weeks and J. O. Baylen, "Admiral James H. Glennon's Mission to Russia, June-July 1917," *New Review* 13 (December 1973): 14–31.

GOLDEN, JOHN OLIVER (1892–1940). Worker. Golden worked on a cotton plantation in Mississippi as a boy. He attended Tuskegee Institute but was expelled after a quarrel with a white official. He joined the Communist Party and went to the Soviet Union in 1925 as a representative of the party. He returned to the United States in 1927. He then formed a group of African-American agricultural experts, signed a contract with the Soviet Ministry of Agriculture, worked in cotton growing near Tashkent, Uzbekistan, and was later an instructor at the Tashkent Institute of Irrigation and Mechanization of Agriculture. He became a Soviet citizen in 1935 and was elected to the Tashkent Soviet. Died 1940 in Tashkent. His granddaughter, Yelena Khanga, wrote her family history (with Susan Jacoby) in *Soul to Soul: A Black Russian American Family, 1865– 1992* (New York, 1992). *Reference*: Paula Garb, *They Came to Stay: North Americans in the U.S.S.R.* (Moscow, 1987), pp. 36–40.

GOLDER, FRANK ALFRED (1877–1929). Historian, born August 11, 1877, near Odessa, Russia. Golder came with his parents to the United States in 1880 and grew up in Bridgeton, New Jersey. He graduated from Bucknell University, taught in a government school in Alaska from 1899 to 1902, and graduated from Harvard University. He wrote *Russian Expansion on the Pacific, 1641–1850* (Cleveland, 1914). He was assistant professor and later professor of history at Washington State College from 1911 to 1920. He went to Russia in 1915 to prepare a guide to materials on American history in Russian archives for the Carnegie Institution and published the results as *Guide to Materials for American History in Russian Archives* (Washington, D.C., 1917–1937). He also secured in St. Petersburg an important collection of unpublished letters of John Paul Jones, which he published in *John Paul Jones in Russia* (Garden City, N.Y., 1927). He returned to Russia in 1917 for the American Geographical Society, to translate and prepare for publication the journals of the explorer Vitus Bering. He was in Petrograd during part of the Russian Revolution. He went to Vladivostok to accompany the Advisory Commission of Railway Experts across Siberia. He later published *Bering's Voyages: An Account of the Efforts of the*

Russians to Determine the Relation of Asia and America (New York, 1922–
1925). He joined the Inquiry commission as a specialist on Russian affairs. He
was in Eastern Europe and Soviet Russia from 1920 to 1923 to collect materials
for the Hoover Library at Stanford University. He was special investigator for
the *American Relief Administration. He was associate professor of history at
Stanford University from 1921 to 1924, professor of Russian history after 1924,
and director of the Hoover Library. He returned to the Soviet Union in 1925
and again in 1927. He was coauthor of *On the Trail of the Russian Famine*
(Stanford, Calif., 1927) and *The Russian Revolution* (Cambridge, Mass., 1918).
Died January 7, 1929, in Stanford, California. *References*: Frank Alfred Golder
Papers, Hoover Institution Archives, Stanford, Calif.; *DAB*; Alain Dubie, *Frank
A. Golder: An Adventure of a Historian in Quest of Russian History* (Boulder,
Colo., 1989); Terence Emmons and Bertrand M. Patenaude, eds., *War, Revo-
lution, and Peace in Russia: The Passages of Frank Golder, 1914–1927* (Stan-
ford, Calif., 1992); *NCAB* 23:204; and Allen Glen Wachhold, ''Frank A. Golder:
An Adventure in Russian History'' (Ph.D. diss., University of California at
Santa Barbara, 1984).

GOLDMAN, EMMA (1869–1940). Anarchist and editor, born June 27, 1869,
in Kovno, Lithuania, and grew up in Konigsberg, East Prussia, and St. Petersburg. She came to the United States in 1885. She worked in a corset factory in
New Haven, Connecticut. She was converted to anarchism in 1889 and moved
to New York City. She was arrested in 1893 for inciting to riot and spent one
year in prison. She went to Europe in 1895 and studied nursing. She edited the
anarchist journal *Mother Earth* after 1906. She opposed U.S. entry into World
War I, was arrested with *Alexander Berkman in 1917, was convicted of conspiracy to obstruct the operation of the military draft, and was sentenced to two
years' imprisonment and a fine of ten thousand dollars. She was deported to
Soviet Russia in 1919. Although she had at first been a supporter of the Russian
Revolution, she became disillusioned, and her opinion of the Soviet experiment
changed within less than a year—to one of intense dislike. She left Soviet Russia
in 1921 and lived in Estonia, Sweden, Germany, England, and after 1926, St.
Tropez, France. She wrote *My Disillusionment in Russia* (Garden City, N.Y.,
1923) and an autobiography, *Living My Life* (New York, 1931). Died May 14,
1940, in Toronto, Canada. *References*: *DAB S2*; Richard Drinnon and Anna
Maria Drinnon, eds., *Nowhere at Home: Letters from Exile of Emma Goldman
and Alexander Berkman* (New York, 1975); *NAW*; *NYT*, May 14, 1940; and
Alice Wexler, *Emma Goldman in Exile: From the Russian Revolution to the
Spanish Civil War* (Boston, 1989).

GOODRICH, JAMES PUTNAM (1864–1940). Public official, born February
18, 1864, in Winchester, Indiana. Goodrich attended DePauw University, studied
law, and was admitted to the bar in 1886. He practiced law in Winchester and
Indianapolis from 1910 to 1914 and then devoted his time to his business interests.
He was governor of Indiana from 1917 until 1921. In 1922, he became a member

and special investigator of the *American Relief Administration, for which he made three trips to Soviet Russia, also acting as unofficial observer of economic and social conditions in Russia for Presidents Warren G. Harding and Calvin Coolidge. He visited the Soviet Union again in 1925 and 1928 and became a member of the *American-Russian Chamber of Commerce. He was a member of the International St. Lawrence Waterways Commission after 1924. Died August 15, 1940, in Winchester, Indiana. *References*: James P. Goodrich Papers, Herbert Hoover Presidential Library, West Branch, Iowa; *CA*; Frederick C. Giffen, "James Putnam Goodrich and Soviet Russia," *Mid-America* 71 (1989): 153–74; and *NCAB* 30:76.

GORTON, WILLARD LIVERMORE (1881–?). Civil engineer, born June 13, 1881, in Eau Claire, Wisconsin. Gorton graduated from the University of Oklahoma. He was in charge of constructing the city water supply and sewers at Chickasha, Oklahoma, with the U.S. Reclamation Service, was chief engineer for the Idaho Irrigation Project in Richfield, Idaho, for J. G. White and Company, and was chief irrigation engineer for the Bureau of Public Works of the Philippines in Manila until 1915. He served with the U.S. Army Engineers during World War I, was chief engineer of the Idaho Public Utilities Commission from 1919 to 1922, and was in private practice after 1922. He was a consultant on reclamation and irrigation projects to the Soviet government and was in charge of constructing an irrigation project in Russian Turkestan from 1930 to 1932. He was also chief consulting engineer for the design and construction of the Vaksh, a large irrigation project for the Glavkhlopkom (Chief Cotton Committee). *References*: Willard L. Gorton Papers, Hoover Institution Archives, Stanford, Calif.; and *WWIN*.

GRAVES, WILLIAM SIDNEY (1865–1940). Army officer, born March 27, 1865, in Mount Calm, Texas. Graves graduated from the U.S. Military Academy in 1899 and was commissioned in the infantry. He served in the Philippine-American War from 1899 to 1902, in the Philippines from 1904 to 1906, and with the General Staff in Washington from 1909 to 1918. He was commander of the American Expeditionary Force in Siberia from 1918 until 1920. He commanded a force of some ten thousand men in Vladivostok, whose purpose was to protect Allied military stores in depots along the Trans-Siberian Railway, to render aid to the Czech army stranded in Siberia, and to discourage any Japanese ambitions to annex Russian territories during the confusion and civil war that had followed the Russian Revolution of 1917. He carried out his orders scrupulously, firmly resisting pressure from British, French, and some American diplomatic officials who wanted him to take action against the Bolsheviks. He wrote *America's Siberian Adventure* (New York, 1931). He was the commanding general of the First Infantry Brigade, the First Division, the Sixth Army Corps Area, the Panama Canal Division, and the Panama Canal Department. He retired in 1928, with the rank of major general. Died February 27, 1940, in Shrewsbury,

New Jersey. *References*: William Sidney Graves Papers, Hoover Institution Archives, Stanford, Calif; *DAB S2*; *DAMIB*; Warren J. Eitler, "Diplomacy of the Graves Mission to Siberia" (Ph.D. diss., Georgetown University, 1953); *NYT*, February 28, 1940; and *WWWA*.

GREENE, FRANCIS VINTON (1850–1921). Army officer, born June 27, 1850, in Providence, Rhode Island. Greene graduated from the U.S. Military Academy in 1870, was commissioned in the artillery, and served at coastal forts in the South until 1872. He was transferred in 1872 to the Corps of Engineers, was involved in the survey of the Canadian boundary from 1872 to 1876, and then served in the office of the secretary of war. He was military attaché in Russia in 1877–1878, observing the Russo-Turkish War with the Russian headquarters in the field. He later prepared a report, *The Russian Army and Its Campaigns in Turkey in 1877–78* (New York, 1879), which filled the information gap in the War Department concerning the organization and capabilities of the Russian Army. He was in charge of public works in the city of Washington until 1886, when he resigned from the army. He was vice-president and later president of the Barber Asphalt Paving Company. He served in the Spanish-American War in the Philippines. He was later managing director of the New Trinidad Lake Asphalt Company, police commissioner of New York City in 1903–1904, and president of the Niagara, Lockport, and Ontario Power Company and the Ontario Power Company in Buffalo, New York, from 1905 to 1915. He wrote *Sketches of Army Life in Russia* (New York, 1881). Died May 15, 1921, in New York City. *References*: *DAB*; *NCAB* 23:23; and *NYT*, May 16, 1921.

GREENER, RICHARD THEODORE (1844–1922). Lawyer and consul, born January 30, 1844, in Philadelphia. Greener graduated from Harvard College. He was principal of the male department of the Institute for Colored Youth in Philadelphia from 1870 to 1872, served in the office of the U.S. attorney for the District of Columbia in 1872–1873, and was professor of mental and moral philosophy and logic at the University of South Carolina from 1873 to 1877. He was admitted to the bar in 1876. He was instructor in the law department of Howard University from 1877 to 1880 and dean in 1879–1880. He was law clerk in the office of the first comptroller of the U.S. Treasury from 1880 to 1882 and practiced law in the District of Columbia from 1882 to 1884. He became a prominent figure in Republican politics. He served as consul in Bombay, India, and was a commercial agent at Vladivostok from 1898 until his retirement in 1905. Died May 2, 1922, in Chicago. *References*: Allison Blakely, "Richard T. Greener and the 'Talented Tenth's' Dilemma," *Journal of Negro History* 59 (1974): 305–21; *DAB*; and *NCAB* 13:577.

GROW, MALCOLM CUMMINGS (1887–1960). Surgeon, born November 19, 1887, in Annapolis, Maryland. Grow graduated from Jefferson Medical College (Philadelphia). He served in the Imperial Russian Army Medical Corps from 1915 to 1917 and wrote *Surgeon Grow: An American in the Russian Fighting* (New York, 1918). He served as surgeon with the 45th Artillery and the 42nd Infantry Division in France during World War I and with the 8th Air Force and later the U.S. Strategic Air Force in the European Theater during World War II. He was surgeon general of the Air Force Medical Service from 1949 until his retirement, with the rank of major general, in 1949. Died October 20, 1960, at Andrews Air Force Base, Maryland. *Reference*: *Journal of the American Medical Association* 172 (January 7, 1960): 62.

GRUBER, RUTH (1911–). Journalist and author, born in Brooklyn, New York. Gruber graduated from New York University and the Universities of Wisconsin and Cologne (Germany). She was special foreign correspondent for the *New York Herald Tribune* during the 1930s and made two trips to the Soviet Union, traveling north of the Arctic Circle (the first foreign correspondent to penetrate the Soviet Arctic) and then through the gulag and Yakutsk. She wrote *I Went to the Soviet Arctic* (New York, 1939). She was special assistant to the secretary of the interior and field representative for Alaska from 1941 to 1946, foreign correspondent of the *New York Times* in 1946, and again special foreign correspondent for the *New York Herald Tribune* from 1947 to 1965. She wrote *Ahead of Time: My Early Years as a Foreign Correspondent* (New York, 1991). *Reference*: *CA*.

GUILD, CURTIS (1860–1915). Public official and diplomat, born February 2, 1860, in Boston. Guild graduated from Harvard University. He joined the staff of *Commercial Bulletin* in 1881, was made partner in 1884, and was sole owner and editor after 1902. He served in the Spanish-American War. He was lieutenant governor of Massachusetts from 1903 to 1905 and governor from 1906 to 1909. He was U.S. ambassador to Russia from 1911 to 1913. He tried, unsuccessfully, to explain to the Russian government the U.S. decision to abrogate the 1832 treaty because of Russian policies toward the Jews. Although he was previously popular in tsarist official circles, that decision made the atmosphere in St. Petersburg so unpleasant that he returned to the United States and resigned. Died April 6, 1915, in Boston. *References*: *DAB*; *NCAB* 14:454; and *NYT*, April 7, 1915.

GUMBERG, ALEXANDER SEMENOVICH (1887–1939). Financier, born in Elizavetgrad, Russian Ukraine. Gumberg emigrated to the United States in 1903 and became a registered pharmacist in 1908. He was also business manager for the radical paper *Novyi Mir*. In 1915, he became a commissioned purchasing agent for the industrial firm of Perelstrous and Storms. He returned to Russia in 1917, became the confidential adviser to *Raymond Robins, head of the American Red Cross delegation in Russia, and acted as a contact between the delegation and the Russian government. He also served as a translator to the *Root Mission. He was the Soviet government's principal contact point for relations with the American embassy, the American Red Cross Commission, and the Russian section of the Committee on Public Information. He returned to the United States in 1918 and served as the North American representative of the Petrograd Telegraph Agency. He then organized the American office of the All-Russian Textile Syndicate and handled large purchases of cotton in the United States. He was in the confidence of both American and Soviet officials. He was adviser to the *Chase National Bank until 1930, when he joined the staff of the Atlas Corporation, a Wall Street investment company. He was adviser to American financial and business concerns on political, economic, and cultural relations with the Soviet Union and was probably the most important U.S. individual promoting American business with the Soviet Union before 1933. Died May 30, 1939, in Norwalk, Connecticut. *References*: Alexander Gumberg Papers, Wisconsin State Historical Society, Madison; James K. Libbey, *Alexander Gumberg and Soviet-American Relations, 1917–1933* (Lexington, Ky., 1977); *MERSH*; and *NYT*, May 31, 1939.

H

HAMMER, ARMAND (1898–1990). Businessman, born May 21, 1898, in New York City. Hammer graduated from Columbia University and its medical school. He then became involved in the family's pharmaceutical company and went to Soviet Russia in 1921 on a business mission for the company. He met V. I. Lenin and proposed to barter a shipment of surplus American wheat in return for Russian furs and caviar. Lenin accepted the deal and offered a concession on an asbestos mine in southern Russia, which was a flop. Hammer was the agent for other American business and had sole sales concession in the Soviet Union for *Ford, U.S. Rubber, Allis-Chalmers, and Underwood Typewriter. In 1925, the Soviet government decided to handle its own foreign trade, and in exchange for his agency concession with thirty-eight American firms, Hammer asked for a manufacturing concession to make pencils in Russia. During his nine years residency in Russia he bought up art objects, acquiring many of the imperial family's priceless treasures. When he was finally forced to leave the Soviet Union in the early 1930s, he took with him a large collection of art treasures, selling them at special shows at Gimbel's and other American department stores. He wrote *The Quest of the Romanoff Treasure* (New York, 1932). He then became involved in the brewing and distilling industry. He bought Occidental Petroleum Company in 1956 and entered the fertilizer business. In the early 1960s, he returned to talk trade with the Soviets and, in 1972, concluded a large fertilizer contract with the Soviet Union. He wrote (with Neil Lyndon) *Hammer* (New York, 1987). Died December 10, 1990, in Los Angeles. *References*: Carl Blumay (with Henry Edwards), *The Dark Side of Power: The Real Armand Hammer* (New York, 1992); John Bryson, *The World of Armand Hammer* (New York, 1985); *CB* 1973; Bob Considine, *The Remarkable Life of Dr. Armand Hammer* (New York, 1975); Joseph Finder, *Red Carpet* (New York, 1983); Philip S. Gillette, "Armand Hammer, Lenin, and the First American Concession in Soviet Russia," *SR* 40 (1981): 355–65; John H. Ingham, *Biographical Dictionary of American Business Leaders* (Westport, Conn., 1983); *NYT*, December 12, 1990; Steve Weinberg, *Armand Hammer: The Untold Story* (Boston, 1989); Robert

C. Williams, *Russian Art and American Money, 1900–1940* (Cambridge, Mass., 1980), ch. 6.

HAMMOND, JOHN HAYS (1855–1936). Mining engineer, born March 31, 1855, in San Francisco. Hammond graduated from the Sheffield Scientific School of Yale University and the Royal School of Mines in Freiberg, Saxony. He was employed in various mining jobs in California from 1879 to 1881, became a consulting engineer in 1881, and served as consulting engineer to the mining department of the Union Iron Works in San Francisco from 1884 to 1891 and as president of the Bunker Hill and Sullivan Mine in the Coeur d'Alene district of Idaho from 1891 to 1893. He went to South Africa in 1893 as manager of mining properties on the Rand in the Transvaal and then was hired by Cecil Rhodes and the British South African Company. After the Jameson Raid of 1896, he was convicted of treason and sentenced to death but was released after serving five months in jail and paying a fine. He was a consulting engineer in London from 1896 to 1899 and in New York City after 1899. He was also a consulting engineer and general manager of the Guggenheim Exploring Company until 1907. He was invited to Russia in 1897–1898 to make a survey of Russia's industrial potentialities and particularly of its mining resources. He returned to Russia in 1910 and 1912, again surveying Russian industrial potentialities. He wrote *The Autobiography of John Hays Hammond* (New York, 1935). Died June 8, 1936, in Gloucester, Massachusetts. *References*: John Hays Hammond Papers, Yale University Library, New Haven, Conn.; W. C. Askew, "Efforts to Improve Russo-American Relations before the First World War: The John Hays Hammond Mission," *SEER* 31 (December 1952): 179–85; *DAB S1*; *NCAB* 26:45; and *NYT*, June 9, 1936.

HAPGOOD, ISABEL FLORENCE (1850–1928). Translator and author, born November 21, 1850, in Boston and grew up in Boston, Jersey City, and Worcester, Massachusetts. Hapgood mastered, in good part on her own, virtually every Germanic and Romance language, as well as Russian, Polish, and Old Church Slavonic. She began her literary career in 1886, translating from French, Spanish, Dutch, and Polish. She was best known, however, for her faithful translations of Russia's greatest writers. Through her, Russian literature first became available directly to the English-reading world. She traveled in Russia from 1887 to 1889, gathering firsthand impressions of the country, its people, and its institutions. She became acquainted with Russian poets and writers and was invited by Count Leo Tolstoy to his family home at Yasnaya Polyana. She wrote *Russian Rambles* (Boston, 1895), *A Survey of Russian Literature* (New York, 1902), and many articles and reviews for magazines and newspapers. She served as foreign correspondent, editorial writer, and reviewer for the *New York Evening Post* and the *Nation*. She made a second trip to Russia in 1917 to collect material for a book (never published) on Russian church music and escaped at the outbreak of the revolution. Died June 26, 1928, in New York City. *References*: Isabel

Florence Hapgood Papers, New York Public Library, New York City; *DAB*; *NAW*; *NCAB* 21:51; and *NYT*, June 27, 1928.

HARPER, SAMUEL NORTHRUP (1882–1943). Educator, born April 9, 1882, in Morgan Park, Chicago. Harper graduated from the University of Chicago and from l'Ecole des Langues Orientales Vivantes in Paris and studied at Columbia University. After 1905, he spent six months in Russia each year, financed by *Charles Richard Crane. He was associate in Russian at the University of Chicago from 1905 to 1909, lecturer in Russian institutional history at the University of Liverpool from 1911 to 1913, assistant professor of Russian language and institutions at the University of Chicago after 1915 and head of the department after 1930. He was recognized as one of the foremost American authorities on the life, and language of the Soviet people. From 1904 until the beginning of 1943, he made eighteen journeys to Russia and studied Russian institutions under both the tsarist and the Communist regimes. He wrote *Civic Training in Russia* (Chicago, 1929), *Making Bolsheviks* (Chicago, 1931), and *Government of the Soviet Union* (New York, 1938). Died January 18, 1943, in Chicago. *The Russia I Believe In: The Memoirs of Samuel N. Harper, 1902–1941*, ed. Paul V. Harper (Chicago, 1945), was published posthumously. *References*: Samuel N. Harper Papers, University of Chicago Library; John Charles Chalberg, "Samuel Harper and Russia under the Tsars and Soviets" (Ph.D. diss., University of Minnesota, 1974); Paul A. Gobel, "Samuel N. Harper and the Study of Russia: His Career and Collection," *Cahiers du Monde Russe et Sovietique* 14 (1973): 608–20; *NYT*, January 19, 1943; and John B. Poster, "A Warmth of Soul: Samuel Northrup Harper and the Russians," *Journal of Contemporary History* 14 (1979): 235–51.

HARRIMAN, WILLIAM AVERELL (1891–1986). Businessman, public official, and diplomat, born November 15, 1891, in New York City. Harriman graduated from Yale University. He worked for the Union Pacific Railroad from 1913 to 1917, then organized the Merchant Shipbuilding Company, and by the mid-1920s had the largest American merchant fleet. In 1920, he founded the investment banking firm of W. A. Harriman and Company, which had some financial dealings with the Soviets and which operated a manganese mining concession near Chiatouri, in the Caucasus, from 1925 to 1928. He was chairman of the executive committee of the Illinois Central Railroad from 1931 to 1942. He was Lend-Lease administrator for Great Britain in 1941–1942. He undertook a special mission to Moscow in 1941 to arrange *Lend-Lease for Russia and another mission in 1942. He attended all the major wartime conferences and established a close personal relationship with Joseph Stalin. He was U.S. ambassador to the Soviet Union from 1943 to 1946. Stalin trusted him to convey faithfully Roosevelt's policies. He played a crucial role in the shaping of U.S. policy toward the Soviet Union in the first weeks of the presidency of *Harry S. Truman. Long concerned about Soviet expansionism and fearful that the

United States was being too accommodating toward Stalin, he advocated a firm but friendly policy on such things as Lend-Lease and postwar economic assistance. He was U.S. ambassador to Great Britain in 1946 and secretary of commerce from 1946 to 1948. He was U.S. special representative in Europe for the Economic Cooperation Administration in 1948 and special assistant to the president for national security affairs. He helped sell *NSC–68 to President Truman and was head of the Mutual Security Agency from 1951 to 1953. He was governor of New York from 1954 to 1958. After 1961, he was roving ambassador, then assistant secretary of state for Far Eastern affairs, and undersecretary of state for political affairs. He negotiated the Partial Test Ban Treaty in 1963. He was chief U.S. negotiator in the Vietnam peace negotiations in 1968–1969. He wrote *America and Russia in a Changing World* (Garden City, N.Y., 1971) and (with Elie Abel), *Special Envoy to Churchill and Stalin, 1941–1946* (New York, 1975). Died July 25, 1986, in Yorktown Heights, New York. *References*: W. Averell Harriman Papers, Manuscript Division, Library of Congress; Rudy Abramson, *Spanning the Century: The Life of W. Averell Harriman, 1891–1986* (New York, 1992); Larry I. Bland, "Averell Harriman, the Russians, and the Origins of the Cold War in Europe, 1943–1945," *Australian Journal of Politics and History* 23 (1977): 403–16; Larry I. Bland, "W. Averell Harriman: Businessman and Diplomat, 1891–1945" (Ph.D. diss., University of Wisconsin, 1972); Larry I. Bland, "W. Averell Harriman: The Liberal Cold Warrior," in Jules Davids, ed., *Perspectives in American Diplomacy* (New York, 1976), pp. 299–320; *CB* 1946; *DADH*; Joseph Finder, *Red Carpet* (New York, 1983); Walter Isaacson and Evan Thomas, *The Wise Men: Six Friends and the World They Made* (New York, 1986); John Daniel Langer, "The Harriman-Beaverbrook Mission and the Debate over Unconditional Aid for the Soviet Union, 1941," *Journal of Contemporary History* 14 (1979): 463–84; *NCAB* G:16; *New Yorker*, May 3, 10, 1952; and *NYT*, July 27, 1986.

HARRIS, EMMA (1870–?). Singer, born in 1870 in Augusta, Georgia. Harris directed a church choir in Brooklyn. In 1901, she joined the "Louisiana Amazon Guards," a vaudeville troupe of seven black women, and toured Europe until 1904. The troupe arrived in Moscow in 1904, performed in theaters in St. Petersburg and Moscow, and then disbanded in 1905 because of revolutionary activities in Russia. She remained in Russia and toured widely as a concert singer for more than a decade. During World War I she became involved with nonmusical activities and never returned to the field. She settled in New York in 1933. Died after 1937 in new York City. *Reference*: Eileen Southern, *Biographical Dictionary of Afro-American and African Musicians* (Westport, Conn., 1982).

HARRIS, ERNEST LLOYD (1870–1946). Consul, born October 26, 1870, in Jasper County, Iowa. Harris attended Iowa (later Grinnell) College and graduated from Cornell College and the University of Heidelberg. He entered the consular service in 1898, served as consular agent and later commercial agent in Eibenstock and Chemnitz, Germany, and was consul and then consul general in

Smyrna, Turkey, and Stockholm until 1916. He left the consular service in 1916 to take a position with the Petrograd office of the National City Bank of New York in 1917. In 1918, he made a survey of the cotton situation in Russian Turkestan. He returned to the consular service in 1918 and was consul general in Irkutsk from 1918 to 1921. He wrote "The Allies in Siberia" (N.p., 1921). He was consul general in Singapore from 1921 to 1925, in Vancouver from 1925 to 1929, and in Vienna from 1929 until his retirement in 1935. Died February 2, 1946, in Vancouver, British Columbia, Canada. *References*: Ernest Lloyd Harris Papers, Hoover Institution Archives, Stanford, Calif.; *NYT*, February 3, 1946; and *WWA*.

HARRIS, FRANKLIN STEWART (1884–1960). Agriculturist, born August 29, 1884, in Benjamin, Utah County, Utah. Harris graduated from Brigham Young University (Provo, Utah) and Cornell University. He was professor of agronomy at Utah State Agricultural College (later Utah State University) and agronomist at the Utah Agricultural Experiment Station in Logan from 1911 to 1916, director of the school of agriculture from 1912 to 1916, director of the experiment station from 1916 to 1921, president of Brigham Young University from 1921 to 1945, and president of Utah State Agricultural College from 1945 until his retirement in 1950. He also served as president of the Utah Rural Rehabilitation Corporation from 1934 to 1937. As agronomist and chairman of a commission of American experts, he traveled to the Soviet Union in 1929 to investigate that country's attempts to establish an agricultural district for the colonization of Jewish people at Birobidzhan. Died April 18, 1960, in Salt Lake City, Utah. *References*: Franklin Stewart Harris Papers, Brigham Young University Library, Provo, Utah; *NCAB* 53:67; *NYT*, April 20, 1960; and *Science* 132 (August 24, 1960): 433–34.

HARRIS, LEVETT (1780?–1839). Merchant and consul, from Philadelphia. Harris was commission agent in various St. Petersburg merchant houses and was U.S. consul general at St. Petersburg from 1803 to 1816. He was secretary to the commissioners to negotiate a treaty of peace under Russian mediation in 1813–1814 and chargé d'affaires at St. Petersburg from 1814 to 1817. Died September 1839 in Philadelphia. His nephew, **JOHN LEVETT HARRIS**, served as U.S. consul in St. Petersburg from 1816 to 1819. *Reference:* Levett Harris Letters, William L. Clements Library, University of Michigan, Ann Arbor; and James Barton Rhoads, "Harris, Lewis, and the Hollow Tree," *American Archivist* 25 (1962): 295–314.

HARRISON, JOSEPH (1810–1874). Mechanical engineer, born September 20, 1810, in Philadelphia. Harrison was apprenticed to a builder of steam engines and then became involved in building locomotives. He became a foreman for Garrett and Eastwick in Philadelphia in 1835 and a partner in Garrett, Eastwick, and Company in 1837 (renamed Eastwick and Harrison in 1839). He originated several important improvements in the locomotive. He went to St. Petersburg in 1843, where, with *Thomas Winans, he concluded a contract with the Russian government for building locomotives and iron trucks of freight cars. Eastwick and Harrison closed their plant in Philadelphia in 1844 and moved a portion of their equipment to St. Petersburg, where the firm of Harrison, Winans, and Eastwick completed the work they had contracted. He returned to the United States in 1852. In 1859 he patented the sectional Harrison Steam Boiler and in 1862 erected a factory in Philadelphia for its manufacture. He wrote *The Iron Worker and King Solomon* (Philadelphia, 1869), which included an account of his business ventures in railroad building in Russia. Died March 27, 1874, in Philadelphia. *References*: *DAB*; *NCAB* 12:495; and J. N. Westwood, *Locomotive Designers in the Age of Steam* (Rutherford, N.J., 1978).

HARRISON, MARGUERITE ELTON BAKER (1879–1967). Journalist, born October 1879 near Baltimore. Harrison graduated from Radcliffe College. After her husband's death in 1915, she became a journalist for the *Baltimore Sun*. In 1918 she joined the Military Intelligence Division, was sent to Europe, and was stationed in Berlin until 1919. In 1920 she was sent to Russia, was arrested as a spy, and remained in prison ten months. She wrote *Marooned in Moscow: The Story of an American Woman Imprisoned in Russia* (New York, 1921), *Unfinished Tales from a Russian Prison* (New York, 1923), and *Red Bear or Yellow Dragon* (New York, 1924). She made a journey around the world in 1922–1923, and an overland journey from Istanbul to Persia in 1924–1925. She wrote an autobiography, *There Is Always Tomorrow: The Story of a Checkered Life* (New York, 1935). Died July 16, 1967, in Baltimore. *Reference*: Elizabeth Fagg Olds, *Women of the Four Winds* (Boston, 1985), pp. 155–230.

HARTMAN, ARTHUR ADAIR (1926–   ). Diplomat, born March 12, 1926, in New York City. Hartman graduated from Harvard University. He was economic officer of the Economic Cooperation Administration in Paris from 1948 to 1952, political-military officer with the U.S. Mission to the North Atlantic Treaty Organization (NATO) and European Regional Organizations in Paris in 1954–1955 and in Saigon from 1956 to 1958. He was international affairs officer with the Economic Organization Affairs Section of the Bureau of European Affairs of the State Department from 1958 to 1961, staff assistant to undersecretary of state for economic affairs in 1961–1962, special assistant in 1962–1963, chief of economic section in the embassy in London from 1963 to 1967, special assistant and staff director to undersecretary of state from 1967 to 1969, deputy director for coordination from 1969 to 1972, deputy chief of mission and minister counselor of the U.S. mission to the Common Market in Brussels from 1972 to 1974, assistant secretary of state for European affairs from 1974 to 1977, and U.S. ambassador to France from 1977 to 1981. He was U.S. ambassador to Moscow from 1981 to 1987. He was later criticized for his management style and for neglecting security at the embassy in Moscow. He was an international business consultant after 1989. *References*: *DADH*; *Washington Post*, February 26, 1988; and *WWA*.

HARVEY, GEORGETTE (1883–1952). Actress and singer, born 1883 in St. Louis. Harvey went to New York in 1901 and began her professional career in stage music in 1905. She formed a female quartet, called "Creole Belles," which was possibly the first black female quartet in the United States. The group went on a European tour but was disbanded in St. Petersburg, the last city on their itinerary. She operated a nightclub in St. Petersburg until 1917, when the outbreak of the Russian Revolution forced her to flee. She escaped to East Asia and spent a few years teaching English in China and Japan. She returned to the United States in 1921 and settled in New York City, appearing in both dramas and musicals. She also sang with community groups and in nightclubs and theaters. Died February 17, 1952, in New York City. *References*: Eileen Southern, *Biographical Dictionary of Afro-American and African Musicians* (Westport, Conn., 1982); and *NYT*, February 18, 1952.

HASKELL, WILLIAM NAFEW (1878–1952). Army officer, born August 13, 1878, in Albany, New York. Haskell graduated from the U.S. Military Academy in 1901 and was commissioned second lieutenant. He served in the Philippines in operations against the Moros tribes, commanded the Army School of Enlisted Specialists of the Signal Corps in Ft. Omaha, Nebraska, and served again in the Philippines until 1914. He participated in the Mexican border campaign and served in France during World War I. He was chief of the Allied mission to Romania attempting to alleviate famine conditions in 1919 and was Allied high commissioner to Armenia in 1919–1920. He was director of the *American Relief Administration in Soviet Russia from 1921 to 1923. With headquarters in Moscow, he organized a Russian relief corps and feeding stations in the famine districts. He wrote of his experiences in the July 1948 issue of *Plain Talk*. He returned to the United States in 1923. He was National Guard liaison officer at Governor Island, New York, from 1923 to 1926. He resigned in 1926 and was commander of the New York National Guard from 1926 to 1940. He returned to active duty in 1940, commanded the 27th Infantry Division in 1940–1941, and organized the Army Emergency Relief Headquarters in 1941–1942. He retired with the rank of lieutenant general in 1942. He was in charge of field operation of the office of Foreign Relief and Rehabilitation Operation in the State Department in 1943–1944 and was national director of the Office of Civilian Defense in 1944–1945. He was vice-president of Save the Children Federation from 1947 until his death. Died August 13, 1952, in Greenwich, Connecticut. *References*: *CB* 1947; *NCAB* 40:516; and *NYT*, August 14, 1952.

HAVEN, WILLIAM ANDERSON (1888–1973). Industrial engineer and businessman, born August 11, 1888, in Swissvale, Pennsylvania. Haven graduated from Pennsylvania State College. He was employed by the United States Steel Corporation from 1909 to 1912 and was general foreman or superintendent of blast furnace plants for various iron and steel companies from 1912 until 1927.

He was vice-president of Arthur G. McKee and Company of Cleveland from 1929 until 1953. In 1930, he supervised the planning of the Magnitogorsk steel plant, the largest in the Soviet Union at the time, and lived in the Soviet Union in 1931–1932, overseeing the construction of this plant. He was later a consultant in the iron and steel industry. Died May 1973, in Cleveland. *Reference*: William Haven Papers and autobiography, Western Reserve Historical Society, Cleveland, Ohio.

HAYWOOD, WILLIAM DUDLEY ("BIG CHILL") (1869–1928). Labor leader, born February 4, 1869, in Salt Lake City, Utah. Haywood began working as a boy in a variety of mining jobs in Utah, Nevada, and Idaho. He was member of the executive board of the Western Federation of Miners and its secretary-treasurer. He was a founding member of the International Workers of the World (IWW) in 1905 and later served as its secretary. He was arrested in 1917 on a charge of seditious conspiracy and was sentenced to twenty years' imprisonment. While awaiting a new trial, he jumped bail in 1921 and fled to Soviet Russia. He was one of the organizers of the *Kuzbas colony. Died May 18, 1928, in Moscow. *Bill Haywood's Book: The Autobiography of William D. Haywood* (New York, 1929) was published posthumously. *References*: Peter Carlson, *Roughneck: The Life and Times of Big Bill Haywood* (New York, 1983); Joseph Robert Conlin, *Big Bill Haywood and the Radical Union Movement* (Syracuse, N.Y., 1969); *DAB*; Melvyn Dubofsky, *"Big Bill" Haywood* (Manchester, 1987); *NYT*, May 19, 1928; and Bryan D. Palmer, " 'Big Bill' Haywood's Defection to Russia and the IWW: Two Letters," *Labor History* 17 (1976): 271–78.

HAZARD, JOHN NEWBOLD (1909–   ). Legal scholar, born January 5, 1909, in Syracuse, New York. Hazard graduated from Yale University and Harvard Law School and studied law at the Moscow Juridical Institute from 1934 to 1937. He was later admitted to the New York bar. He practiced law in New York City from 1939 to 1941. He was deputy director of the Soviet Union branch of the *Lend-Lease Administration in Washington, D.C., from 1941 to 1945. He was professor of public law at Columbia University from 1946 to 1976 and professor of law in 1976–1977. He was adviser on Soviet law to the U.S. prosecutor preparing the indictment of Axis criminals in 1945. He wrote *Soviet Housing Law* (New Haven, Conn., 1939), *Recent Trends in the Treatment of Criminals in the U.S.S.R.* (New York, 1939), *Law and Social Change in the U.S.S.R.* (London, 1953), *The Soviet System of Government* (Chicago, 1957), *Settling Disputes in Soviet Society: The Formative Years of Legal Institutions* (New York, 1960), *Communists and Their Law* (Chicago, 1969), and *Managing Change in the U.S.S.R.: The Politico-Legal Role of the Soviet Jurist* (Cambridge, Mass., 1983) and was coauthor of *The Soviet Legal System: Post-Stalin Documentation and Historical Documentary* (Dobbs Ferry, N.Y., 1962). He also wrote *Recollections of a Pioneering Sovietologist* (New York, 1987). *References*: John N. Hazard Papers, Columbia University Library, New York City; and *WWA*.

HEALD, EDWARD THORNTON (1885–1967). Association official, born September 20, 1885, in Portland, Oregon, and grew up in Peoria, Illinois. Heald graduated from Oberlin College and Western Reserve University. He was student secretary of the *Young Men's Christian Association (YMCA) at Colorado College (Colorado Springs) in 1909–1910 and at Kansas State College (Manhattan) in 1910–1911, membership secretary in Toledo, Ohio, from 1911 to 1914, and general secretary in Davenport, Iowa, from 1914 to 1916. He was international representative of the YMCA in Russia and Siberia from 1916 to 1919. He wrote *The Y.M.C.A. with the Czecho-Slovak Army* (Prague, 1919). He was general secretary in Davenport from 1919 to 1922, in Troy, New York, from 1922 to 1929, and in Canton, Ohio, from 1929 to 1945. He was secretary-treasurer of the Stark County Historical Society in Canton from 1946 to 1954 and its historian after 1954. Died June 1, 1967, in Canton, Ohio. *References*: *CA*; Edward T. Heald, *Witness to Revolution: Letters from Russia, 1916–1919*, ed. James B. Gidney (Kent, Ohio, 1972); and Warren Walsh, ed., ''Petrograd, March–July 1917: The Letters of Edward T. Heald,'' *American Slavic and East European Review* 6 (1947): 116–57.

HENDERSON, LOY WESLEY (1892–1986). Diplomat, born June 28, 1892, in Rogers, Arkansas. Henderson graduated from Northwestern University. He was a member of the American Red Cross Commission to Western Russia and Baltic States in 1919–1920. He entered the foreign service in 1921. He served with the Division of Eastern European Affairs in the State Department in 1925–1926, from 1930 to 1933, and from 1938 to 1941. He served in the U.S. legation in Riga, Kovno, and Tallinn from 1927 to 1929 and at the embassy in Moscow from 1934 to 1938. He was counselor of embassy and charge in Moscow and Kuibyshev in 1942. He played an important role in wartime Moscow, serving as the U.S. representative at a meeting between Winston Churchill and Joseph Stalin in August 1942. He was U.S. ambassador to Iraq from 1943 to 1945, director of Near Eastern and African Affairs in the State Department from 1945 to 1948, first U.S. ambassador to India and Nepal from 1948 to 1951, ambassador to Iran from 1951 to 1955, deputy undersecretary of state for administration from 1955 to 1957, and member of the faculty of the National War College from 1957 to 1960. He was a career ambassador after 1956 and retired in 1961, He was director of the Center for Diplomacy and Foreign Policy at American University from 1961 to 1968. Died March 25, 1986, in Bethesda, Maryland. *References*: George W. Baer, ed., *A Question of Trust: The Origins of U.S.–Soviet Diplomatic Relations: The Memoirs of Loy W. Henderson* (Stanford, Calif., 1986); H. W. Brands, *Inside the Cold War: Loy Henderson and the Rise of American Empire, 1918–1961* (New York, 1991); Thomas R. Maddux, ''Loy W. Henderson and Soviet-American Relations: The Diplomacy of a Professional,'' in Kenneth Paul Jones, ed., *U.S. Diplomats in Europe, 1919–1941* (Santa Barbara, Calif., 1981), pp. 149–61; and *NYT*, March 26, 1986.

HIBBEN, PAXTON (1880–1928). Journalist, editor, and diplomat, born December 5, 1880, in Indianapolis, Indiana. Hibben graduated from Princeton and Harvard universities, studied law, and was admitted to the bar in 1906 but never practiced. He entered the diplomatic service in 1905, was second secretary at the U.S. embassy in St. Petersburg and Mexico City, and was secretary of legation in Bogota, Columbia, and in The Hague until 1914. He was war correspondent of *Collier's Weekly* in 1914–1915 and staff correspondent of the Associated Press from 1915 to 1917. He served in the U.S. Army during World War I and with the American Military Mission to Transcaucasia in 1919–1920, was staff correspondent for the *Chicago Tribune* in Europe in 1920–1921, and was secretary of the Russian Commission of the Near East Relief charged with investigating and reporting on industrial, agricultural, social, and sanitary conditions in Soviet Russia in 1921. He was secretary of the Russian Red Cross Commission in America, organized in 1922, and director of the American Committee for Relief of Russian Children, one of the several small American relief committees sympathetic to bolshevism. He was a vocal critic of *Herbert Hoover and the *American Relief Administration. He wrote *Report on the Russian Famine, 1922* (New York, 1922). He advocated recognition of the Soviet Russian government by the United States and, as a result, was called in 1924 before an army court of inquiry to answer to a charge of unfitness to retain his commission in the reserve corps, but his commission was not revoked. Died December 5, 1928, in New York City. *Reference*: NCAB 22:119.

HINDUS, MAURICE GERSCHON (1891–1969). Author, born February 27, 1891, in Bolshoye Bikovo, Russia, and came to the United States in 1905, settling in New York City. Hindus became a naturalized citizen in 1910. He graduated from Colgate University and studied at Harvard University. He became a free-lance writer and wrote *The Russian Peasant and the Revolution* (New York, 1920). In 1922, he spent several months living with the Russian Doukhobors in western Canada. He was then commissioned by *Century* magazine to go to the Soviet Union and investigate the collective farm system. He wrote *Broken Earth* (New York, 1926), *Humanity Uprooted* (New York, 1930), and *Red Bread* (New York, 1931). He traveled frequently in the Soviet Union throughout his career and wrote *The Great Offensive* (New York, 1933), *Mother Russia* (New York, 1943), and an autobiography, *Green Worlds: An Informal Chronicle* (New York, 1938). Becoming a leading authority on the Soviet Union, he helped to increase American understanding of, and sympathy for, the Soviet Union. He was war correspondent for the *New York Herald Tribune* during World War II. During the Cold War, he became highly critical of the Soviet government. He later wrote *The Cossacks: The Story of a Warrior People* (New York, 1945), *Crisis in the Kremlin* (Garden City, N.Y., 1953), and *House without a Roof: Russia after Forty-Three Years of Revolution* (Garden City, N.Y., 1961). *A Traveler in Two Worlds* (Garden City, N.Y., 1971) was published posthumously. Died July 8, 1969, in New York City. *References*: *DAB S8*; and *NYT*, July 9, 1969.

HIRSCH, ALCAN (1885–1938). Chemical engineer, born February 1, 1885, in Corpus Christi, Texas. Hirsch graduated from the Universities of Texas and Wisconsin. He established a laboratory in New York in 1911 and was consultant to various industrial corporations from 1912 to 1916, consultant to the Japanese government on chemical development from 1916 to 1918, and president of Hirsch Laboratories after 1917. He formed Rector Chemical Company in 1917 and was one of the founders of Molybdenum Corporation of American in 1920. He was chief consultant to the Soviet government on its heavy chemical industry from 1931 to 1933, chief constructing engineer to the Ministry of the Chemical Industry of the Soviet Union (Chemtrust) from 1932 to 1934, and chief adviser to the chemical section of the Commisariat of Heavy Industry of the Soviet Union. He wrote *Industrialized Russia* (New York, 1934). Died November 24, 1938, in New Rochelle, New York. *References*: Alcan Hirsch Biographical Materials, University of Wisconsin Library, Madison; *NYT*, November 25, 1938; and *WWWA*.

HITCHCOCK, ETHAN ALLEN (1835–1909). Businessman and diplomat, born September 19, 1835, in Mobile, Alabama. Hitchcock moved to St. Louis in 1851. In 1860, he went to China and engaged in commission business, becoming a partner in Olyphant and Company of Hong Kong, from which he retired in 1862 with a great deal of wealth. He returned to St. Louis, where he became involved in a variety of business activities from 1874 to 1897. He was U.S. minister to Russia in 1897–1898 and the first U.S. ambassador to Russia in 1898–1899. He was successful in increasing American exports to Russia and was useful in keeping the Russians informed about the Spanish-American War. He was secretary of the interior from 1898 until 1907. Died April 9, 1909, in Washington, D.C. *References*: *DAB*; *DADH*; *NCAB* 11:16; and *NYT*, April 10, 1909.

HOFFMAN, WICKHAM (1821–1900). Diplomat, born April 2, 1821, in New York City. Hoffman graduated from Harvard University, was admitted to the bar in New York in 1841, and practiced law in New York City. He served in the Union army in 1861. He was assistant secretary of legation in Paris from 1861 to 1867, first secretary from 1867 to 1874, and secretary of legation in London from 1874 to 1877. He was secretary of legation in St. Petersburg from 1877 to 1882 and wrote *Leisure Hours in Russia* (London, 1883). He was U.S. minister to Denmark from 1883 until his retirement in 1885. Died May 21, 1900, in Atlantic City, New Jersey. *References*: *DAB*; *NCAB* 12:71; and *NYT*, May 22, 1900.

HOLT, WILLIAM JOSEPH (1829–1881). Physician, born January 13, 1829, in Augusta, Georgia. Holt graduated from South Carolina College (later University of South Carolina) and the Medical College of Georgia and studied in Berlin, Vienna, and Paris. He served as a surgeon with the medical department of the Russian Army during the Crimean War. He was a planter in Lowndes County, Alabama, from 1857 until 1861, served as military surgeon with the Confederate army during the Civil War, and practiced medicine in Montgomery, Alabama, from 1865 until his death. Died April 27, 1881, in Montgomery. *References*: William Joseph Holt Papers, University of South Carolina Library, Columbia; and Emmett B. Carmichael, "William Joseph Holt," *Alabama Journal of Medical Sciences* 1 (1964): 451–54.

HOOVER, CALVIN BRYCE (1897–1974). Economist, born April 14, 1897, in Berwick, Illinois. Hoover served in the U.S. Army during World War I, graduated from Monmouth (Ill.) College and the University of Wisconsin, and studied at the University of Minnesota. He was assistant professor of economics at Duke University from 1925 to 1927, professor from 1927 until 1974, and dean of the graduate school from 1937 to 1947. He was economic adviser to the U.S. Department of Agriculture from 1933 to 1935 and a member of the Research and Analysis Division of the Office of Strategic Services from 1941 to 1944. He spent 1929–1930 in the Soviet Union, studying the Soviet economic system firsthand, and made return visits in 1933, 1939, 1956, and 1958. He wrote *The Economic Life of Soviet Russia* (New York, 1931) and an autobiography, *Memoirs of Capitalism, Communism, and Nazism* (Durham, N.C., 1965). He retired in 1967. Died June 23, 1974, in Durham, North Carolina. *References*: *American Economic Review* 66 (1976): 725–26; *CA*; *EAIE*; and *NYT*, July 12, 1974.

HOOVER, HERBERT CLARK (1874–1964). Mining engineer and president of the United States, born August 10, 1874, in West Branch, Iowa, and grew up in Oregon. Hoover graduated from Stanford University. He worked for an international mining concern from 1897 to 1908, overseeing its operations in Australia and China. He organized his own firm in 1908 and worked in various parts of Russia from 1909 to 1915. He was chairman of the Committee for Relief in Belgium during World War I and U.S. food administrator in 1917–1918. He was then responsible for general civilian relief operations in Europe until 1919. In his capacity as director general of the *American Relief Administration (ARA), he responded favorably for aid to Soviet Russia during the period of famine from 1921 to 1923. He promised food on the condition that Americans then imprisoned in Russian jails be released. He was secretary of commerce from 1921 until 1928 and president of the United States from 1929 to 1933. He wrote *The Memoirs of Herbert Hoover* (New York, 1951–1952) and *An American Epic, Vol. 2: Famine in Forty-Five Nations, 1914–1923* (Chicago, 1961). Died October 20, 1964, in New York City. *References*: David Bruner, *Herbert Hoo-*

ver: A Public Life (New York, 1979); Leo E. Chavez, "Herbert Hoover and Food Relief: An Application of American Ideology" (Ph.D. diss., University of Michigan, 1976); DAB S7; Joan Hoff-Wilson, *Herbert Hoover: The Forgotten Progressive* (Boston, 1975); Eugene P. Trani, "Herbert Hoover and the Russian Revolution, 1917–20," in Lawrence E. Gelfand, ed., *Herbert Hoover: The Great War and Its Aftermath, 1914–23* (Iowa City, Iowa, 1979), pp. 111–42; Benjamin M. Weissman, *Herbert Hoover and Famine Relief to Soviet Russia, 1921–1923* (Stanford, Calif., 1974); and Edward F. Willis, *Herbert Hoover and the Russian Prisoners of World War I: A Study in Diplomacy and Relief, 1918–1919* (Stanford, Calif., 1951).

HOPKINS, HARRY LLOYD (1890–1946). Social worker and government official, born August 17, 1890, in Sioux City, Iowa. Hopkins graduated from Grinnell College. He was involved with the Association for Improving the Condition of the Poor and was executive secretary of the New York City Board of Child Welfare, director of the Gulf Division of the American Red Cross, and executive director of the New York Tuberculosis and Public Health Association. He was executive director of the New York State Temporary Relief Administration from 1931 to 1933 and director of the Federal Emergency Relief Administration from 1933 to 1938. He was secretary of commerce from 1938 to 1940. He was responsible for the *Lend-Lease program in 1941. He was special assistant to the president from 1942 until his retirement in 1945. A close and trusted adviser and confidant of President *Franklin D. Roosevelt, he was sent to the Soviet Union in 1941 to make personal contact with Joseph Stalin and to discuss Soviet supply needs, and he recommended the inclusion of Russia in Lend-Lease. He was sent to the Soviet Union again in 1945 by President *Harry S. Truman to assure the Soviet government that Truman would continue Roosevelt's policy and to work out the arrangements for the *Potsdam Conference. Died January 29, 1946, in New York City. *References*: Harry Hopkins Papers, Franklin D. Roosevelt Library, Hyde Park, N.Y.: Henry M. Adams, *Harry Hopkins: A Biography* (New York, 1977); *DAB S4*; John Daniel Langer, "The Formulation of American Aid Policy toward the Soviet Union, 1940–1943: The Hopkins Shop and the Department of State" (Ph.D. diss., Yale University, 1975); George McJimsey, *Harry Hopkins: Ally of the Poor and Defender of Democracy* (Cambridge, Mass., 1987); Robert Sherwood, *Roosevelt and Hopkins: An Intimate History* (New York, 1948); and Dwight W. Tuttle, *Harry L. Hopkins and Anglo-American-Soviet Relations, 1941–1945* (New York, 1983).

HOPPER, BRUCE CAMPBELL (1892–1973). Educator, born August 24, 1892, in Litchfield, Illinois. Hopper attended the University of Montana, graduated from Harvard University, and studied at the Sorbonne and Oxford University. He served with the American Field Service of the French Army in 1917 and with the U.S. Army Air Service during World War I. He was editor of the

China Press in Shanghai in 1920–1921. He was an observer for the Institute of Current World Affairs in the Soviet Union from 1926 to 1929 and returned in 1930 for an extensive stay. He visited the Soviet Union frequently until the outbreak of World War II. He was assistant professor of government at Harvard University from 1931 to 1937 and associate professor from 1937 until his retirement in 1961. He was attached to the U.S. embassy in Stockholm in 1942–1943, representing the Office of Strategic Services, and to the chief of the historical section of the 8th Air Force from 1943 to 1945. He served as consultant to the commanding general of the air force from 1945 to 1947. He wrote *Pan-Sovietism: The Issue before America and the World* (Boston, 1931). Died July 6, 1973, in Cambridge, Massachusetts. *References*: *NYT*, July 7, 1973; and *WWWA*.

"HOT LINE" AGREEMENT (1963). Memorandum of understanding between the United States of America and the Union of Soviet Socialist Republics regarding the establishment of a direct communications link, signed in Geneva on June 20, 1963. It established a direct communication link between the United States and the Soviet Union. An agreement between the United States of America and the Union of Soviet Socialist Republics on measures to improve the USA-USSR direct communications link (**"HOT LINE" MODERNIZATION AGREEMENT**), signed in Washington on September 30, 1971, established two satellite communication circuits—one Soviet and one American. Memorandum of understanding between the United States of America and the Union of Soviet Socialist Republics on the U.S.-U.S.S.R. direct communications link (**"HOT LINE" EXPANSION AGREEMENT**), signed in Washington on July 17, 1984, added a high-speed facsimile transmission capability. *Reference*: *ACDA*.

HOUGH, DAVID LEAVITT (1865–1938). Civil engineer, born April 27, 1865, in Fort Wayne, Indiana. Hough graduated from the Sheffield Scientific School of Yale University. He was chief engineer and general manager of the East River Gas Company in Long Island City from 1892 to 1895, served in the Spanish-American War, was president and organizer of United Engineering and Contracting Company in New York City from 1899 to 1905, and was president of New York Tunnel Company from 1905 to 1914, building some of the principal tunnels under Manhattan Island and the East River. He was in Russia from 1914 to 1917, involved in several railroad projects. Invited to advise on the cost of constructing a central railroad station in Moscow, he was named managing director of the Moscow Central Station Company, but the plan was scrapped because of World War I. He served in the Quartermaster Corps during World War I. He was employed by the Foundation Company of New York City from 1920 to 1931. Died October 12, 1938, in Amityville, Long Island, New York. *References*: *NYT*, October 13, 1938; *Obituary Record of Graduates Deceased during the Year Ending July 1, 1938* (New Haven, Conn., 1939), pp. 175–76.

HUGHES, JAMES LANGSTON (1902–1967). Author, born February 1, 1902, in Jopkin, Missouri, and grew up in Kansas, Illinois, and Ohio. Hughes attended Columbia University and graduated from Lincoln University. His first volume of poetry was published in 1926 and his first novel in 1930. In 1932, he joined a band of twenty-two young African-Americans who went to the Soviet Union to make a film on race relations in the United States. After the film project collapsed, he traveled extensively in Central Asia and spent a year in the Soviet Union. He described his experiences in *I Wonder as I Wonder: An Autobiographical Journey* (New York, 1956). He settled in Harlem in 1941. Died May 22, 1967, in New York City. *References*: Langston Hughes Papers, Beinecke Library, Yale University, New Haven, Conn.; Faith Berry, *Langston Hughes: Before and Beyond Harlem* (Westport, Conn., 1983); *CA; DAB S8; DANB; NYT*, May 23, 1967; and Arnold Rampersand, *The Life of Langston Hughes* (New York, 1986–1988).

HULLINGER, EDWIN WARE (1893–1968). Author and journalist, born August 13, 1893, in Chicago. Hullinger attended Occidental College, graduated from University of Kansas, and studied at Columbia University School of Journalism. He was a reporter for the *Los Angeles Tribune* and then was foreign correspondent for the United Press in Soviet Russia from 1918 to 1922. He was expelled from Soviet Russia in 1922 after insisting on the rights of correspondents in Moscow to send all news unhampered by a political censor. He wrote *The Reforging of Russia* (New York, 1925). He taught journalism at New York University, the University of Kansas, the University of Miami, and Boston University. He was senior information specialist at the U.S. Department of Agriculture in Washington, D.C., from 1939 to 1941 and assistant director of Foreign Broadcast Intelligence Service of the Federal Communication Commission from 1943 to 1945. He was production manager, executive producer, and president of Hullinger Productions from 1945 until his death. Died October 26, 1968, in Miami. *References*: *NYT*, October 28, 1968; and *WWWA*.

HUNT, WILLIAM HENRY (1823–1884). Public official and diplomat, born June 12, 1823, in Charleston, South Carolina. Hunt attended Yale University, studied law in New Orleans, and was admitted to the bar in 1844. He practiced law in New Orleans from 1844 to 1878 and was attorney general of Louisiana from 1876 to 1878, judge of the U.S. Court of Claims in Washington, D.C., from 1878 to 1881, and secretary of the navy in 1881–1882. He was U.S. minister to Russia, an appointment he considered tantamount to exile, from 1882 until his death. He dealt with cases of persecution against American Jews and protested a law banning the American Bible Society's activities in the Caucasus. Died February 27, 1884, in St. Petersburg. *References*: *DAB; DADH*; Thomas Hunt, *the Life of William H. Hunt* (Brattleboro, Vt., 1922); *NCAB* 4:244; and *NYT*, February 28, 1884.

HURD, EUGENE (1881–1941). Surgeon, born July 7, 1881, in Ft. Atkinson, Wisconsin. Hurd graduated from West Coast College of Medicine and Surgery (San Francisco). He practiced medicine in Seattle after 1906. He was a war correspondent during the Russo-Japanese War and a member of the Washington state House of Representatives in 1913. He went to Russia at the outbreak of World War I. Receiving an army commission, he was appointed captain in the Russian Army in 1914 and was promoted to colonel in 1915, serving as a medical officer with the Russian Army at the front during World War I and operating on more than thirty-one-thousand wounded soldiers. He was surgeon to the *Root Mission in 1917. Escaping to France, he enlisted in the U.S. Army and served in the U.S. Army Medical Corps during World War I. He later resumed his medical practice in Seattle. Died May 19, 1941, in Richardson Springs, California. *References*: *NYT*, May 21, 1941; and *WWWA*.

HUTCHINS, JOHN POWER (1873–1952). Mining engineer, born July 3, 1873, in San Francisco. Hutchins graduated from the University of California. He was hydraulic engineer on the Mother Lode in Nevada in 1898 and examined placer deposits in Alaska from 1898 to 1900. He was an engineer consultant in San Francisco and later opened an office in New York City, examining mines in Colombia and in the western United States. In 1910, he was engaged for similar work by the Russian Mining Corporation of London, England, with headquarters in St. Petersburg, from which he directed the management of the Lena Placer Goldfields in Siberia and examined several mining properties controlled by the tsar. His work was later expanded to include the management of lead and zinc mines in the Altai Mountains in Siberia. He left Russia in 1917, joined the American International Corporation in New York City in 1918, and was its Rome, Italy, manager. Died November 26, 1952, in San Francisco. *Reference*: *NCAB* 42:191.

HUTCHINSON, LINCOLN (1866–1940). Economist, born April 10, 1866, in San Francisco. Hutchinson graduated from the University of California and Harvard University and studied at Stanford University and the University of Leipzig. He was assistant professor of economics at the University of California from 1905 to 1913 and associate professor of commerce after 1913. He served as commercial attaché in Rio de Janeiro in 1914–1915, in the U.S. Army Quartermaster Corps during World War I, in the War Trade Board, and then in the War Industries Board until 1919. He was in charge of the organization of the *American Relief Administration (ARA) in Czechoslovakia in 1919 and was technical adviser to the government of Czechoslovakia in 1920–1921. He was economic investigator for the ARA mission in Soviet Russia from 1921 to 1923 and was coauthor of *On the Trail of the Russian Famine* (Stanford, Calif., 1927). He was later involved in research and writing. Died May 22, 1940, in San Francisco. *References*: *Encyclopedia of American Biography* (New York, 1941), 12:202–4; and *NYT*, May 23, 1940.

I

INCIDENTS AT SEA AGREEMENT (1972). Agreement between the United States of America and the Union of Soviet Socialist Republics on the prevention of incidents on and over the high seas, signed in Moscow on May 25, 1972. The agreement intended to reduce the number of potentially dangerous confrontations between the U.S. and Soviet navies. *References*: *ACDA*; Sean Lynn-Jones, "Applying and Extending the USA-USSR Incidents at Sea Agreement," in Richard Fieldhouse, ed., *Security at Sea: Naval Forces and Arms Control* (Oxford, 1990), pp. 203–19; Sean M. Lynn-Jones, "The Incidents at Sea Agreement," in Alexander L. George, Philip J. Farley, and Alexander Dallin, eds., *U.S.-Soviet Security Cooperation: Achievements, Failures, Lessons* (New York, 1988), pp. 482–509; and Sean M. Lynn-Jones, "A Quiet Success for Arms Control: Preventing Incidents at Sea," *International Security* 9 (Spring 1985): 154–84.

INF TREATY (1987). Intermediate-Range Nuclear Forces Treaty, the treaty between the United States of America and the Union of Soviet Socialist Republics on the elimination of their intermediate-range and shorter-range missiles, signed in Washington on December 18, 1987. The treaty required destruction of the two countries' ground-launched ballistic and cruise missiles with ranges of between five-hundred and five-thousand kilometers, their launchers, and associated support structures and support equipment within three years after the treaty entered into force in 1988. *References*: *ACDA*; Janne E. Nolan, "The INF Treaty," in Michael Krepon and Dan Caldwell, eds., *The Politics of Arms Control Treaty Ratification* (New York, 1991), pp. 355–97; and William B. Vogele, "Tough Bargaining and Arms Control: Lessons from the INF Treaty," *Journal of Strategic Studies* 12 (1989): 257–72.

INSTITUTE FOR SOVIET-AMERICAN RELATIONS. A nonpartisan, non-profit organization based in Washington, D.C., founded in 1983 to promote improved Soviet-American relations and communication, encourage collaborative activities in areas of mutual interest, including environment, economics, education, agriculture, and health, and serve as an information clearinghouse for Soviet-American exchange, with particular emphasis on the private sector. It pioneered in the field of citizen diplomacy as a clearinghouse, cataloguing and covering the private initiatives and concentrating on cooperative projects in the environment, sustainable economics and agriculture, technical assistance and aid, and the development of civil society and indigenous cultural pride. The name was later changed to ISAR, and the organization became dedicated to supporting the democratic process and efforts to improve conditions for people who live in the territory formerly called the Soviet Union.

INTER-ALLIED RAILWAY COMMISSION IN SIBERIA. Organized in March 1919, with *John F. Stevens as president, to provide general supervision of the railways in those regions where Allied troops were operating. It was dissolved on November 1, 1922. *Reference*: Inter-Allied Railway Commission in Siberia Records, National Archives, Washington, D.C.

INTERIM AGREEMENT ON OFFENSIVE ARMS (1972). Interim agreement between the United States of America and the Union of Soviet Socialist Republics on certain measures with respect to the limitation of strategic offensive arms, signed in Moscow on May 26, 1972. The agreement was designed to complement the *ABM Treaty by limiting competition in offensive strategic arms and providing time for more negotiations. It was intended to remain in force for five years so that both countries could continue negotiations for a more comprehensive agreement. It also froze the number of U.S. and Soviet deployed launchers for intercontinental and submarine-launched ballistic missiles. *Reference*: ACDA.

INTERNATIONAL HARVESTER COMPANY. Formed in 1902 by the merger of the McCormick Company with Deering Harvester and three smaller machinery makers. It set up its first overseas factory in 1905. Its plant at Lyubertsy, near Moscow, which was opened in 1911, was the largest plant in prerevolutionary Russia. The Omsk (Siberia) branch was the largest overseas branch operated by the company. It was nationalized by the Soviet government in 1924, and the company suffered a huge loss. *References*: International Harvester Company Corporate Archives, Chicago; Fred V. Carstensen, *American Enterprises in Foreign Markets: Studies of Singer and International Harvester in Imperial Russia* (Chapel Hill, N.C., 1984); Fred V. Carstensen and Richard H. Working, "International Harvester in Russia: A Washington–St. Petersburg Connection?" *Business History Review* 57 (1983): 347–66; and Elizabeth Cowan Pickering, "The International Harvester Company in Russia: A Case Study of a Foreign Corporation in Russia from the 1860's to the 1930's" (Ph.D. diss., Princeton University, 1974).

J

JACKSON AMENDMENT. An amendment attached to the Senate Joint Resolution that ratified the Antiballistic Missile Systems *(ABM) Treaty in 1972. Introduced by Senator Henry M. Jackson (D-Wash.), the amendment provided for Congress to consider any Soviet actions that endangered the survivability of U.S. deterrent forces as grounds for abrogating the treaty; urged the president to see that future treaties would not limit the United States to levels of intercontinental strategic forces inferior to the limits provided for the Soviet Union; and called on the U.S. government to pursue vigorous research and development and modernization programs as required by prudent strategic posture. The Jackson Amendment was considered to be an expression of Senate insistence on equality in any long-term strategic agreements with the Soviet Union. *Reference*: *DINRT*.

JACKSON-VANIK AMENDMENT. An amendment, sponsored by Senator Henry M. Jackson (D-Wash.) and Representative Charles Vanik (D-Ohio), to the Trade Act of 1974. It prohibited extension of U.S. government credits and most-favored-nation trade status to any Communist country that restricted free emigration of its citizens. The amendment was prompted by congressional concern over the Soviet Union's treatment of its Jewish minority. *References*: *DINRT*; William Korey, "The Story of the Jackson Amendment, 1973–75," *Midstream* 21 (March 1975): 7–36; John Sinclair P. Robson, "Henry Jackson, the Jackson-Vanik Amendment, and Détente: Ideology, Ideas, and United States Foreign Policy in the Nixon Era" (Ph.D. diss., University of Texas, 1989); and Paula Stern, *The Water's Edge: Domestic Politics and the Making of American Foreign Policy* (Westport, Conn., 1979).

JANIN, CHARLES HENRY (1873–1937). Mining engineer, born November 16, 1873, in Oakland, California. Janin was a farmer in southern California and then worked as an assistant in his father's engineering office and later for another engineering firm in San Francisco, although lacking any formal engineering training. He opened his own office in San Francisco in 1911, examining mines in the United States, Mexico, Russia, Siberia, Malaya, and other foreign countries until 1930 and specializing in gold dredging. He was in Russia in 1914 as a consultant on gold placer operations in Perm Province and again in 1917, when he was engaged to examine properties of the tsar. He prepared in 1917 "Notes on Russian Mines in the Ural Mountains, Kirghiz Steppe, and Altai Mountains" and wrote of his experiences in Petrograd in an article in the August 4, 1917, issue of *Mining and Scientific Press*. He returned to the United States at the outbreak of the Russian Revolution and served as government consultant during World War I. He was back in Siberia in 1925 and 1929, examining mines for Lena Goldfields and other companies. Died November 30, 1937, in Piedmont, California. *References*: Charles Henry Janin Papers, Huntington Library, San Marino, Calif.; Donald Chaput, "Gold for the Commissars: Charles Janin's Siberian Ventures," *Huntington Library Quarterly* 49 (1986): 385–400; *Mining and Metallurgy* 19 (February 1938): 121–22; and *WWIN*.

JESUP NORTH PACIFIC EXPEDITION (1900–1901). A scientific expedition to the North Pacific and Siberia carried out by the American Museum of Natural History and financed by Morris Ketchum Jesup (1830–1908) to study migrations between Asia and North America and to investigate the relationship between the peoples of northeastern Asia and northwestern North America. The Siberian operations of the expedition began in 1898. Three teams conducted fieldwork, one in southern and two in northern Siberia. The expedition established the close relationship of the populations and strongly supported the view that the ancestors of the American Indians came from Asia. It also produced ethnographies of Siberian peoples and many museum collections. *References*: William W. Fitzhugh and Aron Cromwell, *Crossroads of Continents: Cultures of Siberia and Alaska* (Washington, D.C., 1988); Stanley A. Freed, Ruth S. Freed, and Laila Williamson, "Capitalist Philanthropy and Russian Revolutionaries: The Jesup North Pacific Expedition (1897–1902)," *American Anthropologist* 90 (1988): 7–25; and Stanley A. Freed, Ruth S. Freed, and Laila Williamson, "Scholars amid Squalor," *Natural History* 97 (March 1988): 60–68.

JOHNSON, ALBERT AARON (1880–1963). Agriculturist, born January 1, 1880, near MacFarland, Dane County, Wisconsin. Johnson served during the Spanish-American War and graduated from the University of Wisconsin. He was head of the department of agriculture and biology at the North Georgia Agricultural College from 1907 to 1909. In 1909, he planned and organized the La Crosse School of Agriculture and Domestic Economy at Onalaska, Wisconsin, and was its principal until 1911. He planned and organized the Milwaukee School of Agriculture and Domestic Science in 1911 and was its principal until 1914. He was director of the New State Institute of Applied Agriculture at Farmingdale, Long Island, from 1914 until 1923. He was sent to the Near East in 1921 to investigate agricultural conditions for the Near East Relief, and he visited Turkey, Armenia, and Georgia. He was then appointed chairman of the Russian Commission of the Near East Relief and made a thorough investigation of the conditions of the famine-devastated regions of Soviet Russia, particularly along the Volga River. In his work in Soviet Russia, he gained the confidence of Soviet officials. In 1923, he was manager of an unofficial commission to Soviet Russia consisting of senators and representatives. In 1927, he organized the firm of A. A. Johnson and Associates to furnish an economic service to American manufacturers and bankers in Russia. He wrote *Russia at Work: Economic, Political, and Organization* (Springfield, Mass., 1928) and *The Soviet Union at Work: Past, Present, Future* (Springfield, Mass., 1929). Died May 31, 1963, in Sioux Falls, South Dakota. *References*: Albert Aaron Johnson Papers, State Historical Society of Wisconsin, Madison; *NCAB* A:483; and *NYT*, June 1, 1963.

JOHNSON, BENJAMIN O. (1878–?). Railway engineer, Johnson served as colonel in the *Russian Railway Service Corps from 1917 to 1923 and was president pro tempore of the Inter-Allied Technical Board in 1920–1921. He wrote of his experiences in the May-June 1923 issue of *Military Engineer*. *Reference*: Benjamin O. Johnson Papers, Hoover Institution Archives, Stanford, Calif.

JOHNSON, URAL ALEXIS (1908–). Diplomat, born October 17, 1908, in Falun, Kansas. Johnson graduated from Occidental College and attended Georgetown University School of Foreign Service. He joined the foreign service in 1935 and served in Tokyo, Seoul, Tientsin, and Mukden. He was interned by the Japanese in 1941–1942. He served in Rio de Janeiro from 1942 to 1944 and was consul in Manila in 1945 and in Yokohama from 1945 to 1947 and consul general from 1947 to 1949. He served in the office of Northeast Asian Affairs in the State Department from 1949 to 1951 and was deputy assistant secretary of state for Far Eastern affairs from 1951 to 1953, U.S. ambassador to Czechoslovakia from 1953 to 1958, ambassador to Thailand from 1958 to 1961, deputy undersecretary of state from 1961 to 1964, deputy ambassador to Vietnam in 1964–1965, deputy undersecretary of state for political affairs from 1965 to 1969, undersecretary of state from 1969 to 1973, and ambassador-at-large after 1973. He was chief U.S. delegate at SALT II from 1973 to 1977. He wrote (with Jef Olivarius McAllister) *The Right Hand of Power* (Englewood Cliffs, N.J., 1984). *References*: *DADH*; *NCAB* I:342; and *WWA*.

JOINT DISTRIBUTION COMMITTEE. See AMERICAN JEWISH JOINT DISTRIBUTION COMMITTEE, INC.

JONES, JOHN PAUL (1747–1792). Naval officer, born July 6, 1747, in Kirkcudbrightshire, Scotland. Jones was apprenticed to a merchant shipper in 1759 and then sailed as a cabin boy. He shipped in the slave trade from 1766 to 1768 and commanded his own ship in 1769. He came to the United States in 1773, was commissioned senior lieutenant in the Continental navy in 1775, and served during the revolutionary war. In 1788, he accepted a commission from Tsarina Catherine II as a rear admiral in the Russian Navy. He performed valuable service in the war against Turkey but was the victim of intrigues and was dismissed in 1789. Died July 18, 1792, in Paris, France. *Memoirs of Rear-Admiral John Paul Jones* (Edinburgh, 1830) was published posthumously. *References*: *DAB*; Frank A. Golder, *John Paul Jones in Russia* (Garden City, N.Y., 1927); Samuel Eliot Morison, *John Paul Jones: A Sailor's Biography* (Boston, 1959); and *NCAB* 2: 14.

JORALEMON, IRA BEAMAN (1884–1975). Mining engineer, born July 27, 1884, in Antwerp, New York. Joralemon graduated from Harvard University. He was an engineer and geologist with the Calumet and Arizona Mining Company from 1907 to 1911 and chief geologist from 1911 to 1916. He examined mines in South America for Anaconda Copper Mining Company from 1914 to 1916. He examined mines in Russia and Siberia in 1917. He served with the Aviation Section of the U.S. Army Signal Corps during World War I. He was a consulting mining engineer and geologist in San Francisco from 1923 until his retirement in 1973. Died August 17, 1975, in Berkeley, California. His memoirs, *Adventure Beacons*, ed. Peter Joralemon (New York, 1976), were published posthumously. *References*: Ira Beaman Joralemon Papers, American Heritage Center, University of Wyoming, Laramie; *NYT*, August 23, 1975; and *WWIN*.

JORDAN, PHILIP (1868–1941). Valet. Jordan entered the employ of the Francis family in 1889. He accompanied *David Rowland Francis, the U.S. ambassador to Russia, to St. Petersburg in 1916. He was one of only two African-Americans known to have been an eyewitness to the Russian Revolution and the only one to leave a written account of it. He remained in the employ of the Francis family until his death. *References*: Mrs. Clinton A. Bliss, "Philip Jordan's Letters from Russia, 1917–1919," *Missouri Historical Society Bulletin* 14 (1958): 139–66; and Jamie H. Cockfield, "Philip Jordan and the October Revolution," *History Today* 28 (April 1978): 220–27.

JUDSON, WILLIAM VOORHEES (1865–1923). Army officer, born February 16, 1865, in Indianapolis, Indiana. Judson attended Harvard University, graduated from the U.S. Military Academy in 1888, and was commissioned second lieutenant in the corps of engineers. He was assistant engineer on river and harbor improvements on Lake Erie and the upper Mississippi and at Galveston, Texas, chief engineer and president of the board of public works of Puerto Rico, in charge of river and harbor improvement and portification construction in Georgia and Alabama, instructor in the engineering school, member of the river and harbor board, and assistant to the chief of engineers in Washington, D.C. He was a U.S. military observer with the Russian Army during the Russo-Japanese War in 1904–1905, in charge of harbor and lighthouse construction on Lake Michigan from 1905 to 1909, engineer commissioner of the District of

Columbia from 1909 to 1913, assistant division engineer of the Atlantic division of the Panama Canal in 1913–1914, and then U.S. district engineer in Chicago and Baltimore. He was military aide to the *Root mission. After Elihu Root's return to the United States, Judson remained as chief of the American military mission to Russia and as military attaché at the American embassy at Petrograd until after the overthrow of the Kerensky regime by the Bolsheviks. He returned to the United States in 1918, commanded the 38th Division at Camp Shelby in Hattiesburg, Mississippi, and the port of embarkation in New York, and was district engineer in Chicago until 1922, when he retired. Died March 29, 1923, in Winter Park, Florida. *References*: William Voorhees Johnson Papers, Newberry Library, Chicago; *NCAB* 28:262; "Papers of General Judson," *Newberry Library Bulletin*, no. 3 (December 1945), 8–12; and Jane Gilmer Weyant, "The Life and Career of General William V. Judson, 1865–1923" (Ph.D. diss., Georgia State University College of Arts and Science, 1981).

K

KAL 007 INCIDENT (1983). Korean Air Lines (KAL) flight 007, a passenger aircraft flying from Anchorage, Alaska, to Seoul, South Korea, was shot down on September 1, 1983, by a Soviet fighter jet after it had strayed into Soviet air space. The plane plunged into the Sea of Japan, killing all 269 people aboard, including 61 Americans. It was one of the worst incidents in the Cold War. Although the U.S. government condemned the Soviet act, it refrained from overreaction and continued the negotiations on nuclear arms control. *References*: Alexander Dallin, *Black Box: KAL 007 and the Superpowers* (Berkeley, Calif., 1985); Seymour M. Hersh, *"The Target Is Destroyed": What Really Happened to Flight 007 and What America Knew about It* (New York, 1986); and R. W. Johnson, *Shootdown: Flight 007 and the American Connection* (New York, 1986).

KAMPELMAN, MAX M. (1920–). Lawyer and government official, born November 7, 1920, in New York City. Kampelman graduated from New York University and the University of Minnesota. He was legislative counsel to Senator Hubert H. Humphrey from 1949 to 1955. He practiced law in Washington, D.C., from 1956 to 1985 and again after 1989. He was senior adviser to the U.S. delegation to the United Nations in 1966–1967, U.S. ambassador and chairman of the U.S. delegation to the Conference on Security and Cooperation in Europe in Madrid from 1980 to 1983, ambassador and head of the U.S. delegation to Negotiations on Nuclear and Space Arms from 1985 to 1989, and counselor of the State Department from 1987 to 1989. He wrote *Three Years at the East/West Divide* (New York, 1983) and *Entering New Worlds: The Memoirs of a Private Man in Public Life* (New York, 1991). *References*: *CA*; and *WWA*.

KANTAKUZEN, JULIA DENT GRANT. See CANTACUZENE, JULIA DENT GRANT

KARELIAN FISHING COOPERATIVE. Fishermen of Finnish descent who formed a group in Astoria, Oregon, in 1921 and migrated to Eastern Karelia (an autonomous region in Soviet Russia) in 1922 to establish a fishing cooperative and erect a fish cannery. Much of the equipment sent from the United States was misplaced. The cooperative was dissolved in 1923, and most of its members returned to the United States. *References*: Paul George Hummasti, *Finnish Radicals in Astoria,1904–1940: A Study in Immigrant Socialism* (New York, 1979), ch. 7; and *MERSH*.

KARR, DAVID (1918–1979). Businessman, born August 24, 1918, in New York City. Karr attended American and George Washington universities. He was a journalist until 1945 and partner in a public relations agency from 1945 to 1950. He later established his own public relations agency, Market Relations Network, and was financial vice-president and chairman of the board of Colt Industries in New York City from 1959 to 1964. He established himself as a financial consultant in Paris in 1964, was involved with Trusthouse Forte, a hotel chain, and was then linked with Lazard Freres et Cie. He was chairman of Financial Engineers, a Swiss concern, in Paris after 1974. He started commuting to Moscow in 1972, serving as a broker for Western companies seeking new markets in the Soviet Union and for Soviet agencies seeking new capital and technology. He organized the building of the Kosmos Hotel in Moscow. At the time of his death, he was called one of the leading American businessmen in the East-West trade. On several occasions, he also acted as a private liaison between the United States and the Soviet Union. Died July 7, 1979, in Paris, France. *References*: Roy Rowan, "The Death of Dave Karr, and Other Mysteries," *Fortune* 100 (December 3, 1979): 94–105; "U.S. Entrepreneur's Soviet Ties," *NYT*, October 5, 1979; and *WWWA*.

KEELY, ROYAL ROCKWOOD (1875–1964). Industrial engineer, born September 10, 1875, in Cherryvale, Kansas. Keely graduated from Kansas State and Cornell universities. He was an engineer with Westinghouse, Church, Kerr, and Company, professor of electrical engineering at the University of South Dakota, city engineer in Edmonton, Alberta, and professor of electrical engineering at Nova Scotia Technical College. He went to Russia in 1919 at the invitation of the Soviet government to investigate its industrial and economic conditions. He was arrested in 1920 when he tried to leave the country, was tried and sentenced to two years in a labor camp on the charge of spying, and was imprisoned until 1921, when he was released and returned to the United States. He wrote of his experiences in the December 8, 1921, issue of *American Machinist*. Died February 1964 in Santa Monica, California.

KELLEY, ROBERT FRANCIS (1894–1976). Diplomat, born February 13, 1894, in Somerville, Massachusetts. Kelley graduated from Harvard University and studied at the University of Paris. He was military attaché at the U.S. legation in Copenhagen and in Helsinki and was then stationed in Riga as military observer in the Baltic States, the chief American observation post for developments in

Soviet Russia, from 1920 to 1922. He entered the foreign service in 1922 and served as vice-consul in Calcutta in 1923–1924. He was assistant chief of the Division of Eastern European Affairs in the State Department from 1924 to 1926 and chief of the division from 1926 to 1937. He took the lead in preparing promising young foreign service officers for work in, or in connection with, the Soviet Union and played a crucial role in the institutional molding of the State Department's Russian specialists. He was counselor of the embassy in Ankara from 1937 to 1945, when he retired from the foreign service. He was involved in the establishment of Radio Liberty and served as its chief until 1966. Died June 2, 1976, in Washington, D.C. *References*; Robert F. Kelley Papers, Georgetown University Library, Washington, D.C.; *American Historical Review* 82 (1977): 237–38; *EAIE*; *NYT*, June 3, 1976; and *Washington Post*, June 3, 1976.

KENDALL, DONALD MCINTOSH (1921–   ). Businessman, born March 16, 1921, in Sequim, Washington. Kendall attended Western Kentucky State College. He served in the U.S. Navy during World War II. He was a fountain syrup sales representative of *Pepsi-Cola Company in New York City from 1947 to 1952, vice-president of national sales from 1952 to 1956, vice-president of marketing in 1956–1957, president and chief executive officer from 1963 to 1965, president of Pepsi-Cola International from 1957 to 1963, president and chief executive office of PepsiCo from 1965 to 1971, and chairman of the board and chief executive officer from 1971 until 1986. He persuaded Premier Nikita S. Khrushchev to drink a Pepsi for the cameras at the Moscow Trade Fair in 1959. He went to Russia in 1971 and 1972 and negotiated a ten-year trade agreement with the Soviet Union to make and sell Pepsi Cola in the Soviet Union, in exchange for Russian vodka. *References*: Joseph Finder, *Red Carpet* (New York, 1983); John N. Ingham and Lynne B. Feldman, *Contemporary American Business Leaders: A Biographical Dictionary* (New York, 1990), pp. 283–93; Robert Scheer, "The Doctrine of Multinational Sell," *Esquire* 83 (April 1975): 124–27, 160–64; and *WWA*.

KENNAN, GEORGE (1845–1924). Explorer, journalist, and author, born February 16, 1845, in Norwalk, Ohio. While still a boy, Kennan developed expert proficiency as a telegrapher. He served as military telegrapher in Cincinnati during the Civil War. He was a member of the Siberian expedition of the Western Union Telegraph Company, surveying a possible route for the extension of the telegraph system from American to Europe by way of Alaska and the Bering Strait and across Siberia and Russia. He lived in northeastern Siberia from 1865 to 1867, but the venture was aborted when the laying of the Atlantic cable was completed. He then made a perilous journey of five thousand miles by dogsled to St. Petersburg and later wrote *Tent Life in Siberia and Other Adventures among the Koraks and Other Tribes in Kamchatka and Northern Asia* (New York, 1870). He was in the Russian Caucasus in 1870–1871, studying its people and manners. He was then involved in business in Medina, New York, and New

York City, was assistant manager of the Associated Press in Washington, D.C., from 1877 to 1885, and was also a popular lecturer on the Russian Orient. In 1885, he was commissioned by the Century Company to visit Russia and study prisons in Siberia. Accompanied by *George A. Frost, he went to Siberia, spent a year there, and wrote *Siberia and the Exile System* (New York, 1891), which revealed to the world outside Russia the horrors of the Siberian prisons and the cruel character of the Russian government. He also wrote *A Russian Comedy of Errors, with Other Stories and Sketches of Russian Life* (New York, 1915). Died May 10, 1924, in Elberon, New Jersey. *References*: George Kennan Papers, Manuscript Division, Library of Congress; *DAB*; *NCAB* 1:393; *NYT*, May 11, 1924; and Frederick F. Travis, *George Kennan and the American-Russian Relationship, 1865–1924* (Athens, Ohio, 1990).

KENNAN, GEORGE FROST (1904–   ). Diplomat and historian, born February 16, 1904, in Milwaukee, Wisconsin. Kennen graduated from Princeton University and joined the U.S. foreign service in 1926. He served as vice-consul in Hamburg and Tallinn and as third secretary in Riga, Kovno, and Tallinn from 1929 to 1933. He was third secretary at the embassy in Moscow from 1933 to 1935, consul and second secretary in Vienna in 1935, second secretary in Moscow from 1935 to 1937, and first secretary in Prague in 1938–1939 and in Berlin from 1939 to 1941. He was counselor of legation in Lisbon in 1942–1943 and counselor of the U.S. delegation to the European Advisory Commission in London in 1944–1945. He was minister-counselor of embassy in Moscow in 1945–1946. In 1946, he filed a long dispatch from Moscow in which he analyzed the reasons for Soviet postwar truculence and intransigence. He was director of the Policy Planning Staff of the State Department in 1947–1948. His article "The Sources of Soviet Conduct," published in the July 1947 issue of *Foreign Affairs* (under the pseudonym "X"), proposed a policy of *containment of Soviet expansion. He was deputy counselor and chief long-range adviser to the secretary of state in 1949–1950. He was U.S. ambassador to the Soviet Union in 1952 but was declared *persona non grata* by the Soviet government in that year for some unflattering remarks he made about the Soviet treatment of Western diplomats in Moscow. He was U.S. ambassador to Yugoslavia from 1961 to 1963. He was a member of the Institute for Advanced Study at Princeton after 1950 and professor after 1956. He wrote *Memoirs, 1925–1950* (Boston, 1967), *Memoirs, 1950–1963* (Boston, 1972), *Soviet-American Relations, 1917–1920* (Princeton, N.J., 1954–1958), *Russia and the West* (Boston, 1961), *The Marquis de Custine and His Russia in 1839* (Princeton, J.J., 1968), *The Nuclear Delusion: Soviet-American Relations in the Atomic Age* (New York, 1982), and *Sketches from a Life* (New York, 1989). *References*: George F. Kennan Papers, Princeton University Library, Princeton, N.J.; *Encounters with Kennan: The Great Debate* (London, 1979); *CB* 1959; *EAIE*; Barton D. Gellman, *Contending with Kennan: Towards a Philosophy of American Power* (New York, 1984); J. F. Green, "The Political Thought of George F. Kennan: A Study of the Development and Interpretations of American and Soviet Foreign Policies'' (Ph.D. diss., American University, 1972); Giles D. Harlow and George C. Maerz, eds., *Measures Short of War: The George F. Kennan Lectures at the National War College, 1947– 48* (Washington, D.C., 1991); Daniel F. Harrington, ''Kennan, Bohlen, and the Riga Axioms,'' *DH* 2 (1978): 423–37; Martin F. Herz, ed., *Decline of the West?: George Kennan and His Critics* (Washington, D.C., 1978); Walter L. Hixson, *George F. Kennan: Cold War Iconoclast* (New York, 1989); Walter Isaacson and Evan Thomas, *The Wise Men: Six Friends and the World They Made* (New York, 1986); David Mayers, ''George Kennan and the Soviet Union, 1933–1938; Perceptions of a Young Diplomat,'' *International History Review* 5 (1983): 525–49; Wilson D. Miscamble, *George F. Kennan and the Making of American Foreign Policy, 1947–1950* (Princeton, N.J., 1992); David Myers, *George Kennan and the Dilemma of U.S. Foreign Policy* (New York, 1988); *NCAB* I:308; Michael John Polley, ''George F. Kennan: The Life and Times of a Diplomat, 1925–1975'' (Ph.D. diss., Washington State University, 1984); Michael Polley, *A Biography of George F. Kennan: The Education of a Realist* (Lewiston, N.Y., 1990); Anders Stephanson, *Kennan and the Art of Foreign Policy* (Cambridge, Mass., 1989); Peter Gerard Walsh, ''George F. Kennan's Thoughts on Soviet-American Relations, 1933–1947'' (Ph.D. diss., Carleton University, 1983); Joseph G. Whelan, ''George Kennan and His Influence on American Foreign Policy,'' *Virginia Quarterly Review* 35 (1959): 196–200; and C. Ben Wright, ''George F. Kennan: Scholar-Diplomat'' (Ph.D. diss., University of Wisconsin, 1972).

KENNEDY, JOHN FITZGERALD (1917–1963). President of the United States, born May 29, 1917, in Brookline, Massachusetts. Kennedy graduated from Harvard University, attended Stanford University, and served in the U.S. Navy during World War II. He entered politics in 1946, serving in the U.S. House of Representatives from 1947 to 1953 and in the U.S. Senate from 1953 to 1961. He was president from 1961 until his death. He was surprised by the fierce bluntness of Premier Nikita S. Khrushchev, who thought Kennedy was inexperienced and weak and forced him to deal with a series of challenges in foreign affairs, including the building by East Germany of the Berlin Wall and the *Cuban Missile Crisis in October 1962. The missile crisis was caused by the installation in Cuba of Soviet long-range missiles, which were removed at Kennedy's insistence, in the world's closest approach to nuclear war. He took a significant step toward disarmament in September 1963, when the United States and the Soviet Union signed the limited test ban treaty, banning all but underground tests of explosive nuclear devices. Shot November 22, 1963, on a visit to Dallas, Texas. *References*: Michael R. Beschloss, *The Crisis Years: Kennedy and Khrushchev, 1960–1963* (New York, 1991); *DAB S7*; Bernard J. Firestone, *The Quest for Nuclear Stability: John F. Kennedy and the Soviet Union* (Westport, Conn.: 1982); Louise FitzSimons, *The Kennedy Doctrine* (New York, 1972); Bruce Miroff, *Pragmatic Illusions: The Presidential Politics of John F.*

Kennedy (New York, 1976); Thomas G. Paterson, ed., *Kennedy's Quest for Victory: American Foreign Policy, 1961–1963* (New York, 1989); Glenn Seaborg, *Kennedy, Khrushchev, and the Test Ban* (Berkeley, Calif., 1981); and Richard J. Walton, *Cold War and Counter-Revolution: The Foreign Policy of John F. Kennedy* (New York, 1972).

KENNELL, RUTH EPPERSON (1893–1977). Author, born September 21, 1893, in Oklahoma City, Oklahoma. Kennell attended the University of California at Berkeley. She was children's librarian at the Richmond (Calif.) Public Library from 1914 to 1917. She went to the Soviet Union in the early 1920s as a member of the *Kuzbas colony in Kemerovo, Siberia, and was librarian and secretary at the colony from 1922 to 1924 and correspondent of the *Nation* from 1922 to 1931. She was reference librarian at the International Library in Moscow from 1925 to 1927 and was *Theodore Dreiser's secretary and interpreter during his visit to the Soviet Union in 1927–1928. She was a correspondent in Moscow for the Newspaper Enterprise Association from 1930 to 1932. A writer of children's books and short stories after 1931, she also wrote *Theodore Dreiser and the Soviet Union, 1927–1945: A Personal Chronicle* (New York, 1969) and several children's books about Russian children. Died March 5, 1977. *References*: Ruth Epperson Kennell Papers, University of Oregon Library, Eugene; and *Something about the Author* 6 (1974): 127–28.

KINGSBURY, JOHN ADAMS (1876–1956). Social worker, born August 30, 1876, in Horton, Kansas. Kingsbury attended Washington State College and the University of Washington and graduated from Teachers College of Columbia University. He was principal of schools in Prosser, Washington, superintendent in Georgetown, Washington, and principal of schools in Seattle until 1906. He was assistant secretary of the State Charities Aid Association of New York from 1907 to 1911, general director of the New York Association for Improving the Condition of Poor from 1911 to 1914, commissioner of public charities of New York City from 1914 to 1918, and secretary of the Milbank Memorial Fund from 1921 until his retirement in 1935. During the 1930s, he became an ardent supporter of some health phases of the Soviet system, traveled widely in the Soviet Union from 1930 to 1934, and was coauthor of *Red Medicine: Socialized Health in Soviet Russia* (Garden City, N.Y., 1933). He was chairman of the *National Council on American-Soviet Friendship and helped organize the Russian war relief in 1941. He returned to the Soviet Union in 1950 and 1952 and wrote *Soviet Impressions: After an Interval of Eighteen Years, 1932–1950* (New York, 1951). Died August 3, 1956, in New York City. *References*: John Adams Kingsbury Papers, Manuscript Division, Library of Congress; *NYT*, August 4, 1956; and *WWWA*.

KIRK, ALAN GOODRICH (1888–1963). Naval officer and diplomat, born October 30, 1888, in Philadelphia. Kirk graduated from the U.S. Naval Academy in 1909. He served with the Atlantic and Asiatic fleets, at the Naval Proving Ground in Dahlgren, Virginia, at the Bureau of Ordnance, and on the USS *Maryland* from 1924 to 1926. He was fleet gunnery officer of the Scouting Fleet, commanding officer of the USS *Schenck*, executive officer of the USS *West Virginia*, staff member of the Naval War College in Newport, assistant director of the Ships Movement Division in the Office of the Chief of Naval Operations, and commander of the USS *Milwaukee* until 1937. He served with the Battle Force and then with the U.S. Fleet from 1937 to 1939, was U.S. naval attaché at the U.S. embassy in London in 1939–1940, was director of Naval Intelligence in 1941, commanded convoy escorts and amphibious forces in the Atlantic in 1941–1942, headed the Atlantic Fleet's Amphibious Force in 1943–1944, was commander of the U.S. Naval Task Force in 1944, and was commander of all U.S. naval forces in Europe in 1944–1945. He was U.S. ambassador to Belgium from 1946 to 1949 and ambassador to the Soviet Union from 1949 to 1951. Although he traveled extensively throughout the Soviet Union, Cold War passions made his tenure there generally barren. He met with Premier Joseph Stalin only once and was received officially at the Kremlin only twice during his tenure as ambassador. His wife, **LYDIA KIRK**, wrote a book on their experiences in the Soviet Union, *Postmarked Moscow* (New York, 1952). He was later chairman of the American Committee for the Liberation of the Peoples of Russia and its Radio Liberation and director of the Psychological Strategy Board. He undertook several unofficial missions for President *John F. Kennedy during the Congo crisis and was U.S. ambassador to Nationalist China in 1962–1963 but was forced to resign due to ill health. Died October 15, 1963, in New York City. *References*: *DAB S7*; *DADH*; *NCAB* 50:407; and *NYT*, October 16, 1963.

KISSINGER, HENRY ALFRED (1923–   ). Secretary of state, born May 27, 1923, in Furth, Bavaria, Germany, and came to the United States in 1938. Kissinger served in the U.S. Army during World War II and then graduated from Harvard University. He was a member of the faculty at Harvard University from 1954 until 1969 (professor after 1962). He was also research director of the Council on Foreign Relations from 1954 to 1956. He was special assistant for national security affairs to President *Richard M. Nixon from 1969 to 1973 and secretary of state from 1973 until 1977. His foreign policy was based on the idea of balance of power, and he emphasized the concept of "linkage"—if the Soviets wanted U.S. trade and technology, they should make concessions. The confrontations of the Cold War were replaced by new initiatives directed toward finding areas of cooperation with the Soviet Union, a policy known as *détente. He initiated the Strategic Arms Limitation Talks (*SALT). He wrote his memoirs, *The White House Years* (New York, 1979) and *For the Record* (New York, 1981). He later founded an international consulting group. *References*: Coral Bell, *The Diplomacy of Détente: The Kissinger Era* (New York,

1977); Seyom Brown, *The Crises of Power: An Interpretation of United States Foreign Policy during the Kissinger Years* (New York, 1979); *CB* 1972; Gregory D. Cleva, *Henry Kissinger and the American Approach to Foreign Policy* (Cranbury, N.J., 1989); *DADH*; Seymour M. Hersch, *The Price of Power: Kissinger in the Nixon White House* (New York, 1983); Walter Isaacson, *Kissinger: A Biography* (New York, 1992); David Landau, *Kissinger: The Uses of Power* (Boston, 1972); *PolProf: Nixon/Ford*; Lief Roderick Rosenberger, "The Evolution of the Nixon-Kissinger Policy toward the Soviet Union: An Analysis of the Cold War Legacy and the Ambivalent Pursuit of Détente" (Ph.D. diss., Clarement Graduate School, 1980); Robert D. Schulzinger, *Henry Kissinger: Doctor of Diplomacy* (New York, 1989); Harvey Starr, *Henry Kissinger: Perceptions of International Politics* (Lexington, Ky., 1984); and John G. Stoessinger, *Henry Kissinger: The Anguish of Power* (New York, 1976).

KOEHLER, HUGO WILLIAM (1886–1941). Naval officer, born July 19, 1886, in St. Louis, Missouri. Koehler attended Harvard College and graduated from the U.S. Naval Academy in 1909. He served with the Yangtze Patrol from 1911 to 1913, commanded a tug in the Philippines in 1914–1915, and served with the Atlantic Squadron from 1915 to 1918. He was special agent of the State Department in southern Russia in 1920. He published an account of his mission in the July and August 1921 issues of *World's Work Magazine*. He was naval attaché in Warsaw in 1921–1922. He resigned in 1929, with the rank of commander. Died June 17, 1941, in New York City. *References*: Peter J. Capelotti, ed., *Our Man in the Crimea: Commander Hugo Koehler and the Russian Civil War* (Columbia, S.C., 1991); *NYT*, June 19, 1941; Margaretta Potter, "Memoir of Hugo," University of Rhode Island Libraries, Kingston, R.I.; and Charles J. Weeks and Joseph O. Baylen, "The Aristocrat and the Bolshevik: Hugo Koehler and I. P. Uborevich, Odessa, 1920," *Indiana Social Studies Quarterly* 30 (Spring 1977): 27–40.

KOHLER, FOY DAVID (1908–1990). Diplomat, born February 15, 1908, in Oakwood, Ohio. Kohler attended the University of Toledo and graduated from Ohio State University. He joined the foreign service in 1931 and served in Windsor, Bucharest, Belgrade, Athens, and Cairo until 1941 and in the State Department from 1941 to 1944. He was assistant chief of the Division of Near Eastern Affairs at the State Department in 1944–1945 and first secretary and counselor at the U.S. embassy in Moscow from 1947 to 1949. He was chief of the International Broadcasting Division from 1949 to 1952, counselor of embassy in Ankara from 1952 to 1956, director of the International Cooperation Administration (ICA) from 1956 to 1958, deputy assistant secretary of state for European affairs in 1958–1959, and assistant secretary of state for European affairs from 1959 to 1962, including day-to-day management of the Berlin crisis as director of the Berlin Task Force. He was U.S. ambassador to the Soviet Union from 1962 to 1966. In Moscow he worked to get talks on Berlin and disarmament moving again and sought ways to reduce the chances of nuclear war. He served in Moscow during the *Cuban Missile Crisis, serving as a conduit in the mostly backstage diplomacy that resolved the conflict. He was deputy undersecretary of state for political affairs in 1966–1967. He retired in 1967 and was professor at the Center for Advanced International Studies at the University of Miami from 1968 to 1978. He wrote *Understanding the Russians: A Citizen's Primer* (New York, 1970) and *SALT II: How Not to Negotiate with the Russians* (Miami, 1979), was coauthor of *Soviet Strategy for the Seventies: From Cold War to Peaceful Coexistence* (Coral Gables, Fla., 1973) and *The Role of Nuclear Forces in Current Soviet Strategy* (Coral Gables, Fla., 1974), and was coeditor of *The Soviet Union, Yesterday, Today, and Tomorrow: A Colloquy of American Long Timers in Moscow* (Coral Gables, Fla., 1975). Died December 23, 1990, in Juniper, Florida. *References*: Foy David Kohler Papers, University of Toledo Library, Ohio; *CB* 1951; *DADH*; *NYT*, December 26, 1990; *PolProf: Kennedy*; and *WWA*.

KOREAN AIR LINES INCIDENT (1983). See KAL 007 INCIDENT

KREHBIEL, CHRISTIAN EMANUEL (1869–1948). Clergyman, born September 25, 1869, in Summerfield, Illinois. Krehbiel graduated from Kansas State Normal (Emporia) and studied at the Presbyterian Theological Seminary (Bloomfield, N.J.) and the University of Berlin. He was secretary of the Western Book and Publishing Company (later the Herald Book and Publishing Company) in Newton, Kansas, from 1901 to 1920. He served as field secretary for the Mennonite Central Church from 1921 to 1930 and was involved with its relief work in Soviet Russia in 1922–1923. He was ordained in 1923 and held many offices, including secretary of the General Conference of Mennonite Church from 1926 to 1938 and president from 1938 to 1945. Died June 9, 1948, in Newton, Kansas. *Reference*: *WWWA*.

KUZBAS COLONY. The Autonomous Industrial Colony, "Kuzbas," was established near Kemerovo, in the Kuznetsk Basin (Kuzbas) in Siberia, under a concession granted by Soviet Russia in 1921. American workers were recruited to manage several enterprises in the basin, including coal mines, coke ovens, and a chemical factory, and to increase their productivity. The members of this foreign colony were also promised that they could manage their own affairs. Although three-thousand American skilled workers were promised, only some four-hundred Americans arrived at the colony. Because of the reality of life in the colony and changes in its organizational structure dictated by Soviet authorities, many Americans left the colony in 1923 and returned to the United States. By 1926, less than ten colonists remained. *References*: *MERSH*; and J. P. Morray, *Project Kuzbas: American Workers in Siberia (1921–1926)* (New York, 1983).

L

LANDFIELD, JEROME BARKER (1871–1954). Explorer and editor, born May 7, 1871, in Newark Valley, New York. Landfield graduated from Cornell University. He was in Russia in 1897–1898, exploring mines in the Urals and the Kirghiz steppes and also studying the tribal life of the people of these areas. He obtained a mining claim in the Urals, believed to be the first such claim obtained by an American. He returned to Russia in 1899 for further mining exploration and was in northeastern Siberia in 1900. He was superintendent of a gold mine in Yuma, Arizona, in 1901–1902, and instructor in modern European history at the University of California from 1902 to 1906. In 1907, he joined a group, financed by an English mining syndicate, to explore mining properties in the littoral of northeastern Siberia. He was later engaged in lecturing on current events and in editorial work for the *San Francisco Argonaut* from 1914 to 1917. In 1918, he became adviser on Russian affairs in the State Department and then served as executive secretary of the *American-Russian Chamber of Commerce in New York City. He served as associate editor of the *Weekly Review* and later of the *Independent*. He was engaged in fruit raising and literary pursuits in California from 1929 until his death. Died November 22, 1954, in San Francisco. *References*: Jerome B. Landfield, "Operation Kaleidoscope: A Mélange of Personal Recollections," Bancroft Library, University of California, Berkeley; *NCAB* 44:314; and *NYT*, November 23, 1954.

LANSING, ROBERT (1864–1928). Secretary of state, born October 17, 1864, in Watertown, New York. Lansing graduated from Amherst College, studied law, and was admitted to the bar in 1889. He practiced law after 1890 and served frequently as counsel or agent of the United States before international arbitration tribunals from 1892 to 1914. He was secretary of state from 1915 to 1920. A fervent anti-Bolshevik, he assured American nonrecognition of the Bolshevik regime. He wrote *War Memoirs of Robert Lansing, Secretary of State* (Indianapolis, 1935). He resumed the practice of law in Washington, D.C., in 1921. Died October 30, 1928, in Washington, D.C. *References*: Robert Lansing Papers,

Manuscript Division, Library of Congress; *DAB*; *DADH*; *NYT*, October 31, 1928; Julius W. Pratt, *Robert Lansing* (New York, 1929); Daniel M. Smith, "Robert Lansing," in Norman Graeber, ed., *An Uncertain Tradition: American Secretaries of State in the Twentieth Century* (New York, 1961), pp. 101–27; and William James Walsh, "Secretary of State Robert Lansing and the Russian Revolutions of 1917" (Ph.D. diss., Georgetown University, 1986).

LEDYARD, JOHN (1751–1789). Explorer, born November 1751 in Groton, Connecticut. Ledyard attended Dartmouth College but left to become a sailor in 1773–1774. He participated as a mariner in the voyage of Captain James Cook to the North Pacific from 1776 to 1780 and published a journal of the voyage. In 1787–1788, he embarked on a trip attempting to reach the northwest coast of America by way of Siberia but was arrested by the Russian authorities in Irkutsk and was forced to turn back. He went to Egypt in 1788 to begin an expedition to explore the Niger River. Died January 10, 1789, in Cairo, Egypt. *References*: Helen Augur, *Passage to Glory: John Ledyard's America* (New York, 1946); *DAB*; Eufrosina Dvoichenko-Markov, "John Ledyard and the Russians," *RR* 11 (1952): 211–22; J. K. Munford, *John Ledyard: An American Marco Polo* (Portland, Ore., 1939); *NCAB* 5:122; and Stephen D. Watrous, ed., *John Ledyard's Journey through Russia and Siberia, 1787–1788: The Journal and Selected Letters* (Madison, Wis., 1966).

LEND-LEASE. Passed by Congress on March 11, 1941, the Lend-Lease Act (formally: An Act to Promote the Defense of the United States) empowered the president to lease, lend, or otherwise dispose of arms and other supplies to any country whose defense was deemed essential to the security of the United States. The Soviet Union formally requested Lend-Lease assistance on June 30, 1941. Lend-Lease supplies began flowing to the Soviet Union and were the greatest contribution of the United States to the Soviet war effort, although the Soviet government apparently attempted to hide the part played by the United States from the Soviet people as much as possible. Some eleven billion dollars of aid was provided to the Soviet Union before the program was terminated on September 20, 1945. *References*: *DADH*; Raymond H. Dawson, *The Decision to Aid Russia, 1941: Foreign Policy and Domestic Politics* (Chapel Hill, N.C., 1959); George C. Herring, *Aid to Russia, 1941–46: Strategy, Diplomacy, the Origins of the Cold War* (New York, 1973); Robert Huhn Jones, *The Roads to Russia: United States Lend-Lease to the Soviet Union* (Norman, Okla., 1969); Leon C. Martel, *Lend-Lease, Loans, and the Coming of the Cold War: A Study of the Implementation of Foreign Policy* (Boulder, Colo., 1979); and *MERSH*.

LEVINE, IRVING RASKIN (1922–   ). Journalist, born August 26, 1922, in Pawtucket, Rhode Island. Levine graduated from Brown and Columbia universities. He served in the U.S. Army Signal Corps during World War II. He was foreign news editor of the International News Service in New York City in 1947–1948 and foreign correspondent in Vienna and Paris from 1948 to 1950. He was war correspondent for the National Broadcasting Company (NBC) in Korea from 1950 to 1952, commentator in New York City from 1953 to 1955, and NBC News' chief correspondent in Moscow from 1955 to 1959. He was the first U.S. television correspondent that the Soviet government accredited to work in Moscow. He also reported for the London *Times* and for *Variety* magazine. He was foreign correspondent in Rome from 1959 to 1967, in London in 1967–1968, and again in Rome from 1968 to 1970. He returned to the United States in 1971. He wrote *Main Street, U.S.S.R.* (Garden City, N.Y., 1959), *Travel Guide to Russia* (Garden City, N.Y., 1960), and *The New Worker in Soviet Russia* (New York, 1973). *References*: Irving R. Levine Papers, Syracuse University Library; *CA*; *CB* 1959; and *WWA*.

LEVINE, ISAAC DON (1892–1981). Journalist, born February 1, 1892, in Ozyr, Russia, and came to the United States in 1911. Levine was foreign news editor for the *New York Times* in 1917 and foreign correspondent for the *Chicago Daily News* from 1919 to 1921, for the Hearst Newspaper Syndicate from 1922 to 1924, and for International News Service in Russia from 1922 to 1925. He was editor of *Plain Talk*, an anti-Communist monthly in New York City from 1946 to 1950, was active in forming the American Committee for the Liberation of the Peoples of Russia in the early 1950s, and was European director of Radio Free Europe in Munich in 1951–1952. He was a writer and tobacco farmer in Waldorf, Maryland, from 1952 until his death. He wrote *The Russian Revolution* (New York, 1917), *The Man Lenin* (New York, 1924), *Stalin* (New York, 1931), *Red Smoke* (New York, 1932), *I Rediscover Russia* (New York, 1964), and *Eyewitness to History: Memoirs and Reflections of a Foreign Correspondent for Half a Century* (New York, 1973). Died February 15, 1981, in Venice, Florida. *References*: *CA*; and *NYT*, February 17, 1981.

LEWIS, WILLIAM DAVID (1792–1881). Merchant and banker, born September 22, 1792, in Christiana, New Castle County, Delaware. In 1809, he was apprenticed to merchants in the East India and China trade. In 1813, he joined his brother, John David Lewis, a commission merchant in St. Petersburg, in the merchant house of Lewis and Willing, which his brother had established in 1812. He lived in Russia until 1824. He translated *The Bokchesarian Fountain, by Alexander Pooshkeen, and Other Poems by Various Authors* (Philadelphia, 1849). In July 1817 he was jailed at the request of *John Levett Harris, U.S. consul in St. Petersburg, with whom he had a personal quarrel. He was soon released, but during a trip to the United States, in 1819, he was challenged by Harris to a duel. He accepted and shot his opponent in the thigh when they met at Red Bank, on the Delaware. Shortly thereafter, Harris's uncle, Levett Harris, who had also been consul in St. Petersburg, sued Lewis for slander. After seven years of litigation, a Philadelphia jury awarded Harris one hundred dollars. Lewis was cashier of the Girard Bank from 1832 to 1842, helping finance a number of early Pennsylvania railroads. He was then president of the Pennsylvania

Academy of Fine Arts, president of the Catawissa Railroad Company, and collector of customs for the Port of Philadelphia from 1849 to 1853. He retired from business about 1855. Died April 1, 1881, near Florence, New Jersey. *References*: William David Lewis Papers, Rutgers University Library, New Brunswick, N.J.; William David Lewis Letterbook, Historical Society of Pennsylvania, Philadelphia; *DAB*; James Barton Rhoads, "Harris, Lewis, and the Hollow Tree," *American Archivist* 25 (1962); 295–314; Norman E. Saul, "America's First Student of Russian: William David Lewis of Philadelphia," *Pennsylvania Magazine of History and Biography* 96 (1972): 469–79; Norman E. Saul, "Russian Yankee Doodle," *SR* 33 (1974): 46–54; and Stanley J. Zyzniewski, "A Delawarean's View of Russia in 1816," *Delaware History* 9 (1961): 326–40.

LEYDA, JAY (1910–   ). Filmmaker and author, born February 12, 1910, in Detroit, Michigan, and grew up in Dayton, Ohio. After coming to New York City in 1929, Leyda was an assistant to a photographer and then an independent photographer. Invited to study at State Film Institute in Moscow, he entered Sergei Eisenstein's direction course in 1933. He was theater correspondent for *Theatre Arts Monthly* and joined the crew of Eisenstein's (unfinished) film "Bezhin Meadow" as apprentice director and still photographer. He was assistant curator of the film library of New York's Museum of Modern Art from 1936 to 1940. During World War II, he provided assistance to Artkino, the U.S. distributor of Soviet films, and was technical adviser on Russian subjects filmed at Warner Brothers and MGM in Hollywood. He wrote *Kino: A History of the Russian and Soviet Film* (New York, 1960) and was coauthor of *Eisenstein at Work* (New York, 1982). He left the United States in 1957 and was later employed in the research division of the Berlin Filmarchiv. He edited and translated several works by Sergei Eisenstein, including *The Film Sense* (New York, 1942), *Film Form* (New York, 1957), and *Film Essay and a Lecture* (Princeton, N.J., 1970). *References*: *CA*; and *World Authors, 1950–1970* (New York, 1975).

LIGHT HORSE. A bark, owned by Elias Hasket Derby of Salem. Under the command of Captain Nehemiah Buffington, it went to St. Petersburg in 1784, the first American ship to make a direct, round-trip voyage between the United States and Russia. The voyage was not particularly successful, but it brought to Salem a knowledge of what to take to Russia and started a profitable trade. *Reference*: James Duncan Philips, "Salem Opens American Trade with Russia," *New England Quarterly* 14 (1941): 685–89.

LIMITED TEST BAN TREATY (*LTBT*) (1963). Treaty banning nuclear weapons tests in the atmosphere, in outer space, and under water, signed in Moscow on August 5, 1963. The signatories undertook to refrain from nuclear testing in the atmosphere, outer space, and under water and to refrain from causing, encouraging, or participating in such tests by others. The treaty was open to all states for signature. *References*: *ACDA*; Harold K. Jacobson and Eric Stein, *Diplomats, Scientists, and Politicians: The United States and the Nuclear Test Ban Negotiations* (Ann Arbor, Mich., 1966); Benjamin S. Loeb, "The Limited Test Ban Treaty," in Michael Krepon and Dan Caldwell, eds., *The Politics of Arms Control Treaty Ratification* (New York, 1991); Glenn T. Seaborg, *Kennedy, Khrushchev and the Test Ban* (Berkeley, Calif., 1981); and Ronald J. Terchek, *The Making of the Test Ban Treaty* (The Hague, 1970).

LINCOLN, ABRAHAM (1809–1865). President of the United States, born February 12, 1809, near Hodgenville, Kentucky, and grew up in Spencer County, Indiana. He moved to Illinois in 1830, settling in New Salem. He was admitted to the bar in 1836, served in the Illinois legislature from 1834 to 1841, and practiced law in Springfield after 1837. He served in the U.S. House of Representatives from 1847 to 1849. He was president of the United States from 1861 until his death. He overlooked Russia's suppression of the Polish insurrection of 1863 because Russia supported the Union cause and ignored Confederate representatives. He aided Russia by harboring elements of its Far East and Baltic squadrons in San Francisco and New York in the winter of 1863–1864 so that in case of war in Europe the Russian ships would be available as commerce raiders. Shot April 14, 1865, in Washington, D.C., and died April 15, 1865. *References*: *DAB*; Robert F. Ivanov, *Diplomatiia Avraama Linkol'na* (Moscow, 1987); Hans Rogger, "Russia and the Civil War," in Harold Hyman, ed., *Heard around the World: The Impact Abroad of the Civil War* (New York, 1969), pp. 177–255; and Albert A. Woldman, *Lincoln and the Russians* (Cleveland, 1952).

LOANS TO THE USSR. the Soviet government asked the United States in 1945 to a loan to assist the Soviet Union in recovery from the destruction caused by World War II. Because of Soviet behavior in Eastern Europe and domestic pressures to limit spending, the United States tried to link the loans to demanded political concessions from the Soviet government. The U.S. State Department later claimed to have lost the Soviet loan request. The unsatisfactory loan episode was one of the features shaping the Cold War. *References*: Leon C. Martel, *Lend-Lease, Loans, and the Coming of the Cold War: A Study of the Implementation of Foreign Policy* (Boulder, Colo., 1979); and Thomas G. Paterson, "The Abortive American Loan to Russia and the Origins of the Cold War, 1943–46," *Journal of American History* 56 (1969): 70–92.

LOTHROP, GEORGE VAN NESS (1817–1897). Lawyer and diplomat, born August 8, 1817, in Easton, Bristol County, Massachusetts. Lothrop attended Amherst College, graduated from Brown University, studied law at Harvard University, and was admitted to the Michigan bar in 1843. He practiced law in Michigan, was attorney general of Michigan from 1848 to 1851, and was president of the Detroit Bar Association from 1879 to 1896. He was general solicitor for the Michigan Central Railroad and acquired valuable real estate holdings.

He was U.S. minister to Russia from 1885 to 1888. He was involved in the question of the Russian government's treatment of Russians who had been naturalized in the United States and then returned to Russia. His wife, **ALMIRA STRONG LOTHROP**, wrote *The Court of Alexander III*, ed. William Prael (Philadelphia, 1919). Died July 12, 1897, in Detroit. *References*: George Van Ness Lothrop Papers, Burton Historical Collection, Detroit Public Library; *DAB*; Charles Artemas Kent, "George Van Ness Lothrop, 1817–1897," in William Draper Lewis, ed., *Great American Lawyers* (Philadelphia, 1909), 7:163–99; and *NCAB* 5:160.

LOWN, BERNARD (1921–   ). Physician, born June 7, 1921, in Utena, Lithuania, and came to the United States in 1935. Lown graduated from the University of Maine and Johns Hopkins University. He was assistant in medicine at Peter Bent Brigham Hospital in Boston and director of the Samuel A. Levine Cardiovascular Laboratory, where he was junior associate in medicine, research associate in medicine, associate in medicine, and senior associate in medicine until 1970. He was director of Samuel A. Levine Coronary Unit from 1965 to 1974, physician from 1973 to 1981, and senior physician after 1982. He was also assistant professor of medicine in the department of nutrition, associate professor of cardiology, professor of cardiology after 1974, and director of the cardiovascular laboratory at the School of Public Health of Harvard University. He cofounded the International Physicians for the Prevention of Nuclear War in 1980 and served as its cochairman. He campaigned to publicize the danger that nuclear war poses to human health and worked on ways of preventing it. He was the first president of Physicians for Social Responsibility, from 1960 to 1970, and president of International Physicians for Prevention of Nuclear War after 1980. With the Russian Yevgeny Chazov, he won the Nobel Peace Prize in 1985. *References*: *NYT*, October 12, 1985; Gale Warner and Michael Shuman, *Citizen Diplomats: Pathfinders in Soviet-American Relations and How You Can Join Them* (New York, 1987), ch. 1; and *WWA*.

LOWRIE, DONALD ALEXANDER (1889–1974). Association official, born January 29, 1889, in Chatham, Ohio. Lowrie graduated from Wooster College and Charles University (Prague). He was *Young Men's Christian Association (YMCA) secretary in Cleveland and Hamilton, Ohio, from 1913 to 1916. He served with YMCA in Russia from 1916 to 1919, stationed in Tomsk, Moscow, and Northern Russia. He served with Russian émigrés in Berlin, Riga, Prague, and Belgrade from 1919 to 1933. He was director of United States House, Cite Univesitaire, in Paris, from 1933 to 1946, director of the YMCA Press in Paris from 1946 to 1955 and in Geneva during World War II, and director of the East European Fund in New York City in 1955–1956. He wrote *The Light of Russia: An Introduction to the Russian Church* (Prague, 1923). Died October 12, 1974, in Meadow Lakes, New Jersey. *References*: *CA*; *NYT*, October 15, 1974; and *SR* 33 (1974): 866.

LYONS, EUGENE (1898–1985). Journalist, editor, and author, born July 1, 1898, in Uzlian, Russia, came to the United States in 1907, and was naturalized in 1919. Lyons attended the College of the City of New York and Columbia University. He was a reporter with the *Erie* (Pa.) *Dispatch* in 1919 and the *Boston Telegram* in 1921 and was editor of *Soviet Russia Pictorial* in 1922–1923. He was U.S. correspondent of the Tass news agency from 1923 to 1927. He was United Press correspondent in Moscow from 1928 to 1934. In 1930, he became the first foreign correspondent to obtain an interview with Joseph Stalin after Stalin's rise to power. He became disillusioned with communism and indicted the Soviet system in his memoirs, *Assignment in Utopia* (New York, 1937) and *Moscow Carrousel* (New York, 1935). He was employed by a public relations agency from 1935 to 1939, was editor of *American Mercury* from 1939 to 1944, editor of *Pageant* in 1944–1945, roving editor of Reader's Digest from 1946 to 1962, and senior editor of *Reader's Digest* from 1952 until his retirement in the mid-1970s. He also wrote *Stalin: Czar of All the Russias* (Philadelphia, 1940), *The Red Decade: The Stalinist Penetration of America* (Indianapolis, 1941), *Our Secret Allies: The Peoples of Russia* (New York, 1953), and *Worker's Paradise Lost: Fifty Years of Soviet Communism, A Balance Sheet* (New York, 1967). Died January 7, 1985, in New York City. *References*: *CA*; *CB* 1944; and *NYT*, January 10, 1985.

M

MCCLELLAN, GEORGE BRINTON (1826–1885). Army officer, born December 3, 1826, in Philadelphia. McClellan graduated from the U.S. Military Academy in 1846 and was commissioned in the engineers. He served during the Mexican War and then engaged in several army projects. He studied Russian military methods and operation during the Crimean War in 1855–1856 and wrote *The Armies of Europe* (Philadelphia, 1861), which included a detailed report of the organization of the Russian Army. He served in the Union army during the Civil War, commanding the Army of the Potomac in 1861–1862. He resigned his commission in 1864, was chief engineer for New York City's Department of Docks from 1867 to 1878, and was governor of New Jersey from 1878 to 1881. Died October 29, 1885, in Orange, New Jersey. His autobiography, *McClellan's Own Story* (New York, 1887), was published posthumously. *References*: *DAB*; Warren W. Hassler, *General George E. McClellan: Shield of the Union* (Baton Rouge, La., 1957); *NCAB* 4:140; and Stephen W. Sears, *George B. McClellan: The Young Napoleon* (New York, 1988).

MCCORMICK, ROBERT SANDERSON (1849–1919). Businessman and diplomat, born July 26, 1849, in Rockbridge County, Virginia, and grew up in Illinois. McCormick attended the Universities of Chicago and Virginia. He was involved in the family reaping-machine business until 1889. He was secretary of legation in London from 1889 to 1892, U.S. minister to Austria-Hungary in 1901–1902, and the first U.S. ambassador to Austria-Hungary in 1902. He was U.S. ambassador to Russia from 1903 to 1905. He persuaded the tsar to honor U.S. passports given to Jews and secured permission for the Associated Press to report news from Russia. He also handled Japanese affairs in Russia during the Russo-Japanese War in 1904–1905. He was ambassador to France from 1905 to 1907. Died April 16, 1919, in Hinsdale, Illinois. *References*: William C. Askew, "An American View of Bloody Sunday," *RR* 11 (1952): 35–43; *DAB*; *DADH*; *NCAB* 13:375; and *NYT*, April 17, 1919.

MCCULLY, NEWTON ALEXANDER (1867–1951). Naval officer, born June 19, 1867, in Anderson, South Carolina. McCully graduated from the U.S. Naval Academy in 1887. He served during the Spanish-American War and in the Philippine-American War. He was attached to the Russian forces during the Russo-Japanese War in 1904–1905. He served on the staff of the Naval War College from 1910 to 1912 and commanded the presidential yacht, USS *Mayflower*, from 1912 to 1914. He was naval attaché in Petrograd in 1917–1918. He commanded a patrol squadron off the coast of France in 1918. He was commander of the U.S. Naval Forces in Northern Russia in 1918–1919, served as a special agent for the U.S. State Department in southern Russia in 1919–1920, and was in charge of the evacuation of Sebastopol. The plight of Russian orphans led him to adopt seven of them and bring them back with him to the United States in 1920. He was commanding officer of the U.S. Scouting Fleet from 1923 to 1925, chief of the U.S. Naval Mission to Brazil from 1925 to 1927, and commandant of the Sixth Naval District in Charleston, South Carolina, from 1927 until his retirement, with the rank of vice-admiral, in 1931. Died June 15, 1951, in St. Augustine, Florida. *References*: Richard A. van Doenhoff, ed., *The McCully Report: The Russo-Japanese War, 1904–1905* (Annapolis, Md., 1976); *NYT*, June 15, 1951; Charles J. Weeks, Jr., *An American Naval Diplomat in Revolutionary Russia: The Life and Times of Vice Admiral Newton A. McCully, 1867–1951* (Annapolis, Md., 1993). Charles J. Weeks, "A Samaritan in Russia: Vice Admiral Newton A. McCully's Humanitarian Efforts, 1914–1920," *Military Affairs* 52 (1988): 12–17; and Charles J. Weeks and Joseph O. Baylen, "Admiral Newton A. McCully's Mission in Russia, 1904–1921," *RR* 33 (1974): 63–79.

MACGAHAN, JANUARIUS ALOYSIUS (1844–1878). Journalist, born June 12, 1844, in Perry County, Ohio. MacGahan was a bookkeeper in St. Louis and then went abroad to improve his general education and to continue his study of law. He lived in Brussels, Paris, and Germany. He became special correspondent of the *New York Herald* at the outbreak of the Franco-Prussian War. He accompanied General William T. Sherman to the Caucasus in 1872. He rode into the desert of Central Asia in 1873, defying the Russian embargo on newspapermen and pursued much of the way by Cossacks, to find the expedition of General Constantine Kauffman to the Khanate of Khiva. He remained with the Russian Army during the campaign against Khiva and the war with the Turkomans. He reported the *Virginius* affair in Cuba in 1873, the Carlist campaign in the Pyreness in 1874, and the expedition of the bark *Pandora* to the Arctic in 1875. He wrote *Campaigning on the Oxus and the Fall of Khiva* (New York, 1874) and *Under the Northern Lights* (London, 1876) on the cruise of the *Pandora*. In 1876, he was sent by the London *Daily News* to Bulgaria. His letters from Bulgaria changed British public opinion and contributed to the political reaction that made war inevitable between Russia and Turkey. Since that war gave Bulgaria its independence, he came to be known in that country as "the Liberator." He wrote *The Turkish Atrocities in Bulgaria* (London, 1876) and *War Correspondence of the Daily News* (London, 1877–1878). He followed the Russian-Turkish campaign and, after the fall of Plevna, went to Constantinople to nurse *Francis Vinton Greene through typhoid, only to fall victim to the disease. Died June 9, 1878, in Constantinople. In 1884, his body was brought to the United States on a U.S. cruiser. *References*: *DAB*; *DADH*; *NCAB* 6: 187; and Dale L. Walker, *Januarius MacGahan: The Life and Campaigns of an American War Correspondent* (Athens, Ohio, 1988).

MACGOWAN, DAVID BELL (1870–?). Journalist and diplomat, born June 5, 1870, in Memphis, Tennessee. MacGowan graduated from Washington and Lee University and studied at the Universities of Halle and Berlin. He was a reporter and special correspondent for the *Chicago Tribune* from 1896 to 1898 and correspondent in Berlin in 1899–1900. He was correspondent for the Associated Press in St. Petersburg from 1901 to 1903 and correspondent of the *London Standard* in St. Petersburg from 1904 to 1908. He was editor of the *Knoxville* (Tenn.) *Sentinel* from 1908 to 1914, correspondent of the Associated Press in Galicia, Armenia, Persia, and the Caucasus and in St. Petersburg in 1915. He entered the foreign service in 1915 and served in Moscow from 1915 to 1917. He was consul in Vladivostok from 1920 to 1922, first secretary of legation in Riga, Tallinn, and Kaunas from 1922 to 1932, and supervisor of the Russian Section in Riga. He was consul in Bern from 1932 to 1935, and consul general in 1935, when he retired. *Reference*: *WWWA*.

MCKAY, CLAUDE (1889–1948). Author, born September 15, 1889, in Sunny Ville, Jamaica. McKay was apprenticed to a cabinetmaker and then joined the island constabulary. He began publishing poetry in 1912 and migrated to the United States in that year. He attended Tuskegee Institute and Kansas State University and then settled in Harlem, working as a restaurant owner, longshoreman, porter, bartender, and waiter and continuing to write poetry. He was editor of the *Liberator* in 1922. He traveled in Russia in 1922, where he was lionized and named unofficial delegate to the Fourth Congress of the Communist International. He remained in Russia until 1923. He lived in France from 1923 to 1929 and then traveled in Spain and Morocco. He returned to the United States in the early 1930s. He wrote an autobiography, *A Long Way from Home* (New York, 1937). Died May 22, 1948, in Chicago. *References*: *DAB S4*; James R. Giles, *Claude McKay* (Boston, 1976); and Tyrone Tillery, *Claude McKay: A Black Poet's Struggle for Identity* (Amherst, Mass., 1992).

MALTA SUMMIT (1989). Summit meeting between President *George Bush and President Mikhail S. Gorbachev on December 2–3, 1989, on board a ship in Marsaxlokk Bay in Malta. No concrete agreements were reached, but the two leaders agreed to step up the pace of negotiations on reducing conventional forces and strategic nuclear arms. *References*: *McDonald*; *Weihmiller*; and Joseph G.

Whelan, *Soviet Diplomacy and Negotiating Behavior, 1988–90: Gorbachev, Reagan, Bush Meetings at the Summit* (Washington, D.C., 1991), pp. 213–90.

MARTIN, WILLIAM H. (1931–) and MITCHELL, BERNON F. (1929–). Cryptologists. Martin was born May 27, 1931, in Columbus, Georgia, and grew up in the state of Washington. He attended Central Washington University, then enlisted in the U.S. Navy and served until 1954. He graduated from the University of Washington. He joined the National Security Agency (NSA) in 1957 and worked as a cryptologist in the Office of Research and Development. Mitchell was born March 11, 1929, in San Francisco. He attended California Institute of Technology, then enlisted in the U.S. Navy and served until 1954. He graduated from Stanford University. he joined the National Security Agency in 1957 and worked as a cryptologist in the Office of Research and Development. Martin and Mitchell defected to the Soviet Union in 1960, where they disclosed to the Soviet government highly classified information regarding the NSA and American electronic intelligence operations. They later became Soviet citizens. *References*: James Bamford, *The Puzzle Palace: A Report on America's Most Secret Agency* (Boston, 1982); and *EAIE*.

MARYE, GEORGE THOMAS (1857–1933). Banker and diplomat, born December 13, 1857, in Baltimore and grew up in California. Marye graduated from Trinity College (Cambridge, England), studied law, and was admitted to the bar in 1875. He practiced law in San Francisco from 1875 to 1878. He became a junior partner in the banking house of George T. Marye and Son in San Francisco and Virginia City, Nevada, in 1878. After his father's death in 1883, he continued the business alone until 1892, when he retired. He was U.S. ambassador to Russia from 1914 to 1916. When he reached St. Petersburg, World War I had broken out. He had charge of the diplomatic interests of both Germany and Austria-Hungary, and much of his time was given to caring for the nationals of those countries who were taken prisoner during the war. He resigned because of ill health. He wrote *Nearing the End of Imperial Russia* (Philadelphia, 1920). Died September 2, 1933, in Washington, D.C. *References*: *DADH*; *NCAB* 30: 251; and *NYT*, September 13, 1933.

MATLOCK, JACK FOUST, JR. (1929–). Diplomat, born October 1, 1929, in Greensboro, North Carolina. Matlock graduated from Duke and Columbia universities. He entered the foreign service in 1956, served in Washington from 1956 to 1958 and at the U.S. embassy in Vienna from 1958 to 1960, and was consul general in Munich in 1960–1961. He served in the embassy in Moscow from 1961 to 1963, in Accra from 1963 to 1966, in the consulate in Zanzibar from 1967 to 1969, and in the embassy in Dar es Salaam in 1969–1970. He was country director for the USSR in the State Department from 1971 to 1974, minister-counselor and deputy chief of mission in the embassy in Moscow from 1974 to 1978, and deputy director of the Foreign Service Institute in Washington in 1979–1980. He was chargé d'affaires ad interim in Moscow in 1981, ambassador to Czechoslovakia from 1981 to 1983, and special assistant to the president and senior director of European and Soviet Affairs in the National Security Council from 1983 to 1987. He was U.S. ambassador to the Soviet Union from 1987 to 1991. He compiled and edited *An Index to the Collected Works of I. V. Stalin* (New York, 1971). *References*: *DADH*; L. Elliott, "Our Man in Moscow," *Reader's Digest* 138 (April 1991): 129–33; and *WWA*.

MAYNARD, GEORGE WILLIAM (1839–1913). Mining engineer, June 12, 1839, in Brooklyn, New York. Maynard graduated from Columbia University and studied in Gottingen and in the school of mines at Clausthal. He opened an engineering office and chemical laboratory in New York City in 1864 and worked in Colorado from 1864 to 1867. He was professor of metallurgy and practical mining at the Rensselaer Polytechnic Institute (Troy, N.Y.) from 1868 to 1872. He went to England in 1872, opened an office in London, and served as consulting engineer. He was in Russia for several years, where he erected a copper smelting plant at Voskresensk for a British company. He returned to the United States in 1879 and resumed practice as consulting engineer with offices in New York City. Died February 12, 1913, in Boston. *References*: *DAB*; and *NYT*, February 14, 1913.

MELVILLE, GEORGE WALLACE (1841–1912). Naval engineer, born in New York City. Melville entered the U.S. Navy in 1861 as an assistant engineer. He served with the *Jeannette* expedition to the Arctic in 1879 as an engineer on board the ship. When the ship was crushed by ice in 1881, its party dragged the boats and provisions over the ice toward the Siberian mainland. When the group reached open water, it set out for the Lena Delta in three boats. Melville was the leader of the boat that reached a Russian village on the eastern Lena Delta. In 1882, he found the remains of the second party, led by *George Washington De Long. He wrote *In the Lena Delta: A Narrative of the Search for Lieut.- Commander De Long and His Companions, Followed by an Account of the Greely Relief Expedition and a Proposed Method of Reaching the North Pole* (Boston, 1884). He was engineer in chief of the U.S. Navy from 1887 until his retirement, with the rank of rear admiral, in 1903. Died March 17, 1912, in Philadelphia. *References*: G. W. Grupp, "Rear Admiral George Wallace Melville as man and Engineer-in-Chief of the Navy," *USNIP* 74 (May 1948): 613– 17; F. Hirschfeld, "George W. Melville: Architect of the Steam Navy," *Mechanical Engineering* 102 (July 1980): 24–27; and *NYT*, March 18, 1912.

MENNONITE CENTRAL COMMITTEE (MCC). Organized in 1920 and began relief work in Soviet Russia in 1921. The MCC operated in those parts of Russia where Mennonites lived, but relief was given to the entire population. It terminated its activities in the Soviet Union in 1925. *References*: Mennonite Central Committee Records, Archives of the Mennonite Church, Goshen College, Goshen, Ind.; Peter C. Hielbert et al., *Feeding the Hungry, Russian Famine, 1919–1925: American Mennonite Relief Operations under the Auspices of Mennonite Central Committee* (Scottsdale, Pa., 1929); and John D. Unruh, *In the Name of Christ: A History of the Mennonite Central Committee and Its Service, 1920–1951* (Scottsdale, Pa., 1952).

MEYER, GEORGE VON LENGERKE (1858–1918). Public official and diplomat, born June 24, 1858, in Beacon Hill, Massachusetts. Meyer graduated from Harvard University. He was involved in banking and commercial activity in Boston. He served in the Massachusetts legislature from 1892 to 1896. He was U.S. ambassador to Italy from 1900 to 1905 and ambassador to Russia from 1905 to 1907. He succeeded in cutting through the red tape of Russian bureaucracy to reach Tsar Nicholas II. He effectively presented President Theodore Roosevelt's proposals to end the Russo-Japanese War, using his friendship with Emperor Wilhelm of Germany, who helped persuade the tsar to go along with the peace offer. He was postmaster general from 1907 to 1909 and secretary of the navy from 1909 to 1913. Died March 9, 1918, in Boston. *References*: George von Lengerke Meyer Papers, Manuscript Division, Library of Congress; *DAB*; *DADH*; *NCAB* 14:413; and *NYT*, March 10, 1918.

MICHAEL, LOUIS GUY (1877–1967). Agriculturist, born August 3, 1877, in Hastings, Michigan. Michael graduated from Michigan Agricultural College (later Michigan State University) and the University of Wisconsin and attended Columbia University. He was a chemist at the experiment station and professor of agricultural chemistry at Iowa State College from 1905 to 1909. He went to Russia in 1910 and was in charge of the work of the Corn Selection Commission of the Bessarabian Provisional Government until 1916. In 1917, he made a survey of the production and trade in grain in Russia and the Black Sea ports for a syndicate organized by the *National City Bank. He managed the Peoples' Industrial Trading Company, organized to deal with the Bolsheviks, with headquarters in Riga and Tallinn, in 1919–1920. He was foreign agricultural economist in the Foreign Agricultural Service of the U.S. Bureau of Agricultural Economics from 1924 to 1929. He was agricultural attaché to Yugoslavia, Hungary, Romania, Bulgaria, Greece, and Turkey, stationed in Belgrad from 1930 to 1939, and to the Soviet Union from 1934 to 1939. He represented the Department of Agriculture with the State Department from 1939 to 1943. He was agricultural attaché in the U.S. embassy in Moscow from 1943 to 1946. He served with the Central Intelligence Agency from 1947 to 1961. Died April 15, 1967, in Washington, D.C. His Memoirs, *More Corn for Bessarabia: Russian Experience, 1910–1917* (East Lansing, Mich., 1983) were published posthumously.

MICHELA, JOSEPH ANTHONY (1903-1949). Naval officer, born March 5, 1903, in Iron Mountain, Michigan. Michela graduated from the U.S. Naval Academy in 1928 and from Columbia University. He was assistant military attaché in Moscow in 1940–1941 and military attaché from 1941 until 1943. He had an unusual opportunity to observe the Red Army at close range when he made inspection trips over large sectors of the eastern front with Soviet officers. He served on the Army General Staff from 1943 to 1947. He was military attaché in Prague from 1947 until his death. Died June 12, 1949, in Jiloviste, Czechoslovakia. *References*: *BRDS*; and *NYT*, June 13, 1949.

MIDDLETON, HENRY (1770-1846). Public official and diplomat, born September 28, 1770, in London, England. Middleton was educated in both England and South Carolina. By 1801, he had inherited much wealth and property in South Carolina and Rhode Island. He served in the South Carolina legislature from 1801 to 1810, was governor of South Carolina from 1810 to 1812, and served in the U.S. House of Representatives from 1815 to 1819. He was U.S. minister to Russia from 1821 to 1830, serving as minister to Russia longer than any other American. In 1824, he negotiated a treaty regulating trade and fishing in the Pacific Northwest and establishing a dividing line between Russian and American trading posts but allowing freedom of trade across the dividing line. He was instructed to urge Russian mediation between Spain and her rebellious colonies and to negotiate a general commercial treaty in 1828, but he was not successful in either endeavor. He was remembered as one of the few American representatives who actually enjoyed his residence in St. Petersburg. Died June 14, 1846, in Charleston, South Carolina. *References*: Middleton Family Papers, Middleton Place Foundation, Charleston, S.C.; Harold E. Bergquist, Jr., "Henry Middleton as Political Reporter: The United States, the Near East, and Eastern Europe, 1821–1829," *Historian* 45 (1983): 355–71; Harold E. Bergquist, "Russo-American Economic Relations in the 1820s: Henry Middleton as a Protector of American Economic Interests in Russia and Turkey," *East European Quarterly* 11 (Spring 1977): 27–41; *DAB*; *DADH*; *NCAB* 12:163; and Marc Raeff, "An American View of the Decembrist Revolt," *Journal of Modern History* 25 (1953): 286–93.

MILES, SHERMAN (1882-1966). Army officer, born December 5, 1882, in Washington, D.C. Miles graduated from the U.S. Military Academy in 1905 and was commissioned second lieutenant in the U.S. Army. He served in the cavalry, coast artillery, and field artillery. He served in Cuba in 1907 and was military attaché for Bulgaria, Serbia, Montenegro, and Greece until 1914. He was military attaché in Russia from 1914 to 1916 was a military observer with the Russian Army in the early stages of World War I. He was attached to the U.S. First Army during the major offensives in France and was assistant chief of staff for military intelligence with the Ninth Army. He served in Austria and

Yugoslavia with the American commission for negotiating peace in 1919 and with the Military Intelligence Division of the General Staff at the War Department in Washington from 1919 to 1922. He was military attaché in Turkey from 1922 to 1925 and then served in various military commands in the United States, including the War Plans Division of the General Staff. He was operations officer of the army's Hawaiian Department from 1929 to 1932, assistant chief of the Projects Section of the War Plans Division from 1934 to 1938, assistant chief of staff for intelligence from 1940 to 1942, military attaché in London in 1939–1940, assistant chief of staff of the Military Intelligence Division in the War Department in 1940–1941, chief of the division in 1941–1942, and commander of the First Corps Area in Boston from 1942 until his retirement, with the rank of major general, in 1945. He was a member of the Massachusetts state legislature after 1946. Died October 7, 1966, in Beverly, Massachusetts. *References*: *EAIE*; *NYT*, October 8, 1966; and Rowan A. Williams, "Reporting from Petrograd, 1914–1915," *East European Quarterly* 14 (1980): 335–44.

MILLER, ALVIN JOSEPH (1883–1981). Association official, born December 11, 1883. Miller graduated from Goshen College, Columbia University, and Columbia University Teachers College. He was an instructor at Kent State Teachers College from 1915 to 1919. He served with the American Red Cross (ARC) in France and then was a member of a commission appointed to investigate the possibility of opening a Mennonite relief unit in Central Europe or Soviet Russia, traveling in Soviet Russia in 1919. He did relief work in the Crimea and Constantinople and opened an ARC unit in Simferopol in 1920. He was director of American Mennonite Relief in Soviet Russia from 1921 to 1926. He also represented the *Mennonite Central Committee and served on the staff of Colonel *William Nafew Haskell, director of the *American Relief Administration. He related his activities in Peter C. Hielbert et al., *Feeding the Hungry: Russian Famine, 1919–1925: American Mennonite Relief Operations under the Auspices of Mennonite Central Committee* (Scottsdale, Pa., 1929), ch. 4. He was a member of the faculty of Kent State University after 1936. Died November 9, 1981. *Reference*: A. Warkentin and Melvin Gingerich, *Who's Who among the Mennonites* (North Newton, Kan., 1943).

MITCHELL, ABBIE (1884–1960). Singer and actress, born in New York City and grew up in Baltimore. Mitchell later studied voice and music theory. She first appeared in a musical comedy on Broadway in 1897. She then toured with Black Patti's Troubadors, continued to appear in New York City, and also toured Europe. She was probably the first American to be invited to sing in the Soviet Union. She continued to perform until 1947 and also headed the vocal department at Tuskegee Institute after 1931. Died March 16, 1960, in New York City. *References*: *DANB*; *NAW*; *NYT*, March 20, 1960; and Eileen Southern, *Biographical Dictionary of Afro-American and African Musicians* (Westport, Conn., 1982).

MITCHELL, BERNON F. See MARTIN, WILLIAM H.

MOBY DICK PROJECT. Code name of a program sponsored by the Central Intelligence Agency and carried out by the U.S. Strategic Air Command to develop high-altitude unmanned balloons for overhead photoreconnaissance and to photograph the Soviet Union using these camera-carrying balloons. The program was the result of a desperate need for intelligence on Soviet military and industrial capabilities following the outbreak of the Korean War. The balloon flights over the Soviet Union began in November 1955. The balloons were launched in Western Europe, were recovered near Japan, and produced useful results. The program was abandoned in 1956 when the U–2 reconnaissance aircraft flights over the Soviet Union began. *References*: *EAIE*; and Curtis Peebles, *The Moby Dick Project: Reconnaissance Balloons over Russia* (Washington, D.C., 1991).

MORDECAI, ALFRED (1804–1887). Military engineer, born January 3, 1804, in Warrenton, North Carolina. Mordecai graduated from the U.S. Military Academy in 1823 and was commissioned second lieutenant in the Corps of Engineers. He was assistant engineer in the construction of Fortress Monroe in Virginia, assistant to the chief of engineers, commander of the Washington and the Frankford, Pennsylvania, arsenals, and assistant to the chief of ordnance. He was a member of the U.S. military commission to the Crimean War from 1855 to 1857 and published his observations in *Military Commission to Europe, in 1855 and 1856* (Washington, D.C., 1860). He resigned from the army in 1861 and became a teacher of mathematics in Philadelphia. He was assistant engineer of the Mexico and Pacific Railroad from 1863 to 1866 and treasurer and secretary of canal and coal companies from 1867 to 1887. Died October 23, 1887, in Philadelphia. *References*: Alfred Mordecai Papers, Manuscript Division, Library of Congress; Robert D. Abrahams, *The Uncommon Soldier: Major Alfred Mordecai* (New York, 1958); *DAB*; and *NCAB* 10:443.

MOSCOW SUMMIT (1972). Summit meeting between President *Richard Nixon and General Secretary Leonid I. Brezhnev in Moscow from May 22 to May 29, 1972. The United States aimed to improve U.S. prospects for ending the Vietnam War and to conclude the Strategic Arms Limitation Talks (*SALT) Agreement and a number of other bilateral accords. Nine treaties and agreements were signed, including the Basic Principles of Relations between the U.S. and the U.S.S.R., the Treaty on the Limitation of Anti-Ballistic Missile Systems (*ABM Treaty), and the Interim Agreement on Limitation of Strategic Offensive Arms (now referred to as SALT I). Other agreements concerned cooperative efforts in science and technology, medicine and public health, protection of the environment, collaboration in space exploration, and avoidance of naval incidents at sea. These agreements symbolized the U.S. acceptance of the Soviet Union as an equal nuclear power and as a superpower. *References*: *DADH*; *McDonald*; and *Weihmiller*.

MOSCOW SUMMIT (1974). Summit meeting between President *Richard Nixon and General Secretary Leonid I. Brezhnev in Moscow and Yalta between June 27 and July 3, 1974. The United States aimed to strengthen bilateral relations, to develop areas of cooperation to displace confrontation, and to limit the threat of nuclear war. Numerous agreements were signed, including the Protocol to the Treaty on the Limitation of Anti-Ballistic Missile (ABM) Systems, the Threshold Test Ban Treaty, Treaty and Protocol on the Limitation of Underground Nuclear Weapons, the Long-Term Agreement to Facilitate Economic, Industrial and Technical Cooperation, and agreements on cooperation in energy, housing, and artificial heart research. A decision was made to hold an interim summit to discuss *SALT issues. *References*: *DADH*; *McDonald*; and *Weihmiller*.

MOSCOW SUMMIT (1988). Summit meeting between President *Ronald Reagan and General Secretary Mikhail S. Gorbachev on May 30 to June 3, 1988, in Moscow. Although the meetings were amiable and the two leaders even strolled through Red Square, the Soviet Union record on human rights caused much disagreement. Several minor agreements were signed. *Reference*: Joseph G. Whelan, *The Moscow Summit, 1988: Reagan and Gorbachev in Negotiation* (Boulder, Colo., 1990).

MOSCOW SUMMIT (1991). Summit meeting between President *George Bush and President Mikhail S. Gorbachev in Moscow on July 30–31, 1991. The two leaders signed the *START treaty, committing each side to reduce its nuclear weapons by 30 percent, and the United States granted the Soviet Union the most-favored-nation status. Several additional agreements were also signed, and the two countries agreed to serve as cosponsors of a Middle East peace conference.

MOSCOW SUMMIT (1993). A summit meeting between President George Bush and President Boris Yeltsin in Moscow on January 2–3, 1993. The two leaders signed the *START II treaty on January 3, 1993. The treaty would reduce the two nations' strategic arms by two-thirds, eliminating those that either side might use in a pre-emptive first strike—particularly the land-based missiles with multiple warheads.

MOSELY, PHILIP EDWARD (1905–1972). Educator, born September 21, 1905, in Westfield, Massachusetts. Mosely graduated from Harvard University and carried out historical research in Moscow from 1930 to 1932, which he later described in the April 1965 issue of *Survey*. He was engaged in research in the Balkans in 1935–1936 and was assistant professor and later associate professor in modern European history at Cornell University from 1936 to 1942, professor of international relations at Columbia University from 1946 to 1955, and adjunct professor from 1955 to 1963. He was instrumental in establishing the Russian Institute at Columbia University and was its director. He was assistant chief in the division of political studies and chief of the division of territorial studies in the State Department from 1942 to 1946, adviser to the U.S. delegation at the Moscow Conference in 1945, and political adviser at the *Potsdam Conference in 1945. He wrote *Face to Face with Russia* (New York, 1948), *Russia after Stalin* (New York, 1955), and *The Kremlin and World Politics: Studies in Soviet Policy and Action* (New York, 1960). Died January 13, 1972, in New York City. *References*: Philip E. Mosely Papers, University of Illinois Library, Urbana; Philip E. Mosely Papers, Columbia University Library, New York City; *NCAB* 56:105; and *NYT*, January 14, 1972.

MOTT, JOHN RALEIGH (1865–1955). Association official, born May 25, 1865, near Purvis (later Livingston Manor), Sullivan County, New York, and grew up in Pottsville, Iowa. Mott attended Upper Iowa University (Fayette, Iowa) and graduated from Cornell University. He became affiliated with the *Young Men's Christian Association (YMCA) in 1886 and became its senior student secretary in 1890, the national executive for the American YMCA from 1915 to 1928, and president of the World YMCA in 1926. He was in Russia in 1899 and again in 1909 and was a member of the *Root Mission to Russia in 1917. He shared the Nobel Peace Prize in 1946. Died January 31, 1955, in Orlando, Florida. *References*: John R. Mott Papers, Yale University Divinity School Library, New Haven, Conn.; *CB* 1947; *DAB S5*; C. Howard Hopkins, *John R. Mott: A Biography* (Grand Rapids, Mich., 1979); John W. Long and C. Howard Hopkins, "The Church and the Russian Revolution: Conversations of John R. Mott with Orthodox Church Leaders, June-July, 1917," *St. Vladimir's Theological Quarterly* 20 (1976): 161–80; *NCAB* 44:346; and *NYT*, February 1, 1955.

MULLER, HERMANN JOSEPH (1890–1967). Geneticist, born December 21, 1890, in New York City. Muller graduated from Columbia University and Cornell Medical College. He worked at the University of Texas from 1921 to 1932 and conducted research at Oskar Vogt's Brain Research Institute in Berlin in 1932–1933. He moved his laboratory to the Soviet Union in the early 1930s and worked in Leningrad and Moscow at the Academy of Sciences from 1933 to 1937, concerned chiefly with radiation genetics, cytogenetics, and gene structure. By 1935, he was embroiled in the growing controversy about the work of Trofim D. Lysenko, work that he could not support. Muller hoped to win Soviet sponsorship for basic genetics and for the program of positive eugenics that he presented in his book *Out of the Night* (New York, 1935). After Lysenko won Joseph Stalin's backing, Muller left the Soviet Union, after volunteering to serve in the Spanish Civil War. He worked at the University of Edinburgh in 1938, returned to the United States, and worked at Amherst College and at Indiana

University from 1945 until his death. In 1946, he was awarded the Nobel Prize in physiology and medicine. Died April 5, 1967, in Indianapolis, Indiana. *References*: Hermann Joseph Muller Papers, Lilly Library, Indiana University, Bloomington; Elof Axel Carlson, *Genes, Radiation, and Society: The Life and Work of H. J. Muller* (Ithaca, N.Y., 1981); *DAB S8*; *DSB*; H. J. Muller, *Man's Future Birthright: Essays on Science and Humanity*, ed. Elof Axel Carlson (Albany, N.Y., 1973); and G. Pontecorvo, "Hermann Joseph Muller, 1890–1967," in *Biographical Memoirs of Fellows of the Royal Society* 14 (1968): 349–89.

MUNROE, THOMAS (?–1834). Soldier, born in Washington, D.C. Munroe went to Russia in 1822 to seek a military career. Attaining the rank of colonel in the Imperial Army, he served during the Russo-Turkish War as aide-de-camp to the tsar while the tsar conducted an important peace mission to Constantinople. Died August 1834 at Nikolayev on the Black Sea.

MUTUAL AND BALANCED FORCE REDUCTIONS (MBFR). Negotiations between NATO and the Warsaw Pact concerning reduction of the forces both alliances deployed in Central Europe. The talks began in 1973, following an agreement reached at Moscow in 1972. In subsequent years, agreement was reached on the geographic area in which forces were to be reduced and on the objective of limiting each alliance to a total deployment of nine-hundred-thousand ground and air force troops in the region. The two sides still disagreed on the number of Warsaw Treaty troops in the region, methods for verification of current and future deployments, and the NATO preference that verification of the figures precede troop reductions and not merely follow them. *References*: Coit D. Blacker, "The MBFR Experience," in Alexander L. George, Philip J. Farley, and Alexander Dallin, eds., *U.S.-Soviet Security Cooperation: Achievements, Failures, Lessons* (New York, 1988); Jonathan Dean, *Watershed in Europe: Dismantling the East-West Military Confrontation* (Lexington, Mass., 1987); *DINRT*; Kenneth H. Jacobson, "Mutual and Balanced Force Reductions: The Problem of 'Balance,' " in William W. Whitson, ed., *Foreign Policy and U.S. National Security: Major Postelection Issues* (New York, 1976), pp. 302–14; and John G. Keliher, *The Negotiations on Mutual and Balanced Force Reductions: The Search for Arms Control in Central Europe* (New York, 1980).

N

NATIONAL CITY BANK OF NEW YORK. Established as the First Bank of the United States in 1791 and became the City Bank of New York in 1812 and the National City Bank of New York in 1865. The bank developed close relations with the tsarist government. In 1900, it negotiated, with the New York Security and Trust Company, its first loan to Russia, floating an issue of bonds for a railroad. In 1916, it headed a syndicate that floated two loans to Russia. In 1917, it opened branches in Petrograd and Moscow, the first U.S. bank to open a branch in Russia. It also owned part of several Russian companies. The Russian branches were nationalized by the Bolshevik government in 1917. *References*: Harold van B. Cleveland and Thomas F. Huertas, *Citibank, 1812–1970* (Cambridge, Mass., 1985); and Robert Stanley Mayer, *The Influence of Frank A. Vanderlip and the National City Bank on American Commerce and Foreign Policy, 1910–1920* (New York, 1987).

NATIONAL CONFERENCE ON SOVIET JEWRY (NCSJ). A voluntary, not-for-profit agency comprising nearly fifty national organizations and over three hundred local federations, community councils, and committees, founded in 1971 as the central coordination agency of the organized Jewish community for policy and action in the United States on behalf of the Jews in the Soviet Union. Created in response to the growing anti-Semitism faced by Soviet Jews, its primary purpose was to enable Jews to leave the Soviet Union without obstacles and to ensure that those Jews who chose to remain in the Soviet Union would have access to their Jewish heritage through Jewish cultural and religious institutions.

NATIONAL COUNCIL ON AMERICAN-SOVIET FRIENDSHIP. Founded in 1943 to encourage better relations between the United States and the Soviet Union so that the two powers might cooperate to help bring about world peace and guard against atomic destruction. It provided information concerning major phases of Soviet life and American-Soviet relations through pamphlets, pictorial exhibits, and documentary films. It attempted to increase cultural, educational, and scientific interchange between the two countries, to encourage visits by citizens from each country to the other, to cultivate good business relations, and to promote agreements for the control, limitation, and reduction of armaments.

NEW YORK LIFE INSURANCE COMPANY. Founded in 1841 as the Nautilus Insurance Company and became the New York Life Insurance Company in 1849. It set up a branch in St. Petersburg in 1885. The Soviet government seized the company's Russian offices and terminated its activities in Soviet Russia in 1919. *References*: New York Life Insurance Company Archives, New York City; and Lawrence Fraser Abbott, *The Story of NYLIC: A History of the Origins and Development of the New York Life Insurance Company from 1845 to 1929* (New York, 1930).

NITZE, PAUL HENRY (1907–   ). Government official, born January 16, 1907, in Amherst, Massachusetts. Nitze graduated from Harvard University. He was with Dillon, Read, and Company, investment bankers, in New York City from 1929 to 1937 and was its vice-president from 1939 to 1941. He was financial director to the coordinator of Inter-American Affairs, chief of the Metals and Minerals Branch of the Board of Economic Warfare, director of the Foreign Procurement and Development Branch of the Foreign Economic Administration, and vice-chairman of the U.S. Strategic Bombing Survey from 1944 to 1946. He was deputy director of the Office of International Trade Policy of the State Department in 1946, deputy to the assistant secretary of state for economic affairs in 1948–1949, director of the policy planning staff of the State Department from 1950 to 1953, president of the Foreign Service Educational Foundation in Washington from 1953 to 1961, assistant secretary of defense for international security affairs from 1961 to 1963, secretary of the navy from 1963 to 1967, and deputy secretary of defense from 1967 to 1969. He was a member of the U.S. delegation to the Strategic Arms Limitation Talks (*SALT) from 1969 to 1974, head of the U.S. negotiating team to the Arms Control Talks in Geneva from 1981 to 1984, and special adviser to the president and the secretary of state on arms control matters from 1984 to 1989. He was later diplomat-in-residence at Johns Hopkins University in Washington, D.C. He wrote *From Hiroshima to Glasnost: At the Center of Decision, a Memoir* (New York, 1989). *References*: Ronald Brownstein and Nina Easton, *Reagan's Ruling Class: Portraits of the President's Top 100 Officials* (Washington, D.C., 1982), pp. 518–24; David Callhan, *Dangerous Capabilities: Paul Nitze and the Cold War* (New York, 1990); Steven L. Reardon, *The Evolution of American Strategic Doctrine: Paul H. Nitze and the Soviet Challenge* (Boulder, Colo., 1984); Joseph M. Siracusa, *Rearming for the Cold War: Paul H. Nitze, the H-Bomb, and the Origins of a Soviet First Strike* (Los Angeles, 1983); Strobe Talbott, *The Master of the Game: Paul Nitze and the Nuclear Peace* (New York, 1988): A. Tonelson, ''Nitze's World,'' *Foreign Policy* 35 (Summer 1979): 74–90; and *WWA*.

NIXON, RICHARD MILHOUS (1913–   ). Public official and president of the United States, born January 9, 1913, in Yorba Linda, California. Nixon graduated from Whittier College and Duke University. He served in the U.S. Navy during World War II. He served in the U.S. House of Representatives from 1947 to 1951 and in the U.S. Senate from 1951 to 1953 and was vice-president of the United States from 1953 to 1961. He practiced law from 1961 to 1969. He was president of the United States from 1969 until 1974, when he was forced to resign. Pursuing a policy of improving relations with the Soviet Union, he visited Moscow in 1972, the first time a U.S. president had set foot in Moscow, and General Secretary Leonid I. Brezhnev came to the United States in 1973, initiating a period of détente in U.S.-Soviet relations. Their talks resulted in large grain sales to the Soviet Union and the beginning of talks on limiting strategic nuclear weapons. The Strategic Arms Limitation Talks (*SALT) began in 1969 and resulted in an arms-limitation treaty signed in May 1972. Eighteen other agreements, including the prevention of incidents at sea, as well as medical, scientific, and technological cooperation, were also signed. A final summit meeting took place in Moscow in 1974. He wrote *RN: The Memoirs of Richard Nixon* (New York, 1978). *References*: Stephen E. Ambrose, *Nixon, Vol. 2: Triumph of a Politician, 1962–1974* (New York, 1989); Lief Roderick Rosenberger, "The Evolution of the Nixon-Kissinger Policy toward the Soviet Union: An Analysis of the Cold War Legacy and the Ambivalent Pursuit of Détente" (Ph.D. diss., Claremont Graduate School, 1980); Franz Schurmann, *The Foreign Policies of Richard Nixon: The Grand Design* (Berkeley, Calif., 1987); Ted Szulc, *The Illusion of Peace: Foreign Policy in the Nixon Years* (New York, 1978); and Richard C. Thornton, *The Nixon-Kissinger Years: Reshaping America's Foreign Policy* (New York, 1989).

NONRECOGNITION. The United States refused to recognize the Soviet Union from 1917 to 1933. Adopting the position that recognition implied approval, the U.S. government did not follow its traditional policy and did not enter into diplomatic relations with the Bolshevik government once it became clear that the Bolsheviks controlled Russia. The U.S. government charged that the Bolshevik government had seized power by force and was not representative of the Russian people, that it could not be trusted to carry out its international obligations, and that it supported revolutionary activity throughout the world. *References*: David Glenn Singer, "The United States Confronts the Soviet Union, 1919–1933: The Rise and Fall of the Policy of Non-Recognition" (Ph.D. diss., Loyola University, 1973).

NOYES, GEORGE RAPALL (1873–1952). Educator, born April 2, 1873, in Cambridge, Massachusetts. Noyes graduated from Harvard and studied at the Imperial University in St. Petersburg and in Moscow from 1898 to 1900. He was assistant professor of English at the University of Wisconsin in 1900–1901, assistant professor of English and Slavic philology at the University of California from 1902 to 1907, assistant professor of Slavic philology from 1907 to 1911, associate professor from 1911 to 1919, and professor from 1919 until his retirement in 1943. He wrote *Tolstoy* (New York, 1918) and edited *Masterpieces of the Russian Drama* (New York, 1933). Died May 5, 1952, in Berkeley, California. *References*: *American Slavic and East European Review* 12 (1953): v–vi; Alexander Kaun and Ernest J. Simmons, eds., *Slavic Studies in Honor of George Noyes* (New York, 1943); and *NCAB* 40:439.

NSC–68. National Security Council document issued on April 14, 1950, and largely drafted by *Paul H. Nitze. A comprehensive review of U.S. policy toward the Soviet Union, it based U.S. planning on Soviet capabilities to take certain hostile action and or the assumption that the Cold War was in fact a real war and called for a nonmilitary counteroffensive against the Soviet Union, embracing economic, political, and psychological warfare. It proposed that the United States and its allies should build up their military strength until superior to that of the Soviet Union and its allies and that the United States should postpone negotiations with the Soviet Union until the military buildup had been completed. The outbreak of the Korean War in June 1950 confirmed many of the assumptions in the document, making the danger of Soviet aggression a reality and leading to greatly increased defense spending. *References*: John Lewis Gaddis and Paul Nitze, "NSC–68 and the Soviet Threat Reconsidered," *International Security* 4 (Spring 1980): 164–98; Sam Postbrief, "Departure from Incrementalism in U.S. Strategic Planning: The Origins of NSC–68," *Naval War College Review* 33 (March-April 1980): 34–57; Joseph M. Siracuse, "NSC 68: A Reappraisal," *Naval War College Review* 33 (November-December 1980): 4–14; and Samuel F. Wells, "Sounding the Tocsin: NSC–68 and the Soviet Threat," *International Security* 4 (Fall 1979): 116–48.

NUCLEAR RISK REDUCTION CENTERS AGREEMENT (1987). Agreement between the United States of America and the Union of Soviet Socialist Republics on the establishment of nuclear risk reduction centers, signed in Washington on September 15, 1987. Each country agreed to organize a Nuclear Risk Reduction Center in its capital, to establish a special facsimile communication link between these centers, and to provide additional direct, reliable, high-speed systems for communicating at the government-to-government level. *Reference*: *ACDA*.

O

OLBERG, CHARLES REAL (1875–1938). Hydrological engineer, born August 19, 1875, in St. Paul, Minnesota, and grew up in Washington, D.C. Olberg graduated from George Washington University and the University of California. He was assistant engineer and engineer in the U.S. Reclamation Service from 1902 to 1906, was superintendent of irrigation and supervising engineer of the U.S. Indian Irrigation Service in California and Arizona from 1907 to 1917, served with the U.S. engineers during World War I, and was assistant chief engineer of the U.S. Indian Irrigation Service from 1919 to 1929. He went to the Soviet Union in 1929 and was consulting engineer for the Soviet government in Tiflis. He advised on irrigation, hydroelectric, and drainage problems in Georgia, Armenia, and Azerbaijan and directed the investigation and design of the Mingechaur project, which undertook the irrigation and drainage of the land lying along the Kura River adjacent to the Caspian Sea, the control and regulation of the Kura River, the construction of an earth dam and a power plant, mosquito eradication, river transport, the building of roads, and the settlement of the reclaimed area. He returned to the United States in 1933, was engineer examiner with the U.S. Public Works Administration in Washington, D.C., and later was hydraulic engineer with the U.S. Farm Security Administration. Died April 4, 1938, in Washington, D.C. *Reference*: *NCAB* 28:12.

OLSEN, CLARENCE EDWARD (1899–1971). Naval officer, born October 7, 1899, in Aloha, Michigan. Olsen graduated from the U.S. Naval Academy in 1920 and was commissioned ensign in the U.S. Navy. He was executive officer of several naval ships from 1929 to 1936, served in the Hydrographic Office of the Department of the Navy from 1936 to 1939, and was commander of the USS *Arctic* in 1941–1942. He was chief of the naval division of the U.S. Military Mission to the Soviet Union and served as liaison between the two countries, handling all naval and personnel arrangements for U.S. ships delivering Lend-Lease goods in Murmansk, Molotovsk, Archangel, and Odessa, arranging delivery of U.S. naval vessels to the Soviet Union, arrangement of worldwide weather data exchange, coordination of European and Pacific war activities in cooperation with the military head of the mission, routine intelligence and other duties. He was commander of the USS *Baltimore* in 1945–1946, commanding officer of the naval base in Norfolk, Virginia, from 1948 to 1950 and of the naval base in Newport from 1951 to 1953, and chief of the Military Assistance and Advisory Group to Norway from 1957 until his retirement, with the rank of rear admiral, in 1959. Died November 11, 1971, in Bethesda, Maryland. His memoirs of the *Yalta Conference appeared in the June 1972 issue of *American Heritage*. *References*: "Reminiscences of Rear Admiral Clarence E. Olsen, U.S. Navy (Retired), as They Pertain to the Yalta Conference," oral history, U.S. Naval Institute, Annapolis, Md.; *NCAB* 57:240; and *WWWA*.

"OPEN SKIES" PROPOSAL (1955). A proposal made by President *Dwight E. Eisenhower to the Soviet Union in Geneva on July 21, 1955, for mutual aerial inspection, in which the United States and the USSR would provide each other facilities for aerial photography and aerial reconnaissance. The proposal was rejected by the Soviet Union. *Reference*: W. W. Rostow, *Open Skies: Eisenhower's Proposal of July 21, 1955* (Austin, Tex., 1982).

P

PACKER, EARL LENOIR (1894–). Diplomat, born November 19, 1894, in Ogden, Utah. Packer graduated from George Washington University. He was a clerk in the War Department from 1915 to 1917 and in the U.S. embassy in Petrograd in 1917. He served with the American Military Mission in Petrograd in 1917–1918 and was assistant military attaché therein 1918–1919. He entered the State Department in 1920, serving as a key professional in early U.S. attempts to achieve a realistic understanding of Bolshevik objectives and behavior. He was assistant chief of the Division of Russian Affairs in 1921–1922, served in the Office of the American Commissioner to Russian Provinces and the legation in Riga from 1922 to 1925, and was assistant chief of the Division of Eastern European Affairs from 1928 to 1936. He was consul and first secretary at the U.S. legation in Riga from 1936 to 1939 and in Budapest in 1940, consul in Dresden and first secretary in Dublin in1941 and in Ankara from 1942 to 1945, consul general in Rangoon in 1946–1947, and consul general in Tunis from 1947 to 1950. *Reference*: BRDS.

PARIS SUMMIT (1960). Summit meeting of President *Dwight D. Eisenhower, Premier Nikita S. Khrushchev, Prime Minister Harold Macmillan, and President Charles de Gaulle in Paris from May 15 to May 19, 1960. The issues to be discussed in the conference included Germany and Berlin, disarmament, nuclear testing, and East-West relations. The talks collapsed the first day, after Khrushchev delivered a tirade against the United States for the *U–2 incident. He demanded that Eisenhower publicly apologize, renounce future spy flights, and pass severe judgment on those responsible. Eisenhower was not willing to do any of these things. This was the last attempt to carry out summits on an East-West multilateral basis. All results of the conference were negative, the Cold War resumed and intensified, and the Soviet invitation to Eisenhower for a visit to Moscow was withdrawn. *References*: *McDonald*; and *Weihmiller*.

PARKE, CHARLES ROSS (1823–?). Physician, born June 25, 1823, in Chester County, Pennsylvania. Parke studied medicine at the University of Pennsylvania. He practiced medicine in Concordville, Pennsylvania, and then in Como, Illinois. He served as a surgeon with the Russian medical staff during the Crimean War in 1855–1856. He returned to the United States in 1856. *Reference*: Charles Ross Parke Diary, 1855–1856, Huntington Library, San Marino, Calif.

PEACEFUL NUCLEAR EXPLOSIONS (PNE) TREATY (1976). Treaty between the United States of America and the Union of Soviet Socialist Republics on underground nuclear explosions for peaceful purposes, signed in Washington and Moscow on May 28, 1976, as a companion to the *Threshold Test Ban Treaty (TTBT). The treaty regulated tests by both countries in locations other than their nuclear weapons sites; these tests are, therefore, considered to be for peaceful purposes. The Senate has not ratified either treaty, and the Reagan administration considered the verification provisions of both treaties to be inadequate. The United States and the USSR also promised not to carry out peaceful nuclear explosions with a yield greater than 150 kilotons. *References*: *ACDA*; and *DINRT*.

PEIRCE, HERBERT HENRY DAVIS (1849–1916). Diplomat, born April 11, 1849, in Cambridge, Massachusetts. Peirce attended Harvard University and the Royal School of Mines in London. He entered a business career in 1869 and was in business in Boston and New York City. He was secretary of legation in St. Petersburg from 1894 to 1898 and secretary of embassy from 1898 to 1901. He was third assistant secretary of state from 1901 to 1906. He had charge of the arrangements for deliberations during the Russo-Japanese peace conference in Portsmouth, New Hampshire, in 1905. He was the first U.S. minister to Norway from 1906 to 1911. In 1915–1916, he was temporary special agent assigned to the U.S. embassy in Russia, with the rank of minister, to assist the U.S. ambassador. Died December 5, 1916, in Portland, Maine. *Reference*: *NCAB* 27:273.

PEPSI-COLA COMPANY. Pepsi was invented in 1898, and Pepsi-Cola was registered as a trademark in 1903. It was bought by the Loft Candy Company in 1931 and was merged in 1941 to become Pepsi-Cola Company (PepsiCo in 1965). In 1972, it made a deal with the Soviet government to distribute Stolichnaya vodka in the United States in exchange for Pepsi in the Soviet Union. In 1990, it signed an agreement with the Soviet Union to barter Pepsi-Cola for ships and vodka, the largest deal ever between an American corporation and the Soviet Union. *Reference*: Roger Enrico, *The Other Guy Blinked: How Pepsi Won the Cola Wars* (New York, 1986).

PERLE, RICHARD NORMAN (1941–   ). Government official, born September 16, 1941, in New York City. Perle graduated from the University of Southern California and Princeton University and studied at the University of London. He was staff member of the Subcommittee of National Security of the Senate Committee on Government Operations from 1970 to 1972 and professional staff member of the Permanent Subcommittee on Investigation of the Senate Committee on Government Affairs from 1973 to 1980. He was assistant secretary of defense for international security policy from 1980 to 1987. An anti-Soviet hard-liner, he opposed most arms-control agreements and tried to block accommodation with the Soviet Union. He was later resident scholar at the American Enterprise Institute for Public Policy Research in Washington, D.C. *References*: Ronald Brownsteen and Nina Easton, *Reagan's Ruling Class: Portraits of the President's Top 100 Officials* (Washington, D.C., 1982), pp. 496–504; "Richard Perle: The Pentagon's Powerful Hardliner on Soviet Policy," *Business Week*, May 21, 1984, pp. 130–32; C. Wright, "Perle with a Price?" *New Statesman* 105 (April 22, 1983): 15–16; and *WWA*.

PEYTON, BERNARD (?–?). Merchant, born in Virginia. Peyton went to San Francisco to seek his fortune and became a commission merchant. He made a journey through Russia and Siberia to establish trade relations in 1856–1857. He was superintendent of the California Powder Works in Santa Cruz after 1866. *References*: Bernard Peyton Letters, New York Public Library, New York City; and Norman Saul, "An American's Siberian Dream," *RR* 37 (1978): 405–20.

PICKENS, FRANCIS WILKINSON (1805–1869). Public official and diplomat, born April 7, 1805, in St. Paul's Parish, Colleton District, South Carolina. Pickens attended Franklin College (Ga.) and South Carolina College, studied law, and was admitted to the bar in 1828. He practiced law in Edgefield, South Carolina, served in the state legislature from 1832 to 1834 and in the U.S. House of Representatives from 1834 to 1843, and was a member of the state senate from 1844 to 1846. He was U.S. minister to Russia from 1858 to 1860, serving without special distinction. He was accompanied by his second wife, **LUCY PETWAY HOLCOMBE**, whose influence was responsible for his acceptance of the Russian mission. She made a splendid appearance in the official circles of St. Petersburg and won the special attention of the imperial family, especially after she became pregnant. The empress even assisted with the birth of their daughter. In 1861, she sold the jewels given her by the imperial family to support the Confederacy. A regiment of South Carolina troops was named the Holcombe Legion in her honor, and her picture was engraved on Confederate currency. Pickens was governor of South Carolina from 1860 to 1862. Died January 25, 1869, in Edgefield. *References: BDAC; DAB*; John B. Edmunds, Jr., *Francis W. Pickens and the Politics of Destruction* (Chapel Hill, N.C., 1986); Jack Thorndyke Greer, *Leaves from a Family Album (Holcombe and Greer)*, ed. Jane Judge Greer (Waco, Texas, 1975), pp. 51–58; and *NCAB* 12:173.

PINKNEY, WILLIAM (1764–1822). Public official and diplomat, born March 17, 1764, in Annapolis, Maryland. Pinkney studied law and was admitted to the bar in 1786. He served in the Maryland legislature from 1788 to 1792 and on the state executive council from 1792 to 1795. He was special commissioner to Britain from 1796 to 1804 to adjust claims according to stipulations in Jay's Treaty. He was Maryland attorney general in 1805–1806. He was sent to Britain again in 1806 to join James Monroe in negotiating the Monroe-Pinkney Treaty. He was U.S. minister to Great Britain from 1808 to 1811. He was U.S. minister to Russia in 1817–1818. He failed to negotiate a commercial treaty but succeeded in improving U.S.-Russian relations. Died February 22, 1822, in Washington, D.C. *References*: *DAB*; and *DADH*.

PIPES, RICHARD EDGAR (1923–   ). Historian and government official, born July 11, 1923, in Cieszyn, Poland, came to the United States in 1940, and was naturalized in 1943. Pipes served in the U.S. Army Air Force during World War II. He attended Muskingum College (Ohio) and graduated from Cornell and Harvard universities. He was a member of the faculty of Harvard University after 1950 and was professor of history after 1963. He was associate director of the Russian Research Center from 1962 to 1964 and director from 1968 to 1973. He headed "Team B" in the *Team A/Team B exercise in 1976. He was director of the Eastern European and Soviet Affairs of the National Security Council in 1981–1982. He wrote *U.S.-Soviet Relations in the Era of Détente* (Boulder, Colo., 1981), *Survival Is Not Enough* (New York, 1984), and *Russia Observed: Collected Essays on Russian and Soviet History* (Boulder, Colo., 1989). *References*: J. Alter, "Reagan's Dr. Strangelove," *Washington Monthly* 13 (June 1981): 10–17; and *WWA*.

PNE TREATY. See PEACEFUL NUCLEAR EXPLOSIONS (PNE) TREATY

POINSETT, JOEL ROBERTS (1779–1851). Traveler and diplomat, born March 2, 1779, in Charleston, South Carolina. Poinsett studied in a medical school in Edinburgh and a military academy in Woolwich, England. He traveled to Russia in 1807, became a friend of Tsar Alexander I's, and toured the Caucasus and the Caspian Sea regions (including Baku). He was special diplomatic agent to Buenos Aires and Chile in 1811 and U.S. consul general in Buenos Aires from 1811 to 1815. He served in the South Carolina General Assembly from 1816 to 1820 and in the U.S. House of Representatives from 1821 to 1825. He was special agent to Mexico in 1822 and the first U.S. minister to Mexico, from 1825 to 1829. He was secretary of war from 1837 to 1841. Died December 12, 1851, near Statesburg, South Carolina. *References*: Joel R. Poinsett Papers, Historical Society of Pennsylvania, Philadelphia; *DAB*; James F. Rippy, *Joel R. Poinsett: Versatile American* (Durham, N.C., 1935).

POLAKOV, WALTER NICHOLAS (1879–1937?). Industrial engineer, born July 1879 in Luga, Russia. Polakov graduated from the Royal Institute of Technology in Dresden and studied at the University of Moscow. He came to the United States in 1906. He was an engineer with the American Locomotive Company, with Henry L. Gantt's consulting firm from 1910 to 1912, and with Charles Day's consulting firm from 1912 to 1915. He established Walter N. Polakov and Company, industrial consultants, in 1915 and served as its president. He was management consultant to the Supreme Economic Council of the USSR from 1929 to 1931, working to apply scientific management techniques to Russian industry. He was consulting engineer for the Tennessee Valley Authority after 1933. *References*: Daniel A. Wren, "Scientific Management in the U.S.S.R., with Particular Reference to the Contribution of Walter N. Polakov," *Academy of Management Review* 5 (1980): 1–11; *WWIN*; and *WWWA*.

POOLE, DEWITT CLINTON (1885–1952). Diplomat, born October 28, 1885, at Vancouver Barracks, near Vancouver, Washington. Poole graduated from the University of Wisconsin and George Washington University. He entered the consular service in 1910, serving as vice-consul in Berlin and Paris until 1915, consul in Paris in 1916–1917, and consul in Moscow in 1917–1918. He was special assistant to the U.S. ambassador in Russia in 1918. He witnessed the downfall of the tsarist regime and for a brief period was held prisoner by the Bolshevik government. At that time he was the sole U.S. representative in Russia, as chargé d'affaires until 1919. He was chief of the Division of Russian Affairs in the State Department until 1923, consul general in Cape Town, and counselor at the embassy in Berlin from 1926 until he resigned in 1930. He was a member of the staff of the School of Public and International Affairs at Princeton University from 1930 to 1948 and its director from 1933 to 1939, director of the Foreign Nationalities Branch of the Office of Strategic Services from 1941 to 1945, and president of the National Committee for a Free Europe, an organization funded by the Central Intelligence Agency to sponsor Radio Free Europe, from 1949 to 1951. Died September 3, 1952, in Princeton, New Jersey. *References*: DeWitt C. Poole Papers, State Historical Society of Wisconsin, Madison; *CB* 1950; *EAIE*; *NYT*, September 4, 1952; "The Reminiscences of DeWitt Clinton Poole" (1952), Oral History Collection, Columbia University, New York City; and *WWWA*.

POOLE, ERNEST COOK (1880–1950). Author and journalist, born January 23, 1880, in Chicago. Poole graduated from Princeton University. He was a social worker with the University Settlement on New York's Lower East Side from 1902 to 1904. He returned to Chicago in 1904 and became publicist for the striking stockyard workers. After the St. Petersburg massacre of 1905, he began secretly carrying money and messages for the revolutionaries. In 1906, he made the first trip abroad as a magazine correspondent, visiting remote villages in Russia and sending dispatches for the *Outlook*. He wrote and published his first novel in 1906. He settled in Greenwich Village in 1907, joined the Socialist party, and contributed frequently to its paper, the *New York Call*. In 1914 he reported on World War I from the front lines. He later joined the Committee on Public Information, visited Russia again in 1917, during the provincial government, and wrote articles that were collected in *The Dark People: Russia's Crisis* (New York, 1918), *The Village: Russian Impressions* (New York, 1919), and *The Little Dark Man and Other Russian Sketches* (New York, 1925). His novel *His Family* (New York, 1917) won the first Pulitzer Price for fiction. He wrote an autobiography, *The Bridge: My Own Story* (New York, 1940). Died January 10, 1950, in New York City. *References*: Ernest Poole Papers, Dartmouth College Library, Hanover, N.H.; *DAB S4*; T. Frederick Keefer, *Ernest Poole* (New York, 1966); and *NCAB* 18:420.

POTSDAM CONFERENCE (1945). Summit meeting, held in Potsdam, near Berlin, from July 17 to August 2, 1945, and attended by Premier Joseph Stalin, President *Harry S. Truman, and Prime Minister Winston Churchill (replaced after July 28, 1945, by Prime Minister Clement Attlee). Concerned mostly with postwar Europe and the economic future of Germany, the conference established the military administration of Germany with a central Allied Control Council. The conference was the last of the Big Three meetings during World War II. The American delegation, disturbed by indications of Soviet noncooperation, left Potsdam in a pessimistic mood. *References*: Herbert Feis, *Between War and Peace: The Potsdam Conference* (Princeton, N.J., 1960); John Gimbel, "On the Implementation of the Potsdam Agreement: An Essay on U.S. Postwar Policy," *Political Science Quarterly* 87 (1972): 242–69; and Charles L. Mee, Jr., *Meeting at Potsdam* (New York, 1975).

POWERS, FRANCIS GARY (1929–1977). Pilot, born August 17, 1929, in Jenkins, Kentucky. Powers graduated from Milligan College (Tenn.). He joined the U.S. Air Force in 1950, went through flight training, and was commissioned second lieutenant in 1952. He resigned from the Air Force in 1956 and was then employed by the Central Intelligence Agency (CIA). He learned to fly the high-altitude reconnaissance aircraft and was assigned to the CIA's U–2 Squadron at Incerlik Air Force Base in Adana, Turkey. He flew his first mission over the Soviet Union in 1956 and continued to fly until 1960. He was shot down on May 1, 1960, over Sverdlovsk, in the *U–2 incident. He was held in prison, was put on a publicized trial, and was sentenced to ten years' imprisonment. He was exchanged in 1962 and returned to the United States. He was later an engineering test pilot for Lockheed aircraft and a helicopter traffic reporter for a California radio station. He wrote (with Curt Gentry) *Operation Overflight: The U–2 Spy Pilot Tells His Story for the First Time* (New York, 1970). Killed August 1, 1977, in a crash of his helicopter in Los Angeles, California. *References*: *EAIE*; *NYT*, August 2, 1977; *PolProf: Eisenhower*; and *PolProf: Kennedy*.

PREVENTION OF NUCLEAR WAR AGREEMENT (1973). Agreement between the United States of American and the Union of Soviet Socialist Republics on the prevention of nuclear war, signed in Washington on June 22, 1973. Viewed as a preliminary step toward preventing the outbreak of nuclear was or military conflict, it adopted an attitude of nuclear cooperation, with the two countries agreeing to make the removal of the danger of nuclear war and the use of nuclear weapons an objective of their policies, to practice restraint in their relations toward each other and toward all countries, and to pursue a policy dedicated to stability and peace. *Reference*: ACDA.

PRINCE, NERO (?–?). Servant, from Marlborough, Massachusetts. Prince was one of the founders of the Freemason's African Grand Lodge in Boston in 1791 and became its second grandmaster in 1807. He sailed to Russia in 1810 and worked as a butler for a noble family at the imperial court and subsequently for the tsar. His second wife, **NANCY GARDNER PRINCE** (1799–?), born in Massachusetts, joined him in Russia in 1824 and remained there until 1833. She wrote *A Narrative of the Life and Travels of Mrs. Nancy Prince Written by Herself* (Boston, 1856), an account of black servants' life in Russia from 1824 to 1833. She established a sewing shop, was active in the interdenominational Russian Bible Society, and helped organize an orphanage in St. Petersburg. She left Russia in 1833 because of ill health. Nero Prince died before 1835. *References*: *A Black Woman's Odyssey through Russia and and Jamaica: The Narrative of Nancy Prince*, introduction by Ronald G. Walters (New York, 1990); and Charles H. Wesley, *Prince Hall: Life and Legacy* (Washington, D.C., 1977).

PURINGTON, CHESTER WELLS (1871–1923). Mining engineer, born October 27, 1871, in Boston. Purington graduated from Harvard University. He investigated gold deposits in various places and served with the U.S. Geological Survey. In 1897, he traveled in Russia. He became impressed with its possibilities and made several examinations of gold, iron, and copper deposits in the Ural Mountains. He was a consulting engineer in Denver from 1902 to 1907. He returned to Russia in 1907, investigating mining properties in far eastern Siberia for British companies, and was back in Russia in 1911, examining mines in various parts of Russia as a consulting engineer for Lena Goldfields of London. He became the acknowledged leader of Western mining engineers in Russia before World War I. He organized the American Committee of Engineers in London during World War I and then served with the U.S. military intelligence in Washington, D.C. He again returned to Siberia in 1919, obtained concessions of gold placer properties on the Sea of Okhotsk in Siberia, and made many trips inspecting the area, but he had to postpone any activity because of the political conditions. He then settled in Yokohama, Japan, waiting for the improvement of conditions in Siberia. Killed September 1, 1923, during the earthquake in Yokohama. *References*: Chester Wells Purington Papers, Yale University Library, New Haven, Conn.; *Mining and Metallurgy* 4 (November 1923): 578–79; and *WWIN*.

R

RADIO LIBERTY. Covertly founded by the Central Intelligence Agency (CIA) Clandestine Service in 1951 as Radio Liberation, based in Munich, West Germany. With a transmitter in Lampertheim, it went on the air on March 1, 1953, broadcasting to the Soviet Union. It carried news, information, and entertainment otherwise denied to the radio audiences by the Communist authorities. Its transmissions were jammed by the Soviet Union. Another transmitter began operating in Taipei in 1955, beaming to eastern parts of Siberia and the maritime provinces of the Soviet Union, and another in Playa de Pals, Spain, in 1959. The name was changed to Radio Liberty in 1964. CIA support was terminated in 1973, after which the station was openly funded by the U.S. government through the Board for International Broadcasting. It was merged with Radio Free Europe in 1976. *References*: *EAIE*; Robert T. Holt, *Radio Free Europe* (Minneapolis, 1959); Sig Michelson, *America's Other Voice: The Story of Radio Free Europe and Radio Liberty* (New York, 1983): and Allan Andrew Michie, *Voices through the Iron Curtain: The Radio Free Europe Story* (New York, 1963).

RB–47 INCIDENT (1960). A U.S. Air Force RB–47 reconnaissance plane was shot down by a Soviet fighter over international waters in the Barents Sea, near Kola Peninsula, on July 1, 1960. Four of the six crewmen were killed. The two survivors were captured by the Soviets and became the center of a major diplomatic confrontation between the United States and the Soviet Union. They were finally released on January 21, 1961, as part of a spy exchange. *References*: *EAIE*; *MERSH*; and William L.White, *The Little Toy Dog: The Story of the Two RB–47 Flyers* (New York, 1962).

REAGAN, RONALD WILSON (1911–   ). President of the United States, born February 6, 1911, in Tampico, Illinois. Reagan graduated from Eureka College (Ill.). He worked as a sports announcer for radio stations in Davenport and Des Moines, Iowa, and then had a film career in Hollywood until 1964. He was governor of California from 1967 until 1975 and president of the United

States from 1981 until 1989. He initially adopted a hostile attitude toward the Soviet Union, which he described as the "Evil Empire," calling for the rejection of the SALT II treaty and endorsing the *Zero Option in 1981. He proposed the Strategic Defense Initiative ("Star Wars") to provide the United States with a protective shield from nuclear attack, but he called for arms reduction rather than arms limitation and initiated the Strategic Arms Reduction Talks (*START) in 1982. Capitalizing on the changes occurring in the Soviet Union, he met with General Secretary Mikhail S. Gorbachev in Geneva in 1985, in Reykjavik in 1986, in Washington in 1987, and in Moscow in 1988. He signed the *INF Treaty to remove all intermediate-range nuclear missiles from Europe. The breakthroughs in arms control, the new cooperation in settling Third World disputes, the overall relaxation in tensions, and the rapport between the two leaders led to the thawing of the Cold War. He wrote *An American Life* (New York, 1990). *References*: Coral Bell, *The Reagan Paradox: U.S. Foreign Policy in the 1980s* (New Brunswick, N.J., 1990); Lou Cannon, *President Reagan: The Role of a Lifetime* (New York, 1991); A. Dallin and G. Lapidus, "Reagan and the Russians: American Policy toward the Soviet Union," in Kenneth R. Oye, Robert J. Lieber, and Donald Rothchild, eds., *Eagle Resurgent? The Reagan Era in American Foreign Policy* (Boston, 1987), pp. 193–254; John Lewis Gaddis, "The Reagan Administration and Soviet-American Relations," in David E. Kyvig, ed., *Reagan and the World* (New York, 1990), pp. 17–32; Michael Mandelbaum and Strobe Talbott, *Reagan and the Russians* (New York, 1984); Michael Schaller, *Reckoning with Reagan: America and Its President in the 1980s* (New York, 1992): and Strobe Talbott, *Deadly Gambits: The Reagan Administration and the Stalemate in Nuclear Arms Control* (New York, 1984).

RECOGNITION ISSUE. The United States refused to recognize the Soviet Union from 1917 to 1933. Recognition was finally accorded the Soviet Union in 1933 only because of the realities of the Great Depression. The U.S. government hoped that recognition might bring economic opportunities and a large volume of trade with the Soviet Union. The United States also developed a common interest with the Soviet Union for the need for resist the growing power of Japan and Germany. Furthermore, the policy of nonrecognition did not achieve its objectives of changing the internal configuration or the external behavior of the Soviet Union. The agreement establishing formal diplomatic relations was signed on November 17, 1933. (*See also* Roosevelt-Litvinov Agreements). *References*: Robert E. Bowers, "American Diplomacy, the 1933 Wheat Conference, and Recognition of the Soviet Union," *Agricultural History* 49 (1966): 39–52; Melvin Allan Goodman, "The Diplomacy of Non-Recognition: Soviet-American Relations, 1917–1933" (Ph.D. diss., Indiana University, 1972); John Richman, *The United States and the Soviet Union: The Decision to Recognize* (Raleigh, N.C., 1980); and John Hoff Wilson, "American Business and the Recognition of the Soviet Union," *Social Science Quarterly* 52 (1971): 349–68.

REED, JOHN (1887–1920). Journalist, born October 2, 1887, in Portland, Oregon. Reed graduated from Harvard University. He joined the staff of *American Magazine* in 1911 and the *Masses* in 1913. He was sent to Mexico by *Metropolitan* magazine in 1914 and was war correspondent to Europe after the outbreak of World War I. He wrote *The War in Eastern Europe* (New York, 1916). He married *Louise Bryant in 1917, went to Russia, and was a witness to the Russian Revolution in Petrograd. An enthusiastic supporter of the Bolsheviks, he became a close friend of V. I. Lenin and wrote much of the Bolshevik propaganda intended for the Germans. Indicted for sedition because of his articles in the *Masses*, he returned to the United States in 1918 to help in his defense and was acquitted. He wrote *Ten Days That Shook the World* (New York, 1919), about the events in Russia in 1917. He helped found the Communist Labor Party in 1919, headed the party, and was editor of its journal, *Voice of Labor*. He was back in Soviet Russia in 1919, took an active role in the Second Congress of the Comintern, and was a member of its delegation to the Baku Congress of the Peoples of the East in 1920. Died October 17, 1920, in Moscow. His ashes were buried in the Kremlin wall. *References*: John Reed Papers, Houghton Library, Harvard University, Cambridge, Mass.; *DAB*; Virginia Gardner, ''John Reed and Lenin: Some Insights Based on Mss Collection at Harvard,''*Science and Society* 31 (1967): 388–403; Barbara Gelb, *So Short a Time: A Biography of John Reed and Louise Bryant* (New York, 1973); Granville Hicks, *John Reed: The Making of a Revolutionary* (New York, 1936); Eric Homberger, *John Reed* (Manchester, 1990): Eric Homberger and John Biggart, eds., *John Reed and the Russian Revolution: Uncollected Articles, Letters, and Speeches on Russia* (London, 1992); and Robert A. Rosenstone, *Romantic Revolutionary: A Biography of John Reed* (New York, 1975).

RESWICK, WILLIAM (1889–1954). Journalist, born in the Ukraine and came to the United States as a youth. Reswick graduated from New York University Law School and also studied at the American Academy of Dramatic Arts. He began his newspaper career on the *Warheit* and later went to the *Jewish Morning Journal*. He returned to Soviet Russia in 1922 with the *American Relief Administration. He wrote *I Dreamt Revolution* (Chicago, 1952). In 1923, he became correspondent for International News Service, was later chief of the Moscow bureau of the Associated Press, and covered the Soviet Union until 1934. He also did free-lance writing from Moscow and was associated in several business undertakings there. He was on the staff of the *Jewish Daily Forward* from 1934 to 1941 and joined the *Day* in 1942, where he was employed until his death. Died June 2, 1954, in New York City. *Reference*: *NYT*, June 3, 1954.

REYKJAVIK SUMMIT (1986). Summit meeting President *Ronald Reagan and General Secretary Mikhail S. Gorbachev in Reykjavik, Iceland, on October 11–12, 1986. The talks were to be a discussion on setting the agenda for a summit in the United States. Instead, they turned into intense and detailed negotiations over arms control. A startling plan to reduce nuclear arsenals and, after a time, to destroy them was set aside when President Reagan refused Gorbachev's demand to postpone the Strategic Defense Initiative ("Star Wars"), and the talks collapsed. *References*: E. Haley, "You Could Have Said Yes: Lessons from Reykjavik," *Orbis* 31 (1987): 75–97; and James Schlesinger, "Reykjavik and Revelations: A Turn of the Tide?" *Foreign Affairs* 65 (1986): 426–46.

RICHARDSON, WILDS PRESTON (1861–1929). Army officer, born March 20, 1861, in Hunt County, Texas. Richardson graduated from the U.S. Military Academy in 1884 and was commissioned second lieutenant in the infantry. He served on garrison duty in California and on frontier duty in Apache country and western Nebraska, was instructor in tactics at West Point from 1892 to 1897, served in Alaska from 1897 to 1917, and was president of the U.S. Alaska Roads Commission after 1905 in charge of the government's construction project for Alaska. He commanded the 78th Brigade of the 39th Division in France during World War I. In 1919, he commanded the U.S. forces at Murmansk in Northern Russia, part of an Allied operation aimed at protecting ports and supplies against Bolshevik forces. He retired, with the rank of colonel, in 1920. Died May 20, 1929, in Washington, D.C. *References*: Wilds P. Richardson Papers, U.S. Army Military History Institute, Carlisle Barracks, Pa.; *DAB*; and *WWWA*.

RIDDLE, JOHN WALLACE (1864–1941). Diplomat, born July 12, 1864, in Philadelphia and grew up in St. Paul, Minnesota. Riddle graduated from Harvard University and Columbia University Law School and studied at the Ecole des Sciences Politique and Ecole de France (Paris). He was secretary of legation in Constantinople from 1893 to 1901, secretary of embassy in St. Petersburg from 1901 to 1903, and chargé d'affaires in1903. He presented to the Russian foreign office a petition from the Jews of America deploring the Kishinev pogrom of May 1903, but the Russian government refused to accept the document. He was diplomatic agent and consul general in Egypt from 1903 to 1905, U.S. minister to Rumania and Serbia in 1905–1906, and U.S. ambassador to Russia from 1907 to 1909. Through clever handling and his familiarity with the Russian language and customs, he obtained permission for American Jews to visit their relatives in Russia. He served in the military intelligence division of the general staff of the Army War College during World War I. He was U.S. ambassador to Argentina from 1922 until his retirement in 1925. Died December 8, 1941, in Farmington, Connecticut. *References*: *DADH*; *NCAB* 30:288; and *NYT*, December 9, 1941.

RIGA AXIOMS. Worked out by U.S. foreign service officers in Riga, Latvia, in the 1920s, the axioms interpreted Soviet behavior as based on Marxist ideology and seeking world conquest. Based on the assumptions that the Soviet Union was a revolutionary state and that Soviet foreign policy was rooted in ideology, they concluded that negotiations with the Soviets were pointless and even dangerous. *References*: Daniel F. Harrington, "Kennan, Bohlen, and the Riga Axioms," *DH* 2 (1978): 423–37; and Daniel Yergin, *The Shattered Peace: The Origins of the Cold War and the National Security State* (Boston, 1977).

ROBESON, PAUL (1898–1976). Singer and actor, born April 9, 1898, in Princeton, New Jersey. Robeson graduated from Rutgers University and Columbia University Law School and was admitted to the bar in 1923. He then turned to the theater, joined the Provincetown Players in 1924, and became a prominent actor and singer, appearing on Broadway, throughout the United States, in England and Europe, and in motion pictures. His political beliefs led him to make several trips to the Soviet Union, which he visited in 1934–1935, 1936–1937, 1949, 1958–1959, 1960, and 1961. He wrote an autobiography, *Here I Stand* (New York, 1958). Died January 23, 1976, in Philadelphia. *References*: Robeson Family Archives, Moorland-Spingarn Research Center, Howard University, Washington, D.C.; *CA*; Lenwood G. Davis, *A Paul Robeson Research Guide: A Selected, Annotated Bibliography* (Westport, Conn., 1982); Martin Baumal Duberman, *Paul Robeson* (New York, 1988): *NCAB* 59:233; *NYT*, January 24, 1976; and Susan Robeson, *The Whole World in His Hands: A Pictorial Biography of Paul Robeson* (Secaucus, N.J., 1981).

ROBINS, RAYMOND (1873–1954). Social worker, born September 17, 1873, in Staten Island, New York, and grew up in Ohio, Kentucky, and Florida. Robins graduated from Columbian (later George Washington) University and was admitted to the bar in 1894. He practiced law in San Francisco, then joined the gold rush in Alaska, and remained in Nome, Alaska, until 1901. He settled in Chicago, was superintendent of the Municipal Lodging House from1902 to 1905 and concurrently headworker of Northwestern University Settlement, and was a member of the Chicago Board of Education from 1906 to 1909. He participated in The Men and Religion Forward Movement from 1911 to 1913 and was then involved with the Progressive Party. He was deputy commissioner, with the rank of major in the U.S. Army, of the American Red Cross mission to Russia in 1917 and then was commissioner, with the rank of lieutenant colonel in the U.S. Army, in 1918. He observed from close range the events of the Russian Revolution and developed a remarkably cordial working relationship with V. I. Lenin and Leon Trotsky. He also traveled extensively in Russia, investigating economic and social conditions. He returned to the United States in 1918 and agitated for recognition of the Russian government by the United States. He returned to the Soviet Union in 1933, studying mass production and primary education. Died September 26, 1954, in Chinsegut Hill, New York. *References*: Raymond Robins Papers, State Historical Society of Wisconsin, Madison; Raymond Robins Papers, University of Florida Library, Gainesville; William Hard, *Raymond Robins' Own Story* (New York, 1920); Anne Vincent Meilburger, *Efforts of Raymond Robins toward the Recognition of Soviet Russia and the Outlawry of War, 1917–1933* (Washington, D.C., 1958); *NCAB* 42:11; Neil Victor Salzman, *Reform and Revolution: The Life and Times of Raymond Robins* (Kent, Ohio, 1991);

and William A. Williams, "Raymond Robins and Russian-American Relations, 1917–1938" (Ph.D. diss., University of Wisconsin, 1950).

ROBINSON, GEROID TANQUARY (1892–1971). Historian, born June 21, 1892, in Chase City, Virginia. Robinson graduated from Stanford and Columbia universities. He served in the U.S. Army during World War I. He was then a member of the editorial board of the *Dial* and the *Freeman*. He was a teacher of history at Columbia University from 1924 to 1931 and a member of the faculty of political science after 1931. He was in the Soviet Union from 1924 to 1927, conducting research and studying the Russian agrarian system, and wrote *Rural Russia under the Old Regime: A History of the Landlord-Peasant World and a Prologue to the Peasant Revolution of 1917* (New York, 1932). He was again in the Soviet Union in 1937. He was chief of the Russian Division of the Research and Analysis Branch of the Office of Strategic Services during World War II. He was founder of the Russian Institute at Columbia University in 1946 and its first director until 1951 and was professor of history from 1950 until his retirement in 1960. Died March 30, 1971, in New York City. *References*: Geroid T. Robinson Papers, Columbia University Library, New York City; and John Shelton Curtiss, ed., *Essays in Russian and Soviet History, in Honor of Geroid Tanquary Robinson* (New York, 1963).

ROBINSON, ROBERT (1906–   ). Toolmaker, born June 22, 1906, in Kingston, Jamaica, and grew up in Cuba. Robinson studied toolmaking in Cuba and then came to the United States. He worked for Ford Motor Company in Detroit from 1927 to 1930. He was sent to Russia by Ford in 1930 to work at the Stalingrad tractor factory. He later worked at the First State Ball Bearing Plant in Moscow. He became a Soviet citizen and was elected to the Moscow city soviet. He left the Soviet Union in 1974 and lived in Uganda until 1980, when he returned to the United States. He wrote (with Jonathan Slevin) *Black on Red: My 44 Years inside the Soviet Union: An Autobiography* (Washington, D.C., 1988).

ROCKHILL, WILLIAM WOODVILLE (1854–1914). Diplomat, born April 1854 in Philadelphia. Rockhill graduated from the Ecole Speciale Militaire de St. Cyr, France, and served in the French Army in Algeria until 1876. He was second secretary in the U.S. legation in Peking, secretary of legation from 1884 to 1886, and chargé d'affaires in Korea in 1886–1887. He left the foreign service in 1888 and made scientific expeditions in Mongolia and Tibet. He returned to the foreign service in 1893, serving as chief clerk in the State Department in 1893–1894, third assistant secretary of state from 1894 to 1896, and assistant secretary of state in 1896–1897. He was U.S. minister and consul general to Greece, Romania, and Serbia from 1896 to 1899, director of the International Bureau of the American Republics from 1899 to 1905, and U.S. minister to China from 1905 to 1909. He was U.S. ambassador to Russia in 1910–1911.

His mission to Russia was especially fortuitous because of Russia's activities in East Asia and his knowledge of the area. He was U.S. ambassador to Turkey from 1911 to 1913. Died December 8, 1914, in Honolulu, on his way to China. *References*: *DAB*; *DADH*; *NCAB* 8:129; *NYT*, December 9, 1914; and Paul A. Varg, *Open Door Diplomat: The Life of W. W. Rockhill* (Urbana, Ill., 1952).

ROOSEVELT, FRANKLIN DELANO (1882–1945). President of the United States, born January 30, 1882, in Hyde Park, New York. Roosevelt graduated from Harvard University and Columbia University Law School. He served in the New York state senate from 1911 to 1913, was assistant secretary of the navy from 1913 to 1920, governor of New York from 1929 to 1933, and president of the United States from 1933 until his death. He negotiated the *Roosevelt-Litvinov agreements, which led to the reestablishment of relations between the United States and the Soviet Union in 1933, although the relations soon deteriorated. After the German invasion of the Soviet Union in 1941, he authorized *Lend-Lease aid to the Soviets and sought cooperation with the Soviet Union in the war against the Axis. He conferred with Joseph Stalin at the *Teheran (1943) and the *Yalta (1945) summit conferences, but he did not realize the extent of Soviet ambitions, which led later to the Cold War. Died April 12, 1945, in Warm Springs, Georgia. *References*: Franklin D. Roosevelt Papers, Franklin D. Roosevelt Library, Hyde Park, N.Y.; Edward M. Bennett, *Franklin D. Roosevelt and the Search for Security: American-Soviet Relations, 1933–1939* (Wilmington, Del., 1985); Edward M. Bennett, *Franklin D. Roosevelt and the Search for Victory: American-Soviet Relations, 1939–1945* (Wilmington, Del., 1990); *DAB S3*; Robert Dallek, *Franklin D. Roosevelt and American Foreign Policy, 1932–1945* (New York, 1979); William P. Gerberding, "Franklin D. Roosevelt's Conception of the Soviet Union in World Politics" (Ph.D. diss., University of Chicago, 1959); Warren F. Kimball, *The Juggler: Franklin Roosevelt as Wartime Statesman* (Princeton, N.J., 1991); and Robert J. Maddox, "Roosevelt and Stalin: The Final Days," *Continuity: A Journal of History* 6 (Spring 1983); 113–22.

ROOSEVELT-LITVINOV AGREEMENTS (1933). Agreement signed in 1933 by President *Franklin D. Roosevelt and Soviet Foreign Minister Maxim Litvinov. It established full diplomatic relations between the United States and the Soviet Union. In return, the Soviet Union pledged to grant freedom of worship to Americans in the Soviet Union, to discontinue propaganda and subversive activities in the United States, and to pay at least seventy-five million dollars additional interest on loans for Soviet purchases in the United States. The issue of Soviet debts remained unresolved and was postponed to a later date. The Soviet government did not live up to the pledges made in the agreement, leading to the widely believed notion that "you can't trust the Russians." *References*: Donald G. Bishop, *The Roosevelt-Litvinov Agreements: The American View* (Syracuse, N.Y., 1965); and *DADH*.

ROOT MISSION TO RUSSIA (1917). Formally, the Special Diplomatic Commission of the United States to Russia, created by President *Woodrow Wilson, headed by Elihu Root, and dispatched to the provisional government of Russia in 1917. Other members included *Charles Crane, *John Mott, and *Charles Edward Russell. Concerned that the provisional Russian government would reach a separate peace with Germany, the mission was to assess conditions and needs in Russia, assure the new Russian government of U.S. support, and confer on how the United States could best cooperate in the prosecution of war. The mission was unsuccessful, producing no results. It submitted its final report to the president on August 19, 1917. *References*: Laton Earl Ingraham, ''The Root Mission to Russia, 1917'' (Ph.D. diss., Louisiana State University, 1970); John W. Long and C. Howard Hopkins, ''American Jew and the Root Mission to Russia in 1917,'' *American Jewish History* 49 (1980): 342–54; *MERSH*; Elihu Root, *The Mission to Russia: Political Addresses*, ed. Robert Bacon and James Brown Scott (Cambridge, Mass., 1918); Ronald Radosh, ''American Labor and the Root Commission to Russia,'' *Studies on the Left* 3 (1962): 34–47; and Zosa Szajkowski, ''Jews and the Elihu Root Mission to Russia, 1917,'' *Proceedings of the American Academy for Jewish Research* 37 (1969): 57–116.

ROPES, ERNEST C. (1877–1949). Economist, born in Brooklyn, New York, and grew up in St. Petersburg, Russia, from 1884 and 1892. Ropes graduated from Columbia University. He was then involved in the publishing and bookselling business and was later associated with the paper and pulp industry. He was secretary of the *Young Men's Christian Association (YMCA) in Russia and Estonia from 1919 to 1922 and was attached to the American Expeditionary Forces in North Russia. He joined the U.S. Department of Commerce in 1923 and served as chief of the Russian Unit of the Bureau of Foreign and Domestic Commerce until his retirement in 1947, becoming a leading authority on Soviet-American trade. He made a trip to the Soviet Union for Remington Rand Company in 1928 and visited Moscow in 1946 to confer with Soviet officials on exports to the United States. He was chairman of the board of the American Russian Institute. He was editor and compiler of *Russian Economic Notes* from 1928 to 1940 and wrote many reports issued by the Bureau of Foreign and Domestic Commerce. Died October 13, 1949, in Stratford, Connecticut. *References*: *Encyclopedia of American Biography* (New York, 1952), 23:238–40; and *NYT*, October 14, 1949.

ROPES, WILLIAM (1784–1869). Merchant, born in Salem. Ropes was a clerk in his father's store. He made his first voyage as supercargo on the bark *Mary* to Calcutta in 1806 and another voyage to Canton in 1809. He then went into business in Boston. He started *William Ropes and Company in St. Petersburg in 1832. He settled in London from 1837 until his retirement in 1842. The business in St. Petersburg was carried on by his son, **WILLIAM HOOPER ROPES** (?–1891), who went with his father to St. Petersburg in 1830 and was educated and trained in Russia. He retired in 1889. Died in Tenby, South Wales. *References*: Ropes Family Papers, Baker Library, Harvard University, Cambridge, Mass.; and Harriet Ropes's Cabot, "The Early Years of William Ropes and Company in St. Petersburg," *American Neptune* 23 (1963): 131–39.

ROSEN, JOSEPH A. (1878–1949). Agronomist, born February 15, 1878, in Moscow and apparently grew up in Tula. Rosen attended Moscow University. Suspected of revolutionary activities, he was exiled to Siberia. He escaped, made his way to Germany, and studied at the University of Heidelberg. He came to the United States in 1903, graduated from the Michigan Agricultural College (East Lansing), and attended the University of Minnesota. From 1908 to 1912, he was engaged by the provincial local board of Ekaterinoslav as head of the American Agricultural Bureau in Minneapolis to collect relevant American farming methods with a view to their introduction in Russia and produced ten comprehensive studies. He also obtained large quantities of seeds and implements to be sold to Russian peasants and sold Russian beet seed in the United States. He was agronomist and principal of the Baron de Hirsch Agricultural School in Woodbine, New Jersey, from 1914 to 1916, resumed activities for Ekaterinoslav from 1916 to 1918, and became the New York representative of a Petrograd bank in 1918. In 1921, he joined the *American Relief Administration in Soviet Russia as a representative of the Joint Distribution Committee. In 1922, he took to Soviet Russia a number of American agriculturists and specialists in tractor farming, who acted as traveling instructors to acquaint the Russian farmers with American methods. Concurrently, he arranged for the first sizable shipment of American tractors to be sent to Soviet Russia. His system of centralized repair facilities later served as a prototype for the tractor stations of collectivized Soviet agriculture. He directed the *American Jewish Joint Agricultural Corporation and spent much of his time in the Soviet Union until 1937, when he returned to the United States. He later conducted a resettlement study in British Guiana and directed a resettlement project in the Dominican Republic. Died April 2, 1949, in New York City. *References*: Joseph A. Rosen Papers, Yivo Institute, New York City; *DAB S5*; Dana G. Dalrymple, "Joseph A. Rosen and Early Russian Studies of American Agriculture," *Agricultural History* 38 (1964): 157–60; *NYT*, April 2, 1949; and Zosa Szajowski, *The Mirage of American Jewish Aid in Soviet Russia, 1917–1939* (New York, 1977), ch. 10.

ROSENBERG, JAMES N. (1874–1970). Lawyer and communal leader, born in Allegheny City, Pennsylvania. Rosenberg graduated from Columbia University and Columbia Law School. He worked with the food program of the *American Relief Administration in Soviet Russia and was chairman of the American Joint Distribution Committee in Europe in 1921. In 1924, he founded and was chairman of the *American Jewish Joint Agricultural Corporation, and organization that moved Soviet Jews from the ghetto to the soil in the Crimea. He founded the Soviet for Jewish Farm Settlements in Russia in 1926, directing the population transfer of Jews to Birobidzhan. He wrote *On the Steppes: A Russian Diary* (New York, 1927). He practiced law until 1947, when he retired to devote himself to painting. He wrote *Painter's Self-Portrait* (New York, 1958). Died July 21, 1970, in White Plains, New York. *References*: Maxwell D. Geismer, ed., *Unfinished Business: James N. Rosenberg Papers* (Mamaroneck, N.Y., 1967); *NYT*, July 22, 1970; and *WWWA*.

ROSETT, JOSHUA (1875–1940). Physician, born January 22, 1875, in Ekaterinburg, Russia. Rosett came to the United States in 1891 and became a naturalized citizen in 1896. He graduated from the school of medicine of the University of Maryland. He practiced medicine in Baltimore from 1903 to 1917. In 1918, he was sent by the Committee on Public Information to Vladivostok. There he was first loaned to the War Trade Board to take stock of the immense quantities of goods that had accumulated at that port and was then loaned to the American Red Cross to help in controlling the epidemics of typhoid fever, typhus, and dysentery raging in Siberia. He wrote a pamphlet on the Kolchak counterrevolutionary government. He was instructor in neurology at the College of Physicians and Surgeons of Columbia University in 1919–1920, assistant professor from 1920 to 1935, and professor from 1935 until his death. He was also scientific director of the Brain Research Foundation, Incorporated. Died April 1, 1940, in Merida, Yucatan, Mexico. *Reference*: NCAB 30:222.

ROSS, EDWARD ALSWORTH (1866–1951). Sociologist, born December 12, 1866, in Virden, Illinois, and grew up in Davenport, Cedar Rapids, and Marion, Iowa. Ross graduated from Coe College (Cedar Rapids), studied in Germany, and graduated from Johns Hopkins University. He was professor at Stanford University from 1893 to 1900, at the University of Nebraska from 1901 to 1906, and at the University of Wisconsin from 1906 until his retirement in 1937. He went to Russia in 1917 to report on the revolution. In several magazine articles, in a report to President *Woodrow Wilson, and in the books *Russia in Upheavel* (New York, 1918), *The Russian Bolshevik Revolution* (New York, 1921), and *The Russian Soviet Republic* (New York, 1923), he presented the Bolshevik Revolution in a favorable light. Died July 22, 1951, in Madison, Wisconsin. *References*: Edward A. Ross Papers, State Historical Society of Wisconsin, Madison; *DAB S5*; *NCAB* 18:98; and Julius Weinberg, *Edward Alsworth Ross and the Sociology of Progressivism* (Madison, Wis., 1972).

ROSS, ROBERT (1905–1972). Actor, born in Butte, Montana. Ross went to the Soviet Union in 1928 and was the first African-American to become a Soviet citizen. He played the roles of African-Americans and Africans in Soviet motion pictures, appearing in one of the first Soviet films, *Circus*, in *Uncle Tom's Cabin*, and in *The End of Christie Tucker*. His last film was *Africa Awakes from Sleep*. Died April 7, 1972, in Moscow. *Reference*: New World Review 40 (Spring 1972): 60.

ROWNY, EDWARD LEON (1917–   ). Army officer and government official, born April 3, 1917, in Baltimore. Rowny graduated from Johns Hopkins University and the U.S. Military Academy and was commissioned second lieutenant in the corps of engineers in 1941. He later graduated from Yale and American universities. He was chairman of the North Atlantic Treaty Organization (NATO) military committee working group on the *Mutual and Balanced Force Reductions (MBFR) in Belgium until 1973 and was a representative of the Joint Chiefs of Staff to the *SALT in Geneva from 1973 to 1979. He retired from the army in 1979. He was chief negotiator of the U.S. Arms Control and Disarmament Agency, head of the U.S. delegation, with the rank of ambassador, to the strategic arms control negotiations from 1981 to 1985, and special assistant to the president and secretary of state for arms control from 1985 to 1990. He wrote a memoir, *It Takes One to Tango* (McLean, Va., 1992). *References*: Ronald Brownstein and Nina Easton, *Reagan's Ruling Class: Portraits of the President's Top 100 Officials* (Washington, D.C., 1982), pp. 511–17; and *WWA*.

RUGGLES, JAMES A. (1869–1948). Army officer, born April 1, 1869, in Illinois. Ruggles was commissioned first lieutenant in the infantry in 1898. He served in the U.S. Army in the Philippines and Europe. He was chief of the U.S. military mission in Russia and military attaché at the U.S. embassy in Russia, engaging in counterintelligence work. He retired in 1922, with the rank of colonel. He later served as adjutant of Hollywood American Legion Post 43. Died August 14, 1948, in Los Angeles. *Reference*: *NYT*, August 15, 1948.

RUHL, ARTHUR BROWN (1876–1935). Author, born October 1, 1876, in Rockford, Illinois. Ruhl graduated from Harvard University. He was a reporter for the *New York Evening Sun* from 1899 to 1904 and a special reporter for *Collier's* from 1904 to 1914. He reported from Mexico and then from France, Belgium, and Central Europe in 1914–1915. He was in Russia in 1916–1917 and recorded his experiences in *White Nights and Other Russian Impressions* (New York, 1917). He was in France in 1918 and in the Baltic states in 1919 and was correspondent of the *New York Evening Post* in the Baltic states in 1920–1921. He served with the *American Relief Administration in Russia in 1922–1923. He was later involved in various repertorial and literary pursuits. Died June 7, 1935, in Queens, New York. *References*: *DAB S1*; and *WWWA*.

RUKEYSER, WALTER ARNOLD (1895–1960). Mining engineer, born October 19, 1895, in New York City, Rukeyser graduated from Princeton University and Columbia University School of Mining. He served in the U.S. Navy during World War I. He was a consulting engineer in New York City after 1922, becoming a specialist in the mining of asbestos. He worked in the Soviet Union as a consulting and supervising engineer to the Soviet Asbestos Mining Trust in connection with asbestos production in the Ural Mountains from 1928 to 1930. He wrote *Working for the Soviets: An American Engineer in Russia* (New York,

1932). He served in the U.S. Navy during World War II, was involved in mining developments in Canada after World War II, and was a consultant to Yugoslav officials on the development of asbestos products in the early 1950s. Died October 16, 1960, in Montreal, Canada. *References*: *NYT*, October 19, 1960.

RUSSELL, CHARLES EDWARD (1860–1941). Journalist and author, born September 25, 1860, in Davenport, Iowa. After 1881, Russell held a succession of jobs as reporter or editor in Davenport, Minneapolis, Detroit, and New York City. He was city editor of the *New York World* from 1894 to 1897, managing editor of the *New York American* from 1897 to 1900, and publisher of the *Chicago American* from 1900 to 1902. He wrote for *Everybody's*, *Hampton's*, and *Cosmopolitan* magazines. He joined the Socialist party in 1908 and was Socialist candidate for governor of New York in 1910 and 1912, for mayor of New York City in 1913, and for U.S. senator in 1914. He was a member of the *Root Mission to Russia in 1917. He was expelled from the Socialist party in 1917. He wrote *Unchained Russia* (New York, 1918) and an autobiography, *Bare Hands and Stone Walls: Some Recollections of a Sideline Reformer* (New York, 1933). He later wrote poetry and biography. Died April 23, 1941, in Washington, D.C. *References*: Charles Edward Russell Papers, Manuscript Division, Library of Congress; *DAB S3*; and *NCAB* A:106.

RUSSELL, JOHN MILLER (1768–1840). Merchant. Russell was appointed U.S. consul at St. Petersburg in 1794. He arrived there in the summer of 1795, but the Russian government refused to receive him. In 1795, he became a partner in the St. Petersburg merchant house of Bulkeley Russell and Company, presumably the first American to undertake such a venture in Russia.

RUSSIAN-AMERICAN CONVENTION (1824). Convention regarding navigation, fishing, and trading, and establishments of the northwest coast of America, signed on April 17, 1824, in St. Petersburg. The convention established the boundary between the United States and Russian-America and permitted virtually open U.S. access to both the territorial waters and the shoreline of Russian-America. *References*: Anatole G. Maxour, "The Russian-American and Anglo-Russian Conventions, 1824–1825: An Interpretation," *Pacific Historical Review* 14 (1945): 303–10; and Hunter Miller, ed., *Treaties and Other International Acts of the United States of America* (Washington, D.C., 1933), 3:151–62.

RUSSIAN-AMERICAN INDUSTRIAL CORPORATION (RAIC). Organized in June 1922 by the Amalgamated Clothing Workers of America (ACWA) for the purpose of building clothing factories in Soviet Russia. Several factories were set up, but the Soviet authorities took over full control before 1928. *References*: Robert W. Dunn, "Labor Helped Russian Reconstruction," *New World*

Review 38 (Winter 1970): 153–58; and Zosa Szajowski, *The Mirage of American Jewish Aid in Soviet Russia, 1917–1939* (New York, 1977), ch. 14.

RUSSIAN-AMERICAN TELEGRAPH EXPEDITION (1865–1867). Western Union Telegraph Company decided in 1865 to build an overland cable to Europe via the Bering Strait. Surveys were conducted in Kamchatka and Chukotka. The project was cancelled in 1866, when the Atlantic cable was completed. *References*: Western Union Telegraph Expedition Papers, Smithsonian Institution, Washington, D.C.; Philip H. Ault, "The (Almost) Russian-American Telegraph," *American Heritage* 26 (June 1975): 12–15, 92–98; Rosemary Neering, *Continental Dash: The Russian-American Telegraph* (Ganges, B.C., 1989); and Charles Vevier, "The Collins Overland Line," *Pacific Historical Review* 28 (1959): 237–53.

RUSSIAN-AMERICAN TREATY OF 1832. Treaty of navigation and commerce, signed on December 18, 1832, in St. Petersburg. The treaty extended the principle of the most-favored-nation status to the commercial ships of Russia and the United States, with each nation to enjoy free port calls, favorable customs duties, and other advantages. Both countries pledged to accord the other the same preferences in trade that might in the future be extended to other nations. The treaty was in force until 1913. Because of the Russian government's ill treatment of American Jews visiting Russia and because of anti-Semitic pogroms, the U.S. Congress forced President William Howard Taft's administration to abrogate the treaty as of January 1, 1913. *References*: Nikolai N. Bolkhovitinov, "American-Russian Rapproachment and the Commercial Treaty of 1832," ed. J. Dane Hartgrobe, *Soviet Studies in History* 19 (Winter 1980–81): 3–92; Naomi W. Cohen, "The Abrogation of the Russo-American Treaty of 1832," *Jewish Social Studies* 25 (1–63): 3–41; Clifford L. Egan, "Pressure Groups, the Department of State, and the Abrogation of the Russian-American Treaty of 1832," *Proceedings of the American Philosophical Society* 115 (1971): 328–34; and Hunter Miller, ed., *Treaties and Other International Acts of the United States of America* (Washington, D.C., 3:723–34.

RUSSIAN-AMERICAN TREATY OF 1867. See ALASKA PURCHASE

RUSSIAN BUREAU (1918–1919). The Russian Bureau of the War Trade Board was established in October 1918 to help the Russians to help themselves in stabilizing the economic situation in Russia through encouragement and facilitation of trade between the two countries. Many American hoped that expanded trade relations with Russia would bring out Russia's progressive, democratic potential. The bureau failed to achieve much substantial success and ceased to function in mid–1919. *Reference*: Linda Killen, *The Russian Bureau: A Case Study in Wilsonian Diplomacy* (Lexington, Ky., 1983).

RUSSIAN RAILWAY SERVICE CORPS. A semimilitary unit of American railway engineers founded in September 1917 at the request of the Russian government to install operational changes along the war-wracked Trans-Siberian Railway, which almost ceased to function, and to help maintain Russia's deteriorating railroad system. The Russian provisional government asked for men familiar with methods of railway operations. Some three hundred American railway men were recruited from various American railway positions from 1917 to 1920. The corps consisted only of officers, and its mission was to aid Russian railroaders in the efficient operation of the railways. The men started their assignments in Russia in March 1918. They made some improvements in dispatching techniques and operations and helped the Russians operate the railroad. The real U.S. goal was primarily to protect the interests of the United States and thwart Japanese expansion into Siberia. The corps was withdrawn and returned to the United States in June 1920, but a small group of officers remained until later 1922. *References*: Russian Railway Service Corps Records, National Archives, Washington, D.C.; Judson A. Grenier, "A Minnesota Railroad Man in the Far East, 1917–1918," *Minnesota History* 38 (1963): 310–25; Carolyn B. Grubbs, "American Railroaders in Siberia, 1917–1920," *Railroad History*, no. 150 (1984), 107–14; and *MERSH*.

RUSSIAN SECTION. A center for the study of Soviet affairs, established in 1922 by the U.S. State Department in the U.S. legation in Riga, Latvia, to gather and transmit information relating to Soviet Russia. It was closed down in 1939. *References*: Natalie Grant, "The Russian Section: A Window on the Soviet Union," *DH* 2 (1978): 107–15; and Frederic L. Propas, "Creating a Hard Line toward Russia: The Training of State Department Soviet Experts, 1927–1937," *DH* 8 (1984): 209–26.

RYAN, EDWARD WILLIAM (1884–1923). Sanitarian, born December 14, 1884, in Scranton, Pennsylvania. Ryan graduated from Fordham University. He was an American Red Cross (ARC) worker in Mexico from 1912 to 1914. He was director of the ARC unit in Serbia during World War I and later deputy Red Cross commissioner in Germany. He was the ARC representative in the Baltic states from 1919 to 1922. After he surreptitiously accompanied an Estonian peace commission to Moscow in March 1922, a report on his mission was leaked to the press by U.S. military intelligence, and the resulting publicity compromised the American Red Cross with the Soviet government. He was later a municipal expert in Teheran, Persia. Died September 19, 1923, in Teheran. *References*: *NYT*, September 21, 1923; and *WWWA*.

S

SALISBURY, HARRISON EVANS (1908–   ). Journalist and author, born November 14, 1908, in Minneapolis, Minnesota. Salisbury graduated from the University of Minnesota. He was a reporter for the United Press in St. Paul, Minnesota, and in Chicago, Washington, D.C., and New York City from 1930 to 1942. He was manager of the London bureau from 1942 to 1944 and foreign news editor from 1944 to 1948. He visited the Soviet Union in 1944 and wrote *Russia on the Way* (New York, 1946). He was Moscow correspondent of the *New York Times* from 1949 until 1954. He wrote *An American in Russia* (New York, 1955) and *Moscow Journal: The End of Stalin* (Chicago, 1961). After being barred from the Soviet Union for five years, he visited the Soviet Union and Central Asia in 1959 and in 1961–1962 and wrote *To Moscow—and Beyond: A Reporter's Narrative* (New York, 1960), *A New Russia?* (New York, 1962), and a novel, *The Northern Palmyra Affair* (New York, 1962). He was assistant managing editor of the *New York Times* from 1964 to 1970 and editor of the op-ed page from 1970 until his retirement in 1973. He edited *The Soviet Union: The Fifty Years* (New York, 1967) and wrote *The 900 Days: The Siege of Stalingrad* (New York, 1969), *Black Night, White Snow: Russia's Revolutions, 1905–1917* (New York, 1968), *Russia in Revolution, 1900–1930* (New York, 1978), *Without Fear or Favor* (New York, 1980), *Journey for Our Times* (New York, 1983), and the novel *The Gates of Hell* (New York, 1975). *References*: *CB* 1982; *NCAB* I:210; *PolProf: Johnson*; *PolProf: Kennedy*; and *WWA*.

SALT. The Strategic Arms Limitation Talks were extensive negotiating sessions between the United States and the Soviet Union to promote balanced and adequately verifiable limitations on strategic nuclear weapons in order to increase security by maintaining the strategic balance at a lower, safer, and less expensive level. SALT I opened in Helsinki in 1969. The two parties signed in 1972 the *ABM treaty and an intermin agreement, which froze offensive weapons at existing levels for five years. SALT II negotiations began in Geneva in 1972, attempting to achieve a comprehensive agreement on limiting strategic weapons, to replace the interim agreement. The guidelines for SALT II were agreed on in the *Vladivostok Summit of 1974. It set ceilings of twenty-four hundred strategic delivery vehicles for each side. A three-tier framework for SALT II was agreed upon in Geneva in 1977; the third element of this framework consisted of guidelines for SALT III, scheduled to begin as soon as SALT II agreements were concluded. A SALT II treaty was signed in Vienna in 1979, but ratification of the treaty by the U.S. Senate was indefinitely postponed after the Soviet invasion of Afghanistan in 1979. The administration of President *Ronald Reagan considered the SALT II treaty to be deeply flawed, and new negotiations, which were called *START, were initiated in 1982. *References*: *ACDA*; Dan Caldwell, *The Dynamics of Domestic Politics and Arms Control: The SALT II Treaty Ratification Debate* (Columbia, S.C., 1991); Dan Caldwell, "The SALT II Treaty," in Michael Krepon and Dan Caldwell, eds., *The Politics of Arms Control Treaty Ratification* (New York, 1991), pp. 269–353; *DINRT*; Raymond L. Garthoff, "SALT I: An Evaluation," *World Politics* 31 (October 1978): 1– 25; Roger P. Labrie, ed., *SALT Hand Book: Key Documents and Issues, 1972– 1979* (Washington, D.C., 1979); John Newhouse, *Cold Dawn: The Story of SALT* (New York, 1973); Andrew J. Pierre, "The Diplomacy of SALT," *International Security* 5 (Summer 1980): 178–97; William C. Potter, ed., *Verification and SALT: The Challenge of Strategic Deception* (Boulder, Colo., 1980); Gerald Smith, *Doubletalk: The Story of the First Strategic Arms Limitation Talks* (New York, 1980); Strobe Talbott, *Endgame: The Inside Story of SALT II* (New York, 1980); Mson Willrich and John B. Rhinelander, eds., *SALT: The Moscow Agreements and Beyond* (New York, 1974); and Thomas W. Wolfe, *The SALT Experience* (Cambridge, Mass., 1979).

SANDERS, BEVERLY CHUNE (1808–1883). Merchant, born in Virginia. Sanders was a partner in a retail firm in Baltimore during the 1840s. Hew went to San Francisco in 1850, during the gold rush, and was part owner and the San Francisco agent for *Santa Clara*, the first steamship built in California. He became a leading San Francisco entrepreneur, was involved in founding the San Francisco Savings Bank in 1852, and was president of the American Russian Commercial Company, shipping ice from Alaska to San Francisco. He went to Russia in 1854, reached an agreement with the Russian-American Company, but was unsuccessful in obtaining a contract to build railroads. His bank failed in 1855, and he was ejected from the leadership of the Russian-American Pacific trade. He returned to Baltimore in 1858, was involved in business there, and worked in the New York Customs House during the 1870s. Died December 25, 1883, in Newark, New Jersey. *References*: *NYT*, December 27, 1883; and Norman E. Saul, "Beverly C. Sanders and the Expansion of American Trade with Russia, 1853–1855," *Maryland Historical Magazine* 67 (1972): 156–70.

SAYLER, OLIVER MARTIN (1887–1958). Music critic, born October 23, 1887, in Huntington, Indiana. Sayler graduated from Oberlin College. He was on the staff of the *Indianapolis News* from 1909 to 1920, was a correspondent for the *Boston Evening Transcript* from 1915 to 1920, studied European theaters in 1914 and Russian theaters in 1917–1918, was a lecturer on the theater and on Russia, and conducted a weekly dramatic and literary review on the radio from 1924 to 1929. He revisited Russian theaters in 1924 and 1933 and was the American representative of the Moscow Art Theatre and other theaters in the Soviet Union. He wrote *Russia, White or Red* (Boston, 1919), *The Russian Theatre under the Revolution* (Boston, 1920), *The Russian Theatre* (New York, 1922), and *Inside the Moscow Art Theatre* (New York, 1925). Died October 19, 1958, in Marmaroneck, New York. *References*: *NYT*, October 20, 1958; and *WWWA*.

SAYRE, STEPHEN (1736–1818). Merchant, born June 12, 1736, in Southampton, Long Island, New York. Sayre graduated from the College of New Jersey. He then went to London and became a member of a mercantile house until 1770, when he organized a banking house. His banking house later failed, and he went to Paris. He was secretary to Arthur Lee, diplomatic agent to Berlin from 1777 to 1779, and later lived in Stockholm and again in Paris. He went to St. Petersburg in 1780 and was involved in ship building. He failed to secure the appointment as American agent to St. Petersburg. He tried, unsuccessfully, to develop trade between the United States and Russia. He left Russia in 1781, returned to the United States in 1793, and settled in New Jersey. Died September 27, 1818, in Middlesex County, Virginia. *References*: John R. Alden, *Stephen Sayre: American Revolutionary Adventurer* (Baton Rouge, La., 1983); *DAB*; and *WWWA*.

SCHLEY, REEVE (1881–1960). Banker, born August 28, 1881, in New York City. Schley graduated from Yale and Columbia universities and was admitted to the bar in 1906. He practiced law in New York City from 1906 to 1919 and became vice-president of *Chase National Bank in New York City in 1919. He retired from the bank as senior vice-president in 1946. He served as U.S. fuel administrator for New York City during World War I. He was president of the *American-Russian Chamber of Commerce from 1923 to 1940, heading a group of mercantile and banking interests in starting a campaign for a revival of trade relations between the United States and the Soviet Union. He was *Lend-Lease administrator in charge of sending supplies to the Soviet Union in 1942, a time when shipments had fallen behind schedule. He was mayor of Far Hills, New Jersey, from 1924 to 1936. Died June 26, 1960, in Far Hills, New Jersey. *References*: Reeve Schley Papers, New Jersey Historical Society, Newark; *NCAB* 45:412; *NYT*, June 27, 1960; and *WWWA*.

SCHORR, DANIEL LOUIS (1916–   ). Journalist, born August 31, 1916, in New York City. Schorr graduated from City College of New York. He was assistant editor of the Jewish Telegraphic Agency in New York City from 1934 to 1941 and news editor of the Aneta News Agency in New York City from 1941 to 1943. He served in U.S. Army Intelligence during World War II, was head of European service in Aneta News Agency in the Netherlands from 1945 to 1948, and was a free-lance correspondent in Amsterdam for the *Christian Science Monitor* and the *London Daily Mail* from 1948 to 1950 and for the *New York Times* from 1950 to 1953. He was the Moscow correspondent for Columbia Broadcasting Service (CBS) News from 1955 to 1957, opening the CBS news bureau in Moscow. He conducted the first American television interview with Nikita S. Khrushchev. He was general assignment correspondent for CBS from 1958 to 1960, chief of bureau in Germany and Central Europe from 1960 to 1966, and Washington correspondent from 1966 to 1976. *References: CA; CB* 1978; and *PolProf: Nixon/Ford.*

SCHUYLER, EUGENE (1840–1890). Diplomat, born February 26, 1840, in Ithaca, New York. Schuyler graduated from Yale College and Columbia Law School and was admitted to the bar in 1863. He practiced law in New York City. He was consul in Moscow from 1867 until 1869, consul in Revel, secretary of legation in St. Petersburg, and secretary of legation and consul general in Constantinople until 1878. He translated *Fathers and Sons* (New York, 1867), by Ivan Turgenev and *The Cossacks* (New York, 1878) by Leo Tolstoy. He traveled in Central Asia and wrote *Turkestan: Notes of a Journey in Russian Turkestan, Khokand, Bukhara, and Kuldja* (New York, 1876) and *Peter the Great, Emperor of Russia: a Study of Historical Biography* (New York, 1884). He was U.S. consul in Birmingham in 1878 and consul general in Rome from 1878 until 1880. He was the first U.S. diplomatic representative to Romania from 1880 to 1882 and minister and consul general to Greece, Romania, and Serbia from 1882 until 1884. In 1886, he settled in Alassio, Italy. He was in Cairo in 1889–1890, where he became ill. Died July 16, 1890, in Italy. *References*: Eugene Schuyler Letterbook, Manuscript Division, Library of Congress; James Seay Brown, Jr., "Eugene Schuyler, Observer of Russia: His Years as Diplomat in Russia 1867–1875" (Ph.D. diss., Vanderbilt University, 1971); Marion M. Coleman, "Eugene Schulyer: Diplomat Extraordinary from the U.S. to Russia, 1867–1876," *RR* 7 (1947): 33–48; *DAB*; DADH; *Eugene Schluyer: Selected Essays*, with a memoir of Evelyn Schuyler (New York, 1901); *NCAB* 8:339; and F. G. Siscoe, "Eugene Schulyer, General Kaufman, and Central Asia," *SR* 27 (1968): 119–30.

SCHUYLER, MONTGOMERY (1877–1955). Diplomat, born September 2, 1877, in Stamford, Connecticut. Schuyler graduated from Columbia University. He began his diplomatic career in 1902, serving as second secretary of embassy in St. Petersburg from 1902 to 1904, secretary of legation and consul general in Bangkok from 1904 to 1906, chargé d'affaires to Romania and Serbia in

1906–1907, first secretary and chargé d'affaires in St. Petersburg from 1907 to 1909, first secretary in Tokyo from 1909 to 1911 and in Mexico City from 1911 to 1913, and U.S. minister to Ecuador in 1913–1914. In 1914–1915, he was U.S. special agent to Russia and toured that country, visiting various military fronts. He served in the Ordnance Department and then in the Intelligence Division of the General Staff during World War I and was chief intelligence officer of the American Expeditionary Force in Omsk, Siberia, in 1918–1919. He was U.S. minister to El Salvador from 1921 to 1925 and chief of the division of Russian Affairs in the State Department in 1925. He retired from the diplomatic service in 1925, was partner in Schuyler, Earl, and Company, stockbrokers, from 1926 to 1931, and was president of Roosevelt and Schuyler, champagne importers of New York City. Died November 1, 1955, in Middletown, New York. *References*: *NCAB* 44:225; and *NYT*, November 2, 1955.

SCOTT, JOHN (1912–1976). Journalist and editor, born March 26, 1912, in Philadelphia. Scott attended the University of Wisconsin and was trained as a welder at the General Electric plant in Schenectady, New York. He went to the Soviet Union in 1932 and worked at Magnitogorsk until 1937 as a welder, foreman, and chemist in a coke by-products plant. He married Maria Ivanovna Dikareva (Masha) in 1934. He was later a foreign correspondent in Paris, the Balkans, Berlin, the Near East, Japan, and Moscow. He was expelled from the Soviet Union in 1941 on allegations of "slandering" Soviet foreign policy. He wrote *Behind the Urals* (Boston, 1942). He began working for *Time* in 1941, worked in London, headed the Stockholm bureau until 1945, was assistant to the publisher of *Life* from 1952 until his retirement in 1973, and was vice-president of Radio Free Europe–*Radio Liberty from 1974 until his death. Died December 1, 1976, in Chicago. *References*: John Scott Papers, State Historical Society of Wisconsin, Madison; Pearl S. Buck, *Talk about Russia with Masha Scott* (New York, 1945); Stephen Kotkin, ed. *Behind the Urals: An American Worker in Russia's City of Steel*, enl. ed. (Bloomington, Ind., 1989); and *NYT*, December 3, 1976.

SEWARD, WILLIAM HENRY (1801–1872). Public official and secretary of state, born May 16, 1801, in Florida, New York. Seward graduated from Union College and was admitted to the bar in 1823. He practiced law in Auburn, New York. He served in the New York state senate from 1830 to 1834, was governor of New York from 1838 to 1842, and served in the U.S. Senate from 1849 to 1861. He was secretary of state from 1861 until 1869. In 1867, he negotiated the *Alaska purchase from Russia, at the time called "Seward's folly." Died October 16, 1872, in Auburn, New York. *References*: *BDAC*; *DAB*; Ernest N. Paolino, *The Foundations of American Empire: William Henry Seward and U.S. Foreign Policy* (Ithaca, N.Y., 1973); *Seward at Washington as Senator and Secretary of State: A Memoir of His Life with Selections from His Letters, 1861–1872* (New York, 1891); G. G. Van Dusen, *William Henry Seward* (New York,

1978); and Gordon H. Warren, "Imperial Dreamer: William Henry Seward and American Destiny," in Frank Merli and Theodore Wilson, eds., *Makers of American Diplomacy* (New York, 1974), 1:195–221.

SEYMOUR, THOMAS HART (1807–1868). Public official and diplomat, born September 29, 1807, in Hartford, Connecticut. Seymour studied law and was admitted to the bar in 1833. He practiced law after 1839, was an active member of the Hartford Light Guard, and served as its commander from 1837 to 1841. He served as probate judge for the Hartford district from 1836 to 1839, clerk of the superior court in 1842–1843, and member of the U.S. House of Representatives from 1843 to 1845. He served with the Connecticut Volunteers during the Mexican War. He was governor of Connecticut from 1850 to 1853. He was U.S. minister to Russia from 1854 to 1858. His duties in St. Petersburg were neither onerous nor difficult. Died September 3, 1868, in Hartford, Connecticut. *References*: Thomas Hart Seymour Papers, Connecticut Historical Society, Hartford; *BDAC*; and *DAB*.

SHAPIRO, HENRY (1906–   ). Journalist, born April 19, 1906, in Vaslui, Romania. He was brought to the United States in 1920 and was naturalized in 1928. Shapiro graduated from City College of New York and Harvard University Law School. He was admitted to the bar in 1932 and practiced law in New York in 1932–1933. He was foreign correspondent for the *New York Herald Tribune*, *London Morning Post*, Reuters of London, United Press International, *Atlantic Monthly*, and the American Broadcasting Corporation (ABC) from 1933 to 1973 and was manager of the Moscow bureau of United Press International from 1939 to 1973. He was professor of journalism at the University of Wisconsin from 1973 to 1975. *Reference*: *WWA*.

SHULTZ, GEORGE PRATT (1920–   ). Public official and secretary of state, born December 13, 1920, in New York City. Shultz graduated from Princeton University and Massachusetts Institute of Technology (MIT) and served with the U.S. Marines during World War II. He taught at MIT from 1949 to 1955 and at the University of Chicago from 1957 to 1962 and was dean of the Graduate School of Business there from 1962 to 1969. He was secretary of labor in 1969–1970, head of the Office of Management and Budget from 1970 to 1972, and secretary of the treasury from 1972 to 1974. He was president of the Bechtel Group in San Francisco from 1974 until 1982. He was secretary of state from 1982 until 1989. He helped to negotiate arms agreements with the Soviet Union, including the *INF Treaty in 1987. His stance toward the Soviet Union has been consistently moderate. He was able to establish a dialogue with General Secretary Mikhail S. Gorbachev in 1985. He accompanied President *Ronald Reagan to Reykjavik in 1986 and signed in 1988 an agreement for the withdrawal of Soviet forces from Afghanistan. *References*: *CB* 1988; *DADH*; *PolProf: Nixon/Ford*; and *WWA*.

SIBERIAN INTERVENTION. See AMERICAN EXPEDITIONARY FORCES IN SIBERIA

SIMMONS, ERNEST JOSEPH (1903–1972). Author and educator, born December 8, 1903, in Lawrence, Massachusetts. Simmons graduated from Harvard University. In 1928, he made the first of several research visits to the Soviet Union, lived in Moscow in 1928–1929, and turned to Slavic studies. In 1947 he went to the Soviet Union on a mission for the American Council of Learned Societies to institute a cultural exchange program, but he encountered an utter lack of response, delaying tactics, and outright refusals. He was associate professor and then professor of Slavic languages at Cornell University from 1941 to 1945. In 1943, he directed an intensive study of contemporary Russian civilization. He was professor of Slavic languages at Columbia University after 1946 and chairman of the department and professor of Russian literature until 1959. He wrote *English Literature and Culture in Russia* (Cambridge, Mass., 1935), *Pushkin* (Cambridge, Mass., 1937); *Dostoevski: The Making of a Novelist* (London, 1940), *Leo Tolstoy* (Boston, 1946), and *Chekov: A Biography* (Boston, 1962) and edited *U.S.S.R.: A Concise Handbook* (Ithaca, N.Y., 1947). Died May 3, 1972, in Boston. *References*: *NYT*, May 5, 1972; and *RR* 31 (1972): 437–39.

SIMONS, GEORGE ALBERT (1874–1952). Clergyman and author, born March 19, 1874, in Laporte, Indiana. Simons graduated from Baldwin-Wallace College (Barea, Ohio), New York University, and Drew Theological Seminary. He entered the ministry of the Methodist Episcopal Church in 1899 and was pastor in Brooklyn and New York City from 1899 to 1907. He was superintendent of the Finland and St. Petersburg Methodist Episcopal Church Mission Conference from 1907 to 1911 and superintendent of the Russia Mission from 1911 to 1921. He served as chairman of the American Red Cross Committee in Russia and was a member of the board of American Hospitals for Wounded Russian Soldiers in St. Petersburg during World War I. He was superintendent of the Russia Mission Conference and Baltic Mission from 1921 to 1924 and the Baltic and Slavic Mission Conference from 1924 to 1928. He was also director of the Ministers' Training Institute in Riga, Latvia, from 1923 to 1927. He was minister of Christ Methodist Church in Glendale, Queens, until his death. Died August 2, 1952, in Brooklyn, New York. *References*: John Dunstan, "George A. Simons and the *Khristianski Pobarnik*: A Neglected Source on St. Petersburg Methodism," *Methodist History* 19 (1980): 21–40; Leslie A. Marshall, *The Romance of a Tract and Its Sequel: The Story of an American Pioneer in Russia and the Baltic States* (Rega, Latvia, 1928); *NYT*, August 3, 1952; and *WWWA*.

SINGER SEWING MACHINE COMPANY. Founded in 1851 and sold its first sewing machines in Russia in 1859. By 1892, it had an extensive sales and marketing organization in Russia. It founded Manufakturnaja Kompanija Singer, an independent joint-stock company in Russia in 1897. Singer became a household word in Russia. It built its plant in Russia in 1900 and later operated other plants, warehouses, and retail units in prerevolutionary Russia, where it possessed a near monopoly on the manufacture and sale of sewing machines. Its plants in Moscow and Petrograd were nationalized in 1917 and the plant in Vladivostok in 1923. *References*: Singer Manufacturing Company Records, State Historical Society of Wisconsin, Madison; Fred V. Carstensen, *American Enterprise in Foreign Markets: Studies of Singer and International Harvester in Imperial Russia* (Chapel Hill, N.C., 1984); and Robert Bruce Davies, *Peacefully Working to Conquer the World: Singer Sewing Machines in Foreign Markets, 1854–1920* (New York, 1976).

SISSON, EDGAR GRANT (1875–1948). Editor and author, born December 23, 1875, in Alto, Wisconsin. Sisson studied at Northwestern University. He was staff reporter for the *Chicago Chronicle* until 1898, reporter and drama editor of the *Chicago Tribune* from 1898 to 1901, assistant city editor and then city editor of the *Chicago American* in 1902–1903, and assistant city editor of the *Chicago Tribune* from 1903 to 1909 and city editor from 1909 to 1911. He was managing editor of *Collier's* from 1911 to 1914 and editor of *Cosmopolitan* from 1914 to 1917. He was associate chairman of the U.S. Committee on Public Information in Washington, D.C., from 1917 to 1919 and general director of its foreign section. He organized the publication and distribution of President *Woodrow Wilson's speeches throughout Russia in the winter of 1917–1918. He prepared a report to President Wilson titled *The German-Bolshevik Conspiracy* (Washington, D.C., 1918) (*see* Sisson Documents). He organized the committee's service at the Paris Peace Conference in 1918–1919. He wrote *100 Red Days: A Personal Chronicle of the Bolshevik Revolution, 25 November 1917–4 March 1918* (New Haven, Conn., 1931). He served with the U.S. Office of War Information from 1942 to 1945 and on the editorial staff of the Magazine Corporation of America in 1946. Died March 12, 1948, in New York City. *References*: *NYT*, March 13, 1948; and *WWWA*.

SISSON DOCUMENTS. Named after *Edgar Sisson, who acquired them in 1917. The collection of documents, forged by a Russian journalist in Petrograd in 1917, appeared to prove that the Bolshevik leaders were paid and controlled by the German general staff both before and immediately after the October Revolution. The material was validated by American experts and was published by the U.S. Committee on Public Information as *The German-Bolshevik Conspiracy* (Washington, D.C., 1918) to generate opposition to and intervention against the Soviet regime. *References*: George F. Kennan, "The Sisson Documents," *Journal of Modern History* 28 (1956): 130–54; and *MERSH*.

SMITH, CHARLES EMORY (1842–1908). Editor and diplomat, born February 18, 1842, in Mansfield, Connecticut, and grew up in Albany, New York. Smith graduated from Union College. He served in the office of the adjutant-general during the Civil War. He served on the staff of the *Albany Express* from 1865 to 1870, was associate editor of the *Albany Evening Journal* from 1870 to

1874 and its editor from 1874 to 1880, and was editor of the *Philadelphia Press* after 1880. He was U.S. minister to Russia from 1890 to 1892. He won popularity there by his efficient distribution of American relief funds to famine sufferers, but he was unsuccessful in mitigating the laws that discriminated against Russian Jews. He was postmaster-general from 1898 to 1901. Died January 19, 1908, in Philadelphia. *References*: *DAB*; *DADH*; *NCAB* 11:17; and *NYT*, January 20, 1908.

SMITH, CHARLES HADDEN (1872–1941). Railway engineer, born August 28, 1872, in Rushville, Indiana. Smith attended De Pauw University and the University of Michigan. He went to Alaska in 1897, carrying dispatches for the U.S. government, and remained there until 1899, driving a dog team and prospecting for gold. He was employed by the Great Northern Railway Company, the Chicago, Rock Island and Pacific Railway Company, the Denver, Northwestern and Pacific Railway, and the Missouri Pacific Railroad Company until 1916. He went to Russia in 1916 to buy alfalfa for the U.S. government. Following the Russia Revolution, he was a member of the Advisory Commission of Railway Experts in Russia and was appointed to represent *John F. Stevens on the Russian Railroad Commission. During 1918–1919, he was the American representative on the *Inter-Allied Railway Commission in Siberia and aided in repatriating Czechoslovakian prisoners of war held in Siberia. He was secretary and acting head of the *American-Russian Chamber of Commerce in Moscow from 1927 to 1929, developing favorable connections with the Soviet authorities. He was later representative in Moscow for General Motors Corporation, the Foxboro Manufacturing Company, and other American companies. He was the author of several engineering textbooks in Russian. Died January 23, 1941, in Moscow. *Reference*: *NCAB* 39:65.

SMITH, EDWARD ELLIS (1921–1982). Government official, born August 31, 1921, in West Virginia. Smith graduated from the University of West Virginia. He served in the U.S. Army during World War II and stayed in the War Department as one of its first Russian experts, becoming chief of the Soviet political desk of Army Intelligence and assistant military and economic attaché in Moscow from 1948 to 1951. He was in charge of American Committee for Liberation of the Peoples of Russia and then deputy of the Soviet Russia division of the Central Intelligence Agency (CIA). He was employed at the Moscow embassy from 1954 to 1956 as the first CIA officer to serve in Moscow, under the cover of political attaché. He had an affair with his Russian maid, who turned out to be a colonel in the Soviet KGB. He worked at the Hoover Institution from 1959 to 1962, was vice-president of a California bank, and worked at an international brokerage firm in San Francisco after 1980. Died February 13, 1982, after being hit by a car, in Redwood City, California. *References*: Edward Ellis Smith Papers, Hoover Institution Archives, Stanford, Calif; *BRDS*; *Palo Alto Times Tribune*, February 19, 1982; and Richard Harris Smith, "The First

Moscow Station: An Espionage Footnote to Cold War History," *International Journal of Intelligence and Counterintelligence* 3 (1989): 333–46.

SMITH, GERARD COAD (1914–   ). Government official, born May 4, 1914, in New York City. Smith graduated from Yale University and Yale Law School and was admitted to the bar in 1939. He served in the U.S. Navy during World War II. He practiced law from 1946 to 1950, was special assistant to the Atmoic Energy Commission from 1950 to 1954, and was assistant secretary of state for policy planning from 1957 to 1961. He was a consultant to the Washington Center for Foreign Policy Research from 1961 to 1969. He was director of the U.S. Arms Control and Disarmament Agency from 1969 to 1973 and chief U.S. delegate to all disarmament conferences. He headed the U.S. delegation to the Strategic Arms Limitation Talks (*SALT) with the Soviet Union. He advocated approaching the talks from a position of strength and supported the anti-ballistic missile (ABM) system as a "bargaining chip." He negotiated SALT, the Seabed Arms Control Treaty, and the Nuclear Accident Agreement. He resigned in 1973 and returned to the practice of law. He wrote *Doubletalk: The Story of the First Strategic Arms Limitations Talks* (Garden City, N.Y., 1980). *References*: *CB* 1970; *PolProf: Nixon/Ford*; and *WWA*.

SMITH, HEDRICK LAWRENCE (1933–   ). Journalist, born July 9, 1933, in Scotland. Smith graduated from Williams College and studied at Balliol College, Oxford. He was a reporter for the United Press International in Tennessee and Georgia from 1959 to 1962 and in Cape Canaveral in 1962. He was a reporter for the *New York Times* in Washington in 1962–1963, in Saigon in 1963–1964, and in Cairo from 1964 to 1966 and was diplomatic correspondent in Washington from 1966 to 1971. He was bureau chief in Moscow from 1971 to 1974 and wrote *The Russians* (New York, 1976). He was deputy national editor in 1975–1976 and Washington bureau chief after 1976. *Reference*: *CA*.

SMITH, JESSICA (1895–1983). Editor, born November 29, 1895. Smith graduated from Swarthmore College and was head of the Intercollegiate Socialist Society. She went to Soviet Russia in 1922 as a famine relief worker for the *American Friends Service Committee, working in Soviet villages until 1924. She was also a Federated Press correspondent. She married *Harold Ware in 1925 and worked with the Russian Reconstruction Farm, a Russian-American mixed Company, a project he directed in the Soviet Union, from 1925 to 1927. She was editor of *Soviet Russia Today* (later *New World Review*) from 1936 until 1977 and was founder and vice-chairman of the *National Council on American-Soviet Friendship. She made nine trips to the Soviet Union, the last one in 1971. She wrote *Women in Soviet Russia* (New York, 1928) and *People Come First* (New York, 1948). Died October 17, 1983. *References*: *CA*; *New World Review* 51 (September-October 1983): 4–5.

SMITH, JOSEPH ALLEN (1769–1828). Traveler, born in South Carolina. Smith spent much of his life abroad, traveling in Europe from 1793 to 1808. He was in Russia and the Caucasus from 1802 to 1805, the first American traveler to visit Russia, and dined with the tsar and his family. In 1803, he made an adventurous journey to Astrakhan. He returned to the United States in 1808 and spent the rest of his life in Philadelphia and South Carolina. Died November 29, 1828. *Reference*: Joseph Allen Smith, "Letters from Russia, 1802–1805," ed. George C. Rogers, *South Carolina Historical Magazine* 60 (1959): 94–105, 154–63, 221–27.

SMITH, WALTER BEDELL ("BEETLE") (1895–1961). Army officer and diplomat, born October 5, 1895, in Indianapolis, Indiana. Smith served in the state national guard from 1910 to 1915 and joined the U.S. Army in 1918. During World War II, he served on the staff of General *Dwight D. Eisenhower. He was U.S. ambassador to the Soviet Union from 1946 to 1948. He dealt with tensions caused by the Soviet presence in northern Iran in 1946, participated in the Paris Peace Conference in 1946, and attended the Council of Foreign Ministers meetings in Moscow and in London in 1947. He attempted to end the *Berlin blockade crisis diplomatically, negotiating with Premier Joseph Stalin and Foreign Minister V. M. Molotov. He lived in isolation in the American embassy as relations between the two countries deteriorated. He contributed little to policy-making because the State Department centralized this function in Washington, D.C., and he was called on only to defend U.S. policy and to report the official Soviet reaction to it. He wrote *My Three Years in Moscow* (Philadelphia, 1950). He was director of the Central Intelligence Agency from 1950 to 1953 and undersecretary of state in 1953–1954. He was later vice-chairman of the American Machine and Foundry Company. Died August 9, 1961, in Washington, D.C. *References*: *CB* 1953; *DADH*; *NCAB* G:63; *NYT*, August 10, 1961; *PolProf: Eisenhower*; and *PolProf: Truman*.

SMYSER, HENRY LANIUS (1825–1900). Surgeon, born December 8, 1825, in York, Pennsylvania. Smyser graduated from the University of Pennsylvania. He practiced medicine in Jackson Township, Pennsylvania, and in California during the gold rush. In 1855, he went to Russia and served as surgeon major in the Russian Army during the Crimean War. He later served as a surgeon during the Civil War. Died September 16, 1900, in York, Pennsylvania. *Reference*: Henry L. Smyser Papers, Historical Society of York County, York, Pa.

SNODGRASS, JOHN HAROLD (1868–1943). Consul, born in Marietta, Ohio. Snodgrass attended Cincinnati Law School. He was editor of the *Parkersburg News*, the *Charleston Mail*, and the *Wheeling Intelligencer* in West Virginia from 1893 to 1904. He served during the Spanish-American War. He was consul in Pretoria and Kobe, Japan, and consul general in Moscow from 1909 to 1917. He was involved in helping American businessmen establish business relations with Russia and in popularizing Russia as a market for American goods. He was in charge of German and Austrian commercial interests in Russia and the relief of civilian and military prisoners in Russia, Siberia, and Central Asia from 1914 to 1916. He was coauthor of *Russia: A Handbook on Commercial and Industrial Conditions* (Washington, D.C., 1913). He was head of an investment firm from 1921 to 1930 and of the correspondence department of the Long Island Lighting Company from 1933 to 1936. Died December 19, 1943, in Marietta, Ohio. *References*: *NYT*, December 19, 1943; and *WWWA*.

SONNTAG, GEORGE S. (1786–1841). Soldier, born in Philadelphia. Sonntag went to Russia in 1815 and entered the Russian Army and later became a general. He then joined the Russian Navy and served on the Black Sea. He commanded a regiment of marines during the war against Napoleon from 1812 to 1814 and entered Paris with the allied army. He became an admiral in the Russian Navy, was governor of the port of Odessa, and was admiral of the Black Sea Fleet. Died March 23, 1841, in Odessa, Russia. *Reference*: Sonntag Family Papers, U.S. Army Military History Institute, Carlisle Barracks, Pa.

SPARGO, JOHN (1876–1966). Author, born January 31, 1876, in Stithians, England. He came to the United States in 1901, worked as a social worker in New York City, and settled in 1909 in Bennington Center, Vermont. He became a citizen of the United States in 1907. He was a member of the Socialist Party in the United States, serving as its national executive secretary for several years. In 1918, he was a member of the war mission sent by President *Woodrow Wilson to assist in morale problems among workers in England, France, and Italy, and he served in Rome as a member of the U.S. Committee on Public Information. He became a major architect of the Wilson administration anti-Bolshevik policy. He was an adviser on matters pertaining to the Soviet Union to Presidents Warren G. Harding, Calvin Coolidge, and Herbert Hoover. He wrote *Bolshevism: The Enemy of Political and Industrial Democracy* (New York, 1919), *The Psychology of Bolshevism: A Critical Examination of the Actual Working of Bolshevism in Russia* (New York, 1919), *Russia as an American Problem* (New York, 1920), and *"The Greatest Failure in All History": A Critical Examination of the Actual Workings of Bolshevism in Russia* (New York, 1920). He was founder of the Bennington Museum in 1927 and served as its director-curator until his retirement in 1954. Died August 17, 1966, in Old Bennington, Vermont. *References*: John Spargo Papers, University of Vermont Library, Burlington; *DAB S8*; *NCAB* 52:317; *NYT*, August 18, 1966; and Ronald Radosh, "John Spargo and Wilson's Russian Policy, 1920," *Journal of American History* 52 (1965): 548–60.

STANDING CONSULTATIVE COMMISSION (SCC). Established in accordance with the provisions of SALT I in 1972. The Standing Consultative Commission was empowered to consider *SALT implementation and compliance questions, as well as questions involving interference with national technical means of verification. It has monitored SALT compliance with considerable success. *Reference*: *ACDA*; Robert W. Buchheim and Philip J. Farley, "The U.S.-Soviet Standing Consultative Commission," in Alexander L. George, Philip J. Farley, and Alexander Dallin, eds., *U.S.-Soviet Security Cooperation: Achievements, Failures, Lessons* (New York, 1988), pp. 254–69; Dean Caldwell, "The Standing Consultative Commissions: Past Performance and Future Possibilities," in William C. Potter, ed., *Verification and Arms Control* (Lexington, Mass., 1985), pp. 217–29; and Sidney N. Graybeal and Michael Krepon, "Making Better Use of the Standing Consultative Commission," *International Security* 10 (Fall 1985): 183–99.

STANDLEY, WILLIAM HARRISON (1872–1963). Naval officer and diplomat, born December 18, 1872, in Ukiah, California. Standley graduated from the U.S. Naval Academy in 1895 and was commissioned ensign in 1897. He served during the Spanish-American and the Philippine-American wars, in American Samoa, at Mare Island, California, and at the U.S. Naval Academy until 1919. He was assistant chief of staff to the Battle Fleet commander, head of the War Plans Division in the Office of the Chief of Naval Operations, commander of the USS *California*, and director of naval training. He was chief of naval operations from 1928 to 1930, commander of the fleet's destroyers in 1930–1931 and its cruisers from 1931 to 1933, and chief of naval operations from 1933 until his retirement, with the rank of admiral, in 1937. He returned to active duty in 1941 as a member of the U.S. Production Planning Board. He was a member of the Beaverbrook-Harrimann *Lend-Lease mission to Soviet Russia in 1941 and U.S. ambassador to the Soviet Union in 1942–1943. He had doubts about Soviet good faith and objected to Joseph Stalin's refusal to allow American officials the right to examine firsthand the validity of Russian requests and the uses of the supplies provided by the United States. He was also aggravated by what he perceived as the Soviet government's lack of gratitude for American help. He later wrote (with Arthur A. Ageton) *Admiral Ambassador to Russia* (Chicago, 1955). He served with the Office of Strategic Services in 1944–1945. He became a dedicated foe of communism and joined or supported several right-wing causes. Died October 25, 1963, in San Diego, California. *References*: William Harrison Standley Papers, University of Southern California Library, Los Angeles; William Harrison Standley Papers, Manuscript Division, Library of Congress; *DAB S7*; *DADH*; *NCAB* F:53; and *NYT*, October 26, 1963.

START. The administration of President *Ronald Reagan decided in 1981 that the SALT II treaty was deeply flawed and should not be ratified by the U.S. Senate in its existing form. It then proposed that new negotiations, called START (Strategic Arms Reduction Talks), begin after the administration reexamined the chief elements of America's strategic and long-range nuclear weapons policy. The American proposals for START were announced by President Reagan in 1982. The objectives included a major reduction in the number and destructive potential of nuclear weapons instead of a mere limit on their future growth,

Soviet-American strategic equality, and effective verification of nuclear arms control agreements. START began in 1982, but the talks were broken off in December 1983 because of the deployment of Pershing II and cruise missiles in Europe. In 1985, Soviet and U.S. negotiators resumed talks in Geneva on intermediate-range nuclear weapons, strategic arms, and weapons in outer space. The START Treaty on the Reduction and Limitation of Strategic Offensive Arms, was signed in Moscow on July 31, 1991, and was ratified by the U.S. Senate on October 1, 1992, the most complex arms treaty ever approved. It set a seven-year timetable for the reduction of the nuclear arsenals of the United States and the four republics of the former Soviet Union. The United States would be left with about eighty-five hundred warheads under the treaty. The former republics of the Soviet Union—Russia, Belarus, Ukraine, and Kazakhstan—would cut their combined total to sixty-five hundred warheads. START II treaty was signed in Moscow on January 3, 1993, between Russia and the United States. The treaty would reduce the two nations' strategic arms by two-thirds, eliminating those that either side might use in a pre-emptive first strike. The treaty forsees the elimination of heavy intercontinental ballistic missiles (ICBMs) and land-based ICBMs with multiple warheads. By the year 2003, Russia will be down to three thousand warheads and the United States down to thirty-five hundred warheads. *References*: *DINRT*; Kerry M. Kartchner, *Negotiating START: Strategic Arms Reduction Talks and the Quest for Strategic Stability* (New Brunswick, N.J., 1992); Strobe Talbott, *Deadly Gambits: The Reagan Administration and the Stalemate in Nuclear Arms Control* (New York, 1984); and U.S. Congressional Budget Office, *The START Treaty and Beyond* (Washington, D.C., 1991).

STEFFENS, LINCOLN (1866–1936). Journalist, born April 6, 1866, in San Francisco and grew up in Sacramento, California. Steffens graduated from the University of California. He was later reporter for the *New York Evening Post*, city editor for the *Commercial Advertiser* from 1897 to 1901, and managing editor of *McClure's Magazine* from 1901 to 1906 and of *American Magazine* in 1906–1907. He was a free-lance journalist after 1907. He was in Mexico in 1914. He accompanied *Charles R. Crane to Russia in 1917, studying the war and the social forces unleashed by the Russian Revolution. He returned to Soviet Russia in 1919 as a member of the *William C. Bullitt mission and interviewed V. I. Lenin. He wrote *Autobiography of Lincoln Steffens* (New York, 1931). Died August 9, 1936, in Carmel, California. *References*: Lincoln Steffens Papers, Bancroft Library, University of California, Berkeley, Calif.; Lincoln Steffens Papers, Columbia University Library, New York City; *DAB*; Justin Kaplan, *Lincoln Steffens* (New York, 1974); *NCAB* 14:455; *Letters of Lincoln Steffens*, eds. Ella Winter and Granville Hicks (New York, 1938); Dimitry von Mohrenschild, "Lincoln Steffens and the Russian Bolshevik Revolution," *RR* 5 (Autumn 1945): 31–41; Patrick F. Palermo, *Lincoln Steffens* (Boston, 1971); and Robert Stinson, *Lincoln Steffens* (New York, 1979).

STEINHARDT, LAURENCE ADOLPH (1892–1950). Lawyer and diplomat, born October 6, 1892, in New York City. Steinhardt graduated from Columbia University. After serving in World War I, he practiced law in New York City. A friend of *Franklin D. Roosevelt's, he served on the Democratic national campaign committee in 1932. He was U.S. minister to Sweden from 1933 to 1937, where his primary function was keeping a watch on Soviet affairs, and minister to Peru from 1937 to 1939. He was U.S. ambassador to Russia from 1939 to 1941. He handled the first of the *Lend-Lease shipments to the Soviet Union from the United States, and he was able to provide the U.S. State Department with advance warning of the Soviet-German agreement of August 1939 and of the German attack on Russia in June 1941. The bombing of Moscow forced him and his staff to evacuate the embassy and move to the temporary Russian capital at Kuibyshev in October 1941. He also contributed to the ending of the Russo-Finnish War in March 1940. He was U.S. ambassador to Turkey from 1942 to 1944, ambassador to Czechoslovakia from 1944 to 1948, and ambassador to Canada from 1948 to 1950. Killed in plane crash, March 28, 1950, near Ramsayville, Ontario, Canada. *References*: Laurence A. Steinhardt Papers, Manuscript Division, Library of Congress; *CB* 1941; *DADH*; *NCAB* 40:70; *NYT*, March 29, 1950; and Barry Rubin, "Ambassador Laurence A. Steinhardt: The Perils of a Jewish Diplomat, 1940–1945," *American Jewish History* 70 (1981): 331–46.

STETTINIUS, EDWARD REILLY, JR. (1900–1949). Government official and secretary of state, born October 22, 1900, in Chicago. Stettinius attended the University of Virginia. He worked for General Motors from 1924 to 1934, was vice-president of United States Steel Corporation from 1934 to 1938, and was chairman of the board from 1938 to 1940. He was chairman of the U.S. War Resources Board in 1939–1940 and of the National Defense Advisory Commission in 1940–1941, director of priorities of the Office of Production Management in 1941, administrator of *Lend-Lease from 1941 to 1943, undersecretary of state in 1943–1944, and secretary of state in 1944–1945. He accompanied President *Franklin D. Roosevelt to the *Yalta Conference in 1945. He wrote (with Walter Johnson) *Roosevelt and the Russians: The Yalta Conference* (New York, 1949). He later served as rector of the University of Virginia. Died October 31, 1949, in Greenwich, Connecticut. *References*: Edward R. Stettinius, Jr., Papers, University of Virginia Library, Charlottesville; Thomas M. Campbell and George C. Herring, eds., *The Diaries of Edward R. Stettinius, Jr., 1943–1946* (New York, 1975); Walter Johnson, *Edward R. Stettinius, Jr.* (New York, 1965); Walter Johnson, "Edward R. Stettinius, Jr.," in Norman A. Graebner, ed., *An Uncertain Tradition: American Secretaries of State in the Twentieth Century* (New York, 1961), pp. 210–22; and *NYT*, November 1, 1949.

STEVENS, EDMUND WILLIAM (1910–1992). Journalist, born July 22, 1910, in Denver, Colorado, and grew up in Italy, Illinois, and New York City. Stevens graduated from Columbia University. He went to Moscow in 1934 to study Russian and married a Russian girl in 1935. He worked in a Moscow publishing house as a translator and then was employed by the *American-Russian Chamber of Commerce. He also wrote for the *Manchester Guardian*, the *London Daily Herald*, and the *Observer*. He returned to the United States in 1939. He was correspondent for the *Christian Science Monitor* in Stockholm and then in Romania and Bulgaria from 1939 to 1941 and was war correspondent during World War II. He was in the Soviet Union in 1943–1944 and wrote *Russia Is No Riddle* (New York, 1945). He was again *Christian Science Monitor* correspondent in Moscow from 1946 to 1949 and wrote *This Is Russia, Un-Censored* (New York, 1951). He was the *Monitor*'s chief Mediterranean correspondent from 1950 to 1956. He went back to the Soviet Union in 1956, for *Look* magazine, and stayed for the rest of his life, writing also for *Time, Life, Newsday*, the *Saturday Evening Post*, the *Sunday Times*, the London *Times*, NBC Radio, and the *London Evening News* and becoming the dean of the Moscow press corps. Died May 24, 1992, in Moscow. *References*: *CB* 1950; *Chicago Tribune*, May 27, 1992; and *WWA*.

STEVENS, JOHN FRANK (1853–1943). Civil engineer, born April 25, 1853, near West Gardiner, Maine. Stevens graduated from the State Normal School (Farmington, Mass.). He was involved in railroading in Minnesota, Texas, New Mexico, Iowa, Manitoba, and British Columbia from 1873 to 1886 and was assistant chief engineer of the Great Northern Railway in 1893–1894, chief engineer from 1895 to 1903, and chief engineer of the Chicago Rock Island and Pacific Railway from 1903 to 1906. He was chief engineer of the Isthmian Canal Commission in 1906–1907, vice-president of the New York, New Haven, and Hartford Railroad from 1907 to 1909, president of the Oregon Trunk Railway Company from 1909 to 1911, and a private consultant from 1911 to 1917. He was sent to Russia in 1917 by President *Woodrow Wilson as chairman of the Advisory Commission of Railway Experts to study Russian railways and remained as special advisor to the Russian Ministry of Communications. He organized the *Russian Railway Service Corps to assist in the operation and improvement of the Russian railways. He was president of the Inter-Allied Technical Board, charged with the general supervision and management of the railways in those portions of Siberia and Manchuria in which Allied forces were then stationed, from 1919 to 1922. The board helped preserve the railway lines vital to the economic life of Siberia and kept them in operation. He returned to the United States in 1922. He wrote *An Engineer's Recollections* (New York, 1936). Died June 2, 1943, in Southern Pines, North Carolina. *References*: John Frank Stevens Papers, Manuscript Division, Library of Congress; *DAB S3*; Raymond Estep, "John F. Stevens and the Far Eastern Railways, 1917–1923," *Explorers Journal* 48 (March 1970): 13–24; *NCAB* 32:326; *NYT*, June 3, 1943; and Jacqueline D. St. John, "John F. Stevens: American Assistance to Russian and Siberian Railroads, 1917–1922'' (Ph.D. diss., University of Oklahoma, 1969).

STEVENS, LESLIE CLARK (1895–1956). Naval officer, born February 19, 1895, in Kearney, Nebraska. Stevens graduated from Nebraska Wesleyan University and the U.S. Naval Academy in 1918 and was commissioned ensign in the U.S. Navy in 1918. He also graduated from the Massachusetts Institute of Technology. He served aboard the USS *Balch* during World War I, became a naval aviator in 1924, and served in the Bureau of Aeronautics in the Navy Department and at the Naval Air Station in San Diego until 1934. He was assistant naval attaché at the U.S. embassy in London from 1934 until 1937, served again in the Bureau of Aeronautics, and was on the staff of the commander of the Air Force of the Pacific Fleet and of the commander of Naval Forces in Germany until 1946. He was naval attaché for air at the U.S. embassy in Moscow from 1947 to 1949 and wrote *Russian Assignment* (Boston, 1953). He served in the Office of the Joint Chiefs of Staff in Washington from 1949 to 1951, when he retired, with the rank of vice-admiral. He served as chairman of the American Committee for Liberation from Bolshevism from 1952 to 1954. Died November 30, 1956, in Sanford, Florida. *References: NCAB* 46:333; and *NYT*, December 1, 1956.

STINES, NORMAN CASWELL (1881–1955). Mining engineer, born September 1, 1881, in Detroit, Michigan. Stines graduated from the University of California at Berkeley. He was employed in various mining properties in California, Oregon, Washington, Nevada, Arizona, and Mexico. He was assistant examining engineer for John P. Hutchins in Siberia, general manager of the Sissert Mining District Company in Ekaterinburg in 1915–1916, and managing director after 1916. He also was managing director of the Altai Mines and of the Lenskoi Gold Mining Company and was consulting engineer for the Russian-English Bank in Petrograd. He joined with other engineers in gaining control of a substantial supply of platinum, vital to the American war effort. He served with the U.S. Military Mission to Russia in Petrograd in 1917–1918. He was assistant military attaché to the U.S. legation in Stockholm, was in charge of the Russian section of U.S. intelligence work in Scandinavia in 1918–1919, and was in Paris in 1919. In 1919–1920, he resumed his association with the English group controlling the Russian companies with which he had previously worked and tried, unsuccessfully, to recover those businesses for their owners. He returned to the United States in 1920 and served as consulting engineer until his death. Died March 9, 1955, in Winnemucca, Nevada. *Reference: NCAB* 44:411.

STIRNIMAN, EDWARD JAMES (1892–1974). Agriculturist, born October 23, 1892, in Riceville, Iowa. Stirniman graduated from Iowa State College (Ames). He was instructor and then associate professor in the agricultural engineering department at the University of California in Davis from 1921 to 1929. He was adviser to the Grain Trust of the USSR at Verblud, a demonstration farm in the North Caucasus, from 1929 to 1931. He later resided in Brooklyn, Iowa. Died March 6, 1974, in Grinnell, Iowa. *Reference*: *WWIN*.

STOESSEL, WALTER JOHN, JR. (1920–1986). Diplomat, born January 24, 1920, in Manhattan, Kansas. Stoessel graduated from Stanford University. He joined the foreign service in 1942, served in Caracas, Venezuela, and then served in the U.S. Navy during World War II. He served in Washington, D.C., Moscow, and Bad Nauheim, West Germany, until 1952, was chief of the Division of Soviet and East European Affairs from 1952 to 1956, was adviser to the White House in 1956, was attached to the Paris embassy from 1956 to 1959, was aide to the secretary of state in 1961, and was again in Paris from 1961 to 1963. He was deputy chief of mission in Moscow from 1963 to 1965, deputy assistant secretary of state from 1965 to 1968, U.S. ambassador to Poland from 1968 to 1972, and assistant secretary of state for European affairs from 1972 to 1974. He was U.S. ambassador to the Soviet Union from 1974 to 1976. During this assignment, détente diplomacy brought about a relaxation of tensions and increased trade and optimism about the normalization of U.S.-Soviet relations. He was U.S. ambassador to West Germany from 1976 to 1981, undersecretary of state for political affairs in 1981–1982, and deputy secretary of state from 1982 to 1986. Died December 9, 1986, in Washington, D.C. *References*: *CB* 1970; *DADH*; *NYT*, December 11, 1986; and *WWA*.

STONEMAN, WILLIAM HARLAN (1904–1987). Journalist, born March 15, 1904, in Grand Rapids, Michigan. Stoneman attended the University of Michigan. He served as a foreign correspondent for the *Chicago Daily News* until 1969. He served in Scandinavia and in Rome from 1928 to 1932, was correspondent in Moscow from 1932 to 1935 and in Berlin in 1936, was chief London correspondent from 1936 to 1946 and from 1958 to 1968, and was in Paris in 1968. He was a war correspondent during World War II and adviser to the secretary general of the United Nations from 1946 to 1949. Died April 11, 1987, in Paris, France. *References*: William H. Stoneman Papers, Bentley Historical Library, University of Michigan, Ann Arbor; *CA*; and *NYT*, April 15, 1987.

STORY, RUSSELL MCCULLOCH (1883–1942). Association official born April 9, 1883, in Washburn, Illinois. Story graduated from Monmouth College (Ill.) and Harvard University. He was professor of history at Monmouth College from 1910 to 1914 and assistant professor and associate professor at the University of Illinois from 1914 to 1924. He served with the *Young Men's Christian Association (YMCA) as field secretary in Russia and Siberia during World War I. He was professor of political science at Syracuse University in 1924–1925 and at Pomona College from 1925 to 1937 and was president of Claremont College after 1937. Died March 26, 1942, in Pomona, California. *References*: Russell McCulloch Story Papers, Hoover Institution Archives, Stanford, Calif.; Donald E. Davis and Eugene P. Trani, ''An American in Russia: Russell M.

Story and the Bolshevik Revolution, 1917–1919," *Historian* 36 (1974): 704–21; and *NCAB* 37:438.

STRATEGIC ARMS LIMITATION TALKS. See SALT

STRATEGIC ARMS REDUCTION TALKS. See START

STRONG, ANNA LOUISE (1885–1970). Journalist, born November 24, 1885, in Friend, Nebraska, and grew up in Mt. Vernon and Cincinnati, Ohio, and in Oak Park, Illinois. Strong attended Bryn Mawr College and graduated from Oberlin College and the University of Chicago. She directed child welfare exhibits in various cities from 1911 to 1915 and was involved in socialist politics in Seattle from 1915 to 1921. She went to Poland in 1921 for the *American Friends Service Committee and then to Soviet Russia as a correspondent for Hearst's International News Service. She was in China from 1925 to 1927, returned to the Soviet Union in 1927, and was again in the Soviet Union in 1929–1930 and from 1938 to 1940. She was in the Soviet Union from 1947 to 1949, when she was arrested and deported from that country. She wrote *The First Time in History; Two Years of Russia's New Life* (New York, 1924), *Children of Revolution: The Story of the John Reed Children's Colony on the Volga, Which Is as Well a Story of the Whole Great Structure of Russia* (Seattle, 1925), *Red Star in Samarkand* (New York, 1929), *The Soviets Conquer Wheat: The Drama of Collective Farming* (New York, 1931), *I Change Worlds: The Remaking of an American* (New York, 1935), *This Soviet World* (New York, 1936), *The New Soviet Constitution: A Study in Socialist Democracy* (New York, 1937), *The Soviet Expected It* (New York, 1941), *Peoples of the U.S.S.R.* (New York, 1944), and *The Stalin Era* (Altadena, Calif., 1956). Died March 29, 1970, in Beijing, China. *References*: Anna Louise Strong Papers, University of Washington Library, Seattle; *DAB* S8; David C. Duke, "Anna Louise Strong and the Search for a Good Cause," *Pacific Northwest Quarterly* 66 (1975): 123–37; Philip Jaffe, "The Strange Case of Anna Louise Strong," *Survey: A Journal of Soviet and East European Studies* 53 (October 1964): 129–39; *NYT*, March 30, 1970; Stephanie F. Ogle, "Anna Louise Strong: Progressive and Propagandist" (Ph.D. diss., University of Washington, 1981); and Tracy B. Strong and Helene Keysar, *Right in Her Soul: The Life of Anna Louise Strong* (New York, 1983).

STUART, CHARLES EDWARD (1881–1943). Industrial engineer, born August 29, 1881, in Alexandria, Virginia. Stuart graduated from Virginia Military Institute and studied at the Westinghouse Electric and Manufacturing Company in Pittsburgh. He was employed by Westinghouse from 1902 to 1911 and was senior partner and president of Stuart, James, and Cooke of New York, coalmining consultants, after 1911. He was chief of the Power Conservation Bureau of the U.S. Fuel Administration during World War I. He was a consulting engineer to the government of Russia on the projection of new mines and the rehabilitation of old mines in coal, iron, and copper. In 1927, he made a preliminary inspection of Soviet coal mines, signed technical assistance contracts with Soviet trusts between 1927 and 1930, and prepared a report on the coal mines of the Donets Basin in 1931. He was an active promoter of American assistance to the Soviet Union. He was also executive vice-president of the Export-Import Bank in Washington, D.C., from 1934 to 1936. In 1938, he was considered for the post of ambassador to the Soviet Union. Died June 20, 1943, in New York City. *References*: *NYT*, June 21, 1943; and *WWWA*.

STUCK, RAYMOND WILBER (1897–1981). Industrial engineer, born October 21, 1897, in Wilmot, Ohio. Stuck graduated from Case School of Applied Science. He worked on the design and construction of blast furnaces and coke ovens plants from 1915 to 1918 and was resident engineer on the design and construction of a dirigible hanger in Akron. He was manager and chief engineer in charge of the construction of a steel plant in Magnitogorsk for the firm of Arthur G. Mckee and Company of Cleveland. He served with the U.S. Corps of Engineers from 1934 to 1947 and was later project manager in Argentina and Turkey. Died July 24, 1981, in Winter Haven, Florida.

SUMMERS, MADDIN (1877–1918). Consul, born February 1, 1877, in Nashville, Tennessee. Summers attended Vanderbilt and Columbia universities. He worked as a clerk in a bank in Nashville. He was appointed consular clerk in 1899. He served as vice-counsel and deputy consul general at Barcelona, vice-consul in Madrid, and consul in Belgrade, Santos, and Saõ Paulo from 1900 to 1916. He was consul general in Moscow from 1917 until his death. He directed the activities of consular officers and agents in Russia, extending all the way to Vladivostok. Of senior American officials in Russia, he had the most uncompromising anti-Bolshevik attitude. Died May 4, 1918, in Moscow. *References*: *NYT*, May 6, 1918; and *WWWA*.

SUMMIT CONFERENCES. International political meetings between the heads of government of the United States and the Soviet Union. The meetings were held for substantive purposes. The press first began to use the term *summit conference* in reference to the Geneva Big Four Conference in 1955. Since *Geneva (1955), U.S.–Soviet Union summits have included *Washington (1959), *Paris (1960), *Vienna (1961), *Glassboro (1967), *Moscow (1972), *Washington (1973), *Moscow (1974), *Vladivostok (1974), *Vienna (1979), *Geneva (1985), *Reykjavik (1986), *Washington (1987), *Moscow (1988), *Malta (1989), *Washington (1990), *Moscow (1991) and *Moscow (1993). *References*: *DINRT*; *EAFP*; *McDonald*; Elmer Plischke, *Diplomat in Chief: The President at the Summit* (New York, 1986); and *Weihmiller*.

T

TATE, GEORGE (1745–1821). Naval officer, born June 14, 1745, in London, came with his family to the United States in 1751, and grew up in Stroudwater, Maine. Tate was brought up to the sea. He was commissioned lieutenant in the Russian Navy in 1770 and served in it until his death. He became vice-admiral in 1798 and admiral in 1812. Died in St. Petersburg. *References*: George Tate Papers, Maine Historical Society, Portland, Me.; William David Barry, "Maine's One and Only Russian Admiral," *Down East* 30 (December 1983): 38–39, 67–69; and Francis S. Drake, *Dictionary of American Biography Including Men of the Time* (Boston, 1872).

TAYLOR, BAYARD (1825–1878). Author, traveler, and diplomat, born January 11, 1825, in Kennett Square, Chester County, Pennsylvania. Taylor was apprenticed to a printer in West Chester. He moved to New York City in 1847, where he began to write. He became associated with the *New York Tribune* in 1848. He traveled to Russia in 1858 and wrote *Travels in Greece and Russia* (New York, 1859). He was secretary of legation in St. Petersburg in 1862–1863, working with the U.S. minister, *Cassius M. Clay, to keep Russia sympathetic to the Union during the Civil War. He was U.S. minister to Germany in 1878. Died December 19, 1878, in Berlin, Germany. *References*: Bayard Taylor Papers, Cornell University Library, Ithaca, N.Y.; Richamond Croom Beatty, *Bayard Taylor: Laureate of the Gilded Age* (Norman, Okla., 1936); *DAB*; *DADH*; Marie Hansen-Taylor and Horace E. Scudder, eds., *Life and Letters of Bayard Taylor* (Boston, 1884); *NCAB* 3:454; John Richie Schulz, ed., *The Unpublished Letters of Bayard Taylor in the Huntington Library* (San Marino, Calif., 1937); and Paul C. Wermuth, *Bayard Taylor* (New York, 1973).

TEAM A/TEAM B. Two groups that formulated the 1976 National Intelligence Estimate (NIE). Team B, a group of nongovernment specialists, was mandated by President Gerald Ford's Foreign Intelligence Advisory Board to analyze independently the same raw data available to Team A. Team B was headed by *Richard Pipes, and included *Paul Nitze. Team B's report concluded that Team

A had underestimated the Soviet threat and asserted that the Soviets were seeking overall military superiority and a war-fighting capability. *References*: *DINRT*; Philip A. Peterson, "American Perceptions of Soviet Military Power," *Parameters* 6, no. 4 (1977): 71–82; Richard Pipes, "Team B: The Reality behind the Myth," *Commentary* 82 (October 1986): 25–40; and Robert C. Reich, "Reexamining the Team A–Team B Exercise," *International Journal of Intelligence and Counterintelligence* 3 (Fall 1989): 387–403.

TEHERAN CONFERENCE (1943). Summit meeting of President *Franklin D. Roosevelt, Prime Minister Winston Churchill, and Premier Joseph Stalin, in Teheran, Iran, from November 28 to December 1, 1943. The discussions dealt mostly with military planning for the future invasion of Europe. Decisions regarding the political issues of postwar Europe and East Asia were postponed. *References*: *DADH*; Keith Eubank, *Summit at Teheran: The Untold Story* (New York, 1985); Lukas E. Hoska, Jr., "Summit Diplomacy during World War II: The Conferences at Teheran, Yalta, and Postdam" (Ph.D. diss., University of Maryland, 1966); and Paul D. Mayle, *Eureka Summit: Agreement in Principle and the Big Three at Teheran, 1943* (Newark, Del., 1987).

THACHER, THOMAS DAY (1881–1950). Lawyer, born September 10, 1881, in Tenafly, New Jersey. Thacher graduated from Yale University and attended Yale Law School and was admitted to the bar in 1906. He practiced law in New York City after 1906 and was assistant U.S. attorney for the Southern District of New York from 1907 to 1910. He was a member of the American Red Cross Commission to Russia in 1917–1918. He respected the new Soviet government and vainly urged the U.S. government to cooperate with the Bolshevik leadership and to create an American commission to assist the Soviet government in reorganizing and reconstructing its internal affairs. He served on the U.S. District Court for the Southern District of New York from 1925 to 1930, was solicitor general of the United States from 1930 to 1933, resumed his law practice in 1933, and served on the New York State Court of Appeal from 1943 until his retirement in 1948. Died November 12, 1950, in New York City. *References*: Thomas Day Thacher, "Russia and the War" (1918), New York Public Library; Thomas Day Thacher Papers, Columbia University Library, New York City; Thomas Day Thacher Reminiscences, Oral History Collection, Columbia University, New York City; *DAB S4*; *NCAB* 40:110; and *NYT*, November 13, 1950.

THAYER, CHARLES WHEELER (1910–1969). Diplomat, born February 9, 1910, in Villanova, Pennsylvania. Thayer graduated from the U.S. Military Academy in 1933 and was commissioned second lieutenant in the cavalry but resigned his commission. He went to the Soviet Union to study the Russian language in Moscow. He entered the foreign service, serving as personal secretary to *William C. Bullitt and then as secretary of embassy from 1933 until 1937. He was consul in Berlin and in Hamburg from 1938 to 1940. He returned to

Moscow in 1940 again as secretary of embassy until 1942. He was chargé d'affaires in Afghanistan in 1942–1943, served in the embassy in London in 1943, and headed the U.S. Military Mission to Yugoslavia in 1944–1945. He was chief of the Office of Strategic Services in Austria in 1945–1946, a member of the Joint United States–Soviet Commission on Korea in 1946, director of the International Broadcasting Division of the State Department from 1947 to 1949, political liaison officer to the German government in Bonn in 1950–1951, and consul general in Munich from 1951 to 1953. He resigned in 1953 following an attack on him by Senator Joseph McCarthy. He wrote *Bears in the Caviar* (Philadelphia, 1950), *Hands across the Caviar* (Philadelphia, 1952), *Diplomat* (New York, 1959), and the novel *Moscow Interlude* (New York, 1962) and was coauthor of *Russia* (New York, 1960). Died August 27, 1969, in Salzburg, Austria. *References*: Thomas George Corti, "Diplomat in the Caviar: Charles Wheeler Thayer, 1910–1969" (Ph.D. diss., Saint Louis University, 1988); Thomas G. Corti and T. Michael Ruddy, "The Bohlen-Thayer Dilemma: A Case Study in the Eisenhower Administration's Response to McCarthyism," *Mid-America* 72 (1990): 119–33; *NCAB* 56:370; and *NYT*, August 29, 1969.

THOMAS, GEORGE (?–?). Valet. An African-American, Thomas went to St. Petersburg in 1890 and found employment there as a valet. He adopted the Russian name Fyodor. He later engaged in various amusement enterprises throughout Russia and, by the time of World War I, owned a large amusement complex in Moscow called the Aquarium. In 1917, he fled to Constantinople and established there a Russian cabaret called "Stella." He went bankrupt in the late 1920s and died in debtor's prison.

THOMPSON, LLEWELLYN E., JR. (1904–1972). Diplomat, born August 24, 1904, in Las Animas, Colorado. Thompson graduated from the University of Colorado. He entered the foreign service in 1929, serving as vice-consul in Colombo, Ceylon, and in Geneva from 1929 to 1937 and as consul in Geneva from 1937 to 1939. He was second secretary and consul in Moscow from 1941 to 1944 and in London from 1944 to 1946. He served on the staff of the European Affairs Division of the State Department from 1946 to 1950 and was counselor in the embassy in Rome from 1950 to 1952, U.S. high commissioner to Austria from 1952 to 1955, and ambassador to Austria from 1955 to 1957. He was U.S. ambassador to the Soviet Union from 1957 to 1962. He urged that Premier Nikita S. Khrushchev be invited to the United States. Later, he helped plan the abortive *Paris summit of 1960 and the *Vienna summit of 1961. He was ambassador-at-large from 1962 to 1966 and was involved in the *Cuban missile crisis, the Limited Nuclear Test Ban Treaty of 1963, and East-West trade matters. He was again ambassador to the Soviet Union from 1967 to 1969, during which time the complications of the Vietnam War isolated him somewhat from Soviet leadership, and he was a delegate to the early stages of SALT I from 1969 to 1971. He enjoyed good relations with Soviet leaders, who trusted his integrity and liked the fact that he was fluent in Russian. Died February 6, 1972, in Washington, D.C. *References*: *DADH*; *NCAB* I:326; and *NYT*, February 7, 1972.

THOMPSON, WILLIAM BOYCE (1869–1930). Financier and philanthropist, born May 13, 1869, in Virginia City, Montana, and grew up in Butte, Montana. Thompson attended the School of Mines of Columbia University. He was superintendent of a silver mine, secretary of a lumber company, and a coal dealer until 1897, when he returned to Butte, where he dealt in real estate, mines, and insurance and recovered a considerable amount of copper from the Butte ore dumps. He developed a copper mine in Arizona, opened a broker's office in New York City dealing mostly in copper stocks, launched a silver mine, developed a copper company in Gila County, Arizona, and then became interested in mining properties all over the world. He was director of the Federal Reserve Bank of New York from 1914 to 1919. He was involved in collecting funds for *Herbert Hoover's Belgian relief work during World War I. In 1917, he offered to pay the expenses of the American Red Cross mission to Russia, served initially as the business manager of the mission, and later was its leader. He labored, unsuccessfully, to secure aid from the United States for the provisional government and contributed a million dollars to finance a propaganda campaign designed to keep the Russian Army fighting on the eastern front. After the overthrow of the provisional government, he urged recognition and aid of the new Bolshevik government by the Allies. In 1919, he organized the Farm and Research Corporation for the investigation of plant life (later renamed Boyce Thompson Institute for Plant Research) in Yonkers, New York. Died June 27, 1930, in Yonkers. *References*: *DAB*; Hermann Hagedorn, *The Magnate: William Boyce Thompson and His Time, 1869–1930* (New York, 1935); *NCAB* 22:173; and *NYT*, June 28, 1930.

THRESHOLD TEST BAN TREATY (TTBT) (1974). Treaty between the United States of America and the Union of Soviet Socialist Republics on the limitation of underground nuclear weapon tests, signed in Moscow on July 3, 1974, prohibiting underground nuclear tests above 150 kilotons limits, or threshold. A companion treaty, the *Peaceful Nuclear Explosions (PNE) Treaty in 1976, specifically extended the same limitation to underground tests for peaceful purposes. The Senate has not ratified either treaty, and the Reagan administration considered the verification provisions of both treaties to be inadequate. *References*: *ACDA*; and *DINRT*.

TIMBRES, HARRY GARLAND (1899–1937). Epidemiologist, born April 3, 1899, in Hatfield, Missouri, and grew up in Alberta, Canada. Timbres attended Stanford University, graduated from Haverford College and the School of Medicine of Johns Hopkins University, and studied at the London School of Tropical Medicine and Hygiene. He served with the *American Friends Service Committee in Poland in 1921–1922 and in the Soviet Union in 1922. He was a medical missionary in Santikiniketan, India, from 1929 to 1934. He fought malaria in the Volga region in 1936–1937 and was an assistant in malarial research in Marbumstroy, in the Kazan area, on the Volga River. Died May 12, 1937, at Marbumstroy. His wife, Rebecca Timbres, wrote *We Didn't Ask Utopia: A Quaker Family in Soviet Russia* (New York, 1939). *Reference*: *NYT*, May 17, 1937.

TOLLEY, KEMP (1908–). Naval officer, born April 29, 1908, in Manila, Philippines, to American parents. Tolley graduated from the U.S. Naval Academy in 1929. He served on sea and in foreign duty in China and Japan. He was assistant U.S. naval attaché in Moscow during World War II and later wrote *Caviar and Commissars: The Experience of a U.S. Naval Officer in Stalin's Russia* (Annapolis, 1983). He was director of intelligence at the Armed Forces Staff College in Norfolk, Virginia, from 1951 to 1954, commander of an amphibious group in the Western Pacific in 1956, and commander of fleet activities in Yokosuka, Japan, from 1956 to 1959, when he retired, with the rank of rear admiral. *Reference*: *CA*.

TOON, MALCOLM (1916–). Diplomat, born July 4, 1916, in Troy, New York. Toon graduated from Tufts University and the Fletcher School of Law and Diplomacy. He served in the U.S. Navy during World War II. He entered the foreign service in 1946 and served in Warsaw, Budapest, Berlin, Washington, and London until 1963. He was counselor and political affairs officer in Moscow from 1963 to 1965. There he was falsely accused of being the head of a U.S. spy ring in Russia. He headed the Office of Soviet Affairs in the State Department and was acting deputy assistant secretary of state for east European affairs from 1963 to 1969, U.S. ambassador to Czechoslovakia from 1969 to 1971, ambassador to Yugoslavia from 1971 to 1975, and ambassador to Israel in 1975–1976. Although he was appointed ambassador to Moscow in 1976, the Soviet Union delayed its official approval of the appointment because of lingering distrust dating back to the 1965 spy ring incident. However, Moscow demands for the withdrawal of his appointment were not granted, and he served as U.S. ambassador to the Soviet Union from 1977 until 1979. *References*: *CB* 1978; *DADH*; and *WWA*.

TOWER, CHARLEMAGNE (1848–1923). Financier and diplomat, born April 17, 1848, in Philadelphia. Tower graduated from Harvard University, studied law, and was admitted to the bar in 1878. He practiced law in Philadelphia until 1882, was president of the Duluth Iron Range Railroad Company from 1882 to 1887, and was vice-president of the Finance Company of Philadelphia from 1887 until 1890 and its president in 1890–1891. He was U.S. minister to Austria-Hungary from 1897 to 1899. He was U.S. ambassador to Russia from 1899 to 1902. He negotiated an arbitration agreement over the claims of American sealing vessels seized in the Bering Sea by Russian cruisers. Striving to elevate the U.S.

embassy to an equal status with those of the European powers, in display as well as diplomacy, he ordered uniforms for the embassy staff, thus marking a sharp departure from U.S. diplomatic tradition. He was U.S. ambassador to Germany from 1902 to 1908 and then resumed his business affairs. Died February 24, 1923, in Philadelphia. *References: DAB; DADH; NCAB* 26:124; *NYT*, February 25, 1923; and Fedotoff D. White, "The Charlemagne Tower Collection," *University of Pennsylvania Library Chronicle* 12 (April 1944): 18–25.

TREDWELL, ROGER CULVER (1885–1961). Consul, born January 12, 1885, in Brooklyn, New York. Tredwell graduated from Yale University and studied at the University of Grenoble in France. He was appointed consular assistant in 1909, vice-consul and deputy consul general in Yokohama, deputy consul general in London, and vice-consul and deputy consul at Burslem, England, and Dresden, Germany, until 1912. He served in the State Department in Washington, D.C., and was consul in Bristol, Leghorn, Turin, and Rome from 1913 to 1917. He was assigned to Petrograd in 1917, going to Vologda and Moscow in 1918. He went to Tashkent, Turkestan, in 1918, and was held under arrest by the Soviet government for six months in 1918–1919. He served in the State Department from 1919 to 1924 and was foreign service inspector in 1924–1925. He was consul general in Hong Kong, Sydney, and Stockholm from 1925 to 1933. He retired in 1944. Died July 12, 1961, in Ridgefield, Connecticut. *References: NYT*, July 13, 1961; and *WWWA*.

TRUMAN, HARRY S. (1884–1972). President of the United States, born May 8, 1884, in Lamar, Missouri. Truman was a bank clerk and then farmed. He served in the U.S. Army during World War I. He owned a clothing store. He served on the county court of Jackson County from 1922 to 1924 and again from 1926 to 1928 and was the court presiding judge until 1934. He served in the U.S. Senate from 1935 until 1944, was vice-president of the United States in 1945, and was president of the United States from 1945 to 1953. He initially followed President *Franklin D. Roosevelt's policy of cooperation with the Soviets and participated in the *Potsdam Conference (1945). Becoming frustrated over Soviet behavior when the Soviet Union broke the agreements it had made, he toughened U.S. policy and adopted the policy of *containment. He had to deal with the Soviet activities in Azerbaijan, the *Berlin blockade crisis, and the Korean War. Died December 26, 1972, in Kansas City, Missouri. *References*: Herbert Druks, *Harry S. Truman and the Russians, 1945–1953* (New York, 1966); Keith M. Heim, "Hope without Power: Truman and the Russians, 1945" (Ph.D. diss., University of North Carolina, 1973); Melvyn P. Leffler, *A Preponderance of Power: National Security, the Truman Administration, and the Cold War* (Stanford, Calif., 1992); Robert J. Maddox, *From War to Cold War: The Education of Harry Truman* (Boulder, Colo., 1988); David McCullough, *Truman* (New York, 1992); and William E. Pemberton, *Harry S. Truman: Fair Dealer and Cold Warrior* (Boston, 1989).

TYNES, GEORGE W. (1907–1981). Agriculturist, born in Roanoke, Virginia. Tynes graduated from Wilberforce University and became an expert in poultry and fish husbandry. He went to the Soviet Union in 1932 and became a Soviet citizen in 1939. He served in the Soviet Army during World War II as director of a collective farm. He later worked in Georgia, the Crimea, and the Volga region and was chief of a large duck-breeding farm near Moscow until his retirement in 1974. Died in Moscow. *References:* Robert C. Toth, "Pensioner in Russia with Negro Nationality," *International Herald Tribune*, December 18, 1974; and Robert C. Toth, "Russian Negro from Roanoke," *San Francisco Chronicle*, December 16, 1974.

U

U.S.-SOVIET COMMERCIAL AGREEMENTS (1972). The commercial agreements were signed during the *Moscow summit of 1972. The Soviet Union agreed to make a token payment on its *Lend-Lease debt, and the United States promised to seek credits to finance Soviet purchases in the United States and to restore the most-favored-nation tariff status to imports from the Soviet Union. The *Jackson-Vanik amendment to the Trade Act of 1974 permitted lower tariffs only in exchange for easing the emigration restriction on Soviet Jews. The trade agreements failed when the Soviet Union rejected the *Jackson amendment. *References*: Nancy Howard Stetson, ''Congress and Foreign Policy: The 1972 U.S.-U.S.S.R. Trade Agreement and the Trade Reform Act'' (Ph.D. diss., Columbia University, 1979); and U.S. Congress, Senate Committee on Finance, *Background Materials Relating to the United States–Soviet Union Commercial Agreements* (Washington, D.C., 1974).

U.S.-SOVIET CONVENTIONAL ARMS TRANSFER TALKS (CAT). Four rounds of bilateral negotiations on ways to limit arms sales, held between 1977 and 1979. The talks failed. *Reference*: Janne E. Nolan, ''The U.S.-Soviet Conventional Arms Transfer Negotiations,'' in Alexander L. George, Philip J. Farley, and Alexander Dallin, eds., *U.S.-Soviet Security Cooperation: Achievements, Failures, Lessons* (New York, 1988), pp. 510–23.

U.S.-SOVIET STANDING CONSULTATIVE COMMISSION. See STANDING CONSULTATIVE COMMISSION

U.S.-USSR TRADE AND ECONOMIC COUNCIL. Founded in 1973 by American businessmen and Soviet officials as a binational organization to facilitate trade, tourism, banking, insurance, shipping, aviation, and technology transfer between the United States and the Soviet Union. It maintained a binational staff of trade and economic specialists who worked to develop new business ventures and provide trade assistance services and business support facilities. *Reference*: *US-USSR Trade and Economic Council* (New York, 1977).

U-2 INCIDENT (1960). An American aerial reconnaissance plane, the U-2 was developed to meet the requirements of the Central Intelligence Agency for strategic intelligence on the Soviet Union. The initial flight was made on July 1, 1956. A U-2 plane, flown by *Francis Gary Powers, was shot down by the Soviets over Russia on May 1, 1960, and its pilot captured alive. The Soviet government released details of the flight, displayed the pilot, and forced President *Dwight D. Eisenhower to make a full disclosure of the spy flights and accept responsibility for them. The incident caused the collapse of the *Paris summit between Eisenhower and Premier Nikita S. Khrushchev later that month. The U-2 flights were terminated in the early 1960s but were replaced by a more effective satellite surveillance. *References*: Michael R. Beschloss, *Mayday: The U-2 Affair* (New York, 1986); *DADH*; *EAIE*; Jay Miller, *Lockheed U-2* (Austin, Tex., 1983); and David Wise, *The U-2 Affair* (New York, 1962).

V

VANCE, CYRUS ROBERTS (1917–   ). Lawyer and secretary of state born March 27, 1917, in Clarksburg, West Virginia. Vance graduated from Yale University and was admitted to the bar in 1947. He served in the U.S. Navy during World War II. He practiced law in New York City after 1947. He was associated with Simpson, Thacher, and Bartlett from 1947 to 1956 and was partner after 1956. He was general counsel for the Department of Defense in 1961–1962, secretary of the army from 1962 to 1964, and deputy secretary of defense from 1964 to 1967. He was U.S. negotiator at the Paris Peace Conference on Vietnam in 1968–1969. He also participated in the diplomatic efforts that led to the end of the war in Cyprus. He practiced law again from 1969 until 1976. He was secretary of state from 1977 until 1980. He championed the need for détente with the Soviet Union and played a leading role in the SALT II negotiations. He resumed his law practice and wrote his memoirs, *Hard Choices: Four Critical Years in Managing America's Foreign Policy* (New York, 1983). *References: CA; CB* 1977; *DADH;* David S. McClellan, *Cyrus Vance* (New York, 1985); and *WWA.*

VANDERLIP, WASHINGTON B. (?–?). Mining engineer, born in Elkhart, Indiana. Vanderlip worked as a geologist and engineer in Australia, Burma, Siam, and Korea. In the late 1890s, he was sent to Kamchatka and farther north in Siberia by a British mining company to prospect for gold. In 1898, he found only a few low-grade ores of no commercial value. He possibly revisited Kamchatka in 1903. He wrote (with Homer B. Hulbert) *In Search of Siberian Klondike* (New York, 1903). He later traveled in Alaska and the Philippines for General Electric Company and other U.S. concerns and in Nigeria for the British government. He was back in Soviet Russia in 1920, working for a syndicate that he headed. Because the Soviet government confused him with a distant relative, Frank A. Vanderlip of the *National City Bank of New York, he obtained a concession for exclusive coal, oil, and fisheries in northeastern Siberia, including the entire Kamchatka Peninsula. The concession never went into operation. He published his impressions in the May 1921 issue of *Asia*. He vanished after 1921. *References*: Albert Perry, "Washington B. Vanderlip, the 'Khan of Kamchatka,' " *Pacific Historical Review* 17 (1948): 311–30.

VIENNA SUMMIT (1961). Summit meeting between President *John F. Kennedy and Premier Nikita S. Khrushchev on June 3–4, 1961, in Vienna. The two leaders discussed the status of Berlin, disarmament, and Laos. Kennedy also emphasized the danger of miscalculations and situations that endangered either country's vital interests and from which they could not back down. Khrushchev laid down an ultimatum for resolving the Berlin problem. They agreed to maintain contact on all questions of interest to the two countries and the whole world, and they carried on an active private correspondence for the next two years. The summit did not improve East-West relations, as evidenced by the *Berlin Wall crisis, the resumption of Soviet nuclear testing, and the *Cuban missile crisis. *References*: *McDonald*; and *Weihmiller*.

VIENNA SUMMIT (1979). Summit meeting between President *Jimmy Carter and General Secretary Leonid I. Brezhnev, June 15 to 18, 1979, in Vienna. The occasion marked the success, after years of efforts, in reaching an accord on the limitation of strategic weapons. The SALT II Treaty was signed, and the leaders issued a joint communiqué underlining the importance of summit meetings and promising that such meetings would be held in the future on a regular basis. The Soviet invasion of Afghanistan in 1979 cast a pall over U.S.-Soviet relations, and U.S.-Soviet détente crumpled. The United States viewed Soviet military buildup and activities in the Third World as violations of the "spirit" of détente. No more summits were held until November 1985. *References*: *McDonald*; *Weihmiller*; and Joseph G. Whelan, *Soviet Diplomacy and Negotiating Behavior, 1979–88: New Tests for U.S. Diplomacy* (Washington, D.C., 1988), pp. 67–149.

VLADIVOSTOK SUMMIT (1974) . Summit meeting between President Gerald Ford and General Secretary Leonid I. Brezhnev on November 23–24, 1974, in Vladivostok. The two leaders produced general terms for a SALT II treaty. Ceilings were set on the number of total strategic nuclear launch vehicles, along with a subceiling for vehicles with multiple warheads. They issued a Joint Statement of Strategic Offensive Arms, agreeing to resume SALT II negotiations. *References*: *McDonald*; and *Weihmiller*.

W

WALLACE, HENRY AGARD (1888–1965). Agriculturist and public official, born October 7, 1888, in Adair County, Iowa. Wallace graduated from Iowa State College. He joined his family's magazine, *Wallace's Farmer*, in 1910 as associate editor and was its editor from 1924 to 1928 and editor of *Wallace's Farmer and Iowa Homestead* from 1928 to 1933. He was secretary of agriculture from 1933 to 1940, vice-president of the United States from 1941 to 1945, and secretary of commerce in 1945–1946. Focusing his efforts on the growing tensions between the United States and the Soviet Union, he wanted the United States to work to win Soviet trust through international control of nuclear energy and economic assistance, and he criticized President *Harry S. Truman's "get tough" policy toward the Soviet Union. He was forced to resign in 1946. He was editor of *New Republic* in 1946–1947 and the candidate for president on the Progressive Party ticket in 1948. Died November 18, 1965, in Danbury, Connecticut. *References*: Henry Agard Wallace Papers, University of Iowa, Iowa City; John Morton Blum, ed., *The Price of Vision: The Diary of Henry A. Wallace, 1942–1946*, (Boston, 1973); *DAB S7*; John L. Kelley, "An Insurgent in the Truman Cabinet: Henry A. Wallace's Effort to Redirect Foreign Policy," *Missouri Historical Review* 77 (1982): 64–93; *NCAB* 53:15; *NYT*, November 19, 1965; *Polprof: Truman*; Edward L. Schapsmeier and Frederick H. Schapsmeier, *Prophet in Politics: Henry A. Wallace and the War Years, 1940–1965* (Ames, Iowa., 1971); J. Samuel Walker, *Henry A Wallace and American Foreign Policy* (Westport, Conn., 1976); and Richard J. Walton, *Henry Wallace, Harry Truman, and the Cold War* (New York, 1976).

WALLING, WILLIAM ENGLISH (1877–1936). Author, born March 14, 1877, in Louisville, Kentucky. Walling graduated from the University of Chicago. A man of independent means, he devoted his life to the labor movement. He was factory inspector for the State of Illinois in 1900–1901 and a resident of the University Settlement in New York City's lower East Side from 1901 to 1905. In 1905, he went to Russia to study the country and remained there for two years, interviewing most of the leading revolutionary figures, including V. I. Lenin and Maxim Gorky. He wrote *Russia's Message: The True Import of the Revolution* (New York, 1908). He was later involved in the creation of the National Association for the Advancement of Colored People and was active in the Socialist party. He declined President *Woodrow Wilson's offer of a place on the *Root Mission to Russia in 1917. He was later involved with the American Federation of Labor. The Bolshevik Revolution had a profound and conservative effect on him. By 1921, he collaborated with Samuel Gompers in an anti-Soviet book, *Out of Their Own Mouths: A Revelation and an Indictment of Sovietism* (New York, 1921). Died September 12, 1936, in Amsterdam, Holland. *References*: William English Walling Papers, State Historical Society of Wisconsin, Madison; *DAB S2*; *NYT*, September 13, 1936; and Jack M. Stuart, "William English Walling: A Study in Politics and Ideas" (Ph.D. Diss., Columbia University, 1968).

WALSH, EDMUND ALOYSIUS (1885–1956). Priest, born October 10, 1885, in Boston. Walsh graduated from Woodstock (Md.) College and Georgetown University and studied at the Universities of London, Dublin, and Innsbruck (Austria). He joined the Society of Jesus in 1902 and was ordained in 1916. He was dean of the College of Arts and Sciences of Georgetown University in 1918–1919. He was cofounder of the School of Foreign Service of Georgetown University in 1919 and was its regent until 1952. He served in Soviet Russia in 1922 as a representative of American Roman Catholics to the *American Relief Administration. In June 1922, he was named by the Vatican as director general of the Papal Relief Mission to Soviet Russia and was appointed the Vatican's representative in dealing with the Soviet government regarding Roman Catholic interests in Soviet Russia, and he conducted extensive negotiations with the Soviet leaders. He left Soviet Russia in 1923. He then became an outspoken leader in the fight against world communism. He was president of the Catholic Near East Welfare Association from 1926 to 1931. He wrote *The Fall of the Russian Empire: The Story of the Last of the Romanovs and the Coming of the Bolsheviki* (Boston, 1928), *The Last Stand: An Interpretation of the Soviet Fire-Year Plan* (Boston, 1931), and *Total Empire: The Roots and Progress of World Communism* (Milwaukee, 1951). Died October 31, 1956, in Washington, D.C. *References*: Edmund A. Walsh Papers, Georgetown University Library, Washington, D.C.; Louis Joseph Gallagher, *Edmund A. Walsh, S. J.: A Biography* (New York, 1962); *MERSH*; *NCAB* 47:640; and *NYT*, November 1, 1956.

WARDWELL, ALLEN (1873–1953). Lawyer, born October 4, 1873, in New York City. Wardwell graduated from Yale University and Harvard Law School. He practiced law in New York City after 1898. He was a founder and member of the law firm of Davis, Polk, Wardwell, Sunderland, and Kiendl and predecessor firms after 1909. He was commissioner of the American Red Cross mission to Russia in 1917–1918. He was involved in the efforts to support trade with and aid to Soviet Russia from 1919 to 1924 and was chairman of the Russian Famine Fund in that period. He made another trip to Soviet Russia in 1922 in connection with the famine. He was chairman of the American Red Cross delegation to the Soviet Union in 1941 and participated in the *Averell Harriman mission. Died December 5, 1953, in New York City. *References*: Allen Wardwell Papers, Columbia University Library, New York City; *NYT*, December 21, 1953; and *WWA*.

WARE, HAROLD M. (1890–1935). Agriculturist, born in Woodbury, New Jersey. Ware was involved in vegetable and garden operation, and then in a mushroom house, studied at Pennsylvania State College, owned and ran a farm near Downington, Pennsylvania, from 1911 to 1914 and then sold out, and worked as draughtsman in a shipyard until the end of World War I. He became a member of the Workers' Party. He organized the *American Tractor Brigade, went with it to Russia in 1922, and spent a season at Toikino state farm in Perm Province in the Ural Mountains. He returned to Russia in 1925 and founded the Russian Reconstruction Farm, a Russian-American mixed company at Maslov Kut in the north Caucasus, of which he was the American director until 1928. He was later at the Verblud Sovhoz farm east of Rostov-on-the-Don, in 1929–1930. He returned to the United States in 1931. He conducted a national farm survey in the United States in 1931–1932, then established Farm Research Incorporated, a research center in Washington, D.C., and worked with farmers and farm workers in the United States from 1931 to 1935. Died August 13, 1935, following a car accident, in Harrisburg, Pennsylvania. *References*: Elle Reeve Bloor, *We Are Many: An Autobiography* (New York, 1940), pp. 266–79; and Lement U. Harris, *Harold M. Ware, 1890–1935: Agricultural Pioneer, U.S.A. and U.S.S.R.* (New York, 1978).

WARNKE, PAUL CULLITON (1920–   ). Government official, born January 31, 1920, in Webster, Massachusetts. Warnke graduated from Yale University and Columbia University Law School and was admitted to the bar in 1948. He served in the U.S. Coast Guard during World War II. He practiced law in Washington, D.C., from 1948 to 1966. He was general counsel for the Department of Defense in 1966–1967 and assistant secretary of defense for international security affairs from 1967 to 1969. He resumed the practice of law from 1969 to 1977. He was director of the Arms Control and Disarmament Agency and chief negotiator for the SALT II talks in 1977–1978. The negotiations had moved close to a SALT II agreement in October 1978, when he resigned. *References*: *CB* 1977; *DADH*; and *WWA*.

WASHBURN, STANLEY (1878–1950). Journalist, born February 7, 1878, in Minneapolis. Washburn graduated from Williams College and attended Harvard University Law School. He worked for the *Minneapolis Journal*, *Minneapolis Times*, and *Chicago Daily News*. In 1905, he covered the Odessa mutiny and the disorders of the Russian revolution of that year, and in 1906, he covered the revolutionary disturbances in other parts of Russia. He was war correspondent for *Collier's Weekly* in 1914 and was back in Russia that year as war correspondent for the London *Times*. He was attached to the Russian Army, the only American journalist to have access to the whole Russian front until 1916. He wrote *The Russian Campaign, April to August 1915* (London, 1915), *Victory in Defeat: The Agony of Warsaw and the Russian Retreat* (London, 1916), and *The Russian Offensive* (London, 1917). He served in the U.S. Army during World War I and then was military aide to *John F. Stevens, who headed the Advisory Commission of Railway Experts to Siberia in 1917. He was a member of the *Root Mission in 1917–1918. He settled in Lakewood, New Jersey, and was involved in writing and business interests. Died December 14, 1950, in Lakewood, New Jersey. *References*: Stanley Washburn Papers, Manuscript Division, Library of Congress; *NCAB* 43:41; *NYT*, December 15, 1950; and Stanley Washburn, *On the Russian Front in World War I: Memoirs of an American War Correspondent* (New York, 1982).

WASHINGTON SUMMIT (1959). Summit meeting between President *Dwight D. Eisenhower and Premier Nikita S. Khruschev on September 25 to 27, 1959, in Washington and Camp David, Maryland. The United States aimed to obtain a moratorium of Soviet threats regarding Berlin, underlining that the West intended to stand firm on this issue and that a summit meeting of the Big Four could not be held unless there was a realistic prospect for success. The discussions focused on the *Berlin crisis, but no progress was made on any of the other agenda items, including disarmament, trade and credits, and a nuclear test ban. Khrushchev agreed to lift his ultimatum on Berlin in exchange for Eisenhower's agreement to attend a summit meeting and also to visit Moscow. *References*: *McDonald*; and *Weihmiller*.

WASHINGTON SUMMIT (1973). Summit meeting between President *Richard Nixon and General Secretary Leonid I. Brezhnev on June 18 to 25, 1973, in Washington and San Clemente, California. Eleven agreements and protocols were signed, including the Agreement on the Prevention of Nuclear War and one containing a pledge that the two sides would make serious efforts to work out a permanent agreement on strategic offensive arms by the end of 1974. Other agreements concerned cooperation in the peaceful uses of atomic energy, in agriculture, and in transportation. *References*: *McDonald*; and *Weihmiller*.

WASHINGTON SUMMIT (1987). Summit meeting between President *Ronald Reagan and General Secretary Mikhail S. Gorbachev on December 6 to 9, 1987, in Washington. The two leaders signed the Intermediate-Range Nuclear Forces (*INF) Treaty. They also made some progress on an agreement to reduce strategic (long-range) nuclear weapons.

WASHINGTON SUMMIT (1990). Summit meeting between President *George Bush and President Mikhail S. Gorbachev on May 30–June 2, 1990, in Washington, D.C. The two leaders signed an agreement banning the production of chemical weapons and eliminating most of the existing stockpiles, a trade agreement that normalized trade relations between the two countries, and a long-term grain accord, regulating grain sale to the Soviet Union. *Reference*: Joseph G. Whelan, *Soviet Diplomacy and Negotiating Behavior, 1988–90; Gorbachev, Reagan, Bush Meetings at the Summit* (Washington, D.C., 1991), pp. 291–418.

WEBER, JOHN B. (1842–1926). Government official, born September 21, 1842, in Buffalo, New York. Weber was clerk and bookkeeper for a grain and flour commission house in Buffalo and served in the Union Army during the Civil War. He was assistant postmaster of Buffalo from 1870 to 1873, was sheriff of Erie County from 1874 to 1876, engaged in the wholesale grocery business until 1884, and served in the U.S. House of Representatives from 1885 to 1889. He was commissioner of immigration at the port of New York from 1889 to 1893. In 1891, he served as chairman of a commission that investigated abroad the causes that influenced immigration to the United States, in which capacity he visited Russia in 1892, making extensive investigations of the persecution of the Jews. He was a cashier of the American Exchange Bank of Buffalo after 1895. He wrote *Autobiography of John B. Weber* (Buffalo, N.Y., 1924). Died December 18, 1926, in Lackawanna, New York. *References*: *BDAC*; *NCAB* 24:406; and *NYT*, December 19, 1926.

WESTERN UNION TELEGRAPH EXPEDITION. See RUSSIAN-AMERICAN TELEGRAPH EXPEDITION

WHEATLAND, RICHARD (1762–1830). Sea captain and merchant, born October 20, 1762, in Wareham, Dorset, England. Wheatland lived in London and served in the British Navy. He came to Salem in 1784 and became a shipmaster. He commanded the brig *Vigilant* after 1794 and arrived with it in Archangel in 1798, becoming one of the first Americans to trade at that port. He also sailed to St. Petersburg in 1796 as captain of the *Perseverance*. He actively followed the sea until about 1800. He then engaged in mercantile business in Salem. Died March 18, 1830, in Salem, Massachusetts. *References*: *Vigilant* Logbook, Essex Institute Library, Salem, Mass.; and *Portraits of Shipmasters and Merchants in the Peabody Museum of Salem* (Salem, Mass., 1939).

WHISTLER, GEORGE WASHINGTON (1800–1849). Civil engineer, born May 19, 1800, in Fort Wayne, Indiana. Whistler graduated from the U.S. Military Academy in 1819 and was commissioned second lieutenant in the corps of artillery. He was involved in various topographical surveys until 1833, when he resigned from the army. He then directed various surveys for railroads and oversaw the construction of various lines. He went to Russia in 1842 as consulting engineer for the construction of the railroad from St. Petersburg to Moscow. His advice to the government of Tsar Nicholas I determined the gauge of that railroad and of all railroads built in the Russian Empire thereafter. He supervised the construction of the St. Petersburg–Moscow railroad, which was opened to traffic in 1850. He also supervised the construction of the fortifications, naval arsenal, and docks at Cronstadt, the plans for improving the Dvina River at Archangel, and the iron bridge on the Neva River. Died April 7, 1849, in St. Petersburg. His son, **GEORGE WILLIAM WHISTLER** (1822–1869), civil engineer, was born in New London, Connecticut. He became his father's assistant in 1840. He was superintendent of the Erie and the New York and New Haven railroads and was connected with other lines. He went to Russia in 1856 to complete the St. Petersburg and Moscow railroad in accordance with his father's plans. He remained until 1868, resigned because of ill health, and settled in England. Died December 24, 1869, in Brighton, England. *References*: Anna Matilda McNeill Whistler Diaries 1843–1848, New York Public Library; *DAB*; *MERSH*; *NCAB* 9:48; *NCAB* 9:49; and Albert Parry, *Whistler's Father* (Indianapolis, 1939).

WHITNEY, THOMAS PORTER (1917–). Journalist, born January 26, 1917, in Toledo, Ohio. Whitney graduated from Amherst College and Columbia University. He was social science analyst with the Office of Strategic Services in Washington, D.C., during World War II, attaché and chief of the economic section at the U.S. embassy in Moscow from 1944 to 1947, and staff correspondent for the Associated Press in Moscow from 1947 to 1953. He was foreign news analyst in New York City from 1953 to 1959, president of Whitney Enterprises in New York City from 1966 to 1968, and chairman of the board from 1966 to 1973. He wrote *Russia in My Life* (New York, 1962), *Has Russia Changed?* (New York, 1960), and *Communist Blueprint for the Future: The Complete Texts of All Four Communist Manifestoes, 1848–1961* (New York, 1962), edited *Khrushchev Speaks: Selected Speeches, Articles, and Press Conferences, 1949–1961* (Ann Arbor, Mich., 1963), and translated *One Day in the Life of Ivan Denisovich, First Circle*, and *The Gulag Archipelago* by Aleksandr I. Solzhenitsyn. *References*: *CA*; P. M. Perry, "Interview with Solzhenitsyn's Translator," *Writers Digest* 54 (July 1974): 20–23; and *WWA*.

WILKINS, WILLIAM (1779–1865). Public official and diplomat, born December 20, 1779, in Carlisle, Pennsylvania, and grew up in Pittsburgh. Wilkins attended Dickinson College, studied law, and was admitted to the bar in 1801. He was president of the Bank of Pittsburgh, the Monongahela Bridge Company, the Greensburg and Pittsburgh Turnpike Company, and the Pittsburgh common council until 1819. He served in the state legislature in 1819–1820, was judge of the fifth judicial district of Pennsylvania from 1820 to 1824, was judge of the U.S. district court for western Pennsylvania from 1824 to 1826, and served in the U.S. Senate from 1831 to 1834. He was U.S. minister to Russia in 1834–

1835. His negotiations for a treaty of neutral rights and for the renewal of certain trading rights in North America were unsuccessful. He served in the U.S. House of Representatives from 1842 to 1844, was secretary of war in 1844–1845, and served in the Pennsylvania state senate after 1855. Died June 23, 1865, in Pittsburgh. *References*: *BDAC*; *DAB*; *NCAB* 1:429; and *NYT*, June 24, 1865.

WILLIAM ROPES AND COMPANY. Merchant firm, established in 1832 in St. Petersburg by *William Ropes and carried into the twentieth century by his son, William Hooper Ropes, and other members of the family. The business was broken up in 1913, on the death of the last St. Petersburg partner, Ernest Edward Ropes. *Reference*: Harriett Ropes Cabot, "The Early Years of William Ropes and Company in St. Petersburg," *American Neptune* 23 (1963): 131–39.

WILLIAMS, ALBERT RHYS (1883–1962). Journalist and author, born September 28, 1883, in Greenwich, Ohio, and grew up in Hancock, New York. Williams graduated from Marietta College (Ohio) and Hartford Theological Seminary and studied at Cambridge University and the University of Marburg (Germany). He was minister of a Congregational church in Boston from 1908 to 1914. He was a correspondent for the *Outlook* in Germany during World War I and was arrested by the German authorities on charges of espionage. He went to Petrograd in 1917 as a reporter for the *New York Evening Post*. He became an ardent supporter of bolshevism, met V. I. Lenin, Leon Trotsky, and other Bolshevik leaders, and was one of the best-known sympathizers of Lenin's Bolshevik ideology. He was also a friend and accomplice of *John Reed. He served the Soviet government as assistant in the Commissariat for Foreign Affairs and prepared propaganda to be disseminated among the Germany military forces at the front. He volunteered for service in the Red Army during the early stages of the Russian Civil War and helped create an International Legion, composed of foreigners who were staunch defenders of the Soviet cause. He returned to the United States in 1918. He then lectured and wrote on Soviet affairs, including *Lenin: The Man and His Work* (New York, 1919) and *Through the Russian Revolution* (New York, 1921), a memoir of his experiences in Soviet Russia. He traveled again in Russia from 1922 to 1928, visiting remote areas and attempting to study the impact of the revolution on life in the Russian countryside, and wrote *The Russian Land* (New York, 1928) and *The Soviets* (New York, 1937). He returned to the Soviet Union in 1930, to again study the Russian countryside, and made another trip in 1937. Through the 1930s, he continued to lecture and write about the Soviet Union. He wrote *The Russians: The Land, the People, and Why They Fight* (New York, 1943). He made a final trip in 1959. He later lived in Cedar, Vancouver Island, Canada, in Carmel, California, and in Ossining, New York. Died February 27, 1962, in Tarrytown, New York.

Journey into Revolution: Petrograd, 1917–1918, ed. Lucita Williams (Chicago, 1969) was published posthumously. *References*: *MERSH*; *NYT*, February 28, 1962; and *WWWA*.

WILLIAMS, FRANKWOOD EARLE (1883–1936). Psychiatrist, born May 18, 1883, in Cardington, Ohio. Williams graduated from the University of Wisconsin and the University of Michigan Medical School. He was executive officer and first assistant physician at the Boston Psychopathic Hospital from 1913 to 1915, medical director of the Massachusetts Society for Mental Hygiene from 1915 to 1917, and first assistant and chief of the division of neurology and psychiatry in the Office of the Surgeon General in Washington, D.C., during World War I. He was associate medical director of the National Committee for Mental Hygiene from 1918 until 1922 and its medical director from 1922 until 1931. He then resumed the private practice of psychiatry and psychoanalysis. He visited the Soviet Union in 1931, thought that the Soviet Union was a mental hygienist paradise, and wrote of his experiences in the January 1, 1932, issue of *Survey Graphic*. He also wrote *Soviet Russia Fights Neurosis* (London, 1934) and *Russia, Youth, and the Present-Day World* (New York, 1934). Died September 24, 1936, at sea. *References*: *NCAB* 33:241; and *NYT*, September 26, 1936.

WILLIAMS, SPENCER (1898–1964). Journalist, born in Utica, New York. Williams worked for newspapers in Utica, Rochester, and San Diego. He went to Moscow in 1929 as a special correspondent for Fairchild Publications. He also wrote for the *Manchester Guardian, Wall Street Journal, London Daily Herald*, and Columbia Broadcasting System (CBS). He was a representative of the *American-Russian Chamber of Commerce in Moscow from 1929 to 1940. He then worked in Bucharest for the *Manchester Guardian* and CBS, returned to the United States, and was CBS commentator on Soviet and Balkan affairs. He worked for the United States Information Service as head of foreign broadcast monitoring service operations in the Pacific during World War II. He was director of the worldwide press service of the Radio Liberty Committee after 1950. Died October 24, 1964, in Fort Walton, Florida. *Reference*: *NYT*, October 25, 1964.

WILSON, MILBURN LINCOLN (1885–1969). Agriculturist, born October 23, 1885, in Atlantic, Iowa. Wilson graduated from Iowa State (later University) and the University of Wisconsin. He was professor of agricultural economics at Montana State University from 1926 to 1933 and managing director of the Fairway Farms Corporation of Montana from 1924 to 1933. He served as an adviser for the Grain Trust of the USSR on the organization and management of large-scale mechanized grain farms and was hired by Amtorg as a consultant and to assist in handling orders with American tractor companies. He was in the Soviet Union in 1929 as adviser to Verblud, a demonstration farm in the North Caucasus. In 1929, he served as a technical consultant to the Soviet Union in the handling of mechanized equipment on large-scale wheat operations being started in the Caucasus. He was undersecretary of agriculture from 1937 until 1940 and director of the Federal Extension Service in the Department of Agriculture from 1940 until his retirement in 1953. Died November 22, 1969, in Washington, D.C. *References*: Milburn Lincoln Wilson Papers, Montana State University Library, Bozeman; *NCAB* 55:146; Thomas R. Wessel, "Wheat for the Soviet Masses: M. L. Wilson and the Montana Connection," *Montana* 31 (1981): 42–53; and *WWWA*.

WILSON, WOODROW (1856–1924). President of the United States, born December 28, 1856, in Staunton, Virginia. Wilson attended Davidson College (N.C.) and graduated from Princeton and Johns Hopkins universities. He taught at Bryn Mawr College from 1885 to 1888, was professor of jurisprudence and political economy at Princeton University from 1890 to 1902, and was president of Princeton from 1902 to 1910. He was governor of New Jersey from 1911 to 1913 and president of the United States from 1913 to 1921. Following the overthrow of the Russian monarchy in March 1917, Wilson hastened to do everything in his power to lend support to the new provisional government in Russia. The United States was the first nation to recognize the new Russian regime on March 22, 1917. He began negotiations to extend financial assistance to the new government, arranged to send the *Russian Railway Service Corps and the *Root Mission to confirm American support of the new Russian democracy and to ascertain how the United States could best assist the Russian war effort. He also organized the Russian Bureau of the War Trade Board to provide economic and relief assistance to Russia. In November 1917, he adopted an anti-Bolshevik stance. He agreed to U.S. intervention in North Russia and in Siberia in 1918, sending military expeditions, which were later withdrawn. He continued to work unsuccessfully for a peaceful settlement of the situation in Russia, sending *William C. Bullitt on a secret mission to Moscow to confer with Soviet leaders on peace-related issues but then ignoring Bullitt's proposals. Died February 2, 1924, in Washington, D.C. *References*: *DAB*; Lloyd C. Gardner, *Wilson and Revolutions, 1913–1921* (Philadelphia, 1976); N. Gordon Levin, Jr., *Woodrow Wilson and World Politics: America's Response to War and Revolution* (New York, 1968); Robert J. Maddox, "Woodrow Wilson, the Russian Embassy, and Siberian Intervention," *Pacific Historical Review* 36 (1967): 435–48; Arno J. Mayer, *Wilson vs. Lenin: Political Origins of the New Diplomacy, 1917–1918* (Cleveland, 1964); *MERSH*; Brenda K. Shelton, *President Wilson and the Russian Revolution* (Buffalo, N.Y., 1957); Eugene P. Trani, "Woodrow Wilson and the Decision to Intervene in Russia: A Reconsideration," *Journal of Modern History* 48 (1976): 440–61; Betty Miller Unterberger, "President Wilson and the Decision to Send American Troops to Siberia," *Pacific Historical Review* 24 (1955): 63–68; Betty Miller Unterberger, "Woodrow Wilson and the Bolsheviks: The 'Acid Test' of Soviet-American Relations," *DH* 11 (1987): 71–90; and Betty Miller Unterberger, "Woodrow Wilson and the Russian Revolution," in Arthur S. Lind, ed., *Woodrow Wilson and a Revolutionary World, 1913–1921* (Chapel Hill, N.C., 1982), pp. 49–104.

WINANS, THOMAS DEKAY (1820–1878). Mechanical engineer and inventor, born December 6, 1820, in Vernon, Sussex County, New Jersey, and grew up in Baltimore. Winans was apprenticed to a machinist and became head of the department in his father's establishment. In 1843, his father, Ross Winans (1796–1877), was invited by the Russian government to build the rolling stock for the Moscow and St. Petersburg railroad but declined the invitation in favor of his two sons. In 1843, carrying with him a locomotive built by his father, Winans went to Russia with his brother, William L., to take charge of the mechanical department of the construction of the railroad. He formed a business partnership with *Joseph Harrison and secured a contract to equip the railroad and supply it with locomotives and rolling stock. Establishing the firm of Harrison, Winans, and Eastwick for the Russian enterprise, he fulfilled the contract in 1847, more than a year before the time agreed upon. The firm also provided all the cast iron for the first permanent bridge over the Neva River in St. Petersburg. Winans returned to the United States in 1851, leaving his brother to fulfill the remaining contracts, which were completed in 1862. In 1866, the firm was recalled to Russia under a new contract, but the Russian government took over its interests in 1868. Winans later retired in Baltimore. Died June 10, 1878, in Newport, Rhode Island. *References*: Winans Family Papers, Maryland Historical Society, Baltimore; *DAB*; and *NCAB* 1:239.

WINCHELL, HORACE VAUGHN (1865–1923). Geologist, born November 1, 1865, in Galesburg, Michigan. Winchell graduated from the University of Chicago. He was assistant state geologist of Minnesota from 1889 to 1892 and was later in charge of the explorations of the Mesabi and Vermilion iron ore range for the Minnesota Iron Company. He engaged in general consulting practice as an economic geologist and mining expert from 1893 to 1897, acted as geologist for the Anaconda Copper Mining Company and for other subsidiaries of the Amalgamated Copper Company from 1898 to 1906, and was a consulting geologist to the company from 1906 until his death. He was also chief geologist for the Great Northern Railway Company from 1906 to 1908, when he resumed general consulting practice. In 1917, he conducted a geological exploration in Russia and Siberia, reporting on mineral properties in the Caucasus and elsewhere in Russia and witnessing the Russian Revolution. Died July 28, 1923, in Los Angeles. *References*: *DAB*; *DSB*; and *NCAB* 20:200.

WINKFIELD, JIMMY (1882–1974). Jockey, born April 12, 1882, in Chilesburg, Kentucky. Winkfield was offered a job at the Latonia race track in 1897 and rode his first race for money in 1898. In 1900, he first rode in the Kentucky Derby, and he won the Derby twice, in 1901 and 1902. He was blackballed in 1903 after switching mounts before a stakes race. In 1903, he was offered a job training horses in Russia for an American. He left Russia in 1909 but was lured back in 1913. He escaped to Poland in 1919 and settled in France in 1922. He raced in France until 1930 and then became a trainer. After World War II he returned to the United States and worked as a groom. In 1953 he returned to France and opened a school for training jockeys. Died March 23, 1974, in Paris, France. *References*: *NYT*, March 25, 1974; "The Saga of Jimmy Winkfield," *Ebony* 29 (June 1974): 64–70; and Roy Terell, "Around the World in 80 Years," *Sports Illustrated* 14 (May 8, 1961): 71–88.

WINSHIP, NORTH (1885–1968). Diplomat, born December 31, 1885, in Macon, Georgia. Winship graduated from Mercer University, attended George Washington University, and was admitted to the bar in 1910. He joined the foreign service in 1910, serving as consul in Tahiti from 1910 to 1913, in Owen Sound, Ontario, Canada, in 1913, and in St. Petersburg from 1914 to 1917. He regularly forwarded to Washington detailed and perceptive accounts of what was going on in St. Petersburg, but they arrived late in Washington. President *Woodrow Wilson did not see them and did not act on the basis of the information they contained. Winship was consul in Milan, Bombay, Fiume, Italy, and Cairo from 1917 to 1926, secretary of legation in Egypt from 1926 to 1928, consul general in Copenhagen from 1928 to 1931, counselor in the legation in Copenhagen from 1931 to 1937 and the embassy in Warsaw from 1937 to 1939, counselor in the legation in Pretoria from 1939 to 1931, consul general in Toronto from 1941 to 1944 and in Montreal from 1944 to 1948, and U.S. minister to the Union of South Africa in 1948–1949 and ambassador in 1949–1950. He retired in 1950. Died November 1, 1968, in Macon, Georgia. *References*: *NCAB* 54:391; and *WWWA*.

WITKIN, ZARA (1900–1940). Civil engineer, born December 14, 1900, in Bondsville, Massachusetts. Witkin graduated from the University of California College of Civil Engineering. He was reclamation assistant engineer in Sacramento, plant manager at the Computer Manufacturing Company in San Francisco, maintenance-of-way engineer for the Southern Pacific Company in San Francisco, engineer for the San Francisco Bureau of Governmental Research, construction engineer for MacDonald and Kahn in Los Angeles, chief engineer for a construction firm in Los Angeles until 1924, and engineer and then chief engineer of the Herbert M. Baruch Corporation in Los Angeles from 1924 to 1932. He was consulting engineer for the All-Union Construction Trust of the USSR from 1932 to 1934. In 1934 he founded his own firm in Los Angeles and was president of Fabricated Houses, Incorporated, after 1935. Died June 16, 1940, in Los Angeles. *References*: Michael Gelb, ed., *An American Engineer in Stalin's Russia: The Memoirs of Zara Witkin, 1932–1934* (Berkeley, Calif., 1991); and *WWIN*.

WOLFE, BERTRAM DAVID (1896–1977). Author, born January 19, 1896, in Brooklyn, New York. Wolfe graduated from the College of the City of New York, the University of Mexico, and Columbia University. He was a teacher at the Miguel Lerdo High School in Mexico City from 1922 to 1925 and was one of the founders of the Mexican Communist party. He was expelled from Mexico by the Mexican government for supporting Communist ideals among railroad workers. He was educational director of the Workers School of the American Communist Party in New York City from 1926 to 1928. As a member of the executive committee of the Comintern, he spent 1928 to 1930 in Moscow. He was later a free-lance writer until 1950 and then became chief of the ideological advisory unit of the International Broadcasting Division of the State Department. He was senior fellow in Slavic studies at the Hoover Institution in 1949–1950 and from 1965 to 1968 and was senior research fellow after 1968. He wrote *Three Who Made a Revolution: A Biographical History* (Boston, 1948), *Six Keys to the Soviet System* (Boston, 1956), *The Bridge and the Abyss: The Troubled Friendship of Maxim Gorky and V. I. Lenin* (Stanford, Calif., 1967), and *Lenin* (New York, 1978). *A Life in Two Centuries: An Autobiography* (New York, 1981) was published posthumously. Died February 21, 1977, in Palo Alto, California. *References*: *CA*; Lennard D. Gerson, ed., *Lenin and the Twentieth Century: A Bertram D. Wolfe Retrospective* (Stanford, Calif., 1984); Herbert Hessen, ed., *Breaking with Communism: The Intellectual Odyssey of Bertram D. Wolfe* (Stanford, Calif., 1990); *NCAB* 59:85; and *NYT*, February 22, 1977.

WRIGHT, JOSHUA BUTLER (1877–1939). Diplomat, born October 18, 1877, in Irvington, New York. Wright graduated from Princeton University. He engaged in banking and brokerage business in New York City from 1899 to 1906 and in agriculture and stock raising in Wyoming from 1907 to 1909. He entered the diplomatic service in 1909, serving as secretary of legation in Tagucigalpa and in Brussels, secretary of embassy in Rio de Janeiro, and acting chief of the division of Latin American affairs in the State Department. He was counselor of embassy in St. Petersburg from 1916 to 1918 in charge of the embassy chancery and its day-to-day operations. He was counselor of embassy in London from 1918 to 1923, third assistant secretary of state in 1923–1924, assistant secretary of state from 1924 to 1927, U.S. minister to Hungary from 1927 to 1930, minister to Uruguay from 1930 to 1934, minister to Czechoslovakia from 1934 to 1937, and minister to Cuba from 1937 until his death. Died December 4, 1939, in Havana, Cuba. *References*: *DADH*; *NCAB* 30:196; and *NYT*, December 5, 1939.

Y

YALTA CONFERENCE (1945). Summit meeting at Yalta, in the Crimea, on February 4–11, 1945, attended by President *Franklin D. Roosevelt, Premier Joseph Stalin, and Prime Minister Winston S. Churchill. The three leaders met to make arrangements for a postwar international order and plans for administering Europe. Roosevelt wanted to win Stalin's confidence in American goodwill, to ensure a peaceful postwar world, to nail down the Soviet commitment to enter the Far Eastern war, and to get Stalin's agreement on the creation of the United Nations. The leaders agreed that Germany would be occupied in four separate zones, that the Russian-Polish boundary would move westward and that Poland would be compensated by German territory to the west, and that each liberated country or Axis satellite would have a freely elected democratic government of its own choice. The conference was highly criticized after Stalin broke his promise of free elections in Eastern Europe and installed governments dominated by the Soviet Union. Roosevelt was charged with "selling out" to the Soviets at Yalta. *References*: Russell D. Buhite, *Decisions at Yalta: An Appraisal of Summit Diplomacy* (Wilmington, Del., 1986); Diane Shaver Clemens, *Yalta* (New York, 1970); John L. Snell et al., *The Meaning of Yalta: Big Three Diplomacy and the New Balance of Power* (Baton Rouge, La., 1956); Cyrus Sulzberger, *Such a Peace: The Roots and Ashes of Yalta* (New York, 1982); and Athan G. Theoharis, *The Yalta Myths: An Issue in U.S. Politics, 1945–1955* (Columbia, Mo., 1970).

YOUNG MEN'S CHRISTIAN ASSOCIATION (YMCA). Nonsectarian Christian lay organization, founded in the United States in 1851. The International Committee was formed in 1879. YMCA operations in Russia began in St. Petersburg in 1900 and were generally known under the name *Mayak* (Lighthouse). Financed by James Stokes (1841–1918), Mayak reached a peak between 1917 and 1920, when more than 440 YMCA staffers served in Soviet Russia. The YMCA was forced out of the Soviet Union in 1923. *References*: YMCA of the U.S.A. Archives, University of Minnesota Library, St. Paul; Donald E.

Davis and Eugene P. Trani, "The American YMCA and the Russian Revolution," *SR* 33 (1974): 469–91; Franklin A. Gaylord, "Breaking into Russia," in Frank W. Ober, ed., *James Stokes: Pioneer of Young Men's Christian Association* (New York, 1921), ch. 9; and Kenneth S. Latourette, *World Service: A History of the Foreign Work and World Service of the Young Men's Christian Associations of the United States and Canada* (New York, 1957).

Z

ZERO OPTION. A proposal made by President *Ronald Reagan to the Soviet Union in 1981 concerning intermediate-range land-based nuclear missiles. In the proposal, the United States offered to cancel its planned deployment in Europe of Pershing II and ground-launched cruise missiles if the Soviet Union would dismantle its SS–20, SS–4, and SS–5 missiles. The Soviets counter proposal to freeze both the number and the quality of the nuclear weapons already in place in the European part of the Soviet Union and to place a moratorium on the planned replacement of the existing SS–4 and SS–5 missiles by the new SS–20 models. The Soviet moratorium would have remained in force unless the United States proceeded with the deployment of Pershing II and cruise missiles. Both proposals were rejected. *References*: *DINRT*; and Thomas Risse-Kapper, *The Zero Option: INF, West Germany, and Arms Control* (Boulder, Colo., 1988).

United States Chiefs of Diplomatic Missions in Russia and the Soviet Union

ABBREVIATIONS

AE/P	Ambassador Extraordinary and Plenipotentiary
CdA	Chargé d'affaires
EE/MP	Envoy Extraordinary and Minister Plenipotentiary
MP	Minister Plenipotentiary

REPRESENTATIVES COMMISSIONED TO RUSSIA

John Quincy Adams (1767–1848), MP, 1809–1814
William Pinkney (1764–1822), EE/MP 1816–1818
George Washington Campbell (1769–1848), EE/MP 1818–1821
Henry Middleton (1770–1846), EE/MP 1821–1830
James Buchanan (1791–1868), EE/MP 1832–1834
William Wilkins (1779–1865), EE/MP 1834–1836
John Randolph Clay (1808–1885), CdA 1836–1837
George Mifflin Dallas (1792–1864), EE/MP 1837–1839
Churchill Caldom Cambreleng (1786–1862), EE/MP 1840–1841
Charles Stewart Todd (1791–1871), EE/MP 1841–1846
Ralph Isaacs Ingersoll (1789–1872), EE/MP 1847–1848
Arthur Pendleton Bagby (1794–1858), EE/MP 1848–1849
Neill Smith Brown (1810–1886), EE/MP 1850–1853
Thomas Hart Seymour (1807–1868), EE/MP 1853–1858
Francis Wilkinson Pickens (1805–1869), EE/MP 1858–1860
Cassius Marcellus Clay (1810–1903), EE/MP 1861–1862, 1863–1869
Andrew Gregg Curtin (1815–1894), EE/MP 1869–1872
James Lawrence Orr (1822–1873), EE/MP 1872–1873
Marshall Jewell (1825–1883), EE/MP 1873–1874
George Henry Boker (1823–1890), EE/MP 1875–1878

Edwin Wallace Stoughton (1818–1882), EE/MP 1878–1879
John Watson Foster (1836–1917), EE/MP 1880–1881
William Henry Hunt (1823–1884), EE/MP 1882–1884
Alphonso Taft (1810–1891), EE/MP 1884–1885
George Van Ness Lothrop (1817–1897), EE/MP 1885–1887
Lambert Tree (1832–1910), EE/MP 1889
Charles Emory Smith (1842–1908), EE/MP 1890–1892
Andrew Dickson White (1832–1918), EE/MP 1892–1894
Clifton Rodes Breckinridge (1846–1932), EE/MP 1894–1897
Ethan Allen Hitchcock (1835–1909), EE/MP 1897–1898, AE/P 1898–1899
Charlemagne Tower (1848–1923), AE/P 1899–1902
Robert Sanderson McCormick (1849–1919), AE/P 1903–1905
George von Lengerke Meyer (1858–1918), AE/P 1905–1907
John Wallace Riddle (1864–1941), AE/P 1907–1909
William Woodville Rockhill (1854–1914), AE/P 1909–1911
Curtis Guild (1860–1915), AE/P 1911–1913
George T. Marye (1857–1933), AE/P 1914–1916
David Rowland Francis (1850–1927), AE/P 1916–1918

REPRESENTATIVES COMMISSIONED TO THE UNION OF SOVIET SOCIALIST REPUBLICS

William Christian Bullitt (1891–1967), AE/P 1933–1936.
Joseph Edward Davies (1876–1958), AE/P 1936–1938
Laurence Adolph Steinhardt (1892–1950), AE/P 1939–1942
William Harrison Standley (1872–1963), AE/P 1942–1943
William Averell Harriman (1891–1986), AE/P 1943–1946
Walter Bedell Smith (1895–1961), AE/P 1946–1949
Alan Goodrich Kirk (1888–1953), AE/P 1949–1951
George Frost Kennan (1904–   ), AE/P 1952
Charles Eustis Bohlen (1904–1974), AE/P 1953–1957
Llewellyn E. Thompson, Jr. (1904–1972), AE/P 1957–1962, 1966–1969
Foy David Kohler (1908–1990), AE/P 1962–1966
Jacob Dyneley Beam (1908–   ), AE/P 1969–1973
Walter John Stoessel, Jr. (1920–1986), AE/P 1974–1976
Malcolm Toon (1916–   ), AE/P 1977–1979
Thomas J. Watson, Jr. (1914–   ), AE/P 1979–1981
Arthur Adair Hartman (1926–   ), AE/P 1981–1987
Jack Foust Matlock, Jr. (1929–   ), AE/P 1987–1991
Robert Schwarz Strauss (1918–   ), AE/P 1991–1993

List of Individuals by Profession and Occupation

ACTORS

Aldridge, Ira Frederick
Harvey, Georgette
Mitchell, Abbie
Robeson, Paul
Ross, Robert

AGRICULTURISTS

Campbell, Thomas Donald
Garst, Roswell
Harris, Franklin Stewart
Johnson, Albert Aaron
Michael, Louis Guy
Rosen, Joseph A.
Stirniman, Edward James
Tynes, George W.
Wallace, Henry Agard
Ware, Harold M.
Wilson, Milburn Lincoln

ANARCHISTS

Berkman, Alexander
Goldman, Emma

ARMY OFFICERS. *See also* SOLDIERS

Deane, John Russell
Eisenhower, Dwight David
Faymonville, Philip Ries
Graves, William Sidney
Greene, Francis Vinton
Haskell, William Nafew
Judson, William Voorhees
McClellan, George Brinton
Miles, Sherman
Richardson, Wilds Preston
Rowny, Edward Leon
Ruggles, James A.
Smith, Walter Bedell

ARTISTS

Frost, George Albert

ASSOCIATION OFFICIALS

Anderson, Paul B.
Colton, Ethan Theodore
Gaylord, Franklin Augustus
Heald, Edward Thornton
Lowrie, Donald Alexander
Miller, Alvin Joseph
Mott, John Raleigh
Story, Russell McCulloch

AUTHORS

Berkman, Alexander
Beveridge, Albert Jeremiah
Boker, George Henry
Buel, James William
Bullard, Arthur
Curtin, Jeremiah
Ditson, George Leighton
Dole, Nathan Haskell
Dorr, Rheta Louise Childe
Dreiser, Theodore
Eastman, Max Forrester
Fischer, Louis

Gruber, Ruth
Hapgood, Isabel Florence
Hindus, Maurice Gerschon
Hughes, James Langston
Hullinger, Edwin Ware
Kennan, George
Kennell, Ruth Epperson
Leyda, Jay
Lyons, Eugene
McKay, Claude
Poole, Ernest Cook
Ruhl, Arthur Brown
Russell, Charles Edward
Salisbury, Harrison Evans
Simmons, Ernest Joseph
Simons, George Albert
Sisson, Edgar Grant
Spargo, John
Taylor, Bayard
Walling, William English
Williams, Albert Rhys
Wolfe, Bertram David

BANKERS
Barker, Wharton
Lewis, William David
Marye, George Thomas

BUSINESSMEN
Crane, Charles Richard
Eaton, Cyrus Stephen
Francis, Joseph
Hammer, Armand
Harriman, William Averell
Haven, William Anderson
Hitchcock, Ethan Allen
Karr, David
Kendall, Donald McIntosh
McCormick, Robert Sanderson

CHEMICAL ENGINEERS
Burrell, George Arthur
Hirsch, Alcan

CIVIL ENGINEERS
Bates, Lindon Wallace
Gorton, Willard Livermore
Hough, David Leavitt

Stevens, John Frank
Whistler, George Washington
Witkin, Zara

CLERGYMEN
Krehbiel, Christian Emanuel
Simons, George Albert
Walsh, Edmund Aloysius

COMMUNAL LEADERS
Friedlander, Israel
Rosenberg, James N.

CONSULS. *See* DIPLOMATS

CRYPTOLOGISTS
Martin, William H.
Mitchell, Bernon F.

DANCERS
Bovt, Violette
Duncan, Isadora

DIPLOMATS
Adams, John Quincy
Bagby, Arthur Pendleton
Baker, Henry Dunster
Beam, Jacob Dyneley
Bohlen, Charles Eustis
Boker, George Henry
Breckinridge, Clifton Rodes
Brown, Neill Smith
Buchanan, James
Bullitt, William Christian
Caldwell, John Kenneth
Cameron, Simon
Campbell, George Washington
Clay, Cassius Marcellus
Clay, John Randolph
Cole, Felix
Coleman, Frederick William Backus
Dallas, George Mifflin
Dana, Francis
Davies, Joseph Edward
Durbrow, Elbridge
Francis, David Rowland
Greener, Richard Theodore
Guild, Curtis

Harriman, William Averell
Harris, Ernest Lloyd
Harris, Levett
Hartman, Arthur Adair
Henderson, Loy Wesley
Hibben, Paxton
Hitchcock, Ethan Allen
Hoffman, Wickham
Hunt, William Henry
Johnson, Ural Alexis
Kelley, Robert Francis
Kennan, George Frost
Kirk, Alan Goodrich
Kohler, Foy David
Lothrop, George Van Ness
McCormick, Robert Sanderson
MacGowan, David Bell
Marye, George Thomas
Matlock, Jack Foust, Jr.
Meyer, George von Lengerke
Middleton, Henry
Packer, Earl Lenoir
Peirce, Herbert Henry Davis
Pickens, Francis Wilkinson
Pinkney, William
Poinsett, Joel Roberts
Riddle, John Wallace
Rockhill, William Woodville
Schuyler, Eugene
Schuyler, Montgomery
Seymour, Thomas Hart
Smith, Charles Emory
Smith, Walter Bedell
Snodgrass, John Harold
Standley, William Harrison
Steinhardt, Laurence Adolph
Stoessel, Walter John, Jr.
Summers, Maddin
Taylor, Bayard
Thayer, Charles Wheeler
Thompson, Llewellyn E., Jr.
Toon, Malcolm
Tower, Charlemagne
Tredwell, Roger Culver
Wilkins, William
Winship, North
Wright, Joshua Butler

ECONOMISTS
Brown, William Adams, Jr.
Hoover, Calvin Bryce
Hutchinson, Lincoln
Ropes, Ernest C.

EDITORS
Baker, Henry Dunster
Bess, Demaree Caughey
Dole, Nathan Haskell
Eastman, Max Forrester
Edgar, William Crowell
Goldman, Emma
Hibben, Paxton
Landfield, Jerome Barker
Lyons, Eugene
Scott, John
Smith, Charles Emory
Smith, Jessica

EDUCATORS
Brzezinski, Zbigniew Kazimierz
Counts, George Sylvester
Davis, Jerome
Dewey, John
Duggan, Stephen Pierce
Harper, Samuel Northrup
Hopper, Bruce Campbell
Mosely, Philip Edward
Noyes, George Rapall
Simmons, Ernest Joseph
Sisson, Edgar Grant

EPIDEMIOLOGISTS
Timbres, Harry Garland

EXPLORERS. *See also* TRAVELERS
Collins, Perry McDonough
Danenhower, John Wilson
De Long, George Washington
Kennan, George
Landfield, Jerome Barker
Ledyard, John

FILMMAKERS
Leyda, Jay

FINANCIERS
Gumberg, Alexander Semenovich
Thompson, William Boyce
Tower, Charlemagne

GENETICISTS
Muller, Hermann Joseph

GEOLOGISTS
Winchell, Horace Vaughn

GOVERNMENT OFFICIALS
Brzezinski, Zbigniew Kazimierz
Hopkins, Harry Lloyd
Kampelman, Max M.
Nitze, Paul Henry
Perle, Richard Norman
Pipes, Richard Edgar
Rowny, Edward Leon
Smith, Edward Ellis
Stettinius, Edward Reilly, Jr.
Warnke, Paul Culliton
Weber, John B.

HISTORIANS
Coolidge, Archibald Cary
Fisher, Harold Henry
Golder, Frank Alfred
Kennan, George Frost
Pipes, Richard Edgar
Robinson, Geroid Tanquary

HYDROLOGICAL ENGINEERS
Cooper, Hugh Lincoln
Davis, Arthur Powell
Olberg, Charles Real

INDUSTRIAL ENGINEERS
Calder, John Knight
Haven, William Anderson
Keely, Royal Rockwood
Polakov, Walter Nicholas
Stuart, Charles Edward
Stuck, Raymond Wilber

INVENTORS
Berdan, Hiram
Francis, Joseph
Winans, Thomas DeKay

IRRIGATION ENGINEERS
Davis, Arthur Powell

JOCKIES
Winkfield, Jimmy

JOURNALISTS
Ackerman, Carl William
Barnes, Ralph W.
Beatty, Bessie
Bess, Demaree Caughey
Brooks, Erastus
Browne, Louis Edgar
Bryant, Louise
Buel, James William
Bullard, Arthur
Chamberlin, William Henry
Daniloff, Nicholas
Davis, Malcolm Walter
Denny, Harold Norman [Hobbs]
Doder, Dusko
Dorr, Rheta Louise Childe
Downs, William Randall, Jr.
Duranty, Walter
Edgar, WIlliam Crowell
Farson, [James Scott] Negley
Fischer, Louis
Gilder, William Henry
Gilmore, Lanier King
Gruber, Ruth
Harrison, Marguerite Elton Baker
Hibben, Paxton
Hullinger, Edwin Ware
Kennan, George
Levine, Irving Raskin
Levine, Isaac Don
Lyons, Eugene
MacGahan, Januarius Aloysius
MacGowan, David Bell
Poole, Ernest Cook
Reed, John
Reswick, William
Russell, Charles Edward
Salisbury, Harrison Evans
Schorr, Daniel Louis
Scott, John
Shapiro, Henry

Smith, Hedrick Lawrence
Steffens, Lincoln
Stevens, Edmund William
Stoneman, William Harlan
Strong, Anna Louise
Washburn, Stanley
Whitney, Thomas Porter
Williams, Albert Rhys

LABOR LEADERS
Haywood, William Dudley

LAWYERS
Davies, Joseph Edward
Greener, Richard Theodore
Kampelman, Max M.
Lothrop, George Van Ness
Rosenberg, James N.
Steinhardt, Laurence Adolph
Thacher, Thomas Day
Vance, Cyrus Roberts
Wardwell, Allen

LEGAL SCHOLARS
Hazard, John Newbold

LIBRARIANS
Eddy, Harriet Gertrude

LINGUISTS
Curtin, Jeremiah

MECHANICAL ENGINEERS
Harrison, Joseph
Winans, Thomas DeKay

MERCHANTS
Dobell, Peter
Fisher, Miers, Jr.
Harris, Levett
Lewis, William David
Peyton, Bernard
Ropes, William
Russell, John Miller
Sanders, Beverly Chune
Sayre, Stephen
Wheatland, Richard

METALLURGICAL ENGINEERS
Farney, George Wimbor

METEOROLOGISTS
Abbe, Cleveland

MILITARY ENGINEERS
Delafield, Richard
Mordecai, Alfred

MINING ENGINEERS
Brown, Walter Lyman
Farney, George Wimbor
Fell, Edward Nelson
Hammond, John Hays
Hoover, Herbert Clark
Hutchins, John Power
Janin, Charles Henry
Joralemon, Ira Beaman
Maynard, George William
Purington, Chester Wells
Rukeyser, Walter Arnold
Stines, Norman Caswell
Vanderlip, Washington B.

MUSIC CRITICS
Sayler, Oliver Martin

NAVAL OFFICERS
Danenhower, John Wilson
De Long, George Washington
Glennon, James Henry
Jones, John Paul
Kirk, Alan Goodrich
Koehler, Hugo William
McCully, Newton Alexander
Melville, George Wallace
Michela, Joseph Anthony
Olsen, Clarence Edward
Standley, William Harrison
Stevens, Leslie Clark
Tate, George
Tolley, Kemp

PHILANTHROPISTS
Crane, Charles Richard
Thompson, William Boyce

PHOTOGRAPHERS
Abbe, James Edward

PHYSICIANS
Beeuwkes, Henry
Billings, Frank
Coulter, Herbert McKay
Crawford, John Martin
Grow, Malcolm Cummings
Holt, William Joseph
Hurd, Eugene
Lown, Bernard
Parke, Charles Ross
Rosett, Joshua
Smyser, Henry Lanius

PILOTS
Powers, Francis Gary

POLITICAL SCIENTISTS
Barghoorn, Frederick Charles

PRESIDENTS
Adams, John Quincy
Bush, George Herbert Walker
Carter, James (Jimmy) Earl, Jr.
Eisenhower, Dwight David
Hoover, Herbert Clark
Kennedy, John Fitzgerald
Lincoln, Abraham
Nixon, Richard Milhous
Reagan, Ronald
Roosevelt, Franklin Delano
Truman, Harry S.
Wilson, Woodrow

PRIESTS. *See* CLERGYMEN

PSYCHIATRISTS
Williams, Frankwood Earle

PSYCHOLOGISTS
Gantt, William Andrew Horsley

PUBLIC OFFICIALS
Bagby, Arthur Pendleton
Beveridge, Albert Jeremiah

Breckinridge, Clifton Rodes
Brown, Neill Smith
Byrnes, James Francis
Cameron, Simon
Campbell, George Washington
Clay, Cassius Marcellus
Dallas, George Mifflin
Fox, Gustavus Vasa
Francis, David Rowland
Goodrich, James Putnam
Guild, Curtis
Harriman, William Averell
Hunt, William Henry
Meyer, George von Lengerke
Middleton, Henry
Pickens, Francis Wilkinson
Pinkney, William
Seward, William Henry
Seymour, Thomas Hart
Shultz, George Pratt
Wallace, Henry Agard
Wilkins, William

RAILWAY ENGINEERS
Emerson, George H.
Johnson, Benjamin O.
Smith, Charles Hadden

SANITARIANS
Ryan, Edward William

SCIENTISTS
Churchman, John

SEA CAPTAINS
Wheatland, Richard

SECRETARIES OF STATE
Acheson, Dean Gooderham
Adams, John Quincy
Baker, James Addison III
Buchanan, James
Byrnes, James Francis
Dulles, John Foster
Kissinger, Henry Alfred
Lansing, Robert
Seward, William Henry
Shultz, George Pratt

Stettinius, Edward Reilly, Jr.
Vance, Cyrus Roberts

SERVANTS
Prince, Nero

SINGERS
Arle-Tilz, Coretti
Harris, Emma
Harvey, Georgette
Mitchell, Abbie
Robeson, Paul

SOCIALITES
Cantacuzene, Julia Dent Grant

SOCIAL WORKERS
Bogen, Boris David
Durland, Kellogg
Hopkins, Harry Lloyd
Kingsbury, John Adams
Robins, Raymond

SOCIOLOGISTS
Ross, Edward Alsworth

SOLDIERS. *See also* ARMY
OFFICERS
Munroe, Thomas
Sonntag, George S.

STEAMBOAT CAPTAINS
Few, Simon

SURGEONS. *See* PHYSICIANS

SURVEYORS
Bush, Richard James

TOOLMAKERS
Robinson, Robert

TRANSLATORS
Crawford, John Martin
Dole, Nathan Haskell
Hapgood, Isabel Florence

TRAVELERS
Poinsett, Joel Roberts
Smith, Joseph Allen
Taylor, Bayard

VALETS. *See also* SERVANTS
Jordan, Philip
Thomas, George

WORKERS
Beal, Fred Erwin
Golden, John Oliver

Bibliographical Essay

Several books cover the whole or much of the history of U.S. relations with Russia and the Soviet Union: Thomas A. Bailey, *America Faces Russia: Russian-American Relations from Early Times to Our Day* (Ithaca, N.Y.: Cornell University Press, 1950); Richard J. Barnet, *The Giants: Russia and America* (New York: Simon and Schuster, 1977); Foster Rhea Dulles, *The Road to Teheran: The Story of Russia and America, 1781–1943* (Princeton, N.J.: Princeton University Press, 1944); John Lewis Gaddis, *Russia, the Soviet Union, and the United States: An Interpretive History* (New York: McGraw-Hill, 1990); Oliver Jensen, ed., *America and Russia: A Century and a Half of Dramatic Encounters* (New York: Simon and Schuster, 1962); Thomas B. Larson, *Soviet-American Rivalry* (New York: Norton, 1978); Max M. Laserson, *The American Impact on Russia, 1784–1917: Diplomatic and Ideological* (New York: Macmillan, 1950); Karl W. Ryavec, *United States–Soviet Relations* (New York: Longman, 1989); Nikolai V. Sivachev and Nikolai N. Yakovlev, *Russia and the United States* (Chicago: University of Chicago Press, 1979); Alexandre Tarsaidze, *Czars and Presidents: The Story of a Forgotten Friendship* (New York: McDowell, Obolensky, 1958); and William Appleman Williams, *American-Russian Relations, 1781–1947* (New York: Rinehart, 1952). Eugene Anschel, ed., *American Appraisals of Soviet Russia, 1917–1977* (Metuchen, N.J.: Scarecrow Press, 1978), Eugene Anschel, ed., *The American Image of Russia, 1775–1975* (New York,: Ungar, 1974), Peter G. Filene, ed., *American Views of Soviet Russia, 1917–1965* (Homewood, Ill.: Dorsey, 1968), and Benson Lee Grayson, ed., *The American Image of Russia, 1917–1977* (New York: Ungar, 1978), are collections of essays on this subject.

The eighteenth and nineteenth centuries: Anna Babey, *Americans in Russia, 1776–1917: A Study of the American Travelers in Russia from the American Revolution to the Russian Revolution* (New York: Comet Press, 1938); Nina N. Bashkina et al., eds., *The United States and Russia: The Beginnings of Relations, 1765–1815* (Washington, D.C.: Government Printing Office, 1980); Nikolai N. Bolkhovitinov, *The Beginnings of Russian-American Relations, 1775–1815* (Cambridge: Harvard University Press, 1975); Nikolai N. Bolkhovitinov, *Russia and the American Revolution* (Tallahassee, Fla.: Diplomatic Press, 1976); Joseph Bradley, *Guns for the Tsar: American Technology and the Small Arms Industry in Nineteenth-Century Russia* (DeKalb: Northern Illinois University Press, 1990); Fred V. Carstensen, *American Enterprise in Foreign Markets: Studies of Singer and International Harvester in Imperial Russia* (Chapel Hill: University of North Carolina

Press, 1984); Alfred W. Crosby, *America, Russia, Hemp, and Napoleon: American Trade with Russia and the Baltic, 1783–1812* (Columbus: Ohio State University Press, 1965); Alan Dowty, *The Limits of American Isolationism: The United States and the Crimean War* (New York: New York University Press, 1971); Benson Lee Grayson, *Russian-American Relations in World War I* (New York: Ungar, 1979); David Hecht, *Russian Radicals Look to America, 1825–1894* (Cambridge: Harvard University Press, 1947); John C. Hildt, *Early Negotiations of the U.S. with Russia* (Baltimore: Johns Hopkins University Press, 1906); Ronald J. Jensen, *The Alaska Purchase and Russian American Relations* (Seattle: University of Washington Press, 1975); Walther Kirchner, *Studies in Russian-American Commerce, 1820–1860* (Leiden: Brill, 1975); Howard I. Kushner, *Conflict on the Northwest Coast: American-Russian Rivalry in the Pacific Northwest, 1790–1867* (Westport, Conn.: Greenwood Press, 1975); George S. Queen, *The United States and the Material Advance in Russia, 1881–1906* (New York: Arno, 1976); Norman E. Saul, *Distant Friends: The United States and Russia, 1763–1867* (Lawrence: University Press of Kansas, 1991); Benjamin Platt Thomas, *Russo-American Relations, 1815–1867* (Baltimore: Johns Hopkins University Press, 1930); Arthur W. Thompson and Robert W. Hart, *The Uncertain Crusade: America and the Russian Revolution at 1905* (Amherst: University of Massachusetts Press, 1970); Robert A. Waldman, *Lincoln and the Russians* (New York: Collier, 1961); and Edward H. Zabriskie, *American-Russian Rivalry in the Far East: A Study in Diplomacy and Power Politics, 1895–1914* (Philadelphia: University of Pennsylvania Press, 1946).

Russian Revolution: George F. Kennan, *Soviet-American Relations, 1917–1920* (Princeton, N.J.: Princeton University Press, 1956–1958); Linda Killen, *The Russian Bureau: A Case Study in Wilsonian Diplomacy* (Lexington: University Press of Kentucky, 1983); Christopher Lasch, *The American Liberals and the Russian Revolution* (New York: Columbia University Press, 1962); Arno J. Mayer, *The Politics and Diplomacy of Peacemaking: Containment and Counterrevolution at Versailles, 1918–1919* (New York: Knopf, 1967); Arno J. Mayer, *Wilson vs. Lenin: Political Origins of the New Diplomacy, 1917–1918* (New Haven, Conn.: Yale University Press, 1958); Brenda K. Shelton, *President Wilson and the Russian Revolution* (Buffalo: State University of New York, 1957); and Leonid Ivan Strakhovsky, *American Opinions about Russia, 1917–1920* (Toronto: University of Toronto Press, 1961).

American Intervention: Richard Goldhurst, *The Midnight War: The American Intervention in Russia, 1918–1920* (New York: McGraw-Hill, 1978); Robert J. Maddox, *The Unknown War with Russia: Wilson's Siberian Intervention* (San Rafael, Calif.: Presidio Press, 1977); Benjamin D. Rhodes, *The Anglo-American Winter War with Russia, 1918–1919: A Diplomatic and Military Tragicomedy* (Westport, Conn.: Greenwood Press, 1988); Betty M. Unterberger, *America's Siberian Expedition, 1918–1920: A Study of National Policy* (Durham, N.C.: Duke University Press, 1956); and John A. White, *The Siberian Intervention* (Princeton, N.J.: Princeton University Press, 1950).

The 1920s: Theodore Draper, *American Communism and Soviet Russia: The Formative Years* (New York: Viking Press, 1960); Peter G. Filene, *Americans and the Soviet Experiment, 1917–1933* (Cambridge: Harvard University Press, 1967); Paul Garb, *They Came to Stay: North Americans in the U.S.S.R.* (Moscow: Progress Publishers, 1987); Benjamin M. Weissman, *Herbert Hoover and Famine Relief to Soviet Russia, 1921–1923* (Stanford, Calif.: Hoover Institution Press, 1974); and Joan Hoff Wilson, *Ideology and Economics: United States Relations with the Soviet Union, 1918–1933* (Columbia: University of Missouri Press, 1974).

The 1930s: Edward M. Bennett, *Franklin D. Roosevelt and the Search for Security: American-Soviet Relations, 1933–1939* (Wilmington, Del.: Scholarly Resources, 1985); Edward M. Bennett, *Recognition of Russia: An American Foreign Policy Dilemma* (Waltham, Mass.: Blaisdell, 1970); Donald G. Bishop, *The Roosevelt-Litvinov Agreements: The American View* (Syracuse, N.Y.: Syracuse University Press, 1965); Robert Paul Browder, *The Origins of Soviet-American Diplomacy* (Princeton, N.J.: Princeton University Press, 1953); Thomas R. Maddux, *Years of Estrangement: American Relations with the Soviet Union, 1933–1941* (Tallahassee: University Presses of Florida, 1981); John Richman, *The United States and the Soviet Union: The Decision to Recognize* (Raleigh, N.C.: McCamberleigh Hall, 1980); Hugh De Santis, *The Diplomacy of Silence: The American Foreign Service, the Soviet Union, and the Cold War, 1933–1947* (Chicago: University of Chicago Press, 1980); Andrew J. Schwartz, *America and the Russo-Finnish War* (Washington, D.C.: Public Affairs Press, 1960); and Robert Sobel, *The Origins of Interventionism: The United States and the Russo-Finnish War* (New York: Bookman Associates, 1960).

World War II: Raymond H. Dawson, *The Decision to Aid Russia, 1941: Foreign Policy and Domestic Politics* (Chapel Hill: University of North Carolina Press, 1959); George C. Herring, Jr., *Aid to Russia, 1941–1946: Strategy, Diplomacy, and the Origins of the Cold War* (New York: Columbia University Press, 1973); Robert Huhn Jones, *The Roads to Russia: United States Lend-Lease to the Soviet Union* (Norman: University of Oklahoma Press, 1969); Ralph B. Levering, *American Opinion and the Russian Alliance, 1939–1945* (Chapel Hill: University of North Carolina Press, 1976); Richard C. Lukas, *Eagles East: The Army Air Force and the Soviet Union, 1941–1945* (Tallahassee: Florida State University Press, 1970); Leon Martel, *Lend-Lease, Loans, and the Coming of the Cold War: A Study of the Implementation of Foreign Policy* (Boulder, Colo.: Westview Press, 1979); and Hubert P. Van Tuyll, *Feeding the Bear: American Aid to the Soviet Union, 1941–1945* (New York: Greenwood Press, 1989).

The Cold War: Lynn Etheridge Davis, *The Cold War Begins: Soviet-American Conflict over Eastern Europe* (Princeton, N.J.: Princeton University Press, 1974); Justus D. Doenecke, *Not to the Swift: The Old Isolationists and the Cold War Era* (Lewisburg, Pa.: Bucknell University Press, 1979); Herbert Feis, *From Trust to Terror: The Onset of the Cold War* (New York: Norton, 1970); Denna Frank Fleming, *The Cold War and Its Origins, 1917–1960* (Garden City, N.Y.: Doubleday, 1961); Andre Fontaine, *History of the Cold War: From the October Revolution to the Korean War, 1917–1950* (New York: Pantheon Books, 1968); John Lewis Gaddis, *The Long Peace: Inquiries into the History of the Cold War* (New York: Oxford University Press, 1987); John Lewis Gaddis, *The United States and the Origins of the Cold War, 1941–1947*, (New York: Columbia University Press, 1972); Louis J. Halle, *The Cold War as History* (New York: HarperCollins Publishers, 1991); Paul Y. Hammond, *Cold War and Détente: The American Foreign Policy Process since 1945* (New York: Harcourt Brace Jovanovich, 1975); Paul Y. Hammond, *The Cold War Years: American Foreign Policy since 1945* (New York: Harcourt, Brace and World, 1969); Fraser J. Harbutt, *The Iron Curtain: Churchill, America, and the Origins of the Cold War* (New York: Oxford University Press, 1986); George R. Hess, ed., *America and Russia: From Cold War to Coexistence* (New York: Crowell, 1973); Lynn Boyd Hinds and Theodore Otto Windt, *The Cold War as Rhetoric: The Beginnings, 1945–1950* (New York: Prager, 1991); William G. Hyland, *The Cold War: Fifty Years of Conflict* (New York: Random House, 1992); Roger E. Kanet and Edward A. Kolodziel, eds., *The Cold War as Cooperation* (Baltimore: Johns Hopkins

University Press, 1991); Linda Killen, *The Soviet Union and the United States: A New Look at the Cold War* (Boston: Twayne, 1989); Walter LaFeber, *America, Russia, and the Cold War, 1945–1990* (New York: McGraw-Hill, 1991); Louis Leibovich, *The Press and the Origins of the Cold War, 1944–1947* (New York: Praeger, 1988); Deborah Ralph B. Levering, *The Cold War, 1945–1987* (Arlington Heights, Ill.: Harlan Davidson, 1988); Robert B. McCalla, *Uncertain Perceptions: U.S. Cold War Crisis Decision Making* (Ann Arbor: University of Michigan Press, 1992); Thomas J. McCormick, *America's Half Century: United States Foreign Policy in the Cold War* (Baltimore: Johns Hopkins University Press, 1989); Robert James Maddox, *The New Left and the Origins of the Cold War* (Princeton, N.J.: Princeton University Press, 1973); Lynn H. Miller and Ronald W. Pruessen, eds., *Reflections on the Cold War: A Quarter Century of American Foreign Policy* (Philadelphia: Temple University Press, 1974); Joseph G. Nye, Jr., *The Making of America's Soviet Policy* (New Haven, Conn.: Yale University Press, 1984); Thomas G. Patterson, *On Every Front: The Making of the Cold War* (New York: Norton, 1979); Thomas G. Patterson, *Soviet-American Confrontation: Postwar Reconstruction and the Origins of the Cold War* (Baltimore: Johns Hopkins University Press, 1973); Robert A. Pollard, *Economic Security and the Origins of the Cold War, 1945–1950* (New York: Columbia University Press, 1985); Lisle A. Rose, *After Yalta* (New York: Scribner, 1973); Joseph M. Sircusa, ed., *The American Diplomatic Revolution: A Documentary History of the Cold War, 1941–1947* (Port Washington, N.Y.: Kennikat Press, 1977); Hugh Thomas, *Armed Truce: The Beginning of the Cold War, 1945–46* (New York: Atheneum, 1987); Adam B. Ulam, *The Rivals: America and Russia since World War II* (New York: Viking, 1971); Bernard A. Weisberger, *Cold War, Cold Peace: The United States and Russia since 1945* (New York: American Heritage, 1984); Ralph K. White, *Fearful Warriors: A Psychological Profile of U.S.-Soviet Relations* (New York: Basic Books, 1984); Randall Woods and Howard Jones, *Dawning of the Cold War: The United States' Quest for Order* (Athens: University of Georgia Press, 1991); and Daniel Yergin, *Shattered Peace: The Origins of the Cold War and the National Security State* (Boston: Houghton Mifflin, 1977).

Truman Presidency and Containment: Terry L. Deibel and John Lewis Gaddis, eds., *Containing the Soviet Union: A Critique of U.S. Policy* (Washington, D.C.: Pergamon-Brassey's International Defense Publishers, 1987); Herbert Druks, *Harry S. Truman and the Russians, 1945–1953* (New York: Speller, 1966); Thomas H. Etzold and John Lewis Gaddis, eds., *Containment: Documents on American Policy and Strategy, 1945–1950* (New York: Columbia University Press, 1978); John Lewis Gaddis, *Strategies of Containment: A Critical Appraisal of Postwar American National Security Policy* (New York: Oxford University Press, 1982); Deborah Welch Larson, *Origins of Containment: A Psychological Explanation* (Princeton, N.J.: Princeton University Press, 1985); and Melvyn P. Leffler, *A Preponderance of Power: National Security, the Truman Administration, and the Cold War* (Stanford, Calif.: Stanford University Press, 1992).

Eisenhower Presidency: Michael R. Beschloss, *Mayday: Eisenhower, Khrushchev, and the U–2 Affair* (New York: Harper and Row, 1986); and H. W. Brands, *Cold Warriors: Eisenhower's Generation and American Foreign Policy* (New York: Columbia University Press, 1988).

Kennedy Presidency: Michael R. Beschloss, *The Crisis Years: Kennedy and Khruschev, 1960–1963* (New York: HarperCollins, 1991); Bernard J. Firestone, *The Quest for Nuclear Stability: John F. Kennedy and the Soviet Union* (Westport, Conn.: Greenwood Press, 1982); James M. McSherry, *Khrushchev and Kennedy in Retrospect* (Palo Alto, Calif.:

Open-Door, 1971); and Glenn T. Seaborg, *Kennedy, Khrushchev, and the Test Ban* (Berkeley: University of California Press, 1981).

The 1970s and Détente: Coral Bell, *The Diplomacy of Détente: The Kissinger Era* (New York: St. Martin's Press, 1977); Lawrence T. Caldwell, *Soviet-American Relations: One Half Decade of Détente, Problems and Issues* (Paris: Atlantic Institute for International Affairs, 1976); Raymond L. Garthoff, *Détente and Confrontation: American-Soviet Relations from Nixon to Reagan* (Washington, D.C.: Brookings Institution, 1985); Charles Gati and Tobi Trister Gati, *The Debate over Détente* (New York: Foreign Policy Association, 1977); Terry L. Heyns, *American and Soviet Relations since Détente: The Framework* (Washington, D.C.: National Defense University Press, 1987); Ronald E. Hoyt, *Winners and Losers in East-West Trade: A Behavioral Analysis of U.S.-Soviet Détente (1970–1980)* (New York: Prager, 1983); Louisa Sue Hulett, *Decade of Détente: Shifting Definitions and Denouement* (Washington, D.C.: University Press of America, 1982); William Hyland, *Mortal Rivals: Superpower Relations from Nixon to Reagan* (New York: Random House, 1987); Robert S. Litwack, *Détente and the Nixon Doctrine: American Foreign Policy and the Pursuit of Stability* (Cambridge: Cambridge University Press, 1984); Fred Warner Neal, ed., *Détente or Debacle: Common Sense in U.S.-Soviet Relations* (New York: Norton, 1979); Richard Pipes, *U.S.-Soviet Relations in the Era of Détente* (Boulder, Colo.: Westview Press, 1981); Peter J. Potichnyj and Jane P. Shapiro, eds., *From the Cold War to Détente* (New York: Praeger, 1976); Della W. Shelton, ed., *Dimensions of Détente* (New York: Prager, 1978); Richard W. Stevenson, *The Rise and Fall of Détente: Relaxations of Tensions in U.S.-Soviet Relations, 1953–84* (Urbana: University of Illinois Press, 1985); and Charles E. Timberlake, ed., *Détente: A Documentary Record* (New York: Praeger, 1978).

The 1980s: Seweryn Bialer and Michael Mandelbaum, eds., *Gorbachev's Russia and American Foreign Policy* (Boulder, Colo.: Westview Press, 1988); Dan Caldwell, ed., *Soviet International Behavior and U.S. Policy Options* (Lexington, Mass.: Lexington Books, 1985); Lawrence T. Caldwell and William Diebold, Jr., *Soviet-American Relations in the 1980s: Superpower Politics and East-West Trade* (New York: McGraw-Hill, 1980); Fred Halliday, *The Making of the Second Cold War* (London: Verso, 1983); Terry L. Heyns, *American and Soviet Relations since Détente: The Framework* (Washington, D.C.: National Defense University Press, 1987); George Liska, *Rethinking US-Soviet Relations* (New York: B. Blackwell, 1987); Michael Mandelbaum and Strobe Talbott, *Reagan and Gorbachev* (New York: Vintage, 1987); Richard A. Melanson, ed., *Neither Cold War nor Détente? Soviet-American Relations in the 1980s* (Charlottesville: University Press of Virginia, 1982); Don Oberdorfer, *The Turn: From the Cold War to a New Era, the United States and the Soviet Union, 1983–1990* (New York: Poseidon Press, 1991); Peter Savigear, *Cold War or Détente in the 1980s: The International Politics of American-Soviet Relations* (New York: St. Martin's, 1987); Strobe Talbott, *Deadly Gambits: The Reagan Administration and the Stalemate in Nuclear Arms Control* (New York: Knopf, 1984); and Strobe Talbott, *The Russians and Reagan* (New York: Vintage, 1984).

The 1990s: Michael R. Beschloss and Strobe Talbott, *At The Highest Tide: The Inside Story of the End of the Cold War* (Boston: Little Brown, 1993); John Lewis Gaddis, *The United States and the End of the Cold War: Implications, Reconsiderations, Provocations* (New York: Oxford University Press, 1992); Robert K. German, ed., *The Future of U.S.-U.S.S.R. Relations: Lessons from Forty Years without World War* (Austin, Tex.: Lyndon B. Johnson School of Public Affairs, 1986); Michael J. Hogan, *The End of the Cold War: Its Meaning and Implications* (Cambridge: Cambridge University Press, 1992);

Arnold Horelick, ed., *U.S.-Soviet Relations: The Next Phase* (Ithaca, N.Y.: Cornell University Press, 1986); Nish Jamgotch, Jr., *U.S.-Soviet Cooperation: A New Future* (New York: Praeger, 1989); Robert Jervis and Seweryn Bialer, eds., *Soviet-American Relations after the Cold War* (Durham, N.C.: Duke University Press, 1991); Michael Mandelbaum, ed., *The Rise of Nations in the Soviet Union: American Foreign Policy and the Disintegration of the USSR* (New York: Council on Foreign Relations Press, 1991); and Thomas H. Naylor, *The Cold War Legacy* (Lexington, Mass.: Lexington Books, 1991).

Summit Meetings, Negotiations, and Treaties: Arnold Beichman, *The Long Pretense: Soviet Treaty Diplomacy from Lenin to Gorbachev* (New Brunswick, N.J.: Transaction, 1991); Raymond Bennett and Joseph E. Johnson, eds., *Negotiating with the Russians* (Boston: World Peace Foundation, 1951); Robert J. Einhorn, *Negotiating from Strength: Leverage in U.S.-Soviet Arms Control Negotiations* (New York: Prager, 1985); Alexander L. George, *Managing U.S.-Soviet Rivalry: Problems of Crisis Prevention* (Boulder, Colo.: Westview Press, 1963); Alexander L. George, Philip J. Farley, and Alexander Dallin, eds., *U.S.-Soviet Security Cooperation: Achievements, Failures, Lessons* (New York: Oxford University Press, 1988); Michael Krepon and Dan Caldwell, eds., *The Politics of Arms Control Treaty Ratification* (New York: St. Martin's Press, 1991); John W. McDonald, Jr. *U.S.- Soviet Summitry: Roosevelt through Carter* (Washington, D.C.: U.S. Foreign Service Institute, Department of State, 1987); David D. Newsom, ed., *Private Diplomacy with the Soviet Union* (Washington, D.C.; Institute for the Study of Diplomacy, Georgetown University, 1987); Leon Sloss and M. Scott Davis, eds., *A Game for High Stakes: Lessons Learned in Negotiating with the Soviet Union* (Cambridge, Mass.: Ballinger, 1986); Richard F. Starr, ed., *Public Diplomacy: USA versus Soviet Union* (Stanford, Calif.: Hoover Institution Press, 1986); Gordon R. Weihmiller, *U.S.-Soviet Summits: An Account of East-West Diplomacy at the Top, 1955–1985* (Lanham, Md.: University Press of America, 1986); Joseph G. Whelan, *Soviet Diplomacy and Negotiating Behavior: The Emerging New Context for U.S. Diplomacy* (Boulder, Colo.: Westview Press, 1983); Joseph G. Whelan, *Soviet Diplomacy and Negotiating Behavior, 1979–88: New Tests for U.S. Diplomacy* (Washington, D.C.: Government Printing Office, 1988); and Joseph G. Whelan, *Soviet Diplomacy and Negotiating Behavior, 1988–90: Gorbachev, Reagan, Bush Meetings at the Summit* (Washington, D.C.: Government Printing Office, 1991).

Exchanges and Cooperation: Catherine P. Ailes and Arthur E. Pardee, Jr., *Cooperation in Science and Technology: An Evaluation of the U.S.-Soviet Agreement* (Boulder, Colo.: Westview Press, 1983); Robert F. Byrnes, *Soviet-American Academic Exchanges, 1958– 1975* (Bloomington: Indiana University Press, 1976); Nish Jamgotch, ed., *Sectors of Mutual Benefit in U.S.-Soviet Relations* (Durham, N.C.: Duke University Press, 1985); Herbert Kuperberg, *The Raised Curtin* (New York: Twentieth Century Fund, 1977); J. D. Parks, *Conflict and Coexistence: American-Soviet Cultural Relations, 1917–1958* (Jefferson, N.C.: McFarland, 1983); Yale Richmond, *U.S.-Soviet Cultural Exchanges, 1958– 1986* (Boulder, Colo.: Westview Press, 1987); and Gale Warner and Michael Shuman, *Citizen Diplomats: Pathfinders in Soviet-American Relations and How You Can Join Them* (New York: Continuum, 1987).

Arms Race: Coit D. Blacker, *Reluctant Warriors: The United States, the Soviet Union, and Arms Control* (New York: W. H. Freeman, 1987); Patrick Glynn, *Closing Pandora's Box: Arms Races, Arms Control, and the History of the Cold War* (New York: Basic Books, 1992); George F. Kennan, *The Nuclear Delusion: Soviet-American Relations in* the Atomic Age (New York: Pantheon Books, 1982); Charles R. Morris, *Iron Destinies, Lost Opportunities: The Arms Race between the U.S.A. and the U.S.S.R., 1945–1987* (New York: Harper and Row, 1988); Harland B. Moulton, *From Superiority to Parity: The United States and the Strategic Arms, 1961–1971* (Westport, Conn.: Greenwood Press, 1979); and Keith B. Payne, *Nuclear Deterrence in U.S.-Soviet Relations* (Boulder, Colo.: Westview Press, 1982).

Intelligence: Lawrence Freedman, *U.S. Intelligence and the Soviet Strategic Threat* (Princeton, N.J.: Princeton University Press, 1986); David C. Martin, *Wilderness of Mirrors* (New York: Harper and Row, 1980); John Prados, *Soviet Estimate: U.S. Intelligence Analysis and Russian Military Strength* (New York: Dial Press, 1982); and Jeffrey Richelson, *American Espionage and the Soviet Target* (New York: Morrow, 1987).

Trade: Mikhail V. Condoide, *Russian-American Trade: A Study of the Foreign-Trade Monopoly* (Columbus: Ohio State University Press, 1946); Robert Cullen, *The Post-Containment Handbook: Key Issues in U.S.-Soviet Economic Relations* (Boulder, Colo.: Westview Press, 1990); John Whylen De Pauw, *Soviet-American Trade Negotiations* (New York: Praeger, 1979); Joseph Finder, *Red Carpet: The Connection between the Kremlin and America's Most Powerful Businessmen* (New York: Holt, Rinehart and Winston, 1983); Philip J. Funigiello, *American-Soviet Trade in the Cold War* (Chapel Hill: University of North Carolina Press, 1988); Marshall I. Goldman, *Détente and Dollars: Doing Business with the Soviets* (New York: Basic Books, 1975); James L. Hecht, ed., *Rubles and Dollars: Strategies from Doing Business in the Soviet Union* (New York: HarperBusiness, 1991); James K. Libbey, *American-Russian Economic Relations: A Survey of Issues and References* (Claremont, Calif.: Regina Books, 1989); Bruce Parrott, ed., *Trade, Technology, and Soviet-American Relations* (Bloomington: Indiana University Press, 1985); and Colin White, *Russia and America: The Roots of Economic Divergence* (London: Croom Helm, 1987).

Technological Transfer: Philip Hanson, *Trade and Technology in Soviet-Western Relations* (New York: Columbia University Press, 1981); George D. Holliday, *Technology Transfer to the USSR, 1928–1937 and 1966–1975: The Role of Western Technology in Soviet Economic Development* (Boulder, Colo.: Westview Press, 1979); Robyn Shotwell Metcalfe, *The New Wizard War: How the Soviets Steal U.S. High Technology—and How We Give It Away* (Redmond, Wis.: Tempus Books, 1988); Glenn E. Schweitzer, *Techno-diplomacy: U.S.-Soviet Confrontations in Science and Technology* (New York: Plenum Press, 1989); and Antony C. Sutton, *Western Technology and Soviet Economic Development* (Stanford, Calif.: Hoover Institution Press, 1968–1973).

Space: Dodd L. Harvey and Linda C. Ciccoritti, *U.S. Soviet Cooperation in Space* (Washington, D.C.: Center for Advanced International Studies, University of Miami, 1974).

Human Rights: A. Glenn Mower, Jr., *Human Rights and American Foreign Policy: The Carter and Reagan Experiences* (New York: Greenwood Press, 1987); and Joshua Muravchik, *The Uncertain Crusade: Jimmy Carter and the Dilemmas of Human Rights* (Lanham, Md.: Hamilton Press, 1986).

Soviet Jewry: Gary Dean Best, *To Free a People: American Jewish Leaders and the Jewish Problem in Eastern Europe* (Westport, Conn.: Greenwood Press, 1982); Morris Brafman and David Schimel, *Trade for Freedom: Détente, Trade, and Soviet Jews* (New York: Shengold, 1974); William W. Orbach, *The American Movement to Aid Soviet Jewry* (Amherst: University of Massachusetts Press, 1979); Paula Stern, *Water's Edge: Domestic Politics and the Making of American Foreign Policy* (Westport, Conn.: Greenwood Press, 1979); and Zosa Szajkowski, *The Mirage of American Jewish Aid in Soviet Russia, 1917–1939* (New York: Szajkowski, 1977).

African Americans: Alison Blakely, *Russia and the Negro: Blacks in Russian History and Thought* (Washington, D.C.: Howard University Press, 1986).

Journalists: Whitman Bassow, *The Moscow Correspondent: Reporting on Russia from the Revolution to Glasnot* (New York: William Morrow, 1988).

Art: Robert C. Williams, *Russian Art and American Money, 1900–1940* (Cambridge: Harvard University Press, 1980).

INDEX

Page numbers in **bold** indicate main entries.

Abbe, Cleveland, **1**

Abee, James Edward, **1–2**

ABM Treaty (1972), **2**, 94, 95, 127, 159

Accidents Measures Agreement (1971), **2**

Acheson, Dean Gooderham, **2–3**

Ackerman, Carl William, **3**

Adams, John Quincy, **3–4**

Afghanistan Crisis (1980–1988), **4**, 32, 160, 190

AFSC. *See* American Friends Service Committee

Agro-Joint. *See* American Jewish Joint Agricultural Corporation

Alaska Purchase (1867), **4–5**, 163

Albert Kahn Company, **5**

Aldridge, Ira Frederick, **5**

Alexander I, 140

Alexander II, 4, 15, 63

Altai Mountains, 92, 96

American Committee for Relief of Russian Children, 86

American Committee on East-West Accord, **5**

American Expeditionary Forces in North Russia, **6**

American Expeditionary Forces in Siberia, **6**, 60, 73, 94, 163

American Friends Service Committee (AFCS), **6–7**, 168, 177, 182

American Jewish Joint Agricultural Corporation (Agro-Joint), **7**, 153

American Jewish Joint Distribution Committee, Inc. (JDC), **7**, 21, 64, 153

American National Red Cross, **8**, 20, 37, 38, 75, 85, 126, 149, 154, 158, 165, 180, 182, 192

American Relief Administration (ARA), 6, **8**, 17, 52, 61, 67, 72, 73, 83, 86, 88, 92, 126, 147, 153, 155, 192

American-Russian Chamber of Commerce, **8–9**, 23–24, 73, 111, 161, 167, 174, 198

American-Russian Institute, 9

American Society for Cultural Relations with Russia, **9**

American Special Mission to Russia. *See* Root Mission to Russia

American Tractor Brigade, **9**, 193

Amur River, 35, 61

Anderson, Paul B., **9–10**

Anti-Ballistic Missile Treaty. *See* ABM Treaty

Apollo-Soyuz Test Project (ASTP), **10**

ARA. *See* American Relief Administration

Aral Sea, 63

Archangel, 6, 8, 34, 195, 196

Arle-Tilz, Coretti, **10**

Arthur G. McKee and Company, **10**, 84, 178

ASTP. *See* Apollo-Soyuz Test Project

Austin Company, **10–11**

Autonomous Industrial Colony "Kuzbas." *See* Kuzbas Colony

Azerbaijan Crisis (1946), **11**, 28, 184
Azof, Sea of, 15

Bagby, Arthur Pendleton, **13**
Baker, Henry Dunster, **13**
Baker, James Addison, III, **13–14**
Balkhash, Lake, 29
Ballistic Missile Launch Notification
   Agreement (1988), **14**
Bargaining Chip, **14**, 168
Barghoorn, Frederick Charles, **14–15**
Barker, Wharton, **15**
Barnes, Ralph W., **15**
Basic Principles Agreement (BPA), **15–
   16**
Bates, Lindon Wallace, **16**
Bates, Lindon Wallace, Jr., 16
Beal, Fred Erwin, **16**
Beam, Jacob Dyneley, **17**
Beatty, Bessie, **17**
Beeuwkes, Henry, **17–18**
Berdan, Hiram, **18**
Berkman, Alexander, **18**, 72
Berlin Blockade Crisis (1948–1949), **19**,
   169, 184
Berlin Crisis (1958–1959), **19**, 194
Berlin Wall Crisis (1961), **19**, 105, 190
Bess, Demaree Caughey, **19–20**
Bessarabia, 124
Beveridge, Albert Jeremiah, **20**
Billings, Frank, **20**
Birobidzhan, 81, 154
Black Sea, 16, 124, 170
Bogen, Boris David, **20–21**
Bohlen, Charles Eustis, **21**
Boker, George Henry, **21–22**
Bovt, Violette, **22**
Breckinridge, Clifton Rodes, **22**
Brezhnev, Leonid I., 15, 127, 128, 133,
   190, 194
Brooks, Erastus, **22**
Brown, Neill Smith, **22–23**
Brown, Walter Lyman, 8, **23**
Brown, William Adams, Jr., **23**
Browne, Louis Edgar, **23–24**
Bryant, Louise, **24**, 147
Brzezinski, Zbigniew Kazimierz, **24**
Buchanan, James, **24–25**

Buel, James William, **25**
Bulganin, Nikolai A., 57, 68
Bullard, Arthur, **25–26**
Bullitt, William Christian, 24, **26**, 172,
   180, 199
Burrell, George Arthur, **26**
Bush, George Herbert Walker, 13–14,
   27, 121, 128, 195
Bush, Richard James, **27**
Byrnes, James Francis, **27–28**

Calder, John Knight, **29**
Caldwell, John Kenneth, **29–30**
Cameron, Simon, **30**
Campbell, George Washington, **30**
Campbell, Thomas Donald, **31**
Cantacuzene, Julia Dent Grant, **31**
Cantor, Bernard, 64
Carter, James (Jimmy) Earl, Jr., 24, **31–
   32**, 190
Caspian Sea, 135, 140
CAT. *See* U.S.-Soviet Conventional
   Arms Transfer Talks
Catherine II, 43, 98
Caucasus, 26, 79, 103, 120, 121, 140,
   169, 176, 193, 198, 200
Chamberlin, William Henry, **32**
Chase Manhattan Bank, 32–33
Chase National Bank, **32–33**, 76
Cheliabinsk, 29
Chita, 29
Chukotka, 157
Churchman, John, **33**
Circassia, 49
Clay, Cassius Marcellus, **33**, 179
Clay, John Randolph, **33**
Cold War, 28, 31, **34**, 69, 107, 115,
   134, 137, 151
Cole, Felix, **34**
Coleman, Frederick William Backus, **35**
Collins, Perry McDonough, **35**
Collins Overland Line, 35
Colton, Ethan Theodore, **35–36**
Committee on Public Information ("Creel
   Committee"), 23, 25, **36**, 75, 142,
   154, 166, 170
Committee on the Present Danger, **36**
Containment, **36–37**, 51, 104, 184

Conventional Arms Transfer Talks (CAT). *See* U.S.-Soviet Conventional Arms Transfer Talks
Coolidge, Archibald Cary, 37
Cooper, Hugh Lincoln, 37–38
Coulter, Herbert McKay, 38
Council on Foreign Relations, 38, 107
Counts, George Sylvester, 39
Crane, Charles Richard, 39, 79, 152, 172
Crawford, John Martin, 39–40
Creel Committee. *See* Committee on Public Information
Crimea, 7, 47, 126, 153, 185
Crimean War, 47, 88, 119, 127, 138, 169
Cuban Missile Crisis (1962), 4, 40, 105, 109, 181
Curtin, Jeremiah, 40–41

Dallas, George Mifflin, 43
Dana, Francis, 3, 43
Danenhower, John Wilson, 44
Daniloff, Nicholas, 44
Davies, Joseph Edward, 44–45
Davis, Arthur Powell, 45
Davis, Jerome, 46
Davis, Malcolm Walter, 46
Deane, John Russell, 46–47
Delafield, Richard, 47
De Long, George Washington, 47–48, 133
Denny, Harold Norman [Hobbs], 48
Détente, 15, 48, 107, 133, 176, 189, 190
Dewey, John, 48
Ditson, George Leighton, 49
Dnieprostroi, 38, 68
Dobell, Peter, 49
Doder, Dusko, 49
Dole, Nathan Haskell, 49–50
Donets Basin, 178
Don River, 59
Dorr, Rheta Louise Childe, 50
Downs, William Randall, Jr., 50
Dreiser, Theodore, 50, 106
Dropshot Plan, 51
Duggan, Stephen Pierce, 51
Dulles, John Foster, 21, 51–52, 57
Duncan, Isadora, 52

Duranty, Walter, 52–53
Durbrow, Elbridge, 53
Durland, Kellogg, 53

Eastman, Max Forrester, 55
Eaton, Cyrus Stephen, 56
Eddy, Harriet Gertrude, 56
Edgar, William Crowell, 56–57
Eisenhower, Dwight David, 57–58, 68, 136, 137, 169, 188, 194
Eisenstein, Sergei, 114
Ekaterinburg, 175
Ekaterinoslav, 153
Emerson, George H., 58
Equitable Life Assurance Society of the United States, 58
Esenin, Sergei, 52

Farney, George Wimbor, 59
Farson, [James Scott] Negley, 59–60
Faymonville, Philip Ries, 60
Fell, Edward Nelson, 60
Few, Simon, 60–61
Fischer, Bertha Markoosha, 61
Fischer, Louis, 61
Fisher, Harold Henry, 61–62
Fisher, Miers, Jr., 62
Five-Year Plan, First, 5, 10, 31, 38, 62
Forced Repatriation, 62
Ford, Gerald, 13, 179, 190
Ford Motor Company, 62, 77, 150
Fox, Gustavus Vasa, 62–63
Francis, David Rowland, 63, 98
Francis, Joseph, 63–64
Freyn Engineering Company, 64
Friedlander, Israel, 64
Friends of Soviet Russia, 64
Friends of Soviet Russia Agricultural Relief Unit, 9
Frost, George Albert, 65, 104

Gantt, William Andrew Horsley, 67, 141
Garst, Roswell, 67–68
Gaylord, Franklin Augustus, 68
General Electric Company, 68
Geneva Summit (1955), 57, 68–69, 136
Geneva Summit (1985), 69, 146
Georgia, 185

Gilder, William Henry, **69**
Gilmore, Lanier King, **69–70**
Ginzberg Incident (1894–1896), **70**
Glassboro Summit (1967), **70**
Glennon, James Henry, **70–71**
Golden, John Oliver, **71**
Golder, Frank Alfred, **71–72**
Goldman, Emma, 18, **72**
Goodrich, James Putnam, **72–73**
Gorbachev, Mikhail S., 14, 27, 69, 121, 128, 146, 147, 164, 194, 195
Gorky, Maxim, 192
Gorton, Willard Livermore, **73**
Graves, William Sidney, **73–74**
Greene, Francis Vinton, **74**, 121
Greener, Richard Theodore, **74**
Grow, Malcolm Cummings, **74–75**
Grozny, 26
Gruber, Ruth, **75**
Guild, Curtis, **75**
Gumberg, Alexander Semenovich, **75–76**

Hammer, Armand, **77–78**
Hammond, John Hays, **78**
Hapgood, Isabel Florence, **78–79**
Harper, Samuel Northrup, **79**
Harriman, William Averell, **79–80**, 193
Harris, Emma, **80**
Harris, Ernest Lloyd, **80–81**
Harris, Franklin Stewart, **81**
Harris, John Levett, 81, 113
Harris, Levett, **81**, 113
Harrison, Joseph, **81–82**, 200
Harrison, Marguerite Elton Baker, **82**
Hartman, Arthur Adair, **82–83**
Harvey, Georgette, **83**
Haskell, William Nafew, **83–84**
Haven, William Anderson, **83–84**
Haywood, William Dudley, **84**
Hazard, John Newbold, **84**
Heald, Edward Thornton, **85**
Henderson, Loy Wesley, **85**
Hibben, Paxton, **86**
Hindus, Maurice Gerschon, **86–87**
Hirsch, Alcan, **87**
Hitchcock, Ethan Allen, **87**
Hoffman, Wickham, **87**
Holcombe, Lucy Petway, 139

Holt, William Joseph, **88**
Hoover, Calvin Bryce, **88**
Hoover, Herbert Clark, 8, 23, 86, **88–89**, 170, 182
Hopkins, Harry Lloyd, **89**
Hopper, Bruce Campbell, **89–90**
"Hot Line" Agreement (1963), **90**
"Hot Line" Expansion Agreement, 90
"Hot Line" Modernization Agreement, 90
Hough, David Leavitt, **90**
Hughes, James Langston, **91**
Hullinger, Edwin Ware, **91**
Hunt, William Henry, **91**
Hurd, Eugene, **92**
Hutchins, John Power, **92**
Hutchinson, Lincoln, **92**

Incidents at Sea Agreement (1972), **93**
INF Treaty (1987), **93**, 146, 164, 194
Institute for Soviet-American Relations, **93–94**
Inter-Allied Railway Commission in Siberia, **94**, 167
Interim Agreement on Offensive Arms (1972), **94**
Intermediate-Range Nuclear Forces Treaty. *See* INF Treaty
International General Electric, 68
International Harvester Company, **94**
Irkutsk, 112
ISAR, 94
Ishim River, 60

Jackson, Henry M., 95
Jackson Amendment, **95**, 187
Jackson-Vanik Amendment, **95**, 187
Janin, Charles Henry, **95–96**
JDC. *See* American Jewish Joint Distribution Committee, Inc.
Jeannette, 44, 47, 69, 123
Jesup North Pacific Expedition (1900–1901), **96**
Johnson, Albert Aaron, **96–97**
Johnson, Andrew, 63
Johnson, Benjamin O., **97**
Johnson, Lyndon Baines, 70
Johnson, Ural Alexis, **97**

Joint Distribution Committee. *See* American Jewish Joint Distribution Committee, Inc.
Jones, John Paul, **97–98**
Joralemon, Ira Beaman, **98**
Jordan, Philip, **98**
Judson, William Voorhees, **98–99**

Kahn, Albert, 5
Kahn, Moritz, 5
KAL 007 Incident (1983), **101**
Kamchatka, 49, 157, 189
Kampelman, Max M., **101**
Kantakuzen, Julia Dent Grant. *See* Cantacuzene, Julia Dent Grant
Kara Kum Deesert, 45
Karelian Fishing Cooperative, **102**
Karr, David, **102**
Kazakhstan, 60
Keely, Royal Rockwood, **102**
Kelley, Robert Francis, **102–3**
Kemerovo, 106, 109
Kendall, Donald McIntosh, **103**
Kennan, George, 65, **103–4**
Kennan, George Frost, 36, 38, **104–5**
Kennedy, John Fitzgerald, 40, **105–6**, 107, 190
Kennell, Ruth Epperson, **106**
Kharkov, 10, 16, 68
Khiva, 120
Khrushchev, Nikita, 19, 46, 57, 67, 69, 103, 105, 137, 162, 188, 190, 194
Kingsbury, John Adams, **106**
Kirghiz Steppe, 96
Kirk, Alan Goodrich, **107**
Kirk, Lydia, 107
Kissinger, Henry Alfred, 48, **107–8**
Koehler, Hugo William, **108**
Kohler, Foy David, **108–9**
Korean Air Lines Incident (1983). *See* KAL 007 Incident
Kosygin, Aleksei N., 46, 70
Krehbiel, Christian Emanuel, **109**
Kuibyshev, 85, 173
Kura River, 135
Kuzbas Colony, 84, 106, **109**
Kuznetsk, 64, **109**

Landfield, Jerome Barker, **111**
Lansing, Robert, **111–12**
Ledyard, John, **112**
Lena Delta, 44, 47, 123
Lend-Lease, 47, 60, 79–80, 84, 89, **112**, 135, 151, 161, 171, 173, 187
Lenin, V. I., 17, 46, 55, 77, 147, 149, 172, 192, 197
Levine, Irving Raskin, **112–13**
Levine, Isaac Don, **113**
Lewis, John David, 113
Lewis, William David, **113–14**
Leyda, Jay, **114**
Light Horse, **114**
Limited Test Ban Treaty (LTBT) (1963), 105, **114–15**, 181
Lincoln, Abraham, 30, **115**
Litvinov, Maxim, 23, 151
Loans to the USSR, **115**
Lothrop, George Van Ness, **115–16**
Lown, Bernard, **116**
Lowrie, Donald Alexander, **116**
LTBT. *See* Limited Test Ban Treaty
Lyons, Eugene, **117**
Lysenko, Trofim D., 129

McClellan, George Brinton, **119**
McCormick, Robert Sanderson, **119**
McCully, Newton Alexander, **120**
MacGahan, Januarius Aloysius, **120–21**
MacGowan, David Bell, **121**
McKay, Claude, **121**
McKee, Arthur Glenn, 10
Magnitogorsk, 10, 29, 84, 163, 178
Malta Summit (1989), 27, **121–22**
Martin, William H., **122**
Marye, George Thomas, **122**
Matlock, Jack Foust, Jr., **122–23**
Maynard, George William, **123**
MBFR. *See* Mutual and Balanced Force Reductions
MCC. *See* Mennonite Central Committee
Melville, George Wallace, 44, 47, 69, **123**
Mennonite Central Committee (MCC), 109, **123–24**, 126
Meyer, George von Lengerke, **124**
Michael, Louis Guy, **124**

Michela, Joseph Anthony, **125**
Middleton, Henry, **125**
Miers Fisher and Company, 62
Miles, Sherman, **125–26**
Miller, Alvin Joseph, **126**
Mitchell, Abbie, **126**
Mitchell, Bernon F., 122
Moby Dick Project, **127**
Molotov, V. M., 169
Mordecai, Alfred, **127**
Moscow, 2, 5, 8, 10, 14, 15, 21, 22, 25,
    26, 44, 47, 48, 49, 50, 51, 52, 53, 59,
    60, 61, 70, 80, 84, 85, 90, 91, 93, 94,
    102, 108, 113, 114, 116, 117, 121,
    122, 125, 127, 128, 131, 141, 147,
    150, 152, 158, 159, 162, 163, 164,
    165, 166, 167, 168, 169, 172, 174,
    175, 176, 178, 180, 181, 182, 183,
    184, 185, 196, 198, 200, 202
Moscow Summit (1972), **127–28**, 187
Moscow Summit (1974), **128**
Moscow Summit (1988), **128**, 146
Moscow Summit (1991), 27, **128**
Moscow Summit (1993), 27, **128**
Mosely, Philip Edward, **128–29**
Mott, John Raleigh, 9, **129, 152**
Muller, Hermann Joseph, **129–30**
Munroe, Thomas, **130**
Murmansk, 6, 148
Mutual and Balanced Force Reductions
    (MBFR), **130**, 155

National City Bank of New York, 81,
    124, **131**, 189
National Conference on Soviet Jewry
    (NCSJ), **131**
National Council on American-Soviet
    Friendship, 106, **131–32**, 168
NCSJ. *See* National Conference on Soviet
    Jewry
New York Life Insurance Company, **132**
Nicholas I, 196
Nicholas II, 124
Nikolayev, 59
Nitze, Paul Henry, **132**, 134, 179
Nixon, Richard Milhous, 15, 48, 107,
    128, **133**, 194
Nizhni-Kolymsk, 69

Nizhni Novgorod, 10, 69
Nonrecognition, **133**, 146
Noyes, George Rapall, **133–34**
NSC–68, 80, **134**
Nuclear Risk Reduction Centers Agree-
    ment (1987), 14, **134**

Odessa, 170, 193
Okhotsk, Sea of, 143
Olberg, Charles Real, **135**
Olsen, Clarence Edward, **135–36**
Olympic Games (1980), 4, 32
Omsk, 94, 163
"Open Skies" Proposal (1955), 57, 68,
    136

Packer, Earl Lenoir, **137**
Paris Summit (1960), 19, **137**, 181, 188
Parke, Charles Ross, **138**
Pavlov, Ivan Petrovich, 67
Peaceful Nuclear Explosions (PNE)
    Treaty (1976), **138**, 182
Peirce, Herbert Henry Davis, **138**
Pepsi-Cola Company, 103, **138**
Perle, Richard Norman, **139**
Petrograd, 8, 34, 36, 71, 81, 99, 120,
    131, 137, 153, 166, 175, 184. *See
    also* St. Petersburg
Peyton, Bernard, **139**
Pickens, Francis Wilkinson, **139**
Pinkney, William, **140**
Pipes, Richard Edgar, **140**, 179
PNE Treaty. *See* Peaceful Nuclear Explo-
    sions (PNE) Treaty
Poinsett, Joel Roberts, **140**
Polakov, Walter Nicholas, **141**
Poole, DeWitt Clinton, **141**
Poole, Ernest Cook, **141–42**
Potsdam Conference (1945), 27, 45, 89,
    129, **142**, 184
Powers, Francis Gary, **142**, 188
Prevention of Nuclear War Agreement
    (1973), **143**
Prince, Nancy Gardner, **143**
Prince, Nero, **143**
Protocol to the ABM Treaty, 2, 128
Pulkovo, 1
Purington, Chester Wells, **143–44**

Radio Liberty, 103, **145**, 163
RAIC. *See* Russian-American Industrial
   Corporation
RB-47 Incident (1960), **145**
Reagan, Ronald Wilson, 14, 36, 69, 128,
   138, **145–46**, 147, 160, 164, 171, 194,
   205
Recognition Issue, **146**
Reed, John, 24, **147**, 197
Reswick, William, **147**
Reykjavik Summit (1986), 146, **147–48**,
   164
Richardson, Wilds Preston, **148**
Riddle, John Wallace, **148**
Riga Axioms, **148–49**
Robeson, Paul, **149**
Robins, Raymond, 75, **149–50**
Robinson, Geroid Tanquary, **150**
Ronbinson, Robert, **150**
Rockhill, William Woodville, **150–51**
Roosevelt, Franklin Delano, 27, 45, 89,
   151, 173, 180, 184, 203
Roosevelt-Litvinov Agreements (1933),
   146, **151**
Root, Elihu, **152**
Root Mission to Russia (1917), 8, 9, 39,
   71, 75, 92, 99, 129, **152**, 156, 192,
   194, 199
Ropes, Ernest C., **152**
Ropes, Ernest Edward, 197
Ropes, William, **152–53**, 197
Ropes, William Hooper, 152–53, 197
Rosen, Joseph A., **153**
Rosenberg, James N., **153–54**
Rosett, Joshua, **154**
Ross, Edward Alsworth, **154**
Ross, Robert, **154**
Rostov-on-the-Don, 193
Rowny, Edward Leon, **155**
Ruggles, James A., **155**
Ruhl, Arthur Brown, **155**
Rukeyser, Walter Arnold, **155–56**
Russell, Charles Edward, 152, **156**
Russell, John Miller, **156**
Russian-American Convention (1824),
   156
Russian-American Industrial Corporation

(RAIC), **156–57**
Russian-American Telegraph Expedition
   (1865–1867), 27, 35, 65, 103, **157**
Russian-American Treaty of 1832, 24–
   25, **157**
Russian-American Treaty of 1867. *See*
   Alaska Purchase
Russian Bureau (1918–1919), **157**
Russian Railway Service Corps, 58, 97,
   158, 174, 199
Russian Reconstruction Farm, 168
Russian Section, **158**
Ryan, Edward William, **158**

St. Petersburg, 3, 4, 5, 10, 13, 25, 30,
   33, 34, 40, 43, 49, 59, 71, 75, 81, 83,
   87, 92, 103, 133, 114, 121, 122, 125,
   132, 143, 152, 156, 157, 161, 162,
   163, 164, 165, 179, 195, 196, 197,
   200, 201, 202. *See also* Petrograd
Salisbury, Harrison Evans, **159**
SALT, 14, 32, 97, 107, 127, 128, 132,
   133, 146, 155, **159–60**, 168, 170, 171,
   181, 189, 190, 193
Samara, 6
Sanders, Beverly Chune, **160**
Sayler, Oliver Martin, **161**
Sayre, Stephen, **161**
SCC. *See* Standing Consultative Commis-
   sion
Schley, Reeve, **161**
Schorr, Daniel Louis, **162**
Schuyler, Eugene, **162**
Schuyler, Montgomery, **162–63**
Scott, John, **163**
Seward, William Henry, 4, **163–64**
Seymour, Thomas Hart, **164**
Shapiro, Henry, **164**
Shultz, George Pratt, **164**
Siberia, 3, 6, 9, 16, 25, 27, 29, 35, 36,
   44, 47, 60, 61, 63, 65, 69, 73, 85, 92,
   94, 96, 98, 103, 104, 109, 111, 112,
   133, 139, 143, 144, 153, 154, 158,
   174, 175, 176, 189, 200
Siberian Intervention. *See* American Ex-
   peditionary Forces in Siberia
Simmons, Ernest Joseph, **165**

Simons, George Albert, **165**
Singer Sewing Machine Company, **165–66**
Sisson, Edgar Grant, **166**
Sisson Documents, **166**
Smith, Charles Emory, **166–67**
Smith, Charles Hadden, **167**
Smith, Edward Ellis, **167–68**
Smith, Gerard Coad, **168**
Smith, Hedrick Lawrence, **168**
Smith, Jessica, **168**
Smith, Joseph Allen, **169**
Smith, Walter Bedell, **169**
Smyser, Henry Lanius, **169**
Snodgrass, John Harold, **169–70**
Society of Friends of Soviet Russia, 64
Sonntag, George S., **170**
Spargo, John, **170**
Stalin, Joseph, 1, 52, 55, 70, 79, 80, 89, 107, 117, 129, 169, 171, 180, 203
Stalingrad, 29, 150
Standing Consultative Commission (SCC), 2, **170–71**
Standley, William Harrison, **171**
START, 7, 27, 146, 160, **171–72**
Steffens, Lincoln, **172**
Steinhardt, Laurence Adolph, **173**
Stettinius, Edward Reilly, Jr., **173**
Stevens, Edmund William, **174**
Stevens, John Frank, 94, 167, **174–75**, 194
Stevens, Leslie Clark, **175**
Steward, William H., 4
Stines, Norman Caswell, **175**
Stirniman, Edward James, **175–76**
Stoeckl, Edouard de, 4
Stoessel, Walter John, Jr., **176**
Stoneman, William Harlan, **176**
Story, Russell McCulloch, **176–77**
Strategic Arms Limitation Talks. *See* SALT
Strategic Arms Reduction Talks. *See* START
Strong, Anna Louise, **177**
Stuart, Charles Edward, **177–78**
Stuck, Raymond Wilber, **178**
Summers, Maddin, **178**
Summit Conferences, **178**

Tashkent, 71, 184
Tate, George, **179**
Taylor, Bayard, **179**
Team A/Team B, 140, **179–80**
Teheran Conference (1943), 45, 151, **180**
Thacher, Thomas Day, **180**
Thayer, Charles Wheeler, **180–81**
Thomas, George, **181**
Thompson, Llewellyn E., Jr., **181–82**
Thompson, William Boyce, **182**
Threshold Test Ban Treaty (TTBT) (1974), 128, 138, **182**
Tiflis, 135
Timbres, Harry Garland, **182–83**
Tolley, Kemp, **183**
Tolstoy, Leo, 50, 78
Tomsk, 116
Toon, Malcolm, **183**
Tower, Charlemagne, **183–84**
Trans-Siberian Railroad, 6, 15, 73, 158
Tredwell, Roger Culver, **184**
Trotsky, Leon, 55, 149, 197
Truman, Harry S., 27, 45, 51, 79, 80, 142, **184**, 191
TTBT. *See* Threshold Test Ban Treaty
Turkestan, 45, 73, 81, 184
Tynes, George W., **185**

Ukraine, 7
Ural Mountains, 59, 63, 96, 143, 155, 193
U.S.-Soviet Commercial Agreements (1972), **187**
U.S.-Soviet Conventional Arms Transfer Talks (CAT), **187**
U.S.-Soviet Standing Consultative Commission. *See* Standing Consultative Commission
U.S.-USSR Trade and Economic Council, **187–88**
U-2 Incident (1960), 57, 137, 142, **188**
Uzbekistan, 71

Vance, Cyrus Roberts, **189**
Vanderlip, Washington B., **189–90**
Vanik, Charles, 95
Vienna Summit (1961), 19, 181, **190**
Vienna Summit (1979), 160, **190**

Vladivostok, 8, 29, 38, 73, 74, 121, 154, 160, 166, 178
Vladivostok Summit (1974), 160, **190**
Volga Region, 183, 185
Volga River, 16, 97
Vologda, 184

Wallace, Henry Agard, **191**
Walling, William English, **191–92**
Walsh, Edmund Aloysius, **192**
Wardwell, Allen, **192–93**
Ware, Harold M., 9, 64, 168, **193**
Warnke, Paul Culliton, **193**
Washburn, Stanley, **193–94**
Washington Summit (1959), 19, **194**
Washington Summit (1973), **194**
Washington Summit (1987), **194**
Washington Summit (1990), 27, **195**
Weber, John B., **195**
Western Union Telegraph Expedition. *See* Russian-American Telegraph Expedition
Wheatland, Richard, **195**
Whistler, George Washington, **195–96**
Whistler, George William, 196
Whitney, Thomas Porter, **196**

Wilkins, William, **196–97**
William Ropes and Company, 152, **197**
Williams, Albert Rhys, **197–98**
Williams, Frankwood Earle, **198**
Williams, Spencer, **198**
Wilson, Milburn Lincoln, **198–99**
Wilson, Woodrow, 26, 44, 152, 154, 166, 170, 174, 192, **199–200**, 201
Winans, Thomas DeKay, 82, **200**
Winans, William L., **200**
Winchell, Horace Vaughn, **200**
Winkfield, Jimmy, **200–201**
Winship, North, **201**
Witkin, Zara, **201**
Wolfe, Bertram David, **202**
Wright, Joshua Butler, **202**

Yakutsk, 75
Yalta Conference (1945), 27, 62, 151, 173, **203**
Yeltsin, Boris, 27, 128
Young Men's Christian Association (YMCA), 9, 35–36, 46, 68, 85, 116, 129, 152, 176, **203–4**

Zero Option, 146, **205**

About the Author

DAVID SHAVIT is Associated Professor of library and information studies at Northern Illinois University. His earlier works include *The United States in Asia: A Historical Dictionary* (Greenwood, 1990), *The United States in Africa: A Historical Dictionary* (Greenwood, 1989), and *The United States in the Middle East: A Historical Dictionary* (Greenwood, 1987).